THE SPEAKING CONSTITUTION

A SISYPHEAN LIFE IN LAW

Praise for the book

'*The Speaking Constitution* presents the legal activism of a man dedicated to the struggle for the defense of the rule of law and the rights of citizenship across a wide range of Indian jurisdictions. Its appeal is, however, decidedly universal. Be it because he defended the rights of the young to education, be it because he assisted and inspired grassroots movements for civil liberties, or because he confronted state violence and the atrocities committed against minorities—this is a work that must interest and engage all those across the globe who fight for a just and inclusive society.'

–Gisele Cittadino, Associate Professor, Pontifical Catholic University of Rio de Janeiro

'Sisyphean indeed! This book is a testament of a struggle to humanize the Indian Constitution and the court processes that attempt to undermine it. The blend of civil liberties and social justice that has animated the untiring effort of K.G. Kannabiran is more than remarkable. Since the 1970s his work reads like a haunting war journal: we are taken through the ordeals of the Emergency, the consequences of revolutionary insurgency, of deaths in detention, of encounter killings, of murders and caste discrimination and of minority rights. The book is an indispensable moral testimony so vital for the social sciences and legal studies but also for Human and Social Rights activists beyond India.'

–Ari Sitas, South African Sociologist and Writer, and Emeritus Professor at the University of Cape Town

'This book by the doyen of human rights movement and lawyering in India is a must-read not just for human rights activists but more so for members of judiciary and legal fraternity. This volume grips you from the first page till the end. It not only showcases the heroic battles both in court and outside fought by KGK but also shows that human rights activism is not just about passion but also about craft, courage, conviction, and grounded reality.'

–Mihir Desai, Senior Advocate, Bombay High Court and Vice President, People's Union for Civil Liberties

'This fascinating oral memoir translated from Telugu gives an insider's account of the golden era of human rights mobilization in India. With inspiring words such as "struggle is its own reward" Mr Kannabiran describes how social movements were created in the seventies and the eighties with strong connections to the oppressed and underprivileged. Mr Kannabiran's bravery was recognized when he fought against the Emergency in the 1970s and was particularly defiant in challenging the "encounter killings" of young men during the Naxalite rebellion. A lawyer and a peacemaker, we truly miss him in the South Asia of today.'

–Radhika Coomaraswamy, Former Under Secretary General and Special Representative on Children and Armed Conflict

'*The Speaking Constitution: A Sisyphean Life in Law* is a life of travelling through courts—from the lowest to the highest—to defend the marginalized and secure life for the person condemned to death. K.G. Kannabiran's memoir gives us an invaluable look into the life of a person dedicated to the cause of civil liberties, human rights, justice, and dignity. It was a life that never gave up hope. Rarely we shall get such an account that will reflect faithfully the trajectory of the struggles for justice in the courts of the country for the last seventy years of the Indian republic.'

–Ranabir Samaddar, Political Scientist, Distinguished Chair in Migration and Forced Migration Studies at the Mahanirban Calcutta Research Group

'The legendary proportions of K.G. Kannabiran's contribution to holding powers accountable to the Constitution are brought to life in this book through a reflective autobiography by him and a biographical recounting by Kalpana Kannabiran in her matchless Introduction. The fullness of the account of many battles and court cases he fought as India's foremost rights crusader—his defence of political prisoners, tribals, dalits, religious minorities, victims of fake encounters, of judicial negligence and rape survivors—makes this superbly structured book the most essential reading for anyone concerned with the Constitution and the ideas of justice and freedom.'

–G. N. Devy, Writer and Cultural Activist

'Two of the many boons from [my] assignment [as General Secretary of the People's Union for Civil Liberties] were much more valuable for me than the work itself. I got to see a much wider range of good work being done across the country by people's groups. And to meet persons of exemplary dedication and character, persons I would not have met had I spent time just in my study. The bonds with some of them lasted for decades. Among them was my dear friend K.G. Kannabiran. A lawyer of the highest calibre, he devoted every waking moment to the victims of oppression—of oppression by society as well as the State.'

–Arun Shourie in *The Commissioner for Lost Causes*

K.G. KANNABIRAN

THE SPEAKING CONSTITUTION

A SISYPHEAN LIFE IN LAW

Translated, Compiled, Edited and with an Introduction by
KALPANA KANNABIRAN

Based on the oral memoir,
24 *Gantalu: Atmakadhatmaka Samajika Chitram* (2009, Telugu),
as told to and recorded by N. Venugopal
Commissioned by Devulapalli Publications, and published in *Prajatantra*

HarperCollins *Publishers* India

First published in India by HarperCollins *Publishers* 2022
4th Floor, Tower A, Building No. 10, Phase II, DLF Cyber City,
Gurugram, Haryana – 122002
www.harpercollins.co.in

2 4 6 8 10 9 7 5 3 1

P-ISBN: 978-93-5629-314-4
E-ISBN: 978-93-5629-099-0

Typeset in 10.5/13.5 Adobe Garamond Pro at
Manipal Technologies Limited, Manipal

Printed and bound at
Thomson Press (India) Ltd

MIX
Paper
FSC FSC® C010615

This book is produced from independently certified FSC® paper
to ensure responsible forest management.

For
Vasanth Kannabiran
herstory – history

Contents

A Note on Sources and Translation

THE SPEAKING CONSTITUTION is based on K.G. Kannabiran's 2009 memoir in the Telugu, titled *24 Gantalu: Atmakadhatmaka Samajika Chitram* ('24 Hours: A Personalized Social History'). In working through the Telugu text, the English version presents several points of departure, and is an edited translation that includes detailed footnotes, references and case citations. With the exception of the section in Chapter 16, titled 'Reservations for Muslims', all other notes, references and citations have been introduced by the editor. Chapters have been reorganized thematically and chronologically, and some chapters merged. K.G. Kannabiran wrote in English, and spoke and read Telugu fluently. Where original English drafts of articles that were published in Telugu were available in his personal papers, these have been edited for this work; in a couple of chapters, versions published in English elsewhere have been adapted with the permission of the publishers. *The Speaking Constitution* also makes extensive use of K.G. Kannabiran's personal archives, unpublished notes and court judgments.

Preface

WHEN EMERGENCY WAS declared in June 1975, I was five months short of my fourteenth birthday, with a mysterious new board exam—'tougher than ever before', parents and students were warned—hovering menacingly overhead. Mine was the first batch of the ICSE (Indian Certificate of Secondary Education) in November–December 1975. In the fancy-dress event organized as part of the school's Teachers' Day celebration in September that year, I wore a white cotton sari, powdered my cropped hair, put on a pair of borrowed spectacles and read out Indira Gandhi's speech declaring Emergency. I have a vivid memory of myself reciting the opening lines of that speech: 'The President has proclaimed an emergency. This is nothing to panic about …'

I do not remember discussing what I would do at home. In fact, I don't recall any conversations except about how I would cross the hurdles of this monstrous exam—with my teachers worried I would dent the 100 per cent pass figure that every school desperately wanted (like my parents, I was a mediocre student with no aspiration to excel in school). My mother vexed the teachers at the last parent–teacher meeting with her nonchalant response that she was not really concerned with the school tally. She was caught in a cusp. My father, clearly, was busy keeping another tally—as is evident from his accounts in this book—of prisoners, of those detained in jails, in illegal detention facilities, and those being shot in encounters. In the midst of this, my sister Chitra, a year older, was tasked with chaperoning me and glowering at an ageing rogue tuition master with roving hands, who was entrusted by my somewhat desperate 'harum scarum' mother to teach me math so that I could 'catch up' with the syllabus less than a month before the exam.

On my fourteenth birthday that year, 1 December 1975, in the middle of my board exams, Bhoomaiah and Kishta Goud were hanged in Mushirabad jail in Hyderabad. My parents had both spent the previous night on the pavement outside the jail, and returned home that morning, after the execution, in deep mourning.

In 1977, Emergency was lifted and we had strangers trooping in and out of the house. The home was the world. Among the people who wandered in or came to stay were torture survivors, witnesses of encounters, and political prisoners who had been released. I have a vivid memory of E. Bhikshapathi, who stayed in our home in Domalguda. He was the key witness in the Giraipalli encounter and had come to testify before the Bhargava Commission. A painfully quiet and withdrawing presence, just a few years older than us, he had survived unimaginable torture and was released on the point of death by the police. The other four had been shot in his presence. I don't remember him saying a word during his stay although he lived in our home. The only person he responded to in monosyllables was my father.

My father's office, always the front two rooms of our home till the very end, spilled into the house all the time. Everyone came in, everyone discussed everything—from encounters to tortures, to our personal choices and lives. Sometime around then, our paternal grandmother came to live with us. And I had made a habit of fencing off intrusions and inhabiting a secret life with Mills & Boon and (oftentimes imaginary) rendezvous with friends.

We were used to being asked if we were our mother's children, as she was the most popular English teacher in the largest women's college in the city, Reddy College, and it seemed like every second person we met (including our teachers) had been (or had someone in the immediate family who had been) 'Vasanth madam's student'. She was also the president of the largest college teachers' union in the region: the Telangana Affiliated College Teachers' Association (TACTA). Slowly, however, my father's work, at first hazy, became more and more clear to us—my classmates' parents whom I happened to meet seemed to know him or know of him, and we understood that the work he did was out of the ordinary. Several of the people spoken about in this book—people who were arrested or tortured, leaders of the Naxalite movement, activists in the civil liberties movement, politicians, lawyers, writers and poets—were people we knew and grew up meeting. Public meetings and demonstrations—not parties—were our idea of social gatherings. When we did occasionally meet with families of my parents' friends, it was families that either shared a sense of politics, or were their colleagues—lawyers and Reddy College teachers. My mother ran a community kitchen, besides teaching full-time. There was always food on the table for everyone who came in, announced and unannounced. And we just absorbed everything around us, sometimes resisting people and intrusive talk, while making our individual choices.

Over a decade later, my father received a typed anonymous letter—in early 1994—from someone who claimed to be a policeman and an admirer saying that there was a plot by the police to murder him. The letter named the personnel plotting and those tasked with executing it—in retaliation to the killing of two police officers in January and November 1993, allegedly by Naxalites. It added that that my father's evening walks and self-driven Maruti van were being tracked by a jeep without a licence plate, and asked him to change his car and his walking routine. My mother asked him to go for his walks alone and not take my one-year-old daughter along, as was his habit. A day or two later, when he drove up to my apartment (which was at a T junction) to pick me up, I saw an un-numbered jeep stop at the crossroads and men get out, looking towards his car. They hadn't seen me walking out and he hadn't seen them—I just went up to his side carrying my daughter, told him quietly, and blocked the window while chatting with him. The jeep circled the neighbourhood a couple of times and we stayed like that till they left.

On the night of 2 October 2003, I received a menacing phone call from an anonymous male caller speaking in Urdu who said that my daughters would be abducted on their way to school. This was a day after the Alipiri bomb blast that had targeted then chief minister N. Chandrababu Naidu. We issued a statement widely reported in the press, lodged a police complaint, and took the children off the school bus—resuming our normal routines after a short break. These were but two instances. We had by this time learnt to deal with difficult situations without allowing them to derail us.

I studied sociology and was interested in movements, especially the women's movement, becoming active as an undergraduate student in the late 1970s. I wandered into formal law over a decade later and then directly into the work my father was doing, and into conversations with him around his work—but again, not as a lawyer. I was never interested in inheriting his professional mantle. He was training several other lawyers for that task. Around 1997–98, I began to edit and archive his work in consultation with him, discussing his cases, assisting him in research and drafting, and sitting in on his discussions with clients, friends and seekers of advice who would just walk in. I was more interested in the archives of movements, in the history of jurisprudence around civil liberties and human rights, and in the circulation of an idea of justice—all of this taking shape through my deep immersion in the work of K.G. Kannabiran, my father.

The last case he argued, on 1 May 2009, was a case in the Andhra Pradesh High Court, on the displacement of slum dwellers in Birlagadda in Kurnool district where he forged a settlement in favour of the evacuees. He appeared in court twice after this. On 8 October 2009, a month short of his eightieth birthday, he proudly had me sworn in as advocate in the high court at Hyderabad. I donned the lawyer's habit for the first and last time that day. On our way out, around noon, we met K. Balagopal in the court compound and stopped for a brief chat—the last time we saw him. We lost him that night. A few days later my father returned to the high court one last time to attend the condolence mention of Balagopal by the chief justice.

Working on this memoir has been an experience soaked with memories—of people, of conversations, of grief and loss, of witnessing trauma and pain, of indomitable courage, of growing up under state surveillance as children of a man who had to be surveilled. Importantly, of coming of age with no fear in our hearts because we had heard our father speak of the worst, and had seen him stand tall speaking truth to power in unimaginable ways. And our mother prepared us for the worst, telling us with no fuss whom in their circle of friends we should call if we sensed trouble. This was a personal friend—Jaipal uncle. Dr Jaipal Christian was parent, friend, confidant all rolled into one. With ever open arms he steadied, comforted and reassured us quietly, and with humour at all times. I remember him today with gratitude and love.

A deep, unconditional love and caring, abiding respect, indescribable kindness, and glowing pride in the way we built our lives and work are my most enduring memory of my father. Things were never easy or simple, nor did we agree on everything. We had just made it a habit to stretch the limits of possibility—all of us, individually and together.

It is from this lifelong experience that I approach this text.

—Kalpana Kannabiran

Introduction

Speaking the Constitution: A Biography of Civil Liberties in Independent India

—Kalpana Kannabiran

This unfinished Sisyphean struggle has not made me tire of it but I have been spared of the futile struggle with which Sisyphus was condemned; mine has been the struggle for a better world and the struggle is its own reward.

—K.G. Kannabiran, undated note, c. 2007–08

AS WE ENTER the seventy-fifth year of Indian independence, a close look at the development of the idea of justice through courts in India seems apposite. *The Speaking Constitution* traces this history through cases in courts, tribunals and commissions of different jurisdictions, mostly in the composite state of Andhra Pradesh, but elsewhere as well, mapping in the process a legal geography of civil liberties in India through the work of one of its most committed campaigners, K.G. Kannabiran (1929–2010).

It is also an account of the nature and history of the legal profession told reflexively by seamlessly traversing five decades of court walks.

Coursing through his work is an inimitable and irrepressible sense of humour—the twinkling of his eyes, laughter and his amusement at his own jokes—that is by all accounts one of the most memorable aspects of his court appearances. Dense arguments interlaced with humour that held courts in rapt attention. While it is impossible to dwell on this at any length, for those who knew him and had seen him at work in court, this is an image that endures. In this, he ruptured the staid and stiff construction of 'appropriate lawyerly conduct' making him utterly accessible to all.

In the decidedly polyglot culture of the courtroom, where the vernacular is constitutive of dialogue, we are reminded of Mikhail Bakhtin's observation that laughter draws its object into a zone of proximity that makes it possible to 'break open its external shell, look into its center, doubt it, take it apart, dismember it, lay it bare and expose it, examine it freely and experiment with it … [and] demolishes fear and piety … clearing the ground for an absolutely free investigation'.[1]

The first case K.G. Kannabiran argued—which he writes about in the opening chapter—as a struggling lawyer with no economic support in Madras, was the case of Ansari Begum, challenging a deportation notice under the Foreigners' Act in the immediate aftermath of Partition, in 1958 (Chapter 1).

Straddling the 1977 Bhargava Commission on 'encounter' deaths and the 1978 Muktadar Commission on the Rameeza Bee case of rape and the custodial killing of Ahmed Hussain, her husband (Chapter 7); the Tarkunde Committee's work on encounter deaths in 1977 (Chapter 8); the Naxalite conspiracy cases in the composite state of Andhra Pradesh (Chapter 6); the Shankar Guha Niyogi murder case where he appeared for the Central Bureau of Investigation (CBI) in the Madhya Pradesh High Court in Jabalpur (Chapter 14); the Parliament attack case where he appeared for Shaukat Hussain Guru (Chapter 11); the Coimbatore bomb blasts case (Chapter 16) where he appeared in the trial court for the accused; the 2002 Gujarat massacres where he sat on the Citizens' Tribunal led by Justice Krishna Iyer (Chapter 17); and finally the peace talks between Naxalites and the government in Andhra Pradesh in 2004 (Chapter 18) where he was a key interlocutor, Kannabiran reflects on his experience of confronting human rights violations and the derogation of civil liberties in courts of every jurisdiction, and on the meanings of this critical engagement for the development of a human rights culture on the ground.

In a parallel and intersecting narrative, he speaks of the numerous writ petitions he filed during the Emergency on behalf of dissenters who were communist, Marxist-Leninist, socialist and from the Jana Sangh/Rashtriya Swayamsevak Sangh (RSS), reflecting on the points of law that were material to the cases he argued, marking a

---

1 Bakhtin, M.M. 1990, 'Epic and Novel'. In *The Dialogic Imagination: Four Essays*. Ed. Michael Holquist, trans. Caryl Emerson and Michael Holquist, 4–40. Austin, TX: University of Texas Press. p. 23.

distinction between political prisoners and other prisoners, recounting key elements of the judgments in each case and threading them together in his analysis (Chapters 4 and 5).

After the Emergency, while opposing the Telugu Desam Party's (TDP) repressive regimes under N.T. Rama Rao and N. Chandrababu Naidu, especially on the escalation of extrajudicial murder (Chapter 9), he also represented Congress legislators M. Baga Reddy, P. Janardhan Reddy and Dokka Manikya Vara Prasad in different cases of constitutional significance: internal representation within the party, the right to a corruption-free government, and reservations for Muslim Backward Classes respectively.

The question of accountability of those in elected office was one that Kannabiran was seized of at all times, and he used the courts to foreground the meanings of democratic citizenship and the right to question those in authority. One instance is his cogent arguments on the need for citizens and courts to insist on a code of conduct for elected representatives. On this point, his insights on the English writ of scire facias (later replaced by the writ of quo warranto) in the case of the physical attack on Bangladeshi writer Taslima Nasreen by a mob of fifty men belonging to All India Majlis-E-Ittehadul Muslimeen (AIMIM) led by its leader Akbaruddin Owaisi in a public meeting in Telugu University in the heart of Hyderabad in 2007, are invaluable.[2]

In this introduction, I attempt an approach that draws on the methods of constitutional ethnography to understand K.G. Kannabiran's work. Looking at 'the logics of particular contexts as a way of illuminating complex interrelationships among political, legal, historical, social, economic, and cultural elements', as Kim Lane Scheppele argues, enables a better understanding of 'how constitutional systems operate by identifying the *mechanisms* through which governance is accomplished, and the strategies through which governance is attempted, experienced, resisted and revised, taken in historical depth and cultural context', distilling the '*logics* that link various specific features … into patterns whose traces may also be visible elsewhere'. The idea is to draw attention to 'a set of repertoires that can be found in real cases and that provide insight into how constitutional regimes operate'.[3]

---

2 For a detailed discussion of this petition see Kannabiran, K.G., and Kalpana Kannabiran, Kalpana. 2007. 'Taslima Case: On a Code of Conduct for Elected Representatives' *Economic and Political Weekly*, Vol. 42, No. 36, September 08–14.

3 Scheppele, Kim Lane. 2004. 'Constitutional Ethnography: An Introduction', *Law & Society Review*, Vol. 38, No. 3 September: p. 391.

This is his account of the work he was engaged in as part of a movement for justice that cascaded across the country. The book itself is encompassing in its scope for an understanding of human rights—I do not attempt to anticipate the entirety of his preoccupations. However, the non-linear structure of this introduction mirrors the complexity of Kannabiran's dialogic engagements with law in courts. In the sections that follow, I will present some thoughts on the larger lessons *The Speaking Constitution* holds for us—in terms of our understanding of the state, of the meanings of life, liberty, protections and freedom under the Constitution, of the place of speech, voice and dialogue, and the spatial rootedness of justice, for instance.[4] In doing this, I present my reading of a sprinkling of the thoughts that animate this work, as a way of opening up a larger, deeper, more wide-ranging and vital dialogue. Among a host of other concerns, we might pose the question: What are the liberating energies fostered by an argumentative, insurgent Constitution?

Signposting the Insurgent Constitution

> [Should] the colonial interpretation of the laws ... be followed while interpreting the Constitution? Did the Constitution imply a break with the past, at least with reference to the people and the state and its government? Does the transformation of a person from the status of a 'subject' to that of 'citizen' mean anything at all when interpreting the scope of entrenched rights in the Constitution?[5]

---

4 I refer here to the work of Philippopoulos-Mihalopoulos, who describes spatial justice as 'the ultimate expression of one's spatial and legal claim to a unique corporeal position which by necessity excludes all others: spatial justice emerges from the fact that only one body can occupy a specific space at any specific time. In other words, spatial justice is the struggle between bodies to be in a specific space at a specific time' (p. 176)—extending the argument to the fact that claims to life and liberty are importantly claims established in space and time, that then transcend spatio-temporality to offer enduring precedents for other times and other places. In order to offer an enduring standard, however, the spatio-temporal rootedness of the first claims is a necessary first step in claims to justice. Philippopoulos-Mihalopoulos, Andreas. 2015. *Spatial Justice: Body, Lawscape, Atmosphere*. Oxon: Routledge.

5 Kannabiran, K.G. 2004. *The Wages of Impunity: Power, Justice and Human Rights*. Hyderabad: Orient Longman, p. 59.

In *The Wages of Impunity* (2004), Kannabiran takes a close look at the justice system and the polity, pointing to the long shadows of the colonial period in independent India. Through his sharp interrogation of path dependency in constitutional and criminal jurisprudence after 1950, that drew on colonial methods of interpretation, he reflects on the interiorities of justice and civil liberties as they are expressed through litigation, courtcraft, judicial deliberations and parliamentary/legislative debates. The practices of state repression and the popular and tenacious attempts to thwart it both inside courts and outside bear several lessons for our grasp of the deeply insurgent possibilities the Constitution offers us today. The account is not of one specific moment alone, but a *longue durée* view of the struggle for civil liberties as it gets articulated in and through courts, with each chapter reflecting on specific cases he argued, or tribunals/inquiries he sat on/participated in.

He urged courts to make a clean break with the colonial trajectories of judicial decision making, especially since even laws which continued from colonial to post-colonial India were now tethered to the new Constitution, and had to therefore be interpreted in the light of freedom and Ambedkar's idea of constitutional morality. The Constitution, after all, 'imagines a social order that celebrates freedom, pluralism, non-discrimination, and justice—an order that displaces the unfreedoms internal to the society as well as the unfreedom of colonization'.[6] His interventions in the matter of Kambarigam Mokhasa (Chapter 2) go to the heart of his preoccupation with the urgency of an insurgent jurisprudence in every site in which justice is deliberated on. It was not only courts, as his discussion of this case demonstrates, but importantly, the bureaucracy and the press that could (and did) effectively further the goals of an insurgent Constitution. The 'insurgent administration', far from being an anachronism, was one he actively partnered with, especially in cases involving the rights of Adivasis to autonomy in Schedule V Areas (Chapter 12)—specifically B.D. Sharma, S.R. Sankaran and B.N. Yugandhar; and on the case of reservations for the Muslim Backward Classes it was P.S. Krishnan. Together, they and others similarly situated in different states revalorized the idea of insurgency, recovering it from militarized statist discourses and pressing it into the service of 'reimagining democratic citizenship and reinventing the state', challenging in the process regimes of dominance, authoritarianism and majoritarian/caste supremacy.[7]

On the indivisibility of rights enshrined in the Constitution and the non-negotiability of unhindered access to socio-economic rights, K.G. Kannabiran

6 Kannabiran, Kalpana. 2012. *Tools of Justice: Non-Discrimination and the Indian Constitution*. New Delhi: Routledge, p. 5.

7 Ibid., p. 6.

consistently opposed the interpretive reduction of the Directive Principles of State Policy (Part IV), eschewing the rhetoric of 'non-enforceability'. He drew, instead, a distinction between judicial enforceability and political enforceability, insisting on the urgent and continuous attention of governments to the Directive Principles.[8] Indeed, it was his argument (borne out by his experience in cases and political deliberations) that it was the neglect of Part IV rights—state abandonment—that led to deep unrest and mass resistance, which was then brutally put down by state violence.

K.G. Kannabiran's work was profoundly affected by the vicissitudes of deliberative democracy (dramatic and mundane), and his incessant, untiring effort was to find ways of historicizing the Constitution, rejecting a reductionist, formulaic route to interpretation. Beyond this, importantly, he charts the Emergency way beyond the Emergency, and follows the travails of justice through his penetrative gaze at the law yielding the most unexpected, even startling insights. His frequent resort to the idea of an 'insurgency' in jurisprudence, administration and advocacy, for instance, recognizes the inherent transformative imperative the Constitution of India signals, and the fact that unless courts were explicitly counter-hegemonic, justice could never be done. This idea was articulated stunningly by B.R. Ambedkar in his last speech in the Constituent Assembly where he observed that 'Political democracy cannot last unless there lies at the base of it social democracy … a way of life which recognizes liberty, equality and fraternity as the principles of life …', especially important in a society where graded inequality and the concentration of wealth obstruct even the most minimal egalitarian moves.[9]

In interweaving this idea with his arguments on the writ of the Constitution, Kannabiran was clear that courts needed to take 'insurgent' positions in terms of the social and political contexts within which constitutional jurisprudence must be located. Anything less would only be 'jurisprudential dissociation' at best,[10] at its worst, 'judicial pusillanimity' (to use Justice Leila Seth's unforgettable expression).[11] The questions of philosophy, law and politics embedded in his everyday travels

---

8 Kannabiran, K.G. 2010. 'Development Challenges in Extremist Affected Areas' (unpublished).

9 *Constituent Assembly Debates*, Volume XI, 14–26 November 1949. On 25 November 1949, pp. 978–79, https://eparlib.nic.in/bitstream/123456789/763285/1/cad_25-11-1949.pdf. Accessed on 4 November 2021.

10 Kannabiran, Kalpana. 2012. *Tools of Justice: Non-Discrimination and the Indian Constitution*. New Delhi: Routledge.

11 Quoted in *Navtej Singh Johar vs Union of India*, AIR 2018 SC 4321.

in courts hold several lessons for our understanding of our presents. What are the somatic and semantic meanings of justice as they emerge through courtcraft and public deliberation on civil liberties? The expression 'insurgent Constitution' points to Kannabiran's approach to questions of justice: a Marxist with a very strong affection for communism, he was profoundly influenced by Ambedkar and by Gandhi, engaging deeply with the ideas, acutely conscious of divergences, dissentience, irresolutions and contradictions, and yet forging 'constellations' that spoke to his thought and work in the most unusual ways.[12] In the cases he argued, and in his reasoning on the relationship between justice, equality and liberty (or freedom), he grappled constantly with the complexity of reckoning with insurgent ideas embedded in the Constitution—this is a thought I will return briefly to in the concluding section. As Linda Colley observes so pertinently in another context, constitutions 'only function well to the degree that politicians, the law courts and the populations concerned are able and willing to put sustained effort into thinking about them, revising them when necessary, and making them work. These are also emphatically not innocent devices, and never have been. From the outset … written constitutions have been as much to do with enabling varieties of power as they have been with restricting power.'[13]

The Speaking Constitution opens a window into the micro-practices of insurgent constitutional practice, especially against state arbitrariness, but also in relation to larger political processes in a deliberative, dialogic democracy. In laying bare the everyday practices of repression that then congeal and harden in episodic conflagrations, K.G. Kannabiran presents through the entire work a radical critique of governance and demonstrates through a deep constitutional engagement what concrete steps might lead to the attainment of the fundamental guarantees of life, dignity and liberty in the most minimalist reading.

Policing with Impunity, Debating State Accountability

Through the several layers of our engagements with the Constitution we constantly 'encounter' the exceptional in the everyday, ordinary business of living, dying and surviving/escaping.

12 See Rathore, Aakash Singh. 2017. *Indian Political Theory: Laying the Groundwork for Svaraj*. London and New York: Routledge.

13 Colley, Linda. 2021. *The Gun, the Ship, and the Pen: Warfare, Constitutions, and the Making of the Modern World*. New York and London: Liveright Publishing Corporation, p. 32.

This section discusses briefly Kannabiran's critique of policing arising from his interventions over four decades.

In 1977, the Janata government at the centre designated retired Supreme Court judge Justice Vashishtha Bhargava to constitute a one-man commission of inquiry to look into the torture in custody and murder of political dissenters in encounters during the Emergency, between 1975 and 1977, based on the reports of the Civil Liberties (Tarkunde) Committee.[14] The Congress party remained in power in the composite state of Andhra Pradesh during and immediately after the Emergency. When their brazen attempts to intimidate witnesses and derail the hearings failed, police officers in the state made a representation to Chief Minister M. Chenna Reddy that the morale of the force would be weakened if they were subjected to investigation in an open inquiry. The compliant chief minister ordered that the commission hold in-camera proceedings, resulting in the withdrawal of the Tarkunde Committee and the shutting down of the commission. Although no report was released by Justice Bhargava since the commission had not completed its task, thirty years after Indian independence the Bhargava Commission and the work of the Tarkunde Committee marked a turning point in the popular Indian understanding of state violence, especially witnessed in 'fake encounters'/cold-blooded murders by the state. It marked the beginning of a tenacious fight across the country against extrajudicial murder by the state and against impunity for the police.

As a first step, a Sisyphean return to one of K.G. Kannabiran's core concerns is unavoidable—extrajudicial murder by the state. On the night of 27 November 2019, a young veterinarian, 'Disha', was raped and murdered by unknown persons

14 Justice V. Bhargava was on the Supreme Court bench that had earlier heard and dismissed the case of A. Lakshmanarao challenging his illegal detention by the AP police and challenging the validity of S. 344(1A), CrPC contending that it offends Art. 19(1)(d) of the Constitution in the Parvathipuram Conspiracy Case—as per minority view in *Raj Narain v. Superintendent, Central Jail, New Delhi* (11.09.1970—SC—AIR 1971 SC 178; MANU/ SC/ 0164/1970) written by Justice C.A. Vaidialingam. This was an important minority judgment that spoke directly to the right to personal liberty and the duty of the court to safeguard it: 'when the personal liberty of a person is sought to be restricted or curtailed, rules of the law as well as the forms must be scrupulously observed' (para 37). Justice Bhargava (along with Justice I.D. Dua) hearing the case of A. Lakshmanarao were part of the majority in *Raj Narain*. He was therefore familiar with the history of Naxalites petitioning the courts to intervene and check state arbitrariness and police atrocities. See *A. Lakshmanarao vs. Judicial Magistrate, First Class, Parvatipuram and Ors*. AIR 1971 SC 186. Bench: I.D. Dua, S.M. Sikri, Vashishtha Bhargava.

on her way back home from work. Four suspects were arrested the following day. On 6 December, after a week in custody, the suspects—a lorry driver and cleaners—were taken by the police to the scene of the offence and shot dead. The question of whether they were subjected to torture while in custody remains undetermined. The police claimed that they fired in self-defence against unarmed suspects in custody. There was public jubilation over the encounter. 'Justice' was deemed to have been done. Jyoti Pandey's ('Nirbhaya') mother weighed in from Delhi that she wished her daughter's rapists had also been done to death as swiftly and with such finality as this.[15] The insistence by women's rights groups that there must be an investigation into the encounter led to the Telangana High Court ordering a second post-mortem in the presence of the families of the dead suspects and the constitution of a commission of inquiry by the Supreme Court led by retired Supreme Court judge Justice V.S. Sirpurkar. Two years later, between August and November 2021, the commission, through hybrid hearings open to media and public, heard and cross-examined witnesses and the police personnel responsible for this crime. The Telangana police unsuccessfully petitioned the Telangana High Court to stay the proceedings of the commission. On 20 May 2022, the Supreme Court of India ordered the release of the report of the Justice Sirpurkar Commission for necessary deliberations by the petitioners and the Telangana High Court.[16] The Sirpurkar Commission in its report concluded that three of the four suspects were killed in a fake encounter and that three of the suspects were minors when they were arrested and shot in police custody. It recommended that ten police personnel (named in the report) be tried for murder.[17] Whether the case of the encounters will actually be tried in a court of law on the basis of the report of the commission of inquiry remains to be seen. Despite the diligent work of the commission and the glimmer of hope in the decision of the high court in refusing to derail the commission, and the decision of the Supreme Court to make the report public in spite of a plea by

15 'Hyderabad Encounter: Nirbhaya's Mother Expresses Satisfaction'. 2019. *New Indian Express*, 6 December, https://www.newindianexpress.com/nation/2019/dec/06/hyderabad-encounter-nirbhayas-mother-expresses-satisfaction-2072332.html. Accessed on 1 November 2021.

16 Order of Supreme Court of India in *G.S. Mani and Another vs Union of India and Others*, Writ Petition (Criminal) No. 348/2019, dated 20 May 2022.

17 Report of the Commission of Inquiry (Constituted by the Hon'ble Supreme Court of India by Order. Dated 12.12.2019, in Writ Petition [Criminal] No. 348 of 2019). Justice V.S. Sirpurkar, Chairman; Justice Rekha P. Sondur Baldota, Member; D.R. Karthikeyan, Member, dated 28 January 2022.

the state to the contrary, the critical concern of state complicity in, and condonation of, police violence remains.[18]

The fight for civil liberties has returned to the same point in the same city where the Bhargava Commission sat in 1977—with the state (now Telangana, then part of the composite state of Andhra Pradesh) shielding murderous policemen, rendering citizens increasingly vulnerable to arbitrary arrests, torture in custody, detention and murder with no recourse to law. There is an important difference. We are not in a formally declared state of internal emergency. Rather, what we see in this juxtaposition of the 1970s and 2019, but also in Kannabiran's account of impunity that stretches from the 1960s to the first decade of the millennium, is the folding together of the norm and the exception in post-colonial governance in India, with the exception sitting smugly in the belly of the norm, so to speak. But importantly, within this political context, he underscores the specific rupture a formal state of exception (like a declaration of internal emergency) brings to the interpretive powers of courts that deliberate on the empirical realities of justice and the Constitution in matters of liberty and life (or killable life, as it were). This 'normal exception' stretches across different parties in power in the state and the centre. K.G. Kannabiran's deliberations on constitutional ethics integrated 'principles that rest[ed] both on abstract axioms and on the experience of concrete application'.[19] This experience was not one that petitioners brought before him alone. He recounts his own experience of being physically assaulted, abused and detained by the police in Madurai, Tamil Nadu, when he and V.M. Tarkunde were participating in a public demonstration (Chapter 2). His deep critiques of state arbitrariness dwelt on continuities in *methods* of (mis)rule, across different authoritarian regimes, and the widespread use of the 'legality' of exception, spread over the centre, left, and right, and centre, state and union territories. His critique was directed not merely at political parties and their stated ideologies, nor at particular political regimes in power.

Nasser Hussain provides an excellent account of the colonial genealogies of emergency and observes that 'the problem of emergency, both as an interpretive question in the law, and as an administrative practice, does not disappear with the

18 See, for instance, the responses of leaders from major political parties. https://thewire.in/politics/telangana-rape-accused-encounter-response. Accessed on 7 December 2021.

19 Lazar, Nomi Claire. 2009. *States of Emergency in Liberal Democracies*. Cambridge: Cambridge University Press, p. 6.

end of colonial rule'.[20] It was this long shadow of colonialism that was subjected to radical critique in the cases brought before courts in Andhra Pradesh. Petitioners vetoed judicial/administrative recourse to the palimpsest of exceptionalism rooted in colonial law, pushing courts to reframe the questions of life and liberty as also the meanings of state accountability under a rejuvenated constitutional commitment in independent India. They insisted that the Constitution must guide courts through a *disruption* of precedents that folded the norm and exception together, thereby putting new axioms in place for an understanding of the rule of law. This moment offers us an opportunity to reflect on the national and international strides of the relentless campaign against state impunity in the 1970s—as a way of reinventing resistance in the present.

Radical Critique of Policing

The challenge to impunity and the insistence on state accountability that K.G. Kannabiran speaks of goes beyond an overarching critique of the neoliberal/authoritarian state. Beginning with his efforts as part of the Defence Committee for Naxalite Prisoners in the early 1970s, stretching right up to his close involvement in the peace talks between Maoists and the government in 2004, straddling the treatment of women (Rameeza Bee), minorities (Ansari Begum, Bidar Sikhs, Coimbatore blasts accused), Dalits (Tsundur), Adivasis (Indervelli), political dissenters in custody (conspiracy cases, preventive detention), as well as encounters (Tarkunde Committee, Madhusudan Raj Yadav, among others), his critique of policing rings clear. Torture is ubiquitous in cases of detention and custody. As Koshka Duff argues, the violence of policing is always literally and ideologically hidden from those who are not its targets, and therefore, '[t]o learn the truth about policing, people would have to listen to the testimonies of those who have experienced it'.[21] By criminalizing dissenters and locking them away or 'encountering'/disappearing them, and discrediting them, the voices that may communicate this knowledge are removed from public discourse. This normalization and invisibilization of the violence perpetrated reverses the threat perception in the popular imagination, from the police to those who are the targets—often unarmed, or outnumbered or

20 Hussain, Nasser. 2003. *The Jurisprudence of Emergency: Colonialism and the Rule of Law* Ann Arbor: The University of Michigan Press, p. 137.

21 Duff, Koshka. 2021. 'Introduction'. In *Abolishing the Police*. Ed. Koshka Duff (Illus. Cat Sims). Left Book Club. E-book, p. 12.

in custody or from the most marginalized groups—generating 'the (misleading, ideological) appearance of consent.'[22]

Painstaking fact-finding reports and petitions by civil liberties groups in Andhra Pradesh reveal the inner workings of criminal and lawless policing and open out to view their counter-subversive strategies honed to perfection—surveillance, disruption, chilling effect, secrecy—that coexist with the abandonment of governance by the state and its usurpation by the police. 'State abandonment and state violence are a couple,' as Woodman observes so pertinently.[23] Witness the case of *Kaloji Narayana Rao vs N. Janardhan Reddy & Ors* where Kannabiran challenged Chief Minister N. Janardhan Reddy, the excise commissioner, and the director general of police in court in a writ of quo warranto for erecting liquor auction tents outside police stations in Warangal since Naxalites were obstructing liquor auctions throughout the state. This was at the peak of the anti-arrack movement that eventually brought down the Congress government in power. The chief minister stated in his detailed counter-affidavit filed in court that '[t]he total arrack revenue of Warangal District for the year 1990–91 was Rs 2,147.42 lakhs (rental of Rs 1,435.89 lakhs plus issue price of Rs 711.53 lakhs). In case the shops are not auctioned, the revenue will be affected and the Government will be put to loss to that extent. On the other hand, people who are accustomed to drinking will be deprived of arrack.'[24] The government did not deny that '[i]n view of the threats of extremists, a request was made to the Director General of Police to provide necessary police support for running the Departmental Depots in Mandal Headquarters'.[25]

The abandonment of governance to the police and the blatant violation of Article 47 of the Constitution evident in the auctioning of liquor contracts, not just under police protection but within the premises of a police station, the petitioner said *warranted the enforcement of constitutional obligations by the court*—a task which the court refused to perform. This coupling of governance (specifically excise revenues from the sale of cheap liquor) with coercive policing, as Kannabiran discusses in the chapter on the Shankar Guha Niyogi murder case (Chapter 14), leads to a spiral of false cases, violence and eventually murder that establishes a conspiracy between

22 Ibid., p. 14.

23 Woodman, Connor. 2021. 'Defending the "Liberal–democratic order": The Strategic-Political Logic of Counter-Subversion, pp. 78-82. In *Abolishing the Police*. Ed. Koshka Duff.(Illus. Cat Sims). Left Book Club. E-book.

24 *Kaloji Narayana Rao vs N. Janardhan Reddy and Ors*, 1991 SCC Online AP 391, para 6. I am grateful to K. Parameshwar for drawing my attention to this case.

25 Ibid.

private and public entities—straddling contractors, industrialists, ministers, police personnel and petty criminals at different levels, and even officers in the justice system—demonstrating this coupling of abandonment and violence in chilling detail. It stretches from liquor vending to murder by hired assassins to encounters, with impunity as its hallmark. His prolific efforts, which include the efforts of the Civil Liberties (Tarkunde) Committee and thereafter the Andhra Pradesh Civil Liberties Committee, to 'stem the rot' of extrajudicial murder ('encounters') by the state and to force accountability on the state and political parties of various hues—especially in respect of violence—are constitutive of the history of the civil liberties movement in the country, and indeed of the history of radical (insurgent) constitutionalism.

The Power of Dialogue

It seems like a different era altogether in the life of the nation when there was a debate in the Lok Sabha on 23 February 1973, regarding Naxalite leader Nagabhushan Patnaik's medical treatment while in jail.[26]

> Shri Chintamani Panigrahi (Bhubaneshwar): I would like to bring to your kind notice and the notice of the hon Minister that *one of the finest and most devoted social workers of our country, Shri Nagabhushan Patnaik* who is now in jail in Andhra Pradesh, is fast deteriorating … More than 100 MPs belonging to all sections of this House had made a petition to the hon President and to the Prime Minister and had pleaded for mercy and for commuting his death sentence …
>
> Shri D.K. Panda (Bhaiyanagar): due to ill-treatment, inhuman treatment given inside the Rajahmundry jail to *Shri Nagabhushan Patnaik, who is the finest democrat and social worker*, his health is fast deteriorating …
>
> Shri S.M. Banerjee: You are aware that he belongs to the Naxalite group. *We may differ with his politics.* He along with 32,000 youngmen are in jail throughout the country without any legal defence … There is a petition with the President and the Prime Minister *signed by more than 80 members belonging to all parties including the ruling party … I must congratulate the progressive forces which are at the core of this.* I request that all the 32,000 men should be released immediately …

26 'Re: Medical Treatment of Shri Nagabhushan Patnaik Detained in an Andhra Jail'. 1973. *Lok Sabha Debates: Seventh Session* (Fifth Lok Sabha), 23 February: 236–40.

When there was a discussion on whether he should be treated in Rajahmundry or Hyderabad or brought to AIIMS, Delhi, Shri D.K. Panda, insisting that he be brought to AIIMS, Delhi, observed, '*There must be human feelings in this matter*' (emphasis added).

Even under the most repressive regime, parliamentary deliberations on the rights of political prisoners, their contributions to a democratic polity, detentions, ill-treatment and deaths in custody point to a different time and a different ethic of politics that refused to be silenced by autocratic leadership or governmental/administrative pusillanimity.

On 15 June 1977, after the lifting of the Emergency and the general elections, the release of political prisoners and the report of the Tarkunde Committee were discussed in the Lok Sabha. Union home minister Chaudhary Charan Singh provided detailed responses to members from all parties in terms of state-wise figures, actions initiated towards release of prisoners, and inquiries into state excesses. Of particular relevance to the present purpose is the discussion on the report of the Tarkunde Committee, *before* the Bhargava Commission was constituted to inquire into encounter deaths in Andhra Pradesh.

Under the item 'Release of Persons Detained during Emergency', Mukhtiar Singh Malik sought a response from the home minister on the (a) number of persons released from among those detained under the Maintenance of Internal Security Act (MISA)/Defence of Internal Security of India Rules (DISIR) and other Acts during Emergency; (b) state-wise and category-wise break-ups; (c) deaths of detenus and causes of deaths during Emergency; (d) steps taken by the government to release detained persons. In his point-by-point response, Home Minister Charan Singh told the House that '(a) and (b) During the Emergency 29,795 persons were detained under the Maintenance of Internal Security Act, 1971, by invoking Section 16A of the Act. Out of them 18,892 detenus had been released up to 10th March 1977 and the remaining were released after that date … (c) 59 detenus died while in custody and 14 died while on parole' (p. 16). Gauri Shankar Rai pressed on further: 'Does the Home Minister know that several people have died soon after release from detention, owing to their illness during detention? Will these deaths also be counted as deaths in custody?' (No. 47, pp. 16–17). To which the home minister's response was that *deaths occurring within three months of release would be considered custodial deaths*, and compensation would be given to those families whose economic situation warranted support (No. 47, p. 17).

This debate bears important lessons for how we might understand state practice in the matter of custodial morbidity and custodial death, especially, but not restricted to, political prisoners. The case that immediately comes to mind is the arrest under the draconian Unlawful Activities Prevention Act (UAPA) of octogenarian activist Father Stan Swamy in the Bhima Koregaon case in October 2020, the conditions of his incarceration despite grave risks posed by Parkinson's disease and COVID-19, and his death in July 2021 while under medical treatment in custody on court orders.[27] The chastisement of the Bombay High Court by the additional solicitor general representing the National Investigation Agency (NIA) for its oral tribute to Stan Swamy in court, and the withdrawal of the tribute by the judge with the comment, 'But you see, Mr Singh, we are also human beings', signals the persistent efforts of the violent state to overawe courts.[28] The latter's willingness to sidestep the Constitution, opting to legitimize the rule by exception instead is a judicial trend that we see consolidating itself during the Emergency. And yet, as we must never forget, there were times when this trend was consistently thwarted, evident in several instances recalled in *The Speaking Constitution*.

To return to the parliamentary debate on the excesses during the Emergency, Chitta Basu drew the attention of the House to the 'apprehensions [that] have been expressed by many that many of the deaths in jail are due to police torture and under questionable circumstances' (p. 17), and sought a response whether the government proposed to initiate a judicial inquiry into deaths in custody (No. 47, p. 18). Professor Dilip Chakravarty demanded information about whether an inquiry would be instituted into the 'conspiracy hatched by the Central Home Ministry ["in league with Shri Siddhartha Shankar Ray"] to have the theory of counter violence … as a result [of which] 5000 Naxalites were killed in the streets of West Bengal' (No. 47, p. 19). The home minister had no such information. K. Chandrappan sought information on why the Janata government had released 'almost all the RSS members who were members of a banned organization'; this was not the case with Naxalite detenus. The home minister had figures for Bengal but said that 'the final word lies with the state government. We can only give them advice' (No. 47, pp. 19–20). G.M. Banatwalla pressed on this point: 'Is it not a fact that in the case of RSS detenus the Government pursued the matter vigorously and all of them have been released immediately but in the case of Naxalites, the government is content by giving a mere advice to the states?' To which Chaudhary Charan Singh registers

27 'Stan Swamy: India Outrage over Death of Jailed Activist'. 2021. BBC, https://www.bbc.com/news/world-asia-india-57718361. Accessed on 7 December 2021.

28 Vidya. 2021. 'Justice Shinde Withdraws Comments Praising Late Stan Swamy after NIA Raises Objection.' *India Today*, 23 July, https://www.indiatoday.in/law/story/justice-shinde-withdraws-comments-praising-stan-swamy-1831771-2021-07-23. Accessed on 9 June 2022.

a strong rebuttal: 'I protest against this insinuation. I have been solicitous to the Naxalites rather than the RSS people and the Naxalite leaders themselves will testify to what I have said' (No. 47, p. 22).

The debate also dwelt on the descriptions of torture perpetrated by the police in the encounters investigated by the Tarkunde Committee before moving on to whether Naxalites still believed in the annihilation of class enemies, with the home minister giving the assurance that many of them had eschewed violence and had chosen to 'follow the democratic path' (No. 47, p. 23, in response to P.K. Kodiyan). The most interesting question of all, however, is the one posed by Vinodbhai B. Sheth: '*What is the actual definition of Naxalites? How can you demarcate Naxalites from other criminals?* Is there any change in the attitude of the police departments against the Naxalites?' (No. 47, p. 24, emphasis added). Chaudhary Charan Singh responded with: '*The definition is that they did not commit any crime for their own personal interest. They were actuated by public interest, although they were mistaken in choosing the method they chose in achieving those ends*' (No. 47, p. 24, emphasis added).[29]

This response of the then home minister takes us directly back to a deliberation over this very question, in a case K.G. Kannabiran brought before the Andhra Pradesh High Court. Justice O. Chinnappa Reddy constituted a committee of judges and senior lawyers to deliberate on the case of Naxalite leader Intha Ramana Reddy who had been awarded a death sentence ex parte because he refused to defend himself. The basic formulation Justice Chinnappa Reddy arrived at was that 'in any crime, even if it involves a murder, if there was no personal motive to kill the other person, where there was no personal gain from committing the crime, where the crime is committed in pursuance of a broad based ideology, such a crime may be defined as a political crime/offence'.[30] The Supreme Court rejected this reasoning, affirming Justice V.R. Krishna Iyer's view in the earlier case of Bhoomaiah and Kishta Goud

---

29 'Murder and Torture of Naxalites in Andhra Pradesh'. *Lok Sabha Debates*, Volume II, Second Series. 15 June 1977. New Delhi: Lok Sabha Secretariat. pp. 217-224. Ramchandra Singh, in his prison reminiscences, speaks of a statement to which Naxalite prisoners were made signatories, immediately after Emergency was lifted in 1977, drafted by Naxalite leader S.N. Singh (Satya Narayan Singh) and submitted to the Government of Uttar Pradesh to secure early release of such prisoners. Singh, Ramchandra. 2018. *Thirteen Years: A Naxalite's Prison Diary*. New Delhi: Navayana, pp. 134–35.

30 *Sessions Judge Nellore Referring Officer vs Intha Ramana Reddy* on 12 February 1971. 1972 CriLJ 1485, para 1. Also *State of Andhra Pradesh vs Intha Ramana Reddy and Anr* on 16 November 1976, AIR 1977 SC 708. Author: Justice A. Gupta; bench: A. Gupta, P. Bhagwati, P. Shinghal.

that the Indian Penal Code (IPC) made no such distinction (Chapter 10). The dialogic method in approaching extremely complex and difficult questions of life and liberty, and indeed the possibility of a parliamentary debate on the subject of Naxalites vs RSS and the turns in Naxalite politics that is open and free of acrimony or reductive condemnation is particularly noteworthy.

In response to a question posed as a separate item in the debate by D.B. Chandragowda, the home minister confirmed that the proposal to set up a 'Civil Rights Commission' was under active consideration of the government (No. 395, p. 60). This again, clearly had to do with the Emergency excesses. Bapusaheb Parulekar sought clarifications on the status of Section 16A of MISA and was informed by Chaudhary Charan Singh that the section had been deleted and all those booked under it released (No. 47, p. 22).

The second aspect of this particular debate that bears an immediate relevance to this work is the parliamentary debate on the findings of the Tarkunde Committee on encounters in Andhra Pradesh. In an item titled 'Calling Attention: Large Scale Murder and Torture of Naxalites in Andhra Pradesh' (pp. 217–24), Samar Mukherjee called for a statement from the home minister on 'The reported large-scale murder and torture of Naxalites in Andhra Pradesh during the last few years as revealed by the Civil Rights Committee headed by Shri V.M. Tarkunde.' The home minister noted with grave concern the two reports released by the Tarkunde Committee and made a statement that bears reiteration today:

> 'The House is aware of the serious problem of law and order resulting from the activities of the Naxalites in certain parts of Andhra Pradesh. These activities included cold-blooded murder and other serious offences. In the circumstances, the police were required to deal with a difficult problem. *But law enforcement agencies cannot take law into their own hands whether they are dealing with Naxalites or any other individual or groups. No failure on their part to act strictly according to law can be condoned. The two reports of the Committee give serious misgivings whether the police had acted in accordance with law while dealing with Naxalites*' (emphasis added).

Samar Mukherjee and Ahalya Rangnekar, quoting sections of the Tarkunde Committee report, cautioned the home minister against delegating responsibility for a judicial inquiry to the chief minister of the state as the same chief minister had been shown by the Tarkunde Committee to be complicit in the violence perpetrated by the police. The chief minister at this time was J. Vengal Rao, with the Congress party returning to power after the Emergency in Andhra Pradesh. K.G. Kannabiran discusses the proceedings of the Bhargava Commission (1977–78) which was constituted by the centre in consultation with the state to inquire into the incidents of encounter murders in Andhra Pradesh. This was also the exact time when the Muktadar Commission was constituted under Justice K.A. Muktadar, a sitting judge of the Andhra Pradesh High Court to inquire into the rape in police custody of Rameeza Bee and the death in police custody of her husband Ahmed Hussain in March 1978 (Chapter 8). Kannabiran appeared before the Muktadar Commission as well. In the months of April–May 1978, both commissions were conducting their hearings on police violence. Unlike the Bhargava Commission which folded up without being allowed to complete its task, the Muktadar Commission report[31] was tabled in the Andhra Pradesh Legislative Assembly.[32] The policemen were tried (and acquitted) by the sessions court, Raichur, Karnataka, an acquittal that was upheld by the Karnataka High Court.[33]

That state violence and police impunity, as also the limits (or lack thereof) of state accountability, were debated at such length and with such rigour meant that human lives (dissident lives, importantly) were placed at the centre of an understanding of democracy mindful of all the risks dissidents might pose to government. This stands as a standard worthy of emulation and remembering in a context where the mere idea of parliamentary debate is subjected to ridicule and censorship, with unarmed civilians under unprecedented risk. Witness, for instance, the targeted violence against Muslims (as in the Delhi riots of February 2020); arbitrary arrests of dissenters (especially anti–Citizenship Amendment Act [CAA] protestors); the abrogation of Article 370 and the fragmentation of the state of Jammu and Kashmir into two union territories, under the rule of the central government, followed by mass arrests and internet shutdowns in the Kashmir valley; the gunning down by the army of unarmed coal miners in Nagaland, a state ruled by exception under the Armed Forces Special Powers Act (AFSPA); or the enactment and subsequent repeal

31 Report of the Commission of Inquiry (to enquire into the detention of Sri Ahmed Hussain and Smt. Rameeza Bee, death of Ahmed Hussain, etc.) Constituted under the Notification G.O. Ms. No. 263, General Administration (General-A) Department, Dated 7 April 1978. By The Hon'ble Sri Justice K.A. Muktadar.

32 'Discussion on the Report of Muktadar Inquiry Commission'. 1978. *Andhra Pradesh Legislative Assembly Debates*, Vol VIII, No. 2 (7 September): 196–251.

33 *Sayeed Ahmed & Ors vs State of Andhra Pradesh*, Crl. A. No. 34/82, Crl. A. No. 374/81, Crl. R.P. 40/82, Crl. A. No. 238/1981 and *State of Andhra Pradesh vs T. Surender Singh*, Crl. A. 34/1982. In the Karnataka High Court at Bangalore, 7 and 8 March 1984.

of farm laws—all matters not debated in Parliament. Perhaps more than ever before, we need to recall Milan Kundera: '[t]he struggle of man against power is the struggle of memory against forgetting.'[34]

Laws, Literatures, Courts, Resistance, Lives: The Power of the 'Vernacular'

Sudhir Dhawale, a leader of the Kabir Kala Manch, was arrested in June 2018, facing prosecution under UAPA and various sections of the IPC for incitement to violence and waging war against the state.[35] In the FIR (First Information Report) placed before the court in *Romila Thapar*,[36] performance of the lines from Bertolt Brecht's 1942 play *The Good Person of Szechwan* was understood by the complainant and the investigating officer as a malicious incitement to violence.

> When injustice is done there should be revolt in the city
> And if there is no revolt,
> it were better that the city should perish in fire before night falls.[37]

What is the relationship between the performance of resistance and incitement to violence? Or the difference between incitement and insurgency? And how does literature render palpable the brutality of state repression? How do song and poetry and their collective performance signal the insurgent storms? The defence of writers and poets was central to K.G. Kannabiran's court walks during the Emergency. Who were these people, and why were they detained or imprisoned? How did the

34 Kundera, Milan. 1980. *The Book of Laughter and Forgetting.* Trans. Michael Henry Heim. New York: Alfred A. Knopf.

35 A longer version of this section was published as: 'The Struggle Is Its Own Reward'. 2019. *Seminar,* Vol. 721 'September': pp 29–38. I am grateful to the editor for permission to include a revised version here.'Vernacular' signposts the debates on the ideas of justice, human rights and pluralism that are constitutive of vernacular cultures.

36 *Romila Thapar & Ors vs Union of India & Ors.* Writ Petition in public interest seeking the immediate release of activists raided and arrested in complete violation of their fundamental rights guaranteed under Article 14 and 21 of the Constitution of India. 29 August 2018.

37 Gandhi, Gopalkrishna. 2018. 'When Brecht Speaks as Ambedkar'. *The Hindu.* 21 September, https://www.thehindu.com/opinion/lead/when-brecht-speaks-as-ambedkar/article24998770.ece. Accessed on 1 December 2021.

courts understand creative expression and the politics of speech, and how indeed did they understand the fragilities of the 'security of state'?

In 1971, three poets, Nikhileshwar, Jwalamukhi and Cherabanda Raju[38]—who were part of a group that called itself the Digambara Kavulu—were arrested under the Andhra Pradesh Preventive Detention Act, 1970. J. Vengal Rao, then state home minister, declared in the Assembly that 'these poets are dangerous because they are "verbal Naxalites"'.[39] Nikhileshwar also speaks of a member of the Revolutionary Writers' Association (RWA) being held in police custody for four days 'for the crime of writing a poem and publishing it in a local weekly … two years ago. Later he was fined Rs 50 by the magistrate for "literary crime".'[40]

The Digambara poets were held in custody for fifty days. Arguing in their defence, K.G. Kannabiran persuaded the court to witness the performance of revolutionary poetry:[41]

> The hearing was totally uninhibited and free. The courtroom was packed and our request to permit the poets to read out the poems impugned by the detention orders was acceded to … [T]he best was Cherabanda Raju's reading. It was a fine satire on Indira Gandhi's socialism set to rhythm and

---

38 Cherabanda Raju (1944–1982), born as Baddam Bhaskara Reddy in Ankusapuram in Hyderabad, was a Telugu teacher in a government school in Hyderabad. He earned wide acclaim for his revolutionary songs. He was imprisoned under preventive detention in 1971, again in 1973 under the MISA, and finally implicated in the Secunderabad conspiracy case, all for inciting armed rebellion against the state through his songs. Suspended from his job, he died young and is remembered for singing the revolution as few could. Jwalamukhi (1938–2008), was an active member of the Organisation for People's Democratic Rights. A prolific poet and human rights defender, he was arrested in 1971 under preventive detention. Nikhileshwar (b. 1938), renowned poet and recipient of the Sahitya Akademi Award in 2021, was imprisoned in 1971 under preventive detention. All three were Digambara poets and co-founders of the Viplava Rachayitala Sangham (VIRASAM), also called the Revolutionary Writers' Association.

39 Nikhileshwar, Interview, Hyderabad. 16 January 2019. 'We have travelled now all the way from verbal Naxalites to urban Naxalites,' he commented sardonically during the interview.

40 Nikhileshwar. 1974. 'Dissent and Hypocrisy'. *Frontier Weekly* '23 March' p. 7.

41 Kannabiran, K.G. 2004. *The Wages of Impunity: Power, Justice and Human Rights*. Hyderabad: Orient Longman, p. 300.

> tune. This device demonstrated the untenability of the detention orders against these three poets.

Nikhileshwar recalls the mood in the court—it was the first time poets were asked to perform in a court of law. The poem he read out was 'Bhayam' (Fear).

> Fear
> wears a deathly countenance
> turning blood
> to water, it
> drenches
> the veins
> ...
> Countless die
> each passing day
> some innocent
> some nameless
> others violently
> still others tortured
> brutalised by lead
> each round a mark
> of the enemy's cowardice
> the inhumanity
> of their violence
> thriving evidence
> of the derangement
> of authority
>
> So why live in fear?
> Rather than
> crawl and prey unseen
> like a bedbug or common louse
> and creep about
> like the agents that surveil
> Set yourself free
> and live, why don't you!
> ...

And in your resolve
to change
this wretched system
may you immerse yourself
in the warmth of struggle
knowing always
that in the anatomy of fear
lies the seed
of its inevitable defeat.[42]

The Parvathipuram conspiracy case was the first time communists were tried en masse for 'waging war against the state' in independent India (Chapter 6). Naxalite leader Sivasagar (K.G. Satyamurthy) recited a poem in court in lieu of his statement—challenging the legal definition of the crime of conspiracy itself, recasting it to speak to the conspiracies of those in power,[43] a reasoning Kannabiran echoes in his reflections on conspiracy.

Statement of a 'Conspirator'
Your Lordships!
The sunrise is no conspiracy
The sun no conspirator
Would you call the labour
of a pregnant woman conspiracy?
And the path of the chariot of history?

---

42 Nikhileshwar. 2018. *Nikhileshwar Kavitvam*. Hyderabad: Emesco Books, pp. 108–09. Translated from the Telugu by Ramya K. Tella. The 'atmosphere of fear' is one that Justice Rajinder Sachar speaks about in his account of his eighty-year-old father's arrest under the Emergency, while Sachar was the chief justice of Sikkim. See Sachar, Rajinder. 2020. *In Pursuit of Justice: An Autobiography*. New Delhi: Rupa Publications. Chapter 7: Emergency.

43 K.G. Satyamurthy (1931–2012), born in Krishna district, also known by his pen name, Sivasagar, was a leader of the Communist Party of India (Marxist-Leninist) (CPI [ML]), and an unparalleled revolutionary poet. Co-founder (with Kondapalli Seetaramayya) of the CPI (ML) [PWG], and a long-time leader who spent years underground, he parted ways with the party, inaugurating a serious debate on Ambedkarite philosophy and the rule of caste in the Naxalite movement, drawing on his personal and political experience with revolutionary politics. A prolific writer and philosopher, Sivasagar is an icon of the Dalit movement and a leading figure in contemporary Telugu literature.

Your Lordships!
Demon landlords
rolling up our land like mats
tucking them under their arms conspire
The brokers hawking my country
to foreign countries are conspirators
Soliciting alliance at Kosygin's leprous feet conspiracy
Nixon's food borne hither by ships conspiracy
Devouring Bharat's freedom is conspiracy
The ballot box is a conspiracy
'Garibi Hatao' is a conspiracy
Indiramma's smile a conspiracy
Conspiring to hang the sun
through arrogant half-closed eyes
of injustice is conspiracy
The sunrise of Srikakulam is no conspiracy
The guerilla sun no conspirator!
Sunrise piercing through darkness
spreads warmth and light
Among the people
Your Lordships!
You are indeed good people!
In this evil hour of injustice
Yama Dharmaraja incarnate![44]

Inguva Mallikarjuna Sharma, speaking of his years in prison between 1973 and 1978 as an accused—A-1—in the Secunderabad conspiracy case, narrates this habit of performing the revolution in courts:[45]

---

44 Sivasagar (K.G. Satyamurthy), '"Kutradaru" Vangmulam' read out in court in June 1973. Cherukuri Satyanarayana, *Suryodayam Kutrakaadu* (Sunrise Is No Conspiracy), Tarimela Nagireddy Memorial Committee, Guntur, 2016, pp. 3–4. Translated from the Telugu by Vasanth Kannabiran.

45 Sharma, Mallikarjuna I. 2017. 'Tale of a Roving Rebel'. No. 30, Vol. 50, *Frontier* (28 January–3 February). Vice-President Venkaiah Naidu was an Akhil Bharatiya Vidyarthi Parishad (ABVP) detenu at the time that Sharma was a CPI (ML) undertrial—and Sharma recalls sharing a van and escort with him to court, 'bitter ideological rivals' who 'had some friendly or non-rancorous chat' on the ride to court. The possibility of this 'chat', however fleeting, is foreclosed in the present

> Those days coming and going to court was a sort of cynosure to both us under-trial [sic] accused as also to our visitors. We would sing revolutionary songs, Cherabanda Raju would also begin singing many times, and even give slogans inside the courts despite protests from the judges. Normally no action would be taken for this 'contempt' and 'defiance' but in emergency [sic] things changed. They began to foist cases under criminal law amendment for giving out slogans and that decreased the number of slogan raising [sic] comrades. However, I continued till last—even giving slogans in the court trying such cases!

For forty-nine years, from 1973 to 2022 (the continuing present). Varavara Rao has lived in anticipation of incarceration or in prison, as P. Hemalatha, his wife, recounts. In December 1985, during N.T. Rama Rao's term as chief minister, when there were open threats to his life from the police, Varavara Rao asked for cancellation of bail in order to protect his rights to free speech and life. Towards the end of 1988, his family, in their efforts to secure bail, met Justice V.M. Tarkunde and Arun Shourie (then editor of the *Indian Express*). Shourie asked them to persuade Varavara Rao to write a weekly column in the *Indian Express* that would generate public support for his release:

> Not politics, but about what life is like in prison. The pigeons, birds, trees, flowers, skies, fellow prisoners, their troubles, the books he reads, his thoughts. Varavara Rao is a sensitive person. His writing on these aspects will reach people across the country through [the] *Indian Express*.[46]

Shourie offered to convince the jail authorities to permit this writing. From 25 December 1988 to 16 April 1989, Varavara Rao wrote a weekly column that appeared in Telugu and English—later published as a book in Telugu with a foreword by Kaloji Narayan Rao and in English with a foreword by Ngugi Wa

---

political environment, a foreclosure that signals the hegemonic disruptions of debate, dialogue and multi-sited politics attendant on the rise of right-wing majoritarian nationalism to national government.

46 Hemalatha, P. 2019. 'Marokasari Nirbandha Jnyapakalu (Once More, Prison Reminiscences)' in Varavara Rao, *Sahacharulu*. Navodaya Publications, Hyderabad, p. 5-6. Translation mine.

Thiong'o.[47] Originally published in 1989, the Telugu collection *Sahacharulu* was republished in February 2019 in the context of Varavara Rao's incarceration in the ongoing Bhima Koregaon case.[48]

The throwback to the 1970s through the singular figure of Varavara Rao, now eighty-two years old and out on bail on health grounds but confined to Mumbai, ceases to be a throwback, the past, present and future indistinct from each other, especially in the machinations of penal justice.

It has also been a lifetime of waiting and trips to courts, jails and police stations for P. Hemalatha. Not only seeking the release of Varavara Rao, her husband, but defending her own actions in defence of free speech. A cursory look at her life shows her stunning resilience and grit in the face of continued onslaught by the state under different political regimes. I point to an older, quite spectacular account that lies buried and forgotten,[49] an account which in fact anticipates her life to the present.

> Mrs. P. Hemalatha, 27, lay waiting for the arrival of her third child at the Government Maternity Hospital, Warangal, on April 26, 1974 … Just before coming to hospital she had worked hard with her associates to bring out the May issue of *Srujana*, a Telugu literary monthly. Two thousand copies of *Srujana* devoted to the railway strike were out on the street that day.

Varavara Rao, then a college lecturer, was arrested days after her return from hospital, in the Secunderabad conspiracy case. Three years later, after the Emergency was lifted in 1977, Hemalatha was sentenced to two years in prison for a poem by Satyam titled 'Can the Jails Run the Trains?' in that issue (with Madhu Dandavate, who led the railway strike during the Emergency and was now installed as the railway minister). The sessions judge, Warangal, delivering the judgment observed:

47 Thiong'o, Ngugi Wa. 2010. 'That Which the Imagination Makes Possible'. In *Captive Imagination: Letters from Prison*. Varavara Rao. New Delhi: Penguin, pp. 7–12.

48 Hemalatha. 2019. 'Marokasari Nirbandha Jnyapakalu '(Once More, Prison Reminiscences)'. In *Sahacharulu*. Varavara Rao. Hyderabad: Navodaya Publications, pp. 5–6. Translation mine.

49 Panjwani, Narendra. 1977. 'Prison for a Poem'. *The Times of India*, 21 August. The excerpts that follow on this case are from this report.

> The fact that the accused is the mother of three children warrants a lenient view, *but as she is not repenting on what she did*, we have to be firm to meet the ends of justice …

This account foregrounds the deep contradictions posed by the presence of women in revolutionary/progressive movements. The constant slippage between receding into the invisibility of reproductive labour and conjugal duties in a patriarchal revolutionary imagination on the one hand, and the refusal by women to 'repent' or be contained/confined within that space (being punished by a criminal court for that refusal) on the other, is one that must be disentangled. The prison holds multiple layers of disobedience and speaks to several expressions of the loss of liberty simultaneously—in fact and metaphorically. Prison writings, especially during the Emergency, are a whole different genre that we cannot explore here.

The struggle then, as now, has been to keep furiously writing and resisting state action—'house searches, midnight raids, preventive detention laws, MISA, arrests under terrorist laws, false cases, false witnesses, confessions (approvers) extracted through force and bribery', as K.V. Ramana Reddy observes in 1975 in his prison diary.[50] In the shadow of the punitive state today, we return in troubling fashion to this moment, the past fusing with the present in state action and in the resistance to it.

Debating Dissent in the Courtroom

> But am I a citizen in the true sense of the word? A citizen, by definition, is one who both rules and is ruled. I am only here to be ruled, and as such, a very essential part of citizenship is denied to me, and to that extent, I am only a subject, as all other detenues are. A state which calls itself a democracy

50 Reddy, K.V. Ramana. 2011. *Jaillo Moodnella Mucchata*: *June–October 1974* (Prison Diary). Hyderabad: Jhanjha Publication, 2011, p. 1. K.V. Ramana Reddy (1927–1998) was a political scientist, biographer and editor. A teacher by profession, he was founder secretary of VIRASAM, editor of its journal, *Arunatara*, general secretary of the All India League for Revolutionary Culture, and editor of its journal, *Thunder*. He edited the complete works of legendary Telugu poet Sri K.V.R., faced sedition charges for editing the Telugu anthology *Jhanjha* and was imprisoned twice: during the Emergency and as an accused in the Secunderabad conspiracy case.

> cannot, and ought not to, admit of subject-hood to even the tiniest fraction of its population, and at the same time hope to continue to be a democracy.
>
> ...
>
> What on earth is this Parliamentary Supremacy for? To beat down the Judiciary?
>
> —Court statement of K.V. Ramana Reddy, 23 February 1976[51]

The charge sheet against Nikhileshwar read as follows:

> You are one of those who launched the Digambara (naked) poets.
>
> Along with your friends Jwalamukhi and Cherabanda Raju you prodded Sri Sri into leaving the Progressive Writers' Association and joining the Revolutionary Writers' Association. You are the principal functionary of the Revolutionary Writers' Association.
>
> Through your poem 'Fear' you tried to incite people to class struggle. You preached that they should face death fearlessly in struggle.
>
> In your poem 'Counter-violence' you criticised the Indian government's role in crushing the revolt in Ceylon by satirising it.
>
> You travelled extensively in the state participating and speaking at student, youth, revolutionary writers and civil rights defenders meetings.
>
> You attended the Punjabi writers conference in Jullunder and endorsed its resolutions.[52]

Nikhileshwar responded with a point-by-point rebuttal of the statements in the charge sheet:

> Whatever I might be by profession, as a poet and a writer … defying the evils of caste, creed and race, I wrote along with the other Digambara friends for universalism … The present society is the result of several contradictions. To go to the roots of these contradictions is my responsibility … My writings were within the limits of the freedom of speech and expression provided by the constitution … The contemporary writer finds concrete shape for his

---

51 Reddy, K.V. Ramana. 1977. *Detenu Diary* (Telugu), Kavali: Sarathi Press, pp. 17, 27. Statement in English in the original.

52 Nikhileshwar. 1975. *Walls*, unpublished. On file with author.

> ideal in the humanistic philosophy of Marxism. I can say unhesitatingly that I follow this great philosophy and write to the call of the times.
>
> It is our duty to assail the inequalities in this society and rouse the people. We wrote poetry as part of our responsibility. To say that they are sadistic or obscene is the result of your perverse interpretation. The Police Department lacks the competence to decide what is sadism or obscenity in literature.
>
> The poems 'Fear' and 'Counter-Violence' reflect my views.
>
> We did not defraud Sri Sri. It would be insulting him to say that we prodded him into joining the Revolutionary Writers' Association. He was one of the founders of the Association.
>
> I do not think writing, travel or participation in meetings could constitute a threat to public safety or law and order.[53]

Justice O. Chinnappa Reddy and Justice A.D.V. Reddy, hearing the case in the Andhra Pradesh High Court, found the grounds of the order of detention invalid. In a sharp comment, Justice Chinnappa Reddy observed:[54]

> The first three grounds in the three orders of detention are identical … We are unable to see any relevance between these three grounds and the object of the detention namely, maintenance of public order … *We are also unable to see how their beliefs in Marxism, Leninism and Maoism or their 'vulgar and sadistic' references to certain classes of people in their writings have any rational connection with the object of detention.* Beliefs are not subject to controls and no one can be jailed for his beliefs.

He quoted Chief Justice Patanjali Sastri who two decades earlier had 'lamented':[55]

> … notwithstanding repeated admonition by this court that due care and attention must be bestowed upon matters involving the liberty of the individual, it is distressing to find that such matters are dealt with in a careless and casual manner.

---

53 Ibid.

54 *K. Yadava Reddy, B. Bhaskara Reddy, A.V. Raghavachari vs Commissioner of Police, AP & State of AP*, WP Nos. 3115, 3116 & 3117 of 1971. High Court of Judicature at Hyderabad, September 20 1971. O. Chinnappa Reddy, J. and A.D.V Reddy, J. Para 21. Emphasis added.

55 Ibid., para 27.

After twenty years we find from the grounds furnished in these cases that the position continues to be the same and we can only join the lament of Patanjali Sastri, C.J.

Forty-five years later, it is not unreasonable to join the lament of Justice Chinnappa Reddy and of Patanjali Sastri, chief justice, before him. The responsibility of the state in matters to do with the negation of personal liberty continues to be the most distressing aspect of our political life.

On poetic expression and incitement, Justice Chinnappa Reddy said:

> Poetry is the spontaneous overflow of powerful feelings. It is the record of the poet's struggle from darkness to light and passion and extravagance go hand in hand with it. It is difficult to see how the mere outpourings of a poet's thoughts and emotions in the form of a poem can have any rational connection with public disorder.

In *Jwalamukhi vs State of Andhra Pradesh* the following year again, the dissenting judge, Justice K. Madhava Reddy, observed:[56]

> These poems only educate the literate Telugu people in these ideas and theories, but as observed by Justice Holmes, 'every idea is an incitement' and the propagation of every such idea cannot, in my opinion, be termed seditious.

This dissenting opinion was upheld by Justice V.R. Krishna Iyer in the Supreme Court three years later during the Emergency in *State of Uttar Pradesh vs Lalai Singh Yadav*,[57] which concerned the publication of a Hindi translation of Periyar's work *Ramayana: A True Reading*. The circulation and interweaving between proscription by the state of political dissent by the left and the majoritarian proscription of anti-caste critiques of Hindu religion then and now is an aspect that merits a detailed exploration.

This section presented one small part of the performance of dissent/ constitutional insurgency in the courtroom in Andhra Pradesh in the 1970s. Whether poetic expression constitutes 'good incitement' (after Justice Holmes) or 'criminal incitement' (from the standpoint of a pusillanimous state) was not a settled matter in courts in cases that stretched from before the Emergency to after the Emergency, demonstrating in a sense the paradoxical continuities in the

56 *Jwalamukhi vs State of Andhra Pradesh*, ILR (1973) AP 114.

57 *State of Uttar Pradesh vs Lalai Singh Yadav*, AIR 1977 SC 202.

fragilities of different regimes. What has, however, continued as a constant is the power of literary performance of resistance in rousing constitutional insurgency as we witnessed during the Emergency and again around the anti-CAA and farmers' protests in 2019–2021, for instance.

Criminal Conspiracies: 'Associational Freedoms'/'Associational Offences'

K.G. Kannabiran challenged conspiracy theories and set out evidence of conspiracy, both, in the cases he fought.[58] He dwells on both these aspects of his work, foregrounding the conditions under which conspiracy must be part of the offences perpetrators of violence are prosecuted for, and the conditions under which the accusation of conspiracy 'directly trenches upon the associational freedoms of speech, association and assembly', the latter extensively in political trials. He pointed out to courts that '[i]mplicating writers in the Secunderabad Conspiracy Case was itself a conspiracy … [T]heir removal from employment was part of this conspiracy on the part of the government' (Chapter 5). His account of the Naxalite conspiracy cases demonstrates that the issue in a conspiracy trial is not manifest criminality, 'but the classic concern in the theory of subjective criminality … [and] the demonstration that the conspiracy is at work … [and not] a project still resting solely in the minds of the conspirators … [such that] acts innocent in themselves, such as mailing a letter, or making a telephone call, can constitute the required overt act for a conspiracy'.[59]

Right from the time of its introduction into the IPC in 1913 to deal with the struggle for freedom, till the present time in its pervasive use in political trials, Kannabiran argues, it has been a tool to delegitimize political dissent, quoting George Fletcher:

> The relentless criticism of the doctrine of conspiracy invites some retrenchment in the scope of liability. The primary libertarian concern is that prosecution of political conspiracies trenches too far on protected freedoms

58 See Kannabiran, K.G. 2008. 'Conspiracies of Association: Associational Offences, Associational Freedoms and the Rule of Law'. In *Challenging the Rules of Law: Colonialism, Criminology and Human Rights in India*. Eds Kalpana Kannabiran and Ranbir Singh. New Delhi: Sage.

59 Fletcher, George P. 1978. *Rethinking Criminal Law*. Boston: Little Brown & Co. p. 224. Quoted in K.G. Kannabiran, 2008, p. 382.

> of thought and speech. A sensible restrictive measure would be strengthening the overt act requirement. This would insure that the prosecution stays its hand until a politically dissident group manifests palpable danger to the community.[60]

In mass violence, like in the case of the brutal daylight murder of six Dalits in Melavalavu, Tamil Nadu, on 30 June 1997, the judge convicted eighteen of the forty accused but did not find motive, conspiracy or unlawful assembly. In Tsundur in Andhra Pradesh, where Dalits were murdered in a planned attack by the dominant castes, while there were convictions, the arguments on the offence of conspiracy were not accepted by the judge.[61] There is a similar denial of conspiracy in the case of targeted mass assault against religious minorities, as Kannabiran argues in his chapter (Chapter 16) on religious minorities in the context of Hindutva violence.[62] And yet, in the Naxalite conspiracy trials (Chapter 6), disparate and unconnected cases and incidents purported to have taken place were strung together by the police to concoct the offence of conspiracy, resulting in the acquittals after long-drawn-out trials like the Parvathipuram, Secunderabad and Bangalore conspiracy cases.

> Conspiracy as an offence is supposed to be secretive, and so direct proof may not be available: proof is only possible circumstantially. This legal postulate may be real if the Dalits were to plan the annihilation of an upper caste landlord. But such secrecy is not required in the case of assault by the upper castes on either the Scheduled Castes or the Scheduled Tribes. In the context of fastening criminal responsibility on the members of the upper castes for assault on the Scheduled Castes, conspiracy and other associational offences have to be differently understood. The limitations evolved by a consensus in the Constitution are not recognised as limitations concerning the rights, duties and responsibilities governing our lives in the hierarchical caste structure.[63]

---

60 Fletcher, George P. 1978. *Rethinking Criminal Law*. Boston: Little Brown & Co. p. 225. Quoted in Kannabiran, K.G. 2008, p. 383.

61 Kannabiran, K.G. 2008, 'Conspiracies of Association: Associational Offences, Associational Freedoms and the Rule of Law', pp. 385–91.

62 See ibid., pp. 391–94.

63 Ibid., p. 386.

The problem is especially complex and knotted in the cases of riots–counter-riots and violence–counter-violence (post–Babri Masjid riots and the Mumbai bomb blasts, the Coimbatore blasts, Godhra, post-Godhra, for instance): 'How does one work out Article 14 if in the riot there is shoddy or no investigation and the "counter riot" is ostensibly fully investigated and implicates the counter-rioters? … How does one square Constitutional values with this kind of social violence where majoritarian social violence is let off the hook, while crimes (similar crimes) committed by the minorities purportedly as redress of earlier wrongs are punished?'[64] In this volume, K.G. Kannabiran reflects on the trial in the Coimbatore bomb blasts case, where he represented the accused (Chapter 16).

In a twist, in his arguments in the Shankar Guha Niyogi murder case, Kannabiran pointed out to the Madhya Pradesh High Court that there was every evidence of conspiracy in Niyogi's murder, that had been appreciated by the trial court. The high court disregarded his arguments as well as the verdict of the trial court, and acquitted the industrialists who were accused by the prosecution of hiring an assassin to murder Niyogi (Chapter 14).

Of significance to our understanding of the crime of conspiracy is the manner in which K.G. Kannabiran illuminates the varied contexts of conspiracy—where it is admitted in the case of political dissent through a subjective appreciation of an inchoate offence, but denied in the case of structural mass violence, for which he uses the term 'associational offences'. What, he asks, is 'the relationship between associational freedoms and associational offences, especially the tensions thereof, in the light of the larger understanding of conspiracy in criminal law'?[65]

A Genealogy of *Puttaswamy vs Union of India*

Our present moment is marked by the continuing spate of attacks by the state on human rights defenders, and the rise of impunity in times of extreme political turbulence, with the space for deliberative democracy and dissent virtually disappearing. A draconian law like the UAPA truncates the reach of the Constitution in the play of courtroom politics and 'justice-speak'.[66] On another track, paradoxically, the Supreme Court in 2017 declared the right to privacy to

64 Ibid., p. 392.

65 Ibid., p. 385.

66 For a detailed discussion of repressive laws, the place of the judiciary and the reach of the Constitution, see Kannabiran, K.G. 2004. *The Wages of Impunity: Power, Justice and Human Rights in India*. Hyderabad: Orient Longman.

be a fundamental right in *Justice K.S. Puttaswamy & Ors vs Union of India*.[67] In delineating the scope of this right, the nine-judge bench resurrected what it called the 'Three Great Dissents' and unequivocally affirmed (on hindsight) the rights of citizens to live lives free of surveillance and state interference, upholding the indivisibility and non-negotiability of fundamental rights, the right to liberty, autonomy and dignity. While a detailed discussion of this momentous decision is out of the scope of the present exercise, one of the dissents so resurrected, and immediately relevant to our purpose, is that of Justice H.R. Khanna in the case of *ADM Jabalpur vs Shivkant Shukla*.[68]

The writ petition *P. Venkataseshamma vs State of Andhra Pradesh & Ors*[69] challenged the arrest of Advocate Pattipati Venkateswarlu under the MISA, 1971, on the intervening night of 25–26 June 1975. The petition was filed by K.G. Kannabiran, representing Pattipati Venkateswarlu's wife, the morning after his arrest. The president proclaimed Emergency on 27 June 1975, promulgated the Maintenance of Internal Security (Amendment) Ordinance, 1975, and the Emergency-President's Order Regarding Suspension of the Rights under Articles 14, 21, And 22 of the Constitution of India (G.O. Rt. No. 1650, General Administration (sc. D) 1 July, 1975). By the time Venkataseshamma's petition came up for hearing on 1 July 1975, all the presidential proclamations and orders were in place to hold citizens in a chokehold. It is important to recall excerpts from the judgment in the first case to challenge the Emergency in the country:

> Mr Kannabhiraman, learned counsel for the petitioner, took time and raised additional grounds questioning the validity of the declaration under Cl. (1) of Article 359 of the Constitution and the validity of the First Amendment Ordinance in general and in particular clause (5) thereof by which Section 16A was introduced in the Principal Act. It is contended that this Amendment Ordinance is ultra vires of the powers vested in the President under Article 123 of the Constitution. This amendment 'tampers with the basic structures or the forms of the Constitution' and is, therefore, void. It is also violative of the right conferred on a person by Article 226 of the Constitution for, in effect the right of the detenu to move the Court is taken away. It was also

67 *Justice K.S. Puttaswamy & Ors vs Union of India*, AIR 2017 SC 4161.

68 *ADM Jabalpur vs Shivkant Shukla*, AIR 1976 SC 1207. See Rohinton F. Nariman. 2021. *Discordant Notes: The Voice of Dissent in the Last Court of Resort*. Vol. 1. New Delhi: Penguin Allen Lane pp. 147–91.

69 *P. Venkataseshamma vs State of Andhra Pradesh & Ors*, AIR 1976 AP 1.

> contended therein that even the provisions of the amended ordinance have not been complied with in detaining the detenu and hence the detention was illegal and void.[70]
>
> ...
>
> Mr Kannabhiraman for the petitioner, however, contends that a declaration under Article 359 does not authorise the making of laws which are violative of fundamental rights. Such laws are void in view of Article 13(2) of the Constitution. Neither the Parliament nor any state legislature nor the President or the Governor in exercise of their power to issue Ordinances make laws which are violative of the rights conferred by Part III of the Constitution. Any law which is violative of the provisions of the Chapter III of the Constitution being void ab initio, any action taken thereunder would ipso facto [sic] void and consequently the declaration made under Article 359 of the Constitution cannot stand in the way of the detenu approaching the Court to declare the detention to be illegal and without jurisdiction and obtain a writ of habeas corpus.[71]
>
> ...
>
> Mr Kannabhiraman, learned counsel for the petitioner stresses that *what are suspended by a declaration of the President under Article 359(1) are not the rights conferred under Part III of the constitution of India but only the right to move the Court to enforce the rights conferred by Part III.* In other words ... therefore, the validity of the law on the ground of infringement of fundamental right can be questioned. The law which is void under Article 13(2) is non est and therefore the executive action purported to be taken thereunder is void ab initio.[72]

The writ petition was dismissed by the Andhra Pradesh High Court (Bench: K. Madhava Reddy, A. Gangadhara Rao and K. Jayachandra Reddy, JJ) on 22 August 1975 with the court ruling that

> ... neither the proclamation of emergency under Art. 352(1) of the Constitution nor the declaration of the President that the right to move courts for enforcement of any of the fundamental rights conferred by Part III of the Constitution is suspended, can be questioned in a Court of law. The proclamation of the President dated 25th June, 1975 issued under Art. 352 as

70 Iid., para 8.

71 Ibid., para 27.

72 Ibid., para 31. Emphasis added.

> well as the declaration of the President made under clause (1) of Article 359 on 30th June 1975 are, therefore, immune from attack.[73]

It is against this background that we recapitulate briefly Justice Khanna's judgment delivered eight months later on 28 April 1976, and its interweaving with the civil liberties challenge from Andhra Pradesh. The Union and the states contended that in view of the 'Presidential order dated June 27, 1975 under Article 359 suspending the right of all persons to move any court for the enforcement of the rights conferred by articles 14, 21 and 22 of the Constitution, petitions for issue of writs of habeas corpus were not maintainable'. In particular, it was stressed that 'the right to move the court for enforcement of the right under Article 21 had been suspended' as '[t]he above mentioned presidential order was stated to be an absolute bar to the judicial security of the detention orders'. Nine high courts in the country, including Andhra Pradesh, although undecided and far from unanimous on the remit of judicial scrutiny, nonetheless held that 'the Presidential order did not create an absolute bar to the judicial scrutiny of the validity of the detention'.[74] K.G. Kannabiran reflects on this judicial equivocation and vacillation in his discussion on the numerous cases he argued in Hyderabad during the Emergency, of which *P. Venkataseshamma* was only the first.

Justice Khanna's dissent in *ADM Jabalpur* flags the legal challenges mounted by conscientious resisters in different states in the country, and reiterates the arguments made before courts, whether or not the courts ruled in favour of the petitioners. As it turns out, the majority of opinions/decisions supported the Emergency, and the suspension of fundamental rights (in the high courts, as indeed in the Supreme Court).

Justice Khanna observed:

> I am unable to subscribe to the view that when right to enforce the right under Article 21 is suspended, the result would be that there would be no remedy against deprivation of a person's life or liberty by the State even though such deprivation is without the authority of law or even in flagrant violation of the provisions of law. The right not to be deprived of one's life or liberty without the authority of law was not the creation of the Constitution. Such right existed before the Constitution came into force. The fact that the framers of the Constitution made an aspect of such right a part of the fundamental rights did not have the effect of exterminating the independent

73 Ibid., para 17.

74 Ibid., para 140.

> identity of such right and of making Article 21 to be the sole repository of that right. Its real effect was to ensure that a law under which a person can be deprived of his life or personal liberty should prescribe a procedure for such deprivation or ... such law should be a valid law not violative of fundamental rights guaranteed by Part III of the Constitution. Recognition as fundamental right of one aspect of the pre-Constitutional right cannot have the effect of making things less favourable so far as the sanctity of life and personal liberty is concerned compared to the position if an aspect of such right had not been recognised as fundamental right because of the vulnerability of fundamental rights accruing from Article 359.[75]

In 2017, the nine-judge Constitution bench in *Justice K.S. Puttaswamy vs Union of India* unanimously held that the judgment of the majority in *ADM Jabalpur* was 'seriously flawed', and that

> The right to life being inalienable to each individual, it existed prior to the Constitution and continued in force under Article 372 of the Constitution. Justice Khanna was clearly right in holding that the recognition of the right to life and personal liberty under the Constitution does not denude the existence of that right, apart from it nor can there be a fatuous assumption that in adopting the Constitution the people of India surrendered the most precious aspect of the human persona, namely, life, liberty and freedom to the state on whose mercy these rights would depend. Such a construct is contrary to the basic foundation of the rule of law which imposes restraints upon the powers vested in the modern state when it deals with the liberties of the individual. The power of the Court to issue a Writ of Habeas Corpus is a precious and undeniable feature of the rule of law.[76]

The court went as far as declaring that '[t]he view taken by Justice Khanna must be accepted, and accepted in reverence for the strength of its thoughts and the courage of its convictions.'[77]

During the Emergency and after, Kannabiran argued on the premise that 'A constitution is a political document which gives legal content to a set of pre-existing

75 *ADM Jabalpur*, para 158.

76 Justice D.Y. Chandrachud in *Justice K.S. Puttaswamy & Ors vs. Union of India*, para 119.

77 Ibid., para 120.

rights, secured politically by peoples' struggles'. The view of courts, therefore, that 'a citizen's right to challenge the validity of a law accrued to him or her on account of the Constitution and Fundamental Rights, which fortunately were included in the Constitution', was in his view unhistorical and erroneous.[78] This formed the crux of his arguments in *P. Venkateshamma vs State of Andhra Pradesh* discussed above and his resolute challenge to the Emergency in the months preceding *ADM Jabalpur*.

The 2017 eulogy of Justice Khanna therefore takes us right back to the heart of the concerns K.G. Kannabiran voiced in his legal battles for the protection of civil liberties within courts, especially during the Emergency, but also beyond those years. The cases that he speaks of in *The Speaking Constitution* are catapulted into a rejuvenated articulation of the rule of law today, in the thick of repressive governance, through the reinstatement of Justice Khanna's dissent, which is not merely symbolic or rhetorical. It is a re-statement by the Supreme Court, of the legitimacy of politics, of resistance to unjust rule, of the constitutional value of 'the courage of conviction', of the non-negotiability of fundamental rights even under authoritarian regimes, and even during a state of emergency (declared and undeclared). What is then resurrected by the Supreme Court is the history of the cases citizens brought to courts that asserted their right to life and personal liberty—notwithstanding their uneven reception by judges of that time. For, along with Justice Khanna, what has been resurrected is the unswerving assertion by petitioners and their lawyers in courts that fundamental rights shall not be suspended even under conditions of emergency, a view that a minuscule number of judges across the country affirmed at that time. The minority view historically, in the matter of personal liberty especially, has presented the correct reading of the Constitution—as the court pointed out in its resurrection of dissents, all importantly in the matter of personal liberty, retracing our steps right back to the inaugural constitutional moment of *A.K. Gopalan*.[79] This also leads us to a more nuanced understanding of the 'tyranny of majorities' and the consequences for citizens of such tyranny—whether on the bench or in society generally. It is this aspect of *Puttaswamy* that helps us reclaim rights in the present that are illuminated by a resurrected past.

> Individuals who assert causes which may be unpopular to the echelons of power are yet entitled to the freedoms which are guaranteed by the Constitution. Dissent is a symbol of a vibrant democracy. Voices in

78 Kannabiran, K.G. 2004. *The Wages of Impunity: Power, Justice and Human Rights*. Hyderabad: Orient Longman, p. 41.

79 *A.K. Gopalan vs State of Madras*, 1950 AIR SC 27. For a detailed discussion, see ibid.

> opposition cannot be muzzled by persecuting those who take up unpopular causes. Where, however, the expression of dissent enters upon the prohibited field of an incitement to violence or the subversion of a democratically elected government by recourse to unlawful means, the dissent ceases to be a mere expression of opinion.[80]

We have full and partial judicial dissents in the cases discussed in the earlier section. Within the 1970s courts, the turn from dissent to incitement is far from resolved in the judicial mind, as we saw in the cases of *Srujana*, as also in Justice Chandrachud's observation above. On the other side, despite internal contradictions and differences within movements on the course, strategies and modalities of struggle (which is alluded to in the parliamentary debate on Naxalite politics discussed in a foregoing section), the spaces of the courtroom and the prison acquired a memorably pedagogic quality—where courts, law, the state and oppressive regimes were critiqued through poetry and song, and judges were drawn across the line to dissent. This stands in contrast to the present time where judges take recourse to poetry to speak to questions of dignity, autonomy and liberty, as we saw in *Navtej Singh Johar*.[81] As performative moves, they speak to the radical politics of courtcraft and to revolutionary stirrings in constitutional interpretation. As memory of cultural politics, they evoke possibilities of a different trajectory for negotiating the present—and across it all, it is a memory of a moment charged with emotion, just as the present is too:

> After the high-pitched and at times emotional arguments concluded, each side presenting his case with equal vehemence, we as Judges have had to sit back and ponder over as to who is right or whether there is a third side to the case.[82]

The repression and arrests started immediately after the election victory of Indira Gandhi after the 1971 war leading to a consolidation of the authoritarian regime.

---

80 *Romila Thapar & Ors vs Union of India & Ors*. Writ Petition in public interest seeking the immediate release of activists raided and arrested in complete violation of their fundamental rights guaranteed under Article 14 and 21 of the Constitution of India. 29 August 2018, dissenting judgment, Justice D.Y. Chandrachud, para 29.

81 *Navtej Singh Johar vs Union of India*. AIR 2018 SC 4321.

82 *Romila Thapar & Ors vs Union of India & Ors*. Writ Petition in public interest seeking the immediate release of activists raided and arrested in complete violation of their fundamental rights guaranteed under Article 14 and 21 of the Constitution of India. 29 August 2018, para 19, majority judgment.

Today, in a comparable political climate, Justice D.Y. Chandrachud's dissenting opinion in *Romila Thapar* joins the extremely slim, fragile, yet valuable tradition of dissent in independent India—where political dissent is inextricably interwoven with judicial dissent, together creating illimitable possibilities of hope for a better future, even while we struggle for justice and liberty in the here and now.

Finally, this resurrection of judicial dissents in *Puttaswamy* urges us to examine the relationship, historically in independent India, between political dissent and judicial dissent. With *Gopalan* at one end and *ADM Jabalpur* at the other end (and indeed *Romila Thapar* in the present), with political dissenters in a free, newly democratic state at one end and dissenters under internal Emergency (with or withiout a formal proclamation) at the other, it carves the space for politics in the judicial imagination. How do political dissent and judicial dissent illuminate each other? We may also recall the case of *A. Lakshmanarao* accused in the Parvathipuram Conspiracy Case cited earlier. The petitioner, an accused in a case of Naxalite conspiracy (see Chapter 6), drew on the judicial dissent of Justice C.A. Vaidialingam in the case of *Raj Narain v. Superintendent, Central Jail, New Delhi*, to argue on the infringement of personal liberty in the matter of political prisoners. The court's carnivalesque[83] resurrection of judicial dissent that had particularly to do with authoritarian practices of the state, at a time of resurgence of authoritarian regimes, is itself an intensely subversive act, a constitutional insurgency par excellence that reinstates the right to resist, even as the land seems to shrink into an *anda* cell, surveilled as never before.[84] As Justice Rohinton Nariman observes, 'The dissenting judge reminds the people of India that they are lost only for the time being—the judgment in dissent will hopefully awaken a future generation of judges from the comatose slumber that the dissenting judge sees that the majority have fallen into.'[85]

83 Here, and elsewhere in this chapter, I borrow from Mikhail Bakhtin's work, especially on the *Dialogic Imagination*, as providing the sensibilities for comprehending the 'plurality of unmerged voices and consciousness, a genuine polyphony of fully valid voices', as they emerge in court talk around life and liberty. Dentith, Simon. 1995. *Bakhtinian Thought: An Introductory Reader*. London: Routledge, p. 40.

84 'Anda' cell is 'a colloquial term for a high-security compound inside a prison that is egg-shaped. The cells inside are often tiny and dimly lit, with sparse ventilation and little space for movement. They are … a form of solitary confinement. Its purpose is often to segregate criminals accused of serious offences, such as terror suspects, from the rest of the inmates', as described in Nidhi Suresh. 2019. 'Prisoner Mirza Himayat Baig Recounts Solitary Confinement inside an Anda Cell'. (Source: *Caravan*, 31 October.)

85 Nariman, Rohinton F. 2021b. *Discordant Notes: The Voice of Dissent in the Last Court of Resort*. Vol. 2. New Delhi: Penguin Allen Lane.

A Life in Law: 'Interilluminations' and the Value of Dialogue

> The contexts of dialogue are without limit. They extend into the deepest past and the most distant future. Even meanings born in dialogues of the remotest past will never be finally grasped once and for all, for they will always be renewed in later dialogue. At any present moment of the dialogue there are great masses of forgotten meanings, but these will be recalled again at a given moment in the dialogue's later course when it will be given new life. For nothing is absolutely dead: every meaning will someday have its homecoming festival.[86]

The preceding sections open out a sense (far from complete) of the multiplicity and plurality of voices, sites, languages, rhythms, journeys and contestatory conversations on the meanings of constitutionalism in independent India, underscoring the constitutive force of *dialogue* in deliberations around democracy across time and within/across each of these spaces—physical spaces and sites of knowledge—and meaning-making.[87] In the very first case presented in this work, where Ansari Begum's assertion that she was a *Tamil* woman who belonged to Madras, anticipates the protests by Muslim women in India against the CAA, 2019, notating 'belonging' and intimate citizenship in radically different terms.[88]

On another track, we may consider the case of autonomy and self-governance for scheduled areas that K.G. Kannabiran argued in 1994 in the case of *Arka Vasanth Rao vs State of Andhra Pradesh*, which anticipated the passage of the Panchayat (Extension to Scheduled Areas) Act, 1996, by forestalling the use of the Andhra Pradesh Panchayat Act in scheduled areas in Andhra Pradesh in the panchayat

---

86 Bakhtin, quoted in Holquist, Michael. (1990) 2002. *Dialogism: Bakhtin and His World*. London and New York: Routledge, p. 38.

87 Dialogue, as used in this essay, is neither 'metaphor' nor 'model', nor does it draw from constitutional scholarship on dialogue. In speaking of insurgent modes of constitutional engagements, I take a different route to dialogue, through Bakhtin, for instance. For a review and contestation of the former from within constitutional scholarship see Carolan, Eoin. 2016. 'Dialogue Isn't Working: The Case for Collaboration as a Model of Legislative–Judicial Relations', *Legal Studies*, Vol. 36, No. 2 (June: 209–29). I am grateful to Suryapratim Roy for discussions on this connection.

88 Kannabiran, Kalpana, and Ramya K. Tella. 2022. 'Migration and "Intimate Citizenship": The "Small Voice" of Ansari Begum'. *Social Change*, Vol. No 52, No.2, June.

elections of 1994 (Chapter 12). These arguments find weight and voice in the struggles of Adivasis for autonomy in the context of the threats of eviction from forests in scheduled areas as recently as 2019.[89] His arguments before the Andhra Pradesh High Court in 2003,[90] drawing support from the work of Upendra Baxi[91] that it 'was a fundamental right of every citizen of this country to have a corruption free clean Government', to which the judges responded that they had 'no quarrel with what Mr Kannabhiran wanted to argue on the basis of the opinion of one of the eminent Jurists of this country'[92]—remain relevant today in the context of post-truth declamations by governments on the elimination of corruption through demonetization.[93] The right to resist arbitrary government, the right to protest and the assertion of associational freedoms in the face of state violence and criminalization—indeed, the reinstatement of the right to resist that we witnessed during the Emergency—finds new meaning and expression in the gains of the farmers' resistance against the farm laws in 2020–21.

His critique of political formations was not limited to government and Naxalites, but extended to political parties as well, of all hues. Arguing in the context of the refusal by the Indian National Congress to recognize the Telangana region prior to state reorganization, and underscoring the need for political parties to provide adequate representation to regions within the state in the electoral scheme, K.G. Kannabiran posited a larger argument on the accountability of political parties under the Constitution. This bears urgent recall in the present context of majoritarian rule by executive fiat and the total abandonment of parliamentary debate in matters of legislation and governance. He urged 'that activities of a political party … must

---

89 For a detailed discussion of this case see Kannabiran, Kalpana. 2022. 'Constitution-as-Commons and Spatial Justice in Adivasi India: The Continuing Legacy of Three Legal Cases'. In *State, Law, and Adivasi: Shifting Terrains of Exclusion*. Eds Antje Linkenbach and Vidhu Verma. New Delhi: Sage/Spectrum, pp. 129-152.

90 *P. Janardhan Reddy vs State of Andhra Pradesh and Ors*. 2003 (2) ALT 579. I am grateful to K. Parameshwar for drawing my attention to this case.

91 Baxi, Upendra. 1989. *Liberty and Corruption: The Antulay Case and Beyond*. Lucknow: The Eastern Book Co.

92 *P. Janardhan Reddy vs State of Andhra Pradesh and Ors*. 2003 (2) ALT 579, para 9.

93 Reddy, D. Narasimha. 2021. 'Demonetization, Corruption and Black Money: The Unfolding Dangers of Opportunistic Politics in the Era of Post-Truth'. In *Discourses on Corruption: Interdisciplinary and Intercultural Perspectives*. Eds Kalpana Kannabiran, Bettina Hollstein and Florian Hoffmann. New Delhi: Sage/Spectrum, pp. 92–117.

be held to be within the public sphere and it would be amenable to writ jurisdiction of this Court … [P]olitical parties have been given Constitutional recognition in terms of 10th Schedule of the Constitution and as such the internal affairs of the party cannot be said to be a private affair … [A] political party must so regulate its procedure in terms of Constitutional commitments and thus if it fails to take any action in relation thereto, a writ of mandamus would issue'.[94] His insistence on broadening the reach of the Constitution, and through that the disciplining of public bodies against practices of arbitrariness (on similar terms as the disciplining of the arbitrary state), saw him open up the scope of Article 226 and persuade reluctant courts to deliberate on these questions, even if ultimately they did not concur with his insurgent reading of the Constitution.

In each of these instances, the dialogue is set up by communities in struggle, and citizens variously located, speaking a plurality of languages of resistance, by the tenacity of survivors/victims of violence (especially state violence, also majoritarian violence bolstered by the abdication/abandonment of due diligence by the state) to find resolutions through representations by lawyers in courts. Stepping out of the scaffolding of monologism that has hitherto been the method of law, the courts too, in small, halting measure, attempt to comprehend anew the experiences performed before them. Critical to this process is relations such conversations manifest and establish, where 'differences—while still remaining different—serve as the building blocks of simultaneity'; where 'both speakers are different from each other and the utterance each makes is always different from the other's (even when one appears to repeat the "same" word as the other; and yet all these differences—and many more—are held together in the relation of dialogue'.[95] There is also, importantly, a temporality embedded in this dialogue that is spatially rooted—this is not fixed or frozen, but shifts and changes shape, imbuing constitutional conversations with new meanings from one 'case'/moment to another, 'set[ting] into motion a process of active, mutual cause-and-effect and interillumination'.[96]

Aishwary Kumar's insights into the fashioning of 'radical equality' in the work of Gandhi and Ambedkar, in contested dialogue with each other, are immediately relevant to an understanding of the premises on which Kannabiran approached

94 *M. Baga Reddy vs Sonia Gandhi and Ors.* 2001 (3) ALD 636, para 3.

95 Holquist, Michael. (1990) 2002. *Dialogism: Bakhtin and His World.* London and New York: Routledge, p. 39.

96 Bakhtin, M.M. 1990. 'Epic and Novel'. In The Dialogic Imagination: Four Essays. Ed. Michael Holquist, trans. Caryl Emerson and Michael Holquist. Austin, TX: University of Texas Press, p. 12.

his task.[97] As a lawyer he constantly petitioned the courts in the cause of personal liberty—providing a kaleidoscopic view of the possibilities a deep engagement with Gandhi and Ambedkar opened out to a counter-colonial constitutional jurisprudence. The ideas of self-determination, self-respect and swaraj that Gandhi and Ambedkar deployed in their political work are particularly instructive in understanding the paths Kannabiran chose to tread in his long struggle to realize the goals of the Constitution on the ground. The connection is an illuminating one, considering both Gandhi and Ambedkar were lawyers, contemporaries who returned to India around the same time, with a keen sense of what the task of building a just and free country involved, each with his own distinct and clear vision of the immense possibilities of insurgent interpretations of rights and the methods of law. These are sensibilities that reverberate through Kannabiran's labours on working with, around and in law as a political project. Ambedkar's plural approaches to the abolition of untouchability and the annihilation of caste and the Hindu social order that engaged publishing, protest, petitioning, litigation, voting rights, reservations, and constitutional proscription commencing in right earnest in 1917,[98] and Gandhi's early mobilization of lawyers to document testimonies and evidence on the suffering of indigo farmers in Champaran in 1917 very soon after his return to India,[99] are archives that help us comprehend the contours of the task undertaken by civil liberties advocacy in India during the 1970s and after, and indeed help us map the genealogies of civil liberties on the Indian subcontinent. Especially pertinent is Kumar's discussion on Ambedkar's 'conviction that any understanding of politics must be necessarily insurrectionary in its articulation',[100] his meditations on the 'insurrectionary duties of the citizen'[101] and the relationship he grappled with between 'insurrection and constitution'.[102] The difficult balance

97 Kumar, Aishwary. 2015. *Radical Equality: Ambedkar, Gandhi and the Risk of Democracy*. Stanford, CA: Stanford University Press.

98 Geetha, V. 2021. *Bhimrao Ramji Ambedkar and the Question of Socialism in India*. Switzerland: Palgrave Macmillan.

99 Amin, Shahid, Tridip Suhrud, Megha Todi. 2022. *Thumb Printed: Champaran Indigo Peasants Speak to Gandhi*. Vol.1. New Delhi: National Archives of India, and Ahmedabad: Navjivan Trust.

100 Kumar, Aishwary. 2015. *Radical Equality: Ambedkar, Gandhi and the Risk of Democracy*. Stanford, CA: Stanford University Press, p. 23.

101 Ibid., p. 8.

102 Ibid., p. 3.

both Gandhi and Ambedkar strove to achieve between force and justice,[103] observes Kumar, was premised on their belief that

> the concept of 'force' can never be collapsed into other forms of power, whether military, legislative, or executive ... Instead, force is the condensation of the subject's experience and intense will to act, even at the risk of death, in a moment of unrestrained creativity and immeasurable freedom. Force is the moral firmness (Gandhi's *agraha*) that constitutes the inalienable truthfulness of being; it is existence that is irreducibly free, equal, and fearless (Ambedkar's *samata*). As concept and act, force makes visible (and reclaims) the experience of freedom in its most indivisible form.[104]

That Kannabiran drew on these arguments on the relationship between politics and ethics, and between the force of ideas—moral force—and the aspiration for freedom, persuading courts to ponder over deeply philosophical questions that lay at the heart of a counter-colonial imaginary, is evident from his reflections on several cases discussed in *The Speaking Constitution*. This is particularly the case in the distinction he draws between 'political crime' and 'ordinary crime' in the context of the death penalty, even while he opposed the death penalty absolutely and without exception. This distinction posed a counter-colonial challenge to the IPC (*G. Krishta Goud* and *Intha Ramana Reddy*) forcing a consideration of the place of insurrection/insurgency in the new constitutional imaginary by courts (Chapter 10)—a reasoning picked up in the parliamentary debates on Naxalite politics discussed earlier in this chapter.

While a detailed reading of Kumar's magisterial work and its relevance to understanding the jurisprudence of civil liberties that Kannabiran co-created is outside the scope of this introduction, it is pertinent to connect his work with Kumar's observation that

> both Ambedkar and Gandhi believed that freedom requires a new language of truth, a new order of conceptuality, a semantic, interpretive, and performative coup de force in thought and action that might wrest the truth of existence at its barest back from the obfuscations of juridical, civilizational, and political theologies.[105]

103 Ibid., p. 6.

104 Ibid., p. 29.

105 Ibid., p. 27.

Lawyering was, for K.G. Kannabiran, a deeply political project that offered infinite possibilities for establishing liberty, dignity and freedom of conscience and reinventing languages of justice premised on counter-colonial constitutional imaginations. His participation in movements, politics, negotiations and civil liberties advocacy were mediated by his standing as a lawyer. In asserting this, he transformed the profession and transformed the approach of movements, dissenters petitioners, legislators and political leaders to the profession.

As a practising lawyer, the trial courts, he argued, were the first institutions of justice that deliberate on the Constitution in substantive ways. In persuading judges, in criminal courts especially, to shift their frames of understanding the relationship between the Constitution and criminal law in cases that he argued in these courts, he transformed courtcraft into a vibrant dialogue, and a political education on the Constitution in everyday practice. He did not see the courts as hampered by 'jurisdictional' issues where it came to the Constitution, which, he asserted, provided the overarching ethic for *all courts* in independent India.[106] He did not believe that the Constitution is the exclusive preserve of courts or the legal profession alone and urged public engagement with the spirit of the Constitution. He also refused consistently to confine himself to any one branch of law, and no court/tribunal was out of bounds. The community of litigants and petitioners he gathered around him was as a result very large and very diverse. There was an important aspect of his interpretation of his profession and the ethics that undergirded it. He believed that every citizen has a stake in the Constitution and must assert that stake and reclaim it—in courts and outside. This conversation—dialogue—between litigants/petitioners, citizens, courts and state was one he stirred to stunning effect.

The Speaking Constitution gives us a flavour of K.G. Kannabiran's deep immersion in the Constitution as politics and as everyday courtcraft, as also his ruminations on a philosophy of justice and its praxis—its multiple intersecting and simultaneous locations.

106 For an account of his work in this direction within the legal profession see the contributions in Kannabiran, Kalpana, ed. 2022. *Insurgent Constitutionalism, Transformative Courtcraft: K.G. Kannabiran Lectures, 2020-21*. Hyderabad: Asia Law House.

1

Childhood, Youth and Education

Early Memories

AT SEVENTY-FIVE, AFTER spending fifty years in the legal profession, I have a wealth of unforgettable memories, thoughts about society, about human rights, about struggles—there is so much to talk about. Writing about a life that has been so fully lived, to relive the events and experiences that have shaped my life, can be an extremely arduous undertaking. And so I feel that the story of my life should not revolve around me and my personal struggles. There are countless experiences that have shaped me as a person, a civil liberties activist, a lawyer and a democrat. My relationships with countless people, my conversations and exchanges over the years, have moulded my personality. My life in this Telugu land, my dialogues with left-wing armed movements, my services as a lawyer sought by this society, my struggles to bring justice to people in struggle and ensure the protection of their rights, my insistence on standing with victims of human rights violations in every corner of the country, and my efforts to bring specific reliefs to victims and create a general environment in our society where human rights are respected have all shaped me as a person. They are a part of my life that cannot be viewed in isolation, each by itself. To recount my life and reflect on it is necessary, no doubt. But my life story must be the story of the struggles for a better society that I have been engaged in. What were the myriad ways in which I was drawn into that social history? How did I understand that history even as I was playing a part in its making? It is this reflection that I attempt to share through this narration of my life story.

My forebears were Tamils who had migrated to Nellore several centuries ago and settled there. I was born into a fairly well-to-do family. My father, Dr K.G. Iyengar, an ophthalmologist in King Edward Memorial Hospital (now Gandhi Hospital) in Secunderabad, was in government service (Madras Presidency) and was transferred to the British resident's service in the Secunderabad Cantonment of the erstwhile Nizam state. He was known as an 'England-returned Doctor'. He established himself quite well, and as bigamy was not prohibited among Hindus, he married a second time—his second wife a child widow and teacher (who after marriage taught in Keyes High School, Secunderabad). This marriage was preceded by tremendous domestic violence on my mother, his first wife, a defiant woman who refused to submit to his wishes. She had no parental family, except for her elder sister, who was widowed in adolescence, had a posthumous child, and lived amidst great penury. My mother left her husband and moved with her children to his joint family house at Nellore. A strong-willed woman, she supported herself and her children on the income from the little ancestral land in Nellore, fending for herself and her children amidst the hostility of her husband's extended family. With this our economic condition slid to the lower middle class.

I studied in Nellore in the Telugu medium till the sixth form. After completing Secondary School Learning Certificate (SSLC), I moved to Madras, and stayed with my maternal cousin whom we affectionately called Rajappa. It was towards the end of the freedom struggle that I joined Pachaiyappa College in Madras to do my Intermediate. The Cabinet Mission to India led by Lord Pethick-Lawrence placed its proposal for the transfer of power to India, and in that context also visited our college when I was there. At that time, there were a few factors that influenced me greatly. One was reading books and literature voraciously—especially English literature. By the time I passed out of law college, I had read all the English literature there was to read.

In Hyderabad state, around this time, there was a severe repression on communists. Vasanth's granduncle, A.S.K. Iyengar,[1] who was organizing workers in Hyderabad, had to go underground to avoid arrest. He came to Madras in hiding. Rajappa provided shelter to ASK. Because of his standing in the official cricket establishment, Rajappa wielded considerable influence. Perhaps it was because of this that ASK's period underground passed uneventfully. ASK also introduced me

1 A.S.K. Iyengar (1907–1978), CPI leader of the Madras Harbour Workers' Union.

to a lot of books. It was on his suggestion that I read Maurice Dobb's *Studies in the Development of Capitalism* (1946).

College and the Political Environment

After completing my Intermediate in Pachaiyappa College, I joined Vivekananda College in Madras for BA (Hons.), specializing in economics, political science and industrial labour. The political atmosphere in Madras during those four years was electric. There was not much to study in college. There were student competitions in college. The Dravidian movement was very strong in Pachaiyappa College and outside. It was the Dravida Kazhagam that first sounded the warning that India was a plural society that could not be confined within any single identity. This was the first challenge that confronted the national freedom movement. The Tamil lecturer in Pachaiyappa College, Anbazhagan, was a Dravidian movement leader.[2] Our college was the centre of the Dravida Kazhagam student wing.

Periyar E.V. Ramasamy Naicker was a revered figure and a great orator. The influence of the self-respect movement and the anti-Brahmin movement was visible on the streets. In Madras, there were demonstrations before hotels serving 'Brahmin meals' to drop the word 'Brahmin', as a result several of them replaced 'Brahmin' with 'vegetarian'. During this time, Nehru visited Madras to inaugurate the Indian Science Congress. There was a huge black-flag demonstration against him. The anti-Brahmin movement also opposed Hindi. Hindi boards at railway stations were blackened with tar. The Tamil people declared that they would not recognize Hindi as the national language. The opposition to Hindi also turned into an opposition to leaders from the north. Nehru, who under normal circumstances drove in an open-top vehicle, stopped this practice in Madras. Notwithstanding the shifts in the Dravida Kazhagam movement later, in the initial stages it was invigorating. It was not a movement that was triggered by one or two people. It was a movement based on a deep faith in, and aspirations for, a different world. Although born a Brahmin, and unable to secure a BA seat in Pachaiyappa College for that reason, I recognized the Dravidian anti-Brahmin movement as one that worked for the development of Tamil society. That was, as a matter of fact, a movement anchored in the values of a different order that resurrected the Tamil people. The non-Brahmin middle classes would never have been able to occupy positions of authority were it not for that movement. The strength of the movement was evident from the fact that it was possible for an unknown law student to defeat the famous Kamaraj Nadar.

---

2 K. Anbazhagan, 1922–2020.

I was always a mediocre student. I did not have any aspirations of excelling in studies. After completing an MA in economics, I had limited options before me: prepare for the competitive exams and appear for the Indian Administrative Service (IAS) and Indian Foreign Service (IFS) examinations; join oil companies like Burmah Shell, Caltex or Esso; or study law and become a lawyer. Seats in law college were easy to get, so that was the only option that seemed doable to me. It is of course possible to appear for competitive examinations while studying law. I did that but failed in the interview. I have the unusual distinction of securing zero marks in the personality test. Even today, I am baffled by the way in which my personality was measured in such strict arithmetical terms.

Rajappa, Chellappa, Ramji

Along with the influence of literature and movements, I was also greatly influenced by my brother Rajappa.[3] A posthumous child, Rajappa built his life surmounting many troubles. He was ten years older than me. A very democratic and progressive person, he had established a legal practice in Madras—a self-made lawyer. By the time I began to study law, Rajappa had already earned a good reputation in the profession. Even in those days, he earned in four figures—which meant you had entered the elite classes. He bought himself a car and started building his own library. This was every lawyer's aspiration: a car and a personal library. For anyone without the backing of family or property, achieving this took ten years of hard labour. Apart from law, Rajappa was a good cricketer and was very active in the cricket establishment. In those days, he was a member of the Triplicane Cricket Club that earned a name as the 'A' Division League Team. Test cricketeers Gopalan and Rangachari were also part of that club.[4]

His desire when I joined the law course that I should work with him, I believe, played a significant role in the paths I chose. I studied law and made Rajappa happy. The two years I spent studying law were the happiest years of my student life. I could treat my friends to coffee and tiffin often. I also had money to buy books and go to the movies with my friends.

By the time I completed my law degree, Rajappa had risen in the cricket establishment and became the secretary of the Board of Control for Cricket in India (BCCI). Occupying that position meant setting aside the legal profession and spending evenings taking care of the administrative responsibilities of the BCCI

3 T. Srinivasa Raghavan (Rajappa) (1919–1956), K. Seshadri (Chellappa) (1921–2006), and K.G. Ramanathan (Ramji) (1926–2014).

4 M.J. Gopalan (1909–2003) and C.R. Rangachari (1916–1993).

and travelling frequently. He had only one junior in his lawyer's office, T. Arjunan, but this person was not capable of arguing very well in courts. He would do his best to take care of matters in the office, but could never hold his own against Rajappa's clerk, Malaiyappa Iyer. In those days, pleaders' clerks were very powerful people. They decided whether a client should meet the lawyer or not. Some clerks were so high-handed that clients even thought they were the lawyers. The clerks had total control over the pleader's office. The location of files, the details of cases—they were the ones who had all the information. Whether or not the pleader instructed them, the clerks would stand in wait at railway stations, figure out prospective clients and bring them to their lawyers. They could tell on looking at a person whether he was a prospective client or not. Malaiyappa Iyer was that kind of clerk.

Rajappa's preoccupation with the BCCI and Malaiyappa's addiction to the races threw his office into disarray. Rajappa never had time to meet his clients. It was normal for clients not to have access to their pleaders. No client ever complained that the pleader was negligent, or that he was corrupt in money matters. To put it plainly, the relationship between the pleader and his client is an amoral one. The first lesson a pleader learns is not to judge the cases a client brings, to be 'impartial' and 'neutral'. Therefore the question of principles is not relevant in accepting a case. A lawyer is not expected to think about the fairness or unfairness (justice/injustice) of the case he is taking up. In other words, a lawyer must view the world around him in dual terms: one world is that of his client and the case; the second is his personal life. In his relationships with his family, other lawyers and friends, he has a certain perspective of the world—one of his choosing. As a lawyer rises in eminence, his personal world keeps shrinking, and his clients' worlds keep expanding. In a world of free competition, the lawyer descends into cut-throat competition. In the early days, lawyers, with their expertise, their erudition and their learning, would win arguments over the opposing party. There were many exemplary lawyers during that time. This was a source of self-fulfilment for them. It was not focussed on maximizing earnings as it is today. Yet, neither then nor now are there ladders that make it possible for lawyers to climb up in the profession. When a young lawyer embarks on practice, the president of the Bar Association in his welcome address solemnly describes how Sir Alladi Krishnaswami began his career from the very bottom. He tells young lawyers that anyone can rise to the top. But in society, for every Alladi who rises to the top, there are countless Alladis who fail.

With no access to ladders, they are reduced to helplessness. I realized, as soon as I entered the profession, that there is a huge gap between the harsh realities of the legal profession and the hoary, noble traditions that are part of solemn declamations.

I sometimes think that lawyers inhabit an illusory world, because they are unable to reconcile this duality that the profession imposes on them.

My interest in literature was kindled by my eldest brother, K. Seshadri, whom we called Chellappa. He was by that time a communist and a leader of the Safai Karamchari Union in Nellore. A voracious reader, he would keep giving me his books to read, asking me to tell him what I had read. On Chellappa's suggestion, I read the philosophical works of J.H. Jackson. I had an essential readings list. Despite a nine-year age gap, we were very close. But when I think back now, I feel his revolutionary zeal bordered on absurdity. Any attachment, whether to left ideals or anti-development ideas, when espoused in extreme ways, reaches levels of the absurd. Therefore, although he influenced me, I did not take to his extreme positions—his influence was limited to my reading and critical thinking.

Apart from Rajappa and Chellappa, I must speak about my older brother Ramji (K.G. Ramanathan). He worked as a clerk in the office of the tahsildar in Madras. He earned Rs 5 per month and bought me my first pair of slippers. He would take me out and treat me to masala dosais. In those days, we were lucky if we had two sets of clothes. He was very short-tempered and yet went to any length to help people. It is for this reason, I think, that although he is now eighty years old, there are forty or fifty friends who still greet him every day. Ramji left the tahsildar office after some days and joined Hindustan Insurance Company. In 1956, when insurance companies were nationalized, Ramji became part of the Life Insurance Corporation (LIC) and a trade union leader there. He had not completed his intermediate level, and yet led the union. He became the secretary, southern zone, of the All India Insurance Employees Union. At that time, Mohan Kumaramangalam was the president. I grew close to Kumaramangalam through Ramji. Owing to his preoccupation with union activities, Ramji kept refusing promotions. Right till his retirement he remained a clerk with the LIC. Perhaps this trait ran in our blood. Ramji, Chellappa and I lived our lives modestly and according to our principles. At one point I had the opportunity of earning a huge income, but I lived by the rule that I would never earn beyond my needs.

It was through Ramji that I got to know V.G. Row, who became famous through the case *V.G. Row vs State*.[5] V.G. Row ran a law firm in Madras called Row and Reddy. He was joined by A.V. Reddy, who later became a high court judge. Row ran the office to provide support to left parties and to poor people who could not afford litigation costs. Although I did not join the office, their work influenced me. In 1952, when there was a ban on the People's Educational Society, Madras, Row successfully challenged it. On the grounds that the society was communist, the

5 *V.G. Row vs State of Madras*, AIR 1951 Mad 147.

Prakasam Pantulu government banned it under the Criminal Law Amendment Act, 1908. Despite the fact that Chittaranjan Das and Congress leaders had opposed this Act during the freedom struggle, the moment they came to power, they began to impose the same Act. Relying on V.G. Row's arguments, the Supreme Court struck down the law. In a strange twist, in May 1992, the Nedurumalli Janardhan Reddy government in Andhra Pradesh banned the People's War Group (PWG) and six organizations under the same law. When we challenged the ban on the ground that the Act had already been struck down in 1952 and was therefore non-existent, the government hastily promulgated the Andhra Pradesh Public Security Ordinance in June 1992 and banned these organizations under the new ordinance. This was later enacted as law.

I graduated from law college in 1953, and enrolled in the Madras High Court in November 1954. Rajappa had me sworn in as an advocate in the first court of Chief Justice P.V. Rajamannar. Two months after my enrolment, Rajappa died in an air crash in Nagpur in January 1955. I had dropped him off the previous evening at the Deccan Airways office on Mount Road. I received a call the next morning from the airlines office informing me that the aircraft had crashed near Nagpur and that there were no survivors. Rajappa was forty-two years old when he died. Our well-built, long-limbed Rajappa was brought back in a five-and-a-half foot coffin. A.S.K. Iyengar identified his body and accompanied him back. With Rajappa's death I was orphaned. I had just entered the profession, and lacked the experience to handle his cases. His clients did not feel they could entrust their cases to this young lawyer. So I gave up the cases, one after another, and vacated his office space. I experienced extreme poverty. I made it a habit to walk along the Beach Road to Mylapore. A friend would walk with me till Triplicane. In the days when I used to walk back home, an old man befriended me on the beach and started walking with us till Triplicane. He told me that he was a very bright student, and a lawyer, but could not find his feet in the profession. He was homeless and living on the beach. He said he had no money to have his sick wife treated, that he gave his son up in adoption because he could not raise him, and admitted his daughter in Seva Sadan. Had we not seen his body on the beach one morning, a few days later, we might not have believed his stories. My professional life as a lawyer began in this tortuous manner in Madras, and carried on in the same way for the next couple of years.

Ansari Begum and Partition

There was, of course, also a sprinkling of happy, memorable experiences; for example, the Ansari Begum case. After Rajappa's death, I joined the office of another senior.

Ansari Begum's case came to me around then in 1958. In those days, I would leave my coat and gown in advocate A.K. Balakrishnan's office. As I was going in one day, I saw a Muslim woman roaming anxiously near the gate, hesitant to enter. When she saw me, she came up and, giving me a piece of paper, asked if I could help her. She was Ansari Begum.[6] She held a Pakistani passport, and had been served a deportation notice under the Foreigners' Act. This was the piece of paper she handed me.

Hearing the painful story of this Tamil Muslim woman, I realized that she was being punished for acts she was not responsible for. Given her circumstances, she could only entrust her case to a lawyer just a bit better off than herself, with a professional standing of a mere two years.

After Partition, there were countless men who chased the illusion that they would enjoy a better life in Pakistan, and moved with entire families. Beyond recall are the hapless women who had no option but to follow their fathers, husbands and sons. Ansari Begum was one such woman. She was 100 per cent a Tamil woman. After going to Pakistan, she was unable to adjust to that unfamiliar environment. Alongside hunger and poverty, she faced hostility from the local people, which was rooted in the fear that the exodus of refugees would dispossess them of their livelihoods. It was owing to these circumstances that Ansari Begum decided to return.[7] When she left this country, she was a full Indian citizen. When she returned, her own personal circumstances had not changed. Authorities did not foresee the possibility that people who crossed the border would return as refugees. Those that returned faced hostility and harassment from officials. In fact, governance simply folded into governmental harassment. Ansari Begum did not know that the document handed to her was a passport that declared she was a citizen of Pakistan. She could no

---

6 The case was reported in *The Hindu* on 21 August 1958. The name of the petitioner was Ansari not Asiya, as Kannabiran refers to her in *24 Gantalu*. The editor is grateful to J. Jeyaranjan and A.S. Panneerselvan for access to this news report. For a detailed discussion of this case see Kannabiran, Kalpana and Ramya K. Tella. 2022. 'Migration and "Intimate Citizenship": The "Small Voice" of Ansari Begum.' *Social Change*, Vol. 52, No.2, June.

7 In her affidavit filed before the court, Ansari Begum said that due to 'absolute misguidance', her husband 'opted out for Pakistan'. 'But soon afterwards, we found that the atmosphere [there] was neither congenial nor to our taste and habit of living. We found there was nothing in common between our ways of living and those of Pakistan. So, after nearly four years, in 1954, we finally decided at the earliest opportunity to return to Madras, which is our native place and the only place to which we belong.' *The Hindu*, 21 August 1958.

longer assert her Indian citizenship. She lost the right to say that the land she and her forebears were born and lived in was where she belonged. She became instead a citizen of a strange country in which she had only lived a short while. How might a lower-middle-class, uneducated Muslim woman even make sense of this situation, leave alone extricate herself from it?

During this period, the Citizenship Act, 1955, was passed. According to this law, the passport was incontrovertible proof of a person's citizenship. Holding a foreign passport meant relinquishing Indian citizenship. In defining citizenship in this manner, the Indian government made a mockery of the basic tenets of democracy. The self-respect and dignity that vested in people's membership of a society was totally eroded.

I did not have a library of my own. I used the court library and my senior's library and studied the Citizenship Act closely. I had still not learnt how to present arguments in court, so my arguments focused on the impenetrable labyrinths of this law and its injustice.

The chief presidency magistrate heard the case. I argued for two hours that the deportation notice must be struck down. I argued that it is ridiculous that she is declared a Pakistani citizen when she does not understand what Partition means. She migrated only in search of livelihood, with no intention of settling there permanently. The court accepted my arguments and struck down the deportation order served on Ansari Begum. Since this case pertained to the period immediately after the enactment of the Citizenship Act, 1955, newspapers carried detailed reports of this case, my arguments and the judgment. *The Hindu* carried a detailed report.[8]

However, although she got a favourable judgment, Ansari Begum was not very happy with the result. She had been grappling with insecurity and fear of the future. These are struggles that are never visible to us. At least half of those who left for Pakistan would have been women. Ansari Begum was just one of those countless, invisible, anonymous women. Partition witnessed the largest human migration. There were camps for refugees set up all over the country. Close to Madras, in Avadi, there were several such camps that I personally visited. The focus on looking at cases

8 The magistrate, who gave her a 'lenient sentence'—'imprisonment till the rising of the Court'—observed in his ruling: 'The accused was born and bred in India. Unfortunately, her husband migrated to Pakistan in a weak moment. It is also significant to note that the husband of the accused has secured employment in the Indian Railways, although on a temporary basis. The accused is a mother of three children and her application for citizenship is still pending with the government.' *The Hindu*, 21 August 1958.

like this cannot be on jurisprudence. It must be on human rights. By virtue of being members of a society, people have inherent rights. National borders and sovereign powers cannot be allowed to defeat those rights. When there is large-scale migration of people who leave their native land and move to unfamiliar destinations, it is the responsibility of governments to recognize their human rights at the most difficult times during human crises. In several instances, migrants may not think through the consequences of moving, or may not understand them. Governments cannot take advantage of such ignorance or unfamiliarity and violate their human rights. Partition imposed unimaginable suffering on the people. Clearly, the leaders had not anticipated the magnitude of harm and suffering it would bring in its wake. Or is it the case that they decided that political decisions of this kind need not take account of human suffering? Governments on both sides did not deliberate on a planned and phased move of people who opted to move from one side to the other.

Moving to Hyderabad

Since I had a very limited practice in the Madras High Court even after practising for close to five years, I thought I would join Mohan Kumaramangalam (1916–1973) as a junior. He was then a senior lawyer. He refused, saying he had shut down his office and only accepted senior engagements. After Kumaramangalam's refusal, I joined the office of R.M. Seshadri, another renowned senior lawyer, on senior advocate A.V. Balakrishnan's advice but left a few months later. I then worked at TVS Motors in Madras as personnel officer and moved to Vijayawada as branch manager. In those days, TVS was not a large business. When I reached Vijayawada, the company had only two trucks. In the nine months that I worked there, the business grew, and at the time I left there were about sixty trucks plying.

I married Vasanth in May 1959 and decided to move to Hyderabad in 1960.[9]

While I was in Madras, I used to know a senior advocate called V.C. Gopalaratnam. He was a very affectionate and jovial man. All of us young lawyers would gather around him every day. He was fond of cutting jokes. Along with other books, he always carried a book of jokes and a bag full of different kinds of pens. When I decided to set up practice in Hyderabad, I went to him and told him of my decision. He said to me: 'Initially you will have no practice. But the world must know that there is a lawyer by your name. Set up an office. Sit in a place where everyone who passes by can see you. Have a cupboard behind you with some second-hand law books. You must

9 See Kannabiran, Vasanth. 2020. *Taken at the Flood: A Memoir of a Political Life*. New Delhi: Women Unlimited.

be seen reading. Passers-by must register that there is a pleader here who is accessible and looks trustworthy and reliable. When they have a problem or their friends have a problem, they should immediately recall you and bring their problems to you.' I followed his advice in letter and spirit.

When I look back, although it was by fortuitous circumstance that I argued and got a favourable ruling in Ansari Begum's case, the political, social and philosophical impact of that case on my own thinking was significant. My perspective at the time I argued the case fifty years ago paved the way for my lifelong work in defending civil liberties.

2
Legal Practice in Andhra Pradesh

Early Years in Hyderabad

I WENT THROUGH considerable hardship to establish myself in legal practice in the early days. I faced many obstacles. But those details are not material to the way in which I wish to recount my life journey here.

Vasanth took up a job as a lecturer in Reddy College for a monthly salary of Rs 150. We rented a house in Chikkadpalli for Rs 50 per month.

Right from the beginning, I think I possessed the skill to present arguments effectively. By 1968–69, my office grew quite big. I got several cases. However, my experiences in the profession in those seven or eight years, the principles I had set out for myself, my friends in Hyderabad—all these played an important part in my life thereafter. At that time, I worked for a brief while in the office of the second government pleader. 'I want to join your office. You need not pay me a single paisa. If you give me a lot of work so that I can learn the lawyer's craft, that is enough,' I said to him. He agreed and stayed true to his word by giving me a lot of work and no money at all. In six months, I had learnt everything I needed to learn about the lawyer's profession. I familiarized myself with all the courts and acquainted myself with the judges, who now began to recognize me.

Thereafter, I made a beginning in my profession.

I set up an office in Marredpalli. A young lawyer called Narasimha Chary joined me as a junior. A few months later, A.K. Ahmed joined me. Gradually, my office gained recognition. I started getting a lot of cases. Around that time, a friend of mine, Kripal Singh, was working in Parry and Company. He and I had met and become friends when we were cricketers. On his suggestion, Parry and Company appointed me as its lawyer. Several companies then appointed me as their legal advisor. I began to get a lot of civil litigation cases.

At that point, I set myself a rule with regard to my income. Irrespective of who the litigant was, I would not amass wealth. I would not fall into the trap of earning money indiscriminately. Even for company matters, I never charged fees that were higher than my normal fee. In other cases, I simply took what the client gave me. I never asked for a fee. In fact, whether in this legal profession, or in my life outside the profession, I have never asked anybody for anything, either for me or for my family.

Vasanth's college was far away from where we lived and it was hard for her, so in 1969 I shifted my home and office to Hyderabad. In all the years that we lived in Hyderabad, we shifted house around eight times. Precisely at this time, in 1968, there were far-reaching changes in national politics and social life. The impact of these changes on courts and on intellectuals became increasingly evident.

I had been observing national politics closely—Partition, the Dravidian movement and its political consequences in Tamil Nadu and earlier in Madras state, the toppling of the Kerala government, and the growing chaos in governance—and my critical engagement with the changes that were now occurring grew. I observed Mohan Kumaramangalam shift his position slowly towards the Congress and Indira Gandhi. When he came to Hyderabad soon after he agreed to be the advocate general of Madras in 1966, I met him at the Ritz Hotel where he was staying and told him I was unhappy with his decision. Later, in 1971, when he became a minister in Indira Gandhi's cabinet, I wrote to him criticizing his move.

The Constitution and the Justice System

By the late 1960s, the justice system was beginning to change. In the years that followed, justices and chief justices of India like V.R. Krishna Iyer and P.N. Bhagwati were speaking of barefoot lawyers, about taking justice to the doors of the common people, of taking law to the people.

Lawyers rose in protest against the fact that the justice system was not fulfilling the noble ideals set out in the Constitution. There were political and social causes for this churning that had begun in the halls of justice. It is necessary to understand the relationship between these causes and my involvement in the civil liberties movement.

I believe that we have not taken our Constitution as seriously as we should have. We are paying the price for that neglect. The Constitution is not merely another piece of legislation. It is a political declaration. The people are behind the Constitution. Peoples' movements are behind it. People's aspirations guide it. Our failure to understand the Constitution in this manner has resulted in our negation of its power as a political declaration. This has also resulted in the complete disconnect we see today between the judgments from our courts and the values of the freedom struggle and the Constitution. We have written the principle of equality into the Constitution in its inaugural moment, but have been unable to understand its true import. The justice system has failed to understand and deliberate productively on the issues that confront the country today.

Even while the Constitution was being drafted, the imprisonment of A.K. Gopalan[1] for waging war against the state in the newly independent nation and soon thereafter, immediately after the coming into force of the Constitution, and the case of *Champakam Dorairajan vs State of Madras*,[2] illustrate the deep contradictions between the values of the freedom struggle and governance in independent India. Preventive detention placed limitations on the constitutional guarantee of personal liberty.

If we step back into history briefly, we realize that courts were used by the colonial government as instruments of oppression, and functioned in that manner throughout colonial rule. After Independence, there was no attempt to change the fundamental character of these institutions in the justice system.

It was not only the justice system—there were no attempts at transforming the social order either. The government of independent India did not confiscate the estates and wealth of zamindars and princes. Where it did confiscate properties, it paid out heavy compensation. In the transition from colonial rule to Independence, the oppressor classes did not suffer any loss. The wealth that they had accumulated through the exploitation of common people over generations remained with them. They were the ones who became ministers, parliamentarians and legislators. Instead of realizing the ideals of the freedom struggle to establish an egalitarian society, inequalities rose in India. A new class of landlords emerged in the country. All the basic institutions in the country—political, social, parliamentary, judicial—saw a spiralling downwards right from the 1950s. Misgovernance eroded and

1 For a detailed analysis of the A.K. Gopalan case, see Kannabiran, K.G. 2004. *The Wages of Impunity: Power, Justice and Human Rights*. Hyderabad: Orient Longman. For the judgment, *A.K. Gopalan vs State of Madras* 1950 AIR SC 27.

2 *State of Madras vs Champakam Dorairajan* AIR 1951 SC 226.

dismantled political and legally mandated institutions. Parliament progressively failed in fulfilling its political responsibilities. The office of the governor was misused. Election commissions became the medium for election propaganda. Political debate stagnated and the level of political discourse fell sharply. There were warning signs of this state of affairs right from the 1950s. M.R. Radha was an actor in Madras. In those days, his dialogue from the film *Raktha Kanneer* (1954) became popular: 'The Congress is a clever party. If you win from the Congress party you will become a minister, if you lose you will become a governor.'

For a few years after Independence, it seemed as if the country was moving along the path of development. The zamindari system was abolished. Heavy industries were set up in the public sector. There was a visible rise in employment. People were hopeful that the economy would grow. And yet there was a simmering political discontent. It was this political and social discontentment that paved the way for alternative visions for my generation and those that followed. If I look back now, I feel the poverty I experienced in my childhood and youth and the widespread social discontent that I witnessed in my early days as a lawyer shaped my perspectives on society.

Representing Colliery Workers

Perhaps because of my association with Ramji, V.G. Row and Kumaramangalam, I became associated with the Singareni Workers' Union immediately after moving to Hyderabad. The Indian National Trade Union Congress (INTUC) leader Srinivasan was part of the union. There was a wage dispute over increments between the management and the workmen. It was, I think, about the withdrawal of a Rs 5 increment given to the workmen. Suddenly after one or two years, the management withdrew this increment and this move was contested by the workmen, leading to the dispute being referred to the tribunal. The dispute ended in favour of the management. In those days, the collieries used to be represented by Mr Narsing, an advocate practising in Dhanbad who specialized in mining laws. He was a management lawyer for the collieries located in and around Dhanbad.

I drafted the writ petition on behalf of the workmen and filed it. I was quite new to this court when I appeared in the case. It came up for final hearing before Justice Gopal Rao Ekbote, who had risen from an advocate's clerk to teacher to lawyer to minister in the Hyderabad government to member of Parliament (MP) and then to high court judge. He turned out to be quite a competent judge and later the chief justice of the Andhra Pradesh High Court. For the workmen, the denial of the disputed increment presented an enormous problem. It also meant working out deductions of payments in respect of all accounts that were paid by the management. It would be Rs 60 (Rs 5 every month for twelve months) multiplied by the number of years, and by the number of the workmen. There were other consequences as well. Our case was quite simple and straightforward. This increment was granted by the management without there being either a demand or a dispute. It formed part of the workmen's wages. Therefore, there could be no deduction excepting those that were permitted by either the Payment of Wages Act or some other statute. It was also contended that the increment amounted to a gift in terms of civil law and a gift could only be unconditional and absolute. Even if considered from that angle the increment granted could not be withdrawn. The tribunal award against the workmen was set aside. The writ petition was also keenly contested. The matter was carried by an appeal and it was before the first bench: Chief Justice Manohar Pershad and Justice Mohammed Mirza. Manohar Pershad was a judge in Hyderabad state and was continued after a successful screening by two Supreme Court judges sitting at Hyderabad. Mr Siaddat Ali Khan, the judge before whom this case was argued in the tribunal, was a victim of the screening process and had to work as an industrial tribunal judge. He was as competent as Manohar Pershad and more of a scholar. Justice Kumarayya and Justice Jaganmohan Reddy were the other judges who managed to get through the screening process.

In the course of the hearing by the first bench, I became aware of the fact that Justice Manohar Pershad and Justice Gopal Rao Ekbote had differences that were evident in their courtroom conduct. However, reversing the judgment delivered by Justice Ekbote was not an easy task. It demanded a thorough familiarity with this branch of law, and an understanding of the basis of the claims—the fact that a daily worker need not always be a temporary worker, or that work is measured by the day and wage computed. To get around the problem, Justice Manohar Pershad insisted that I bring about a settlement in the matter. I told him that if it could be settled, I would be the first to agree. The matter was adjourned and we went to the collieries at Kothagudem where Raj Bahadur Gour joined us to negotiate with the management. When no negotiation was possible and we went back to the high court to report failure, Justice Pershad was quite beside himself, for he was not willing to write a reversing judgment. All of a sudden, he suggested a settlement of Rs 5 lakh to be shared by the workers eligible to receive a share.

The next major engagement was the dispute raised by the workmen in the fixation and fitment into wage scales awarded by the National Coal Wage Board (NCWB). Pursuant to the recommendations made in the Second Five-Year Plan, the government appointed a wage board for the coal mining industry. The NCWB's report was published and the refixation of wages was deemed not possible in the Singareni mines. Fitment posed problems because the jobs to be performed in each category were different. Applying the wage board recommendations, if left to the management, would lead to very arbitrary fixation. Srinivasan of the INTUC again approached me and suggested that the claim statement prepared by his union should be settled by Comrade V.G. Row, who had by then retired and was living in Bangalore. We fixed an appointment but could not complete our work on the draft claim statement before we left for Bangalore. Srinivasan was a stenographer, and a very good one at that. I had instructed him to get a typewriter and papers so that I could dictate the statement. Over a six- to eight-hour train ride, we completed the drafting of the claim statement. V.G. Row spent the entire forenoon with us, sought clarifications, and approved the draft without any corrections.

The presiding judge of the tribunal during most part of the wage board dispute was Tarimela Chandrasekhara Reddy, a first cousin of Comrade Tarimela Nagi Reddy. He was, in his earlier days, with the Indian National Congress and like many old Congress party members, committed to liberal politics and values. As a judge, he used to conduct himself in a very dignified manner. He was never harsh or brusque or dismissive of a counsel's arguments. Advocate Koka Srinivasa Murthy appeared for the management.

The proof of fitment of jobs and skills was quite a heavy task. It led me to visit the mines quite often to see the workmen perform, their place of work and the surrounding conditions in which they worked. I recollect the job of tub-fillers inside the mine, a very arduous task. This aspect comes after the blasting of the coal face. The coal is gathered and loaded into the tubs that are on rails. Before the blasting, the mining sardars dress the coal face and fix shots, and the blasting is done by shot-firers, yet another category. These coal tubs are transported up to the coal-screening plant where the coal is sorted out in sizes. The entire mine is fraught with risk to lives every day. Apart from that, if you stay inside the mine or at the coal-screening plant even for a short period, you will find yourself exhaling smoke for one or two days. In those days, although they had updated bathing facilities for underground mine workers, many of them did not use these facilities. The five-hour underground work was so oppressive that immediately on coming overground they rushed straight to the toddy shops located close by. In my earlier years in Madras I had read *The Road to Wigan Pier* by George Orwell (1937),[3] where he wrote a lucid account of mine workers. I could see that life reflected in the collieries. I decided to examine a few of the workmen in each category.

I requested the judge to have one or two sittings at Kothagudem. I remember that in the first sitting I examined around 100 to 110 witnesses. The examination of witnesses continued for three days. Mr Chandrasekhara Reddy and K. Srinivasa

3 Orwell, George. 1937. *The Road to Wigan Pier*. London: Victor Gollancz.

Murthy stayed in the company's guest house. On the workers' insistence, I stayed in the hotel they had arranged for me. It was an old building which was converted into a lodging house. There were two rooms adjacent to each other with a connecting door. One was intended to be used when I met the workmen. Tiffin and coffee was supplied by a hotel in the neighbourhood. Of course, a visit to the Bhadrachala Ramudu temple could not have been avoided. Although I was reluctant, for that has never been part of my life or my tour agenda, Mr Chandrasekhara Reddy insisted that I accompany them. The temple routine completed, we left for Hyderabad. Somewhere along the way, Srinivasan of the INTUC handed over the brief to Comrade Komarayya of the All India Trade Union Congress (AITUC), and from then on I was handling union matters until the Emergency in 1975. The tub-fillers went on a lightning strike during the pendency of the dispute. The management declared a lockout. Srinivasa Murthy told me he had advised the management to declare the lockout. I simply said, 'Good.' The company would incur heavy losses if the coal stocks were not made ready for dispatch. The management was forced to enter into an agreement with the tub-fillers in respect to their claim, and they were advised to resume duty immediately. Following this example, I advised Komarayya to plan a section-wise series of strikes, and by strikes and settlements the entire dispute was covered. I had the matter disposed of earlier than I had expected.[4]

In this manner, even while I was engaged in civil litigation, I argued several cases of industrial disputes. Later, when I took up civil liberties cases, my experience of appearing for trade unions stood me in good stead.

The Case of Kambarigam Mokhasa, Srikakulam

Kambarigam, a village in Srikakulam district, was part of the Tarla Zamindari.[5] It was now under the control of Parasuram Choudary, who belonged to the dominant Kalinga clan in the area. The members of the clan are predominantly employed in the police department in the state, and have contested the elections and wield political clout. Parasuram Choudary was a *jagirdar* under the Tarla

4 For a discussion on trade unionism, see Kannabiran, K.G. 2004. *The Wages of Impunity: Power, Justice and Human Rights*. Hyderabad: Orient Longman, pp. 272–78.

5 The editor is grateful to J. Hari Narayan for documents relating to Kambarigam. The land in question is described variously and interchangeably in documents as 'jagirdari', *inam*, zamindari, and 'mokhasa'. All of these terms refer to Kambarigam, a village consisting of 450 acres of unsurveyed land, in the uninterrupted possession of a single family from the mid-nineteenth century.

Zamindari. Both the zamindari and the *inams* within the zamindari were gifted by the British government. Although zamindaris were abolished after Independence and the coming into force of the Constitution, the inams themselves remained undisturbed. There was a legal battle between the Tarla Zamindar and Parasuram Choudary that dragged on for almost half a century. The jagirdar (*mokhasadar*) claimed the land was his and appealed to the courts to return it to him. Parasuram Choudary asserted that he had obtained the title to the land lawfully and that it was his property. In this litigation that dragged on for decades, the terms on which the British government gave the zamindari to the Tarla Zamindar were not disclosed or made public by the zamindar, nor did Parasuram Choudary demand that this be made public.

Choudary had in his possession 450 acres of unsurveyed land. The then agent to the governor in Ganjam had signed the gift deed dated 1802, prior to the Permanent Settlement, which was validated as a grant anterior to the Permanent Settlement Regulations, 1802, and survived autonomously even after the abolition of the Tarla Zamindari, merely shifting the payment of a paltry '*kattubadi*' (tax) from the zamindari to the government. The inam settlement commissioner, who was tasked with enfranchising inams under the Inam Settlement Rules, 1859, did not apply the rules to the Kambarigam jagir as it was under litigation from 1856 to 1864. With the enactment of the Estates Abolition Act, 1948, the jagirdar petitioned the Madras High Court that his jagir was exempt from the application of this Act, and received a favourable ruling. Again, in 1964, when the state government petitioned the Andhra Pradesh High Court, the court ruled in favour of the jagirdar (mokhasadar). In 1980, when the revenue department attempted to carry out a suo motu inquiry, the jagirdar obtained an injunction from the court. There were no government land records for the village, and neither the collector nor the revenue officials could enter the land without the permission of the jagirdar. Therefore, he argued, the Land Ceiling Act would not apply to him till the survey was done. Running through the middle of this unsurveyed land was an irrigation canal. He argued that since the canal flowed in his land, he was not liable to pay water cess. There was a branch of the Lions Club in the village; there was also a school in the village. The teacher in the school doubled as the village postmaster—the only sign of modernity.

It was but natural then for the tenant-cultivators to wage a struggle for their rights to the land—a struggle that drew the attention of the constitutionally constituted state government. On the request of the government, the district collector of Srikakulam, J.M. Girgilani, submitted a report. I still remember one sentence from Girgilani's report. He said that the police in that village were working like the private army of the zamindar. Senior Indian Police Service (IPS) officers provided full protection to the Kambarigam mokhasadar Parasuram Choudary, as did courts of every jurisdiction across three states: Orissa, Tamil Nadu and Andhra Pradesh.

The case of the zamindari also needs to be viewed in the historical context of the grant of zamindaris to loyal servants of the British who protected colonial interests against the growing resistance in the colony. It was the blind adoption of colonial laws in independent India without review or amendments given the changed status of the country that paved the way for the original Parasuram Choudary's descendent, the present Parasuram Choudary, to assert his claims in a court of law in independent India. He used a legal provision pertaining to 'lost/misplaced gift deeds', which was generally used by all zamindars to their advantage, employing the justice system to perpetuate injustice. Courts in independent India also fell in line by vesting control of the 450 acre inam with Parasuram Choudary. When he argued that he was personally cultivating the entire land without any tenants, his lawyers and the judges hearing the case did not raise a question. On the whole, the courts delivered a judgment in favour of Parasuram Choudary and against the tenants.[6]

A journalist, T. Madhusudana Rao, published the story of Kambarigam in four parts in the *Indian Express* in February 1982 when Arun Shourie was the editor of the paper.[7] Madhusudana Rao wrote that Kambarigam 'was an independent country by itself' where the Constitution had no jurisdiction.[8] I toured Srikakulam several times with Madhusudana Rao. Shortly after his reports on Kambarigam were published, I met my young friend J. Hari Narayan, the then district collector of Srikakulam, and told him that the saving on 'lost/misplaced gift deeds' was responsible for the

6 *D. Parasuram Choudary & Ors vs Mandal Revenue Officer, Palasa, Srikakulam district*, WP No. 17494/2002 & WP No. 14008/2002, dated 4 July 2002. For recent litigation on the jagirdari, see *Pinninti Kistamma and Ors vs Duvvada Parasuram Choudary and Ors* (08.01.2010: SC) (2010) 2 SCC 452; MANU/SC/0039/2010; and *Duvvada Parasuram Choudary vs Santha Dalayya*, 2014 (4) ALT 71; MANU/AP/0073/2014.

7 T. Madhusudana Rao, (i) 'Fief which Survives by Law', Sunday Edition, *Indian Express*, 7 February 1982; (ii) 'Litigation Overwhelms Legislation', *Indian Express*, 8 February 1982; (iii) 'Tillers Termed Trespassers', *Indian Express*, 9 February 1982; (iv) 'Lone Crusader', *Indian Express*, 10 February 1982. These reports provide detailed information on the history of Kambarigam and have been relied on by the author in his account of the case.

8 T. Madhusudana Rao, 'Fief which Survives by Law', Sunday edition, *Indian Express*, 7 February 1982.

illegal occupation and possession of land by landlords, and that this provision must be repealed. In the course of our long discussion on this, it emerged that the gift deed might be in the old records repository in Orissa. Part of the litigation on Kambarigam took place in the Berhampur court. We also wondered if we might find the papers in Madras since the area was part of the Madras Presidency. Or we might find it in the office of the Tarla Zamindari. Hari Narayan immediately called his steno and dictated a letter to the office of the Tarla Zamindari, directing the production of the gift deed given to it. Curiously enough, the Tarla Zamindari office submitted the deed to the collector almost immediately on receipt of this letter. It was in good condition and not in the least damaged. The conditions and limitations were very clearly stated. The deed recognized the presence of tenants on the land. Hari Narayan immediately sent me a copy. By then the final judgment in the Kambarigam case had already been delivered. The tenant-cultivators were not part of this litigation. It was final, even though the claim that the gift deed was lost was now a false claim.

The Preamble to the Constitution of India envisages a just society—these laws in force make a mockery of this, and protect the interests of the powerful. If we do a comparative analysis of the debates on the right to property and the right to personal liberty and individual freedoms, we will understand which of these is foundational. Despite this, the arbitrariness embedded in the laws in force obstruct our efforts to build a better society.

Ignoring the litigation on Kambarigam, I met CPI leader Dasari Nagabhushana Rao and discussed the matter with him. He then met the villagers and mobilized a struggle against the landlord.[9]

Parasuram Choudary was advised by his lawyers to file a defamation case against Madhusudana Rao and the management of the *Indian Express* for the exposé on Kambarigam. The *Indian Express* requested me to appear for it. In my written arguments on this case, I traced the history of both the Parasuram Choudarys and the gift deed which I now had. I made Parasuram Choudary stand in the witness box for two days in a row for eight hours and cross-examined him. He admitted that he was not personally cultivating the land and that he had tenant-cultivators. After he had admitted to all the points I raised in my cross-examination, he approached me for an out-of-court settlement. I generally agreed to out-of-court settlements in cases where this was legally permissible and I felt it would be feasible. I agreed to a settlement in this case and said I wanted Justice K. Punnaiah to join me as a

9 'Arrest of Ryots in Kambarigam Village', *Andhra Pradesh Legislative Assembly Debates: Official Report*, 13 September 1985, pp. 511–15.

mediator. I wanted to clinch the settlement before he changed his mind. I told him that I would mediate if he agreed to make over at least 300 acres of the land in his possession to the tenant-cultivators. By then the struggle for land in Kambarigam had been going on for a very long time. The government teacher–postmaster who was leading the struggle by the villagers was murdered around this time.[10]

The next day, I travelled by taxi from Srikakulam town to Kavali village in Srikakulam district not far away with Madhusudana Rao to meet Justice Punnaiah at his home. As the road was not motorable after a point, we walked the last 8–10 kilometres. We described the situation to him and persuaded him to be a mediator. But Parasuram Choudary went back on his word. All the judgments till then were in his favour and had reinforced his authority—so he was unwilling to go through with a mediation in which he would stand to lose. I suspect his turnabout was based on the advice of his lawyers.

Reminiscing Two Human Rights Violations in Madurai

Justice V.M. Tarkunde and I, Madurai, October 1982

The violence of the state silences people. We are unwilling to recognize people's rights as a limitation on power and that a properly structured rights discourse may lead to social change with less violence. Courts have come around to the implicit conclusion that anarchic state violence is the only justifiable method to contain and cope with the violence of political movements. My memory goes back to 1982. Justice Tarkunde and I were in Madurai on 31 October 1982 to participate in a public meeting in the forenoon, followed by a silent procession in the evening around 5 p.m. After the meeting, around 4.30 p.m., the processionists gathered near a huge statue of Muthuramalinga Thevar, a well-known leader of the Thevar community in the 1950s. Tarkunde and I were in the first row leading the procession, and as it was a silent procession we had black ribbons tied over our mouths. Among the processionists was a journalist with a camera. As we were getting ready, a contingent of over 100 riot policemen arrived in vans and stood in a row at attention, staring menacingly at us and awaiting orders. The journalist took a few shots of the processionists, and when he began taking shots of the police force, the inspector objected and ordered him to surrender his camera. As he refused, force was used to secure the camera. The journalist, dodging attack, came running to us, seeking

10 T. Madhusudana Rao, 'Lone Crusader', *Indian Express*, 10 February 1982.

our protection. The inspector too came running towards us. The conversation that followed between Tarkunde and the inspector ran somewhat along these lines:

> Tarkunde: Why are you chasing the young man?
>
> Inspector: He took photographs of the police force, which he cannot do. So he must surrender his camera.
>
> Tarkunde: Which law restrains a person from taking photographs of the police force?
>
> Inspector: The provisions of the CrPC [Code of Criminal Procedure].
>
> Tarkunde: I have been a judge of a high court for quite a few years and had occasion to deal with the CrPC. Which section of the CrPC restrains a person from taking photographs of the police force sent to regulate a procession?

The inspector, on hearing the credentials of Mr Tarkunde, and finding himself inadequate, called upon the additional superintendent of police (SP), Mr Mohammed Ali, to deal with Mr Tarkunde. The additional SP, guessing that Mr Tarkunde was not from Madras, bluffed to him that the Madras Police Standing Orders restrained the taking of photographs of a police force sent to regulate a procession. I intervened and said that I had some acquaintance with the Standing Orders and asked him for details. I said this in Tamil. Mr Mohammed Ali thought, 'Enough is enough', and immediately turned around to the police force and ordered them in Tamil, 'Beat up the bastards.'

Mr Tarkunde and I, along with others, were thrashed, pushed into the police van stationed nearby, and carted to the police station. We were made to stand in a row before the station writer's table and our names were recorded in the register. Mr Tarkunde was the first accused. When the police realized they had beaten up a former high court judge, the Q Branch moved in and told Mr Tarkunde to leave. When he refused to leave without the others who were in the lock-up, he was dragged out by his shirt collar and shoved into a city bus passing by. We were all produced before the chief judicial magistrate on the charge that we assaulted the police force and caused some of them injury. They produced medical evidence to support their allegations.

The principal actors in this unprovoked assault were the inspector of police, the additional SP, Mr Mohammed Ali, the station house officer and the government doctors who gave false medical certificates to some of the armed constables.[11] The court may assume that every one of them is a responsible officer. The court, while adjudicating, may even reject Tarkunde's evidence as unreliable and accept instead the official version. These empirically unsupported assumptions have, in my experience, been consistently drawn upon in all cases of personal liberty by courts. Yet, for courts under the constitutional scheme to continue with such attitudes would be to dispense with the vigil which is a mandatory requirement in a sentinel on the qui vive.

Nallakaman's Struggle for Human Rights, Madurai, 1982–2006

I learnt of the Nallakaman case in Madurai by sheer coincidence during my trips to Coimbatore to argue the bomb blasts case around the year 2000. By then, the case had been shuttling between different courts for eighteen years. Lawyers B.B. Mohan, Raju and others felt that although it was a small case in Madurai, it would be good if I appeared.[12] On the face of it, the case appears like a personal dispute, but it was in fact an out-of-the-ordinary case with serious human rights implications.

There were three kinds of investigations conducted for a single case. There were therefore three different judgments. The first case had to do with the private complaint Nallakaman filed against Sub-Inspector Prem Kumar of the Vadipatti police station in Madurai district. The second was the case registered by the police on a complaint against Nallakaman for a matter within the jurisdiction of the Vadipatti police station. The third case was based on the report of the revenue divisional officer on the incident which recommended the prosecution of Sub-Inspector Prem Kumar and three constables.[13]

---

11 For another eyewitness account of this incident see Henri Tiphagne, 2021. 'Defending Human Rights, Challenging State Impunity', K.G. Kannabiran Lectures, *Livelaw*, 13 February 2021. https://www.livelaw.in/columns/defending-human-rights-challenging-state-impunity-henri-tiphagnes-talk-at-kannabiran-lecture-169816. Accessed on 6 May 2022.

12 See B.B. Mohan, 2020. 'Criminal Law and Human Rights: "Distinctive Discrimination" and Article 21 Rights to Fair Trial'. K.G. Kannabiran Lectures, *Livelaw*, 25 December 2020, https://www.livelaw.in/columns/criminal-law-and-human-rights-distinctive-discrimination-and-article-21-rights-to-fair-trial-167651. Accessed on 31 December 2021.

13 *K. Prem Kumar vs The Revenue Divisional Officer, Usilampatti, Madurai District* (16.11.1987: MADHC): MANU/TN/0399/1987. Justice G. Maheswaran; *K. Prem Kumar vs The Revenue Divisional Officer, Madurai and Ors* (06.06.2002:

The same Prem Kumar rose to the rank of SP and gained prominence as the head, Special Investigation Team (SIT) in the *Sankaracharya* case.[14]

The incident

Nallakaman was an ex-serviceman. He had given Bairava Singh, a reserve assistant sub-inspector, a loan of Rs 5,000. In return, he stayed in the house of Bairava Singh, and the arrangement was treated as a lease, which was a common practice in that area. No interest would be payable on the loan. Bairava Singh could pay up his loan and ask Nallakaman to vacate without notice. However, instead of asking Nallakaman to vacate, Bairava Singh filed a complaint in the Vadipatti police station that Nallakaman was refusing to vacate his premises. On the basis of the complaint, Sub-Inspector Prem Kumar immediately summoned Nallakaman to the police station. The police who went to summon Nallakaman assaulted him, stripped him to the waist, and paraded him half-naked on the streets in handcuffs. When he was threatened by the police sub-inspector for the first time and ordered to vacate the house, Nallakaman insisted that he would vacate if his loan was repaid. The incident occurred on 1 February 1982. V.M. Tarkunde and I were assaulted in the same district the same year in October.

Apprehending arrest, Nallakaman secured anticipatory bail from the sessions court. Although the police were trying to convert a civil dispute into a criminal case, Nallakaman only saw it as a civil case. He sent an appeal to the Ex-Servicemen Welfare Board to help him secure the full repayment of his loan. Instead of donning his uniform and arming himself with his rifle to assault Bairava Singh, the assistant director of the board, like an ordinary law-abiding citizen, sent a letter to the local police station to amicably resolve the dispute, saying that he did not wish to take the law into his hands, and wanted the matter of repayment of loan to Nallakaman

---

MADHC): MANU/TN/0905/2002. Justice M. Karpaga Vinayagam; *P. Santhanarajan vs State of Tamil Nadu and Ors* (23.11.2005: MADHC): MANU/TN/2429/2005. Justice P.D. Dinakaran.

14 The Sankaracharya petitioned the Supreme Court to transfer the case outside the state of Tamil Nadu on eight grounds. Prem Kumar's track record was the eighth ground. Clause 5 (viii): 'Shri Prem Kumar, who is heading the Special Investigating Team, is not a fair and upright officer and superior courts have passed strictures against him several times in the past for his uncalled for actions in going out of the way to implicate innocent persons in criminal cases.' *Jayendra Saraswathy Swamigal, Tamil Nadu vs State of Tamil Nadu and Ors* (26.10.2005: SC): MANU/SC/1488/2005; AIR 2006 SC 6.

settled peacefully. On receipt of such communication, all that the receiving authority is expected to do is investigate the matter and direct it to the appropriate authority for settlement. That local police officer was the same Prem Kumar.

The procedure on the treatment of persons during investigation is set out in great detail in the CrPC—especially in terms of the treatment of an accused person. Articles 14 and 21 of the Constitution of India too are to be understood in the same terms. The presence of a lawyer representing the accused person is a guarantee under Article 22 (1) and (2). The Supreme Court emphasized the point on the treatment of accused in a criminal case in the *Nandini Satpathy* case.[15] Although this is a matter that has come up for discussion in our courts on innumerable occasions, this kind of barbaric treatment is commonplace throughout the country.

Nallakaman's wife, Seeniammal, a teacher, was also summoned to the police station by three women constables at school while she was at work. Prem Kumar resorted to foul verbal abuse when she repeated Nallakaman's reasons for not vacating the premises. She told him respectfully that she was old enough to be his mother and that she held a respectable job as teacher in a school and that he should treat her with respect. When she said this, not only did Prem Kumar abuse her even more, he also pulled her sari and rained blows on her back with his lathi. When Nallakaman attempted to intervene, he was assaulted again, and both of them—Nallakaman and Seeniammal—were handcuffed and thrown in the lock-up. When their son Madhivannan heard this, he came running to the police station. He was also beaten up. Nallakaman was then paraded in chains on the main road to the Vadipatti bus stand and back, the police assaulting him on the way in full public view. These were the atrocities—human rights violations—perpetrated on Nallakaman and all the members of his family. There were eighteen injuries on Nallakaman's body and five injuries on his son's body. Despite Nallakaman securing anticipatory bail for himself and his wife immediately on being summoned to the police station, Prem Kumar went ahead undeterred.

The following day, 2 February, 500 panchayat union teachers walked in a procession protesting against this incident. This was a peaceful demonstration. On 3 February, all local political parties called for a bandh in Vadipatti. On 4 February, the teachers organized another procession and protest. In this demonstration, the union of primary school teachers under the leadership of the state president of the union went in a procession to the collector's office and submitted a representation. The day after that, 5 February, an all-party demonstration and a huge public meeting

15 *Nandini Satpathy vs P.L. Dani and Ors* (07.04.1978: SC): MANU/SC/0139/1978; AIR 1978 SC 1025.

was held in Vadipatti condemning this incident and demanding action. The collector took note of this public protest and ordered an inquiry by the revenue divisional officer (RDO). On 17 February, the daily newspapers carried an announcement that anyone who wished to record statements on the police atrocity on Nallakaman's family should do so before the RDO of Usilampatti. On the whole, 289 persons came forward to express willingness to record statements. When the inquiry was being conducted, 212 persons recorded their statements in person. Just looking at these details gives us an idea of how much this incident had agitated the town. The RDO sent a detailed report to the collector on the manner in which Nallakaman and his family were tortured by the police.

Nallakaman then filed a private complaint against the police personnel who assaulted him and his family. Prem Kumar registered a case against Nallakaman for obstructing a government servant from performing his official duty and alleged that Nallakaman had attempted to murder him. In the meantime, the collector sent the RDO's report to the government, which sanctioned legal proceedings against Sub-Inspector Prem Kumar. On the basis of the collector's orders, the RDO registered a criminal complaint against Prem Kumar and the constables. Prem Kumar petitioned the high court that the collector's report was inadmissible. He kept filing one petition after another to delay the proceedings. The high court struck down the collector's report. Nallakaman appealed to the Supreme Court against this decision. The Supreme Court held that it was incorrect to strike down the collector's report and ordered that the three cases be heard together.

One incident, three cases. This was like Akira Kurosawa's legendary film, *Rashomon*.

Through this entire period, not only was Prem Kumar not suspended, but he was awarded promotion after promotion and eventually promoted to the rank of SP. He spared no effort to prolong the case in the hope that Nallakaman would just withdraw, frustrated from the proceedings. When none of his efforts met with any success, he had himself transferred to Madurai as SP. Immediately on taking charge, he started his attempts to derail the case.

Between November 1995 and March 2003, there were thirteen non-bailable warrants (NBWs) that were kept pending without Prem Kumar being arrested. The NBW secured by Nallakaman on 23 April 2001 had not been executed for one year—the only reason why the warrant had remained pending, according to Nallakaman, was because the police officers responsible for its execution were subordinate to SP Prem Kumar.

It was after one such warrant that Prem Kumar petitioned the high court that the investigation should be closed due to inordinate delays. In this case, Nallakaman was not named as a respondent. The high court observed that the facts of the case demonstrated the scant respect Prem Kumar and his colleagues had for the law. Prem Kumar was also censured for misrepresenting facts and not mentioning Nallakaman as a party.[16]

In the year 2000, the sessions court pronounced judgments on all three cases. Nallakaman was found guilty of obstructing a public servant in the performance of his duties, but he was released under the provisions of the Probation of Offenders Act. The sessions court also found that as per the collector's report, Prem Kumar was guilty but he was not sentenced under Section 3 of the Probation of Offenders Act. The private complaint filed by Nallakaman was struck down. Appeals were filed against all the three sessions court judgments—and they came before Justice Jayapalan in the Madurai Bench of the Madras High Court. He heard the arguments but was transferred to Madras before he delivered the judgment. It was at this stage that I argued the case. Again, the judge who heard me got transferred after the arguments were heard. I had to repeat my arguments before yet another judge. I was appearing before the Madurai Bench of the Madras High Court.

I presented my arguments for close to three hours on 13 March 2006, and submitted my written arguments on 16 March 2006. There was evidence of unlawful assembly because witnesses testified that Sub-Inspector Prem Kumar and a few constables were present. Bairava Singh was also there—all those present on that occasion knew that he was responsible for this entire incident. But he was not named anywhere. Only Nallakaman named him in his complaint and showed Bairava Singh as an accused, and detailed how Bairava Singh had provoked the police into attacking Nallakaman and his family. I argued that there were more than five persons present at the time that Nallakaman was being publicly assaulted and it must be treated as an unlawful assembly and sentences awarded accordingly. I also argued that it was not an isolated incident and that the people of the town had risen in one voice against it, and therefore there was evidence of public outrage. It was without doubt a human rights violation. When a police officer is guilty of violation of human rights, under which law could he be set free under the Probation of Offenders Act? This was my question to the court. I argued that the provisions of the Probation of Offenders Act could never apply to a police officer under any circumstances. In the early days of the Narmada Bachao Andolan led by Medha Patkar, there was an incident like this where a person was arrested and paraded in chains. We have Justice Sengupta's judgment in the Supreme Court on this

16 *K. Prem Kumar vs The Revenue Divisional Officer, Madurai and Ors* (06.06.2002: MADHC): MANU/TN/0905/2002. Justice M. Karpaga Vinayagam.

matter. Similarly, Madras High Court judge Rathnavel Pandian's judgment speaks of the same issue. I cited both these judgments and detailed what the procedure established by law should be. These are not technical matters that only lawyers know, nor even matters that only lawyers can argue. These are facts that ordinary citizens should know. It is important to put the legal reasoning aside and look at the bare facts of the Nallakaman case. On the face of it, it seems like a case pertaining to non-repayment of a loan, a civil dispute. But a closer look reveals that fundamental rights, human rights, police atrocities, arbitrary conduct on the part of the police, public protest, the callousness of courts, and the tenacity of an individual's struggle are all defining elements in this incident.

Because the RDO's report was very detailed, I relied on that report for my arguments. I pointed out that Prem Kumar did not behave like a government servant. Bairava Singh had not registered any formal complaint against Nallakaman or Seeniammal at any stage. What this meant was that Prem Kumar interfered in a private dispute over which he had no jurisdiction. His actions, therefore, could not be considered as part of his discharge of official duties. Further, since the government had sanctioned legal proceedings against Prem Kumar, he could no longer claim that he was discharging his official duties. None of his actions could be deemed to be in furtherance of his duties. Not only did Prem Kumar and his constables interfere in a matter beyond their writ, they conducted themselves like rowdies. I argued that a police officer found guilty of a human rights violation could not be released under the Probation of Offenders Act. In a country that is signatory to the International Covenant on Civil and Political Rights, 1966, can the state ignore the blatant violation of civil and political rights by a government servant? The Supreme Court has ruled in several cases that strict adherence to the procedure established by law is the only way in which state authorities who are in a position of power in a criminal investigation may be disciplined and prevented from violating human rights.

I argued that taking all these facts into consideration, the court should complete the long-pending proceedings at the earliest.

Two weeks after I submitted my written arguments, the Madurai Bench of the Madras High Court delivered its judgment in this case. The judgment reached three different conclusions on the three cases. Although my arguments on Nallakaman's innocence were not accepted, his release by the trial court under the Probation of Offenders Act was confirmed. They accepted my argument that the Probation of Offenders Act would not apply to Prem Kumar. He was sentenced to imprisonment for one month. They struck down Nallakaman's plea that the sentence should be enhanced. In a way, this judgment is a victory. Prem Kumar will have to go to jail for a criminal offence for one month, which means he will be dismissed from service. This case is not about Prem Kumar alone. There are several policemen across the country who have made a habit of violating human rights. This is a warning to them all. Nallakaman wants to go up in appeal against the judgment of the Madurai Bench, first, because although he was not sentenced to imprisonment, he was held guilty; and second, to seek enhancement of Prem Kumar's sentence. In any case, Prem Kumar would have to go up in appeal to the Supreme Court as his job was at risk.[17]

Nallakaman waged a courageous battle in defence of human rights that stretched for over twenty long years. While the case was still going on, Nallakaman's wife, Seeniammal, died. He must be in his late sixties. One of his sons is a lawyer, another is an armyman. They did not want him to wage this stubborn, long battle for justice. But he persisted.[18] If every one of us is able to defend human rights in this tenacious, disciplined fashion, we can make a significant difference to unlawful conduct by the police. We must continue this long struggle without giving up midway, regardless of the consequences. If we do this, we will not need police reforms; the police establishment will be forced to mend its ways.

If anyone deserves a human rights award in south India, I believe it is Nallakaman.

Nallakaman was not a Naxalite, he was not a political dissenter or a human rights defender. He was an ex-serviceman and an ordinary, law-abiding citizen. This is the reason why I feel this case is a good example of human rights violations. This case also teaches human rights defenders that they should not work within the prescribed limits of news reports and fact-finding, that there are several innovative ways in

---

17 The final verdict was delivered in 2006 and Prem Kumar was dismissed from service. See Tiphagne, Henri. 2021. 'Defending Human Rights, Challenging State Impunity'. K.G. Kannabiran Lectures. *Livelaw*, 13 February 2021, https://www.livelaw.in/columns/defending-human-rights-challenging-state-impunity-henri-tiphagnes-talk-at-kannabiran-lecture-169816. Accessed on 31 December 2021.

18 Prem Kumar died in 2010. In 2012 Nallakaman petitioned the Madras High Court for compensation from the state. He died aged 78 years in 2021. Forty years after he was subjected to torture by the police, in February 2022, the Madras High Court awarded Rs 2 Lakh compensation posthumously to his kin holding that 'the custodial torture was recorded by the Revenue Divisional Officer in the inquiry report. When deprivation of human rights is patently proved by record and through evidence, the state ought to have taken action on their own.' https://www.thehindu.com/news/cities/Madurai/hc-directs-state-to-pay-compensation-to-family-members-of-man-tortured-in-police-custody-in-1982/article38392734.ece. Accessed on 10 June 2022.

which human rights may be defended. Through radically different approaches we will be able to embed the culture of human rights in our society. We will be able to force governments, public authorities and courts to reckon with what it means to respect human rights. This is what Nallakaman achieved.

A Glimpse of My Travels through Different Courts in India

I have argued thousands of cases in these fifty years—criminal cases, civil cases, service matters, political cases—in practically every branch of law. In criminal matters, I took up both original sessions cases and appeal cases. However, of the appeals that I took up, a large number were cases where I represented prisoners who wrote to me from jail. Even of the criminal sessions cases I took up, the largest number were cases pertaining to the Marxist–Leninist movement. In general, however, I rarely refused a criminal case. I am known in the profession for arguing any case where there was an urgent need for justice.

I have argued cases in courts of different jurisdictions across the state and the country. I appeared in several cases in Tamil Nadu; I appeared in a petition in 1997 demanding a judicial inquiry into the 'encounter' killings in Kolkata in 1968–69, the disappearance in 1971 of revolutionary poet Saroj Dutta and the custodial death of Charu Mazumdar[19]—both in the Calcutta High Court and the Supreme Court. Charu Majumdar's son, Abhijit Mazumdar, met me and asked me to appear in that case.[20] I appeared in the Allahabad High Court at the instance of advocate

19 See Banerjee, Sumanta. 1980. *In the Wake of Naxalbari: A History of the Naxalite Movement in India*. Calcutta: Subarnarekha, pp. 419–22 for biographical notes on Saroj Dutta and Charu Majumdar. Also, Sen, Ilina. 2018. 'The Life and Times of Saroj Dutta, Communist Poet and Thinker'. *Wire*, 3 October, https://thewire.in/film/the-life-and-times-of-saroj-dutta-communist-poet-and-thinker.

20 *Sujato Bhadra and Abhijit Mazumdar vs State of West Bengal*. Writ petition in the matter of indiscriminate and widespread genocide of Naxalites in West Bengal between 1968 and 1972, including prominent leaders of the Naxal Movement by the police administration of the state in utter violation of their human rights and fundamental rights enshrined in the Constitution of India. In the High Court at Calcutta, 1997–98. Draft petition on file. See also Suchitra, M. 2017. 'Charu and Son: Revisiting the Legacy of a Revolutionary Father 50 Years after Naxalbari'. *Wire*, 14 July, https://thewire.in/government/naxalbari-abhijit-mazumdar-charu-mazumdar. Accessed on 23 September 2021. Abhijit Mazumdar refers to the petitions in the high court and Supreme Court in 1997, demanding a judicial inquiry into the deaths of Charu Majumdar, Saroj Dutta and others.

Ravi Kiran Jain of the PUCL who filed a writ petition seeking the establishment of a State Human Rights Commission in Uttar Pradesh.[21] I appeared in the Shankar Guha Niyogi case in Jabalpur.[22] I appeared in Bombay before Judge Gaikwad in the designated court in a Narcotic Drugs and Psychotropic Substances (NDPS) Act case involving Sri Lankan Tamil Elango Natarajan in 1994–95, at the same time that Sanjay Dutt was being tried in the special designated court of Judge J.N. Patel next door.[23] When Elango was convicted for ten years by the Bombay court, I represented him in the Supreme Court and got the sentence reduced to time served in jail. I also appeared for the accused in the Coimbatore bomb blasts case in 2006.[24] I never thought I would appear in the Parliament attack case. However, when there was a boycott of the accused by lawyers in Delhi, Gautam Navlakha and Nitya Ramakrishnan requested me to appear—I agreed. [25] In several cases, I contested the naming of an offence as 'terrorist'—through my cases and my writing on cases. In the course of the trial and appeals in the case of the bomb blasts in the RSS headquarters in Madras in 1993, for instance, I asserted that an attack on the RSS headquarters cannot be construed as a terrorist activity and that the case should not be tried under terrorist laws. It is my belief that if an attack on a political and cultural organization is construed as a terrorist offence, every political conflict will be labelled a terrorist activity, and all political activity will be labelled 'terrorism'.[26]

---

21 *People's Union for Civil Liberties vs State of UP and Ors*. 2000 (1) AWC 729. Decided on 12 January 2000.

22 See Chapter 14.

23 Advocate Colin Gonsalves appeared in this case with K.G. Kannabiran. Kannabiran's response to Sanjay Dutt's trial is published as 'Sanjay Dutt in First Person', in Kannabiran, K.G. 2004. *The Wages of Impunity: Power, Justice and Human Rights*. Hyderabad: Orient Longman, pp. 163–67.

24 See Chapter 16 on religious minorities.

25 For an account of this trial and Kannabiran's role, see Ramakrishnan, Nitya. 2020. 'Trial Lessons from K.G. Kannabiran'. K.G. Kannabiran Lectures. *Livelaw*, 5 December, https://www.livelaw.in/columns/kannabiran-nitya-ramakrishnan-parliament-attack-case-pota-166860. Accessed on 21 September 2021. K.G. Kannabiran appeared for Shaukat Hussain Guru in the trial court. The Supreme Court judgment in this case: *State (NCT Delhi) vs Navjot Sandhu* (2005) 11 SCC 600.

26 The accused were, however, tried under TADA (Terrorist and Disruptive Activities [Prevention] Act) and eventually acquitted by the Supreme Court in December 2010, on the grounds of insufficient evidence linking them to the offences. The larger argument by Kannabiran on the definition of offence as 'terrorist' remains

I went to any court that required my presence, and in cases where the question of justice was urgent. I never trawled for cases. I never set down conditions on the kinds of cases I wished to argue. The cases came searching for me—I argued them, and ensured justice. In some situations, cases came to me when litigants needed a guarantee of an incorruptible lawyer. I had a large office. At one point of time, I had seven juniors in my office, and there was enough work to be able to pay their salaries. I never at any point placed an expectation on my juniors to do the kind of work I did. In all the years when I was arguing political matters, they were handling ordinary cases. I was very particular that none of them should feel that I was using them for my ends, although I always discussed questions of law and justice with all of them. My reputation as a lawyer was not built on these cases alone. I had already established myself by 1969–70—long before I started taking up these cases. However, I have no doubt that my life course changed with doing these cases—in terms of values and ethics especially. I cannot imagine what my life would have been like had I not done these cases.

---

unaddressed. For the Supreme Court judgment in this case, see *Abubucker Siddique and Ors vs State represented by the Deputy Superintendent of Police, CBI/SCB/Chennai, Tamil Nadu*, AIR 2011 SC 91.

3

The Civil Liberties Movement in Andhra Pradesh

The Naxalite Prisoners' Defence Committee

THE CIVIL LIBERTIES movement was not the creation of a single individual or group. It was the product of a specific socio-historical context. There were no doubt civil liberties struggles in India before the 1970s. I remember, for instance, attending a civil liberties meeting held in the MLA (Member of the Legislative Assembly) quarters in Hyderabad in 1964. It ended with sharp differences between sympathizers of the Communist Party of India (CPI) and the Communist Party of India (Marxist) (CPI-M). There is a distinction between the trajectories of the struggles before and after the 1970 movement. The Naxalite armed struggle had declared the annihilation of class enemies. The government unleashed severe repression on the activists in that movement. By then, there had already been a downslide in governance and an erosion of the institutions of law, justice and politics. Parliament had abdicated on its political responsibilities. The office of the governor was corrupted. Election systems and electoral politics had dipped deplorably. Political discourse hit rock bottom.

Indira Gandhi recognized that there was no option but to rethink her political approach. She introduced populist measures and began to speak about the need to implement the Directive Principles of State Policy. However, even while introducing the debate, she craftily introduced a separation between Fundamental Rights and

Directive Principles, triggering an adversarial discourse between Parliament and the justice system, and engaged in political propaganda based on half-truths. In the matter of the Constitution, she propagated the view that the non-justiciable Directive Principles in Part IV of the Constitution were more important than, and prior to, the justiciable rights enshrined in Part III, the chapter on Fundamental Rights. There were several takers for her views. My own view in this matter has always been that Fundamental Rights are indispensable to the realization of Directive Principles. But by the time these wedges were put in place, the justice system had become incapable of leading social transformation. The commercialization of legal practice in the Supreme Court and the exorbitant fees charged hourly by lawyers made it impossible for the poor, ordinary citizen to approach the Supreme Court. The social obligations of the legal profession paled from view. The medical and teaching professions also witnessed the same trends. When there is such deep and simmering discontent, it is natural for movements to rise. Young activists in the communist movement were unable to hold back any longer. After intense debates and discussions, they reached the conclusion that there was no alternative to armed struggle. Disenchanted with the view that socialism would come at some point in the future, they firmly believed that force was the only cure. They had the Chinese experience before them. However, they erred in not recognizing the vast difference between social contexts in China and in India.

After Independence, the unfettered powers vested in the new ruling classes, the police and the military led to the merciless repression and decimation of the armed struggle in its early phases through the widespread use of 'encounters' and mass arrests. Approximately 5,000 Adivasis were put in jail. Two or three talukas in Srikakulam district were converted into detention camps. The state entrapped hundreds of activists and sympathizers of this movement in the Secunderabad conspiracy case,[1] Nagi Reddy conspiracy case and Parvathipuram conspiracy case. Advocate Ravi Subba Rao, despite his affiliation with the CPI, argued Naxalite cases in the Andhra Pradesh High Court even prior to 1970. He was a good man with whom I had a very convivial relationship—I argued a few cases with him. I also made a monthly contribution towards support for CPI cadre. It was through him that I was introduced to Naxalite and civil liberties cases. In a context of severe state

1 *Inguva Mallikarjuna Sharma vs State of Andhra Pradesh*, 1977 (1) ALT 638. For a detailed report, see Menon, Amarnath K. 1985. 'Secunderabad Conspiracy Case: Special Court Faces Uphill Task', *India Today*, 15 July, https://www.indiatoday.in/magazine/nation/story/19850715-secunderabad-conspiracy-case-special-court-faces-uphill-task-770200-2013-12-23. Accessed on 19 October 2021.

repression, it was necessary to gather the support of lawyers who would appear in courts. However, a significant section of the Naxalite cadre took the position that they would not defend themselves in bourgeois courts—and lost the opportunity to be represented. In order to garner the support of lawyers to represent revolutionaries, Bhakti Bhushan Mandal[2] travelled to Hyderabad from Calcutta, probably at the invitation of Ravi Subba Rao. They organized a speech by Bhakti Bhushan Mandal in Haridwar Hotel. I attended the meeting with Ravi Subba Rao. There were about forty lawyers present there. This was just before 1970. It was one of the earliest attempts at building a civil liberties movement in the state. Mandal's speech that day was inspiring. At the end of the meeting we resolved to take some concrete steps towards an organized legal effort.

The Naxalite Prisoners' Defence Committee was formed and I was made convenor.[3] The organizing committee was constituted by B.P. Jeevan Reddy, C. Padmanabha Reddy, Ravi Subba Rao and Pattipati Venkateswarlu. We were in our forties at that time. Jeevan Reddy became a judge soon after. Ravi Subba Rao died in 1980. Padmanabha Reddy and Venkateswarlu continued in the legal profession. We travelled all over the state to appear in cases. I had no experience of working outside the city. I had never delivered a speech in a public meeting. I only had the experience of working in courts. After the Haridwar Hotel meeting—the origin of the civil liberties movement so to speak—I resolved to devote my energies to the defence of movement activists unlawfully placed under detention by the

---

2 1920–2004, Member of the All India Forward Bloc, he represented the Dubrajpur seat in the West Bengal Legislative Assembly in the years 1962–1967, 1969–1971 and 1977–2001. See also Kannabiran, K.G. 2004. *The Wages of Impunity: Power, Justice, and Human Rights*. Hyderabad: Orient Longman, p. 328.

3 This was the second Defence Committee for communist prisoners set up in Andhra Pradesh after Independence. The first was set up in 1952, to provide legal representation to the roughly 30,000 people active in the communist movement who had been jailed and/or arrested for varying periods between 1944 and 1955. In the words of Ch. Rajeshwar Rao, 'The classical and historic peoples' movement which earned the support of the democratic public opinion all over the world, was defended at every stage by a well-organized panel of advocates right from the lower courts to the high court and the special courts. Eminent Lawyers of the Hyderabad state were helped by legal luminaries from Bombay and Delhi', Foreword, in Saxena, Manohar Raj, ed. 2000. *Historic Telangana Peasants' Struggle and the Legal Battle*. Hyderabad: Telangana Martyrs' Memorial Trust. Supreme Court Advocate A.S.R. Chari (1908–1972) who represented Nagabhushan Patnaik briefly was a member of this Defence Committee (See Chapter 10 on the death penalty).

state. If my memory serves me right, I filed 250 writ petitions on behalf of the defendants in the Parvathipuram conspiracy case the day after the Haridwar Hotel meeting. Although the case was registered long before, the investigation had not commenced. The travesties of justice perpetrated in the name of conspiracy need to be spoken about.

The Parvathipuram conspiracy case is a medley of several individual criminal cases.[4] The FIR in this case, registered in January 1970, provided a template for the conspiracy cases that followed. The FIRs in subsequent cases were simply a reproduction of this one with the names of the accused and other specific details replaced. For doing this work two investigating officers secured promotions to the IPS cadre. There were 148 accused in the Parvathipuram case. The witnesses for the prosecution exceeded 1,000. Revolutionary writers in particular were sharp in their interrogation of the notion of conspiracy. How can an offence by 148 persons witnessed by 1,000 persons amount to conspiracy, they would ask. The charge sheet filed in October 1970 stated that a conclave was held in Boddupadu village in October 1968; pursuant to the conspiracy hatched in that conclave, over the next year and a half, there were thirty murders, 100 robberies and 200 other crimes. We argued in our writ petition that given the large number of accused and the even larger number of witnesses, the investigation would take an inordinately long period, therefore, those placed under detention must be released pending investigation. B.P. Jeevan Reddy and I argued the writ petition. Pursuant to our arguments in the writ, the government set up a special court to hear the Parvathipuram conspiracy case. Similarly, another special court was set up in Hyderabad to hear the Nagi Reddy conspiracy case. Even while the Parvathipuram case was being heard, there were splits in the Naxalite movement, and different sections appointed different lawyers. The largest numbers of accused were non-literate Adivasis (Girijans)—several of us lawyers distributed the work amongst ourselves to ensure representation to all. In preparation for this case, the kin of the accused and political leaders would visit the

---

4 *State represented by DSP, Crime Branch CID, Hyderabad vs Choudary Tejeswara Rao and 74 Others,* Sessions Case No. 46/1973. In the court of additional sessions judge, Visakhapatnam. Judgment delivered on 30 August 1976. Criminal Appeals in Andhra Pradesh High Court: *Dr Bathula Sivarama Reddy and Ors vs State of Andhra Pradesh,* Cr. A. Nos. 814, 843, 847, 848, 953, 957, 958, 962, 963, 964, 965, 966 of 1976; Cr. A. Nos. 141, 177, 369, 542, 572 of 1977; and 807 of 1978. Decided on 27 April 1979. Justices P. Ramachandra Raju and Seetharam Reddy. For an account of the case and the people accused in the Parvathipuram conspiracy case, see Satyanarayana, Cherukuri. 2016. *Suryodayam Kutrakaadu* (Sunrise Is No Conspiracy), Guntur: Tarimela Nagireddy Memorial Committee.

lawyers often. Tarimela Nagi Reddy took a keen interest in the work of the Defence Committee, and would frequently visit me at home. Over countless Charminar cigarettes and tea, he would discuss the case threadbare. When we became part of the Defence Committee, as lawyers we had no internal differences. But gradually, Nagi Reddy suspected that Pattipati Venkateswarlu was getting close to Charu Majumdar. I expressed my disagreement with the irreconcilable approach they took to political differences—then and now. People from all factions came to me. The Defence Committee did a commendable job in securing bail and challenging conditional bail. A large section of lawyers offered their support; a new group of young lawyers stepped forward; a culture of working selflessly in defence of activists in mass struggles emerged.

I met Jwalamukhi around that time. He used to visit me in my office and give me lectures on the annihilation of class enemies. I would argue: 'When will you ever finish the task of individually eliminating class enemies? This is not the right approach. There should just be a deluge that will wash this rot away, but individual annihilation is not the path.'

Later, in 1971, Jwalamukhi, Nikhileshwar and Cherabanda Raju were arrested under the Preventive Detention Act. They were part of VIRASAM (Viplava Rachayitula Sangham—the Revolutionary Writers' Association) which was formed in 1970. The three of them recited their revolutionary poetry often. Their books of poems were banned by the government. The poetry anthology *March*, released on 4 July 1970, the day VIRASAM was formed, and the anthology *Jhanjha,* released in October 1970, were both banned. I filed a writ petition challenging these bans in March 1971. The sessions court in Warangal investigated the ban on *March*. In the high court, however, two judges on the three-judge bench, consisting of Justice Obul Reddy, Justice Sriramulu and Justice Madhava Reddy, confirmed the ban. I argued challenging the ban on *March* and *Le*. Advocate Pattipati Venkateswarlu challenged the ban on *Jhanjha*. The judges who confirmed the ban on *March* and *Jhanjha* struck down the ban on *Le*. The court defined the offence of 'waging war against the state' in a complicated manner. Justice Madhava Reddy, one of the few judges who was very attentive to the arguments of lawyers, did not concur with this view. He wrote a stellar dissent, in which he observed:

> These poems only educate the literate Telugu people in these ideas and theories, but as observed by Justice Holmes, 'every idea is an incitement' and the propagation of every such idea cannot, in my opinion, be termed seditious.[5]

5 *Jwalamukhi alias A.V. Raghavachari vs State of Andhra Pradesh* ILR (1973) AP 114.

The Supreme Court, in another case during the Emergency in 1976, decided on the basis of Justice Madhava Reddy dissent.[6]

When Jwalamukhi, Nikhileshwar and Cherabanda Raju were arrested under the Preventive Detention Act in 1971, we challenged the arrests and argued that the Preventive Detention Act itself derogated the Constitution. Justice O. Chinnappa Reddy and Justice A.D.V. Reddy concurred with our arguments and struck down a section in the Preventive Detention Act, and as a result, the Preventive Detention Act itself fell apart. Justice O. Chinnappa Reddy described poetry as a spontaneous outpouring of emotion:

> These cannot have any rational connection with public disorder. Were these three poets creating public disorder by breaking with poetic tradition and writing about social forces at [war] with status quo? Can their writings be dissociated from the revolutionary movement and described in the abstract as outpourings of restless souls looking for light? If the Constitution itself provides the objectives and the obligations, should forces working for change be condemned as criminal?[7]

In 1974, the Organization for the Protection of Democratic Rights (OPDR) was formed under the leadership of senior advocate Vadari Venkataramaiyya. It held its inaugural meeting at Vivek Vardhini College in Hyderabad. Nagi Reddy invited me to join the OPDR. By then, parting ways with Nagi Reddy's politics, I was closely

---

6 *The State of Uttar Pradesh vs Lalai Singh Yadav*, 1976 SCC (Cri) 556. For a detailed discussion of these cases see Kannabiran, K.G. 2004. *The Wages of Impunity: Power, Justice and Human Rights*. Hyderabad: Orient Longman, pp. 270–317.

7 *Hindustan Times*, 'Andhra Detention Clause Quashed; Poets Freed', 21 September 1971. 'Hyderabad, Sept. 20 (UNI): The Andhra Pradesh High Court today struck down Section 6(A) of the State Prevention Detention Act of 1970 as Violative of Article 22 (5) of the constitution.' *K. Yadava Reddy, B. Bhaskara Reddy, A.V. Raghavachari vs Commissioner of Police, AP & State of AP*, WP Nos. 3115, 3116 and 3117 of 1971. High Court of Judicature at Hyderabad, 20 September 1971. Justices O. Chinnappa Reddy and A.D.V. Reddy. Nikhileshwar, Cherabanda Raju and Jwalamukhi are the pen names of the three petitioners respectively. Nikhileshwar (b. 1938), renowned poet for over six decades, was imprisoned in 1971 under preventive detention. All three were Digambara poets and co-founders of the Viplava Rachayitala Sangham (VIRASAM) also called the Revolutionary Writers' Association (RWA).

involved in the campaign against the death penalty awarded to J. Bhoomaiah and G. Kishta Goud, who were part of the Charu Majumdar group.[8]

In every one of the conspiracy trials, we were able to establish that the entire case was not supported by facts. In all the cases I have argued, our effort was to dislodge the status quo. The Andhra Pradesh Civil Liberties Committee (APCLC) was formed in Guntur the same year. I did not think I would become a part of the APCLC either. I did not want to be identified with any one group. A few months later, Emergency was declared at midnight on 25–26 June 1975 under Article 370 of the Constitution by President Fakhruddin Ali Ahmed. This meant the suspension of Fundamental Rights under the Constitution and the derailment of the rule of law. It became impossible for both the OPDR and the APCLC to function.

Although the Constitution of India had been in force for twenty-five years and Emergency provisions were also part of it, the people were totally unprepared to deal with the actual proclamation of Emergency and did not foresee what it might entail. On the day the Emergency was declared, we were all totally immersed in the struggle to have the death sentence awarded to Bhoomaiah and Kishta Goud commuted. We had a huge meeting in May 1975 to demand the commutation of the death penalty in that case. Even at that moment, we little imagined that Emergency would soon follow. By then there was already an external emergency in place. Although emergency had earlier been declared during the Indo-China war in 1962, and again in 1971, and there were simmering questions about state arbitrariness and misrule, there was no demand to repeal the emergency provisions. There was a renewal of this debate in the context of the internal emergency declared in 1975.

Andhra Pradesh Civil Liberties Committee

Sri Sri was elected the president and Pattipati Venkateswarlu the general secretary of the APCLC in 1974, but during the Emergency, the Defence of India Rules made it almost impossible for the organization to function. Added to this was the fact that at a time of severe suppression of civil liberties, the APCLC president expressed his support for the Emergency. The general secretary was the first to be arrested during that time. This was cause for considerable discomfort. The year after emergency was lifted, in 1978, the APCLC met in Warangal where it was decided that there was

---

8 *G. Krishta Goud and Ors vs State of Andhra Pradesh and Ors* (03.10.1975 - SC), (1976) 1 SCC 157. Justices A.C. Gupta and V.R. Krishna Iyer. The petitioner was also referred to as Kishta Goud. See Chapter 10 on the death penalty.

need for some restructuring and a change in leadership. One thing led to another and I was requested to agree to be the president at least for one term, two years.

Till that point, the APCLC consisted of representatives of various Naxalite groups, and its primary task was seen as protecting the civil liberties of Naxalites. The posts in the executive would be filled by consensus on their distribution and rotation between various groups. I agreed to step in for two years and ended up being the president for fifteen. In 1980, when we met in Hyderabad, I was requested to continue for another two years. Chandra Pulla Reddy met me and requested me to continue: 'You have really made the APCLC well known. It is now recognized throughout the country. You must continue.' But I learnt that although it was made to appear as if I was the unanimous choice of all parties, in fact I was seen as close to a particular group. I was determined to free the APCLC from the grip of these parties. I said that Varavara Rao and B. Pradeep should leave it. It is true that they played a vital role in the founding and growth of the civil liberties movement. However, their membership in Naxalite parties opened the APCLC to criticism that it was a Naxalite group that only protected the rights of Naxalites. I remember having this discussion with Varavara Rao in Dr Ramanadham's house in Warangal. I wanted this to change, and accomplished my objective in my third term.

In the third meeting that took place in Khammam in 1983, K. Balagopal was unanimously elected the general secretary, and I got re-elected a third time as the president. Both of us took on the task of expanding the work of the organization. Several people joined us in this effort.

There were difficulties. I remember one case of a person who was arrested on charges of theft and tortured by the police. Unable to bear the torture, he went up to the roof of the control room and jumped to his death. The dead man was the son of a constable. An inspector, under whom this constable worked, met me and asked me to take up this case. Evidently, he had heard about my work and approached me. I agreed. I sent details of the case to the CPI(M) leaders. They said, 'He was a thief. How can we take up this case?' I went ahead and filed the petition. It came up before a very liberal judge, Justice Venkatarama Sastry. He was very angry and issued a notice saying, 'From where does the police get the power to just kill at will? Is this what you call investigation?' A short while later, we had an APCLC meeting in Nalgonda. Our executive member from Nalgonda, Guruva Reddy, asked me at the meeting, 'How can a civil liberties organization take up cases of thieves?' I told him there was no difference between him and the CPI(M), and asked him how he could arrive at the conclusion that the person was a thief before the investigation was complete. Further, if it did turn out that he was a thief, should he have been tortured? Most people did not agree with my reasoning that day. But I understood that the APCLC was on a weak footing.

Civil liberties cannot be defined as the liberties of members of one's own group, and this needs to be broadened. This happened after Dr Ramanadham's murder in 1985. He was a very close friend. It is necessary to contextualize his death. Warangal was, from the very beginning, an epicentre of the Naxalite movement. State repression in the district was high as a result. This repression was not limited to Naxalites, but also extended to ordinary people. In confronting the repression on Naxalites and the repression on ordinary people, the Warangal unit of the APCLC did very good work. Dr Ramanadham was particularly active in broadening the base of the civil liberties movement. When there were floods in Krishna district, he took activists and writers from Warangal with him and opened a relief camp there. This was at a time when the government was taking no steps to mitigate the effects of the natural disaster on the people.

In 1980, when government doctors went on strike, the MG Memorial Hospital, Warangal, was closed. The burden was especially heavy on patients who were poor. Dr Ramanadham, while supporting the doctors' strike, opened a health camp outside the gate of the hospital. He was of the view that doctors must protest against government policy and as a civil libertarian he must ensure that no patients go unattended. He was well known throughout Warangal district as a paediatrician. In 1984, after NTR returned to power, the police repression in Warangal grew alarmingly. Arrests and torture became a daily affair. Encounter deaths started to increase. There were daily reports of torture in custody and disappearances of movement activists. This political situation certainly had a deep impact on Dr Ramanadham. At that time, Balagopal, who had been elected the general secretary of the APCLC the previous year, was also living in Warangal. Both of them got together and decided to confront the growing repression and began to campaign on the issue.

This work became an eyesore for the police. Dr Ramanadham was shot dead by the police on 3 September 1985—but the anger of the police had been brewing for some years prior. In January 1985, he was falsely implicated in a case and arrested. If we retrace our steps to when Dr Ramanadham became a target, we could perhaps go to the disappearance from police custody in Kazipet in December 1984 of Kodavati Sudershan, a native of Kadipikonda village and the protest against this. Sudershan was working as a railway gang labourer in the Kazipet railway station. On 18 December 1984, he was picked up by Sub-Inspector Yadagiri Reddy from Somidi village near Kazipet. Nobody knows what happened to the young man after that. Newspapers reported that he had been tortured to death and his body disposed of by the police. There were eyewitnesses to his being taken away, and the cycle taxi owner who recovered the cycle rented to Sudershan from the police gave a statement to reporters. Some of these people also testified in the inquiry initiated by the RDO and before the Justice T.L.N. Reddy Commission of Inquiry which was constituted by the Telugu Desam Party (TDP) government in 1989 to enquire into forty-seven cases of missing persons.[9] The TDP government had constituted a Cabinet Subcommittee to review and discuss our proposals for improving the human rights situation in the state. We had recorded twenty-eight cases of 'disappearances' from police custody before the commission, and filed a writ petition in the high court concerning ten of the twenty-eight persons missing. While disposing of our writ petition, the high court observed that all the cases be referred to the same commission. There was no response on this from the government. As our discussions were under way, the TDP was defeated in the assembly elections in 1989 and Marri Chenna Reddy became chief minister, leading the Congress government.[10] We resubmitted this list of twenty-eight 'missing persons' to Chief Minister Chenna Reddy, with a memorandum tracing the history of these cases in court in 1990. But although both the TDP and the Congress, as they assumed power in the state, paid lip service to improving the situation on the ground, the repression and violence continued unabated. In 1992, the Justice T.L.N. Reddy Commission was tasked additionally with inquiring into the killing of journalist Gulam Rasool and Vijaya Prasada Rao.[11] In 1994, after I stepped down as president,

9 See also Balagopal, K. 1991. 'Two Missing Women of Karimnagar', *Economic and Political Weekly*, Vol. 26, No. 5, 2 February, pp. 201–05.

10 See Kannabiran, K.G. 1990. 'State of Civil Liberties in AP: An Open Letter to Chief Minister'. Also published in Legal Resources for Social Action, *Legal Perspectives*, Documentation File No. 18, pp. 13–23, http://www.unipune.ac.in/snc/cssh/HumanRights/01%20STATE%20DEMOCRACY%20AND%20LAW/51.%20Legal%20Perspectives%20Legal%20Resources%20for%20Social%20Action%20(LRSA),%20Documentation%20File%20No.%2018,%20Tamil.pdf. Accessed on 25 October 2021.

11 Government of Andhra Pradesh, General Administration (SC-A) Department, G.O. Ms. No. 78, dated 19 February 1992, appointing Justice T.L.N. Reddy, retired judge of the Andhra Pradesh High Court as a one-man Commission of Inquiry under the Commission of Inquiry Act, 1952, 'to inquire into circumstances leading to the death of Gulam Rasool'. The commission submitted its report on 30 June 1993, on the basis of which the government, led by Chief Minister K. Vijayabhaskar Reddy, placed a memorandum before the state assembly in 1995, which stated that '(a) Gulam Rasool (part-time Reporter) and Vijaya Prasada Rao (un-employed post-Graduate) had links with extremist organisations and were collecting funds for the party; (b) In an encounter between police and extremists on 28-12-1991, the two persons died and others escaped; and (c) the

APCLC, I petitioned the National Human Rights Commission (NHRC) as the vice-president, PUCL, that the T.L.N. Reddy Commission had not published the two reports even two years after the inquiries were completed.[12]

The disappearance was reminiscent of the disappearances that we had heard about in South America. It created disquiet. Claude Alvares wrote an article in the *Illustrated Weekly*. On 18 January 1985, the radical students' groups gave a call for a Warangal bandh to protest against the disappearance of Sudershan. That morning, the Hanamkonda police arrested Varavara Rao, not even giving him time to change his clothes—he was made to walk in his lungi and vest from the Hanamkonda crossroads to the police station. There was no warrant or FIR. No complaint either. Therefore, it was an illegal arrest. When her husband was arrested in this manner, Varavara Rao's wife, Hemalatha, petitioned the district collector, R.P. Singh, at noon that day. She was asked to go to the SP. On her behalf, Dr Ramanadham and K. Seetharama Rao, a teacher in Kakatiya University and a member of the APCLC, went to the SP's office. The Warangal SP was K. Aravind Rao. He was very brusque with the civil liberties' representatives and had them arrested in his office premises. The SP then released a statement to the press that he had prior information that Varavara Rao, Ramanadham and some others were planning to commit an offence and that he had arrested them under Section 151 of the CrPC. Aravind Rao's antics were reported in all newspapers. Balagopal petitioned the Lokayukta against this repression in 1985. Writer and VIRASAM leader Chalasani Prasad filed a similar complaint against the same Aravind Rao for similar actions in 2005. This meant that there had been no change in the lawless conduct of police officers from 1985 to 2005.

Dr Ramanadham was implicated in a false case for the first time then—he spent a few days in jail. Less than a week later, a false case was filed against Balagopal and he was put in solitary confinement. Even while this was happening, on 12 January, goons belonging to the ABVP killed the district secretary of the APCLC, Gopi

---

police firing is justified and hence no action against the police need be initiated.' General Administration (SC-A) Department, Andhra Pradesh, Hyderabad. 1994. 'Memorandum of Action taken on the Report of Justice Sri T. Lakshminarayana Reddy, Commission of Inquiry, to inquire into the circumstances leading to the death of Gulam Rasool and his associate Vijaya Prasadarao on 28-12-91 in Rangareddy district.'

12 See Ray, Arun. 2004. 'Complaint regarding non-publication of reports of Justice T.L.N. Reddy Commission of Inquiry relating to "disappearance" of 43 persons from police custody and alleged killing of two persons by police', *National Human Rights Commission of India: Formation, Functioning and Future Proposals*, Vol. I. New Delhi: Khama Publications, p. 152.

Rajanna.[13] At the time, Balagopal, Kodandaram and I were investigating police atrocities in the villages in Sircilla Taluk. We got the news while we were there. Gopi Rajanna was the first person killed in the state for working with the APCLC. Since then, six APCLC members have been killed. That is why when APCLC leader and senior advocate in Nalgonda, Raghava Ranga Rao, died, I wrote that it was the first natural death of a civil liberties activist. Let us return to Dr Ramanadham.

After the disappearance of Kodavati Sudershan, Dr Ramanadham entered the hit list of the police, along with Varavara Rao and Balagopal. They only needed a pretext, which they got when the Kazipet sub-inspector, Yadagiri Reddy, was killed in the Kazipet railway station by Naxalites on 2 September 1985. Smitu Kothari's article in the *Illustrated Weekly* after Dr Ramanadham's death listed all the independent inquiries that had confirmed Yadagiri Reddy's role in many cases of custodial torture, deaths and disappearances. This is not to rationalize Yadagiri Reddy's murder. It is only to point out that when a policeman acts with brazen impunity, he creates many enemies. Immediately after Yadagiri Reddy was killed, we released a statement from the APCLC condemning the murder and stating unequivocally that the APCLC did not support retributive violence or murder. We also stated that all these crimes must be investigated and tried following the principles of due process.

On 3 September, Yadagiri Reddy's body was being taken to his native village after the post-mortem. The procession was led by Deputy Inspector General (DIG) Janak Raj and SP K. Aravind Rao of Warangal. There were around 200 policemen in uniform and in mufti in that procession. Slogans that Naxalites and civil liberties leaders would be killed rent the air. Balagopal and Varavara Rao were specifically named. Although there were these public announcements of the intention to commit murder in a procession led by the top police officers in the district, no preventive measures were taken. Neither Balagopal nor Varavara Rao lived along the route of the procession. But Dr Ramanadham's clinic was on it. His house was also along the route. His friends had warned him not to go to the clinic that day because the atmosphere in the town was tense. But he disregarded them saying he was a doctor who even treated the children of constables—nothing would happen to him. As the procession was passing his clinic, around twenty men who were part

13 Lokayan, 1985. 'The State vs. Civil Liberties Organisations: The Case of APCLC.' Delhi: Lokayan. https://lokayan.net/wp-content/uploads/2021/10/3.3-7-The-State-vs.-Civil-Liberties-Organisation-The-Case-of-APCLC.pdf. Accessed on 6 May 2022.

of it barged into his clinic, pushed the compounder and patients aside and shot him. The assassins, after finishing their job, rejoined the procession.[14]

If one had to take a lawful view of the attack on Dr Ramanadham, there should have been a case registered against the processionists and the leaders of the procession. The post-mortem report said that there were two bullet injuries on his body, fired at close range from a service revolver. Dr Ramanadham's death was condemned by both the ruling TDP and the Congress. The Opposition demanded a judicial inquiry into his murder. NTR refused this suggestion. He said a Criminal Investigation Department (CID) investigation would be sufficient. I addressed press conferences in Hyderabad and Delhi that a CID investigation would mean the police conducting an inquiry on themselves. Dr Ramanadham's murder is a milestone in the civil liberties movement in this country. With this attack, the police had declared war on all those who campaigned for civil liberties.

On 7 November 1987, Japa Lakshma Reddy, a senior civil liberties leader from Karimnagar who had been active in peoples' movements since the days of the Telangana armed struggle, was killed as revenge for the murder of DSP Butchi Reddy by the People's War Group. Lakshma Reddy had systematically exposed and opposed state violence in the district. Similarly, on 7 December 1991, Narra Prabhakar Reddy, a young civil liberties leader in his thirties active in Warangal, was killed in Hanamkonda as revenge for the murder of Congress leader Hayagrivachari. He was a sarpanch in his village, and also the secretary of the District Bar Association. After Balagopal was forced to move out of Warangal following Dr Ramanadham's murder in 1985, Prabhakar Reddy continued to mobilize on civil liberties issues in Warangal from 1985 till his murder in 1991.

Till this point, the police were killing civil liberties activists using violence by the People's War Group as a pretext. After these three deaths, however, the police in Andhra Pradesh no longer needed a pretext. They raised mercenary gangs that acted on their behalf and delegated the murder of civil liberties leaders to these gangs. T. Purushottam and Azam Ali were killed in this manner. Every single person who was suspected to be sympathetic to peoples' movements or to the Naxalite movement became the target of police violence.

14 Menon, Amarnath K. 1985. 'Naxalite terror and official attempts to counter it make news in Andhra Pradesh again'. *India Today*, 30 September. https://www.indiatoday.in/magazine/crime/story/19850930-naxalite-terror-and-official-attempts-to-counter-it-make-news-in-andhra-pradesh-again-802015-2014-01-08. Accessed on 6 May 2022.

It was so terrible. I never used to go for work to Delhi for more than one day. I would return immediately. I was afraid of leaving town because something may happen here. That fear was also partly responsible for my not taking up any work in the Supreme Court. The fear that something might happen in my state. Some young friend of mine would be done to death or some carnage would take place. We were committed to human rights work and we meant business. We wanted to stop this. We wanted to stem this rot.

By no stretch can the APCLC be called an organization sympathetic to Naxalites. It is because the civil liberties of Naxalites and leaders of mass movements were violated the most by the police that these cases figured prominently in civil liberties campaigns. The primary goal of the APCLC was to ensure the rule of law and strict adherence to the Constitution. The risk to life was so great that it became a challenge for new leaders to come forward. This is perhaps why even though I stepped in as the president for only one term, I ended up in the post for fifteen years. I also did not want to leave the organization when the situation was worsening to this extent. Finally, in 1993, when I stepped down from the position in the Kurnool meeting, the APCLC had become known for the work we all did together, throughout the country and abroad. This was the time when we were faced with the question of whether we should only confront state violence or private violence as well. It became part of an international debate. Amnesty International, for instance, began to ask whether we would condemn terrorist violence. It is a question that must be answered.

There was a churning within the APCLC on this question, and an animated debate. Executive meetings would last ten to twelve hours at times. We had several confrontations in the discussions and there were a lot of different opinions being voiced. But none of those differences resulted in any personal animosity among members—the discussions were essentially democratic. I felt the diversity of opinions was extremely important if we were to find a solution. While we were having these discussions, the People's War Group kidnapped a group of IAS officers, among whom S.R. Sankaran was one. The Gurthedu kidnapping took place on 27 December 1987. Bojja Tarakam and I went to Rampachodavaram in East Godavari to negotiate the release of the officers.[15]

15 Menon, Amarnath K. 1988. 'Naxalites Put Andhra Pradesh Government on Tenterhooks'. *India Today*, 31 January, https://www.indiatoday.in/magazine/indiascope/story/19880131-Naxalites-put-andhra-pradesh-government-on-tenterhooks-769006-2013-11-21. Accessed on 25 November 2021.

After securing their release and returning home, APCLC members Kodandaram and Mallikarjun met me and asked why I intervened in that situation. They came home to ask me this question. I told them to place the question before the state executive, and offered to explain myself there. Thereafter, the executive meeting was convened in Khammam. There was a six-hour discussion on this issue. I said:

> I am a lawyer, and I work among people. I have been occupying the same seat in the same room in my office since 1985. Everyone knows where they can find me. In that situation, when there is a crisis, anyone can walk in for my help. I cannot at that stage consult the executive and ask them, what I should do since Sankaran has been kidnapped. Is it possible for me to act only with the formal approval of the executive? There are many times when I need to think and come to a decision immediately. If you disagree, you can convene a meeting later and place it for discussion. If you think I have erred, you can ask me to step down, or I can resign, but when people come to me with the confidence that this person from this organization will help us, I cannot but act immediately. That, in my opinion, is also for the good of the movement.

This debate continued till the Kurnool meeting in 1993, where it crystallized into irreconcilable differences among members and led to voting on issues. I think a discussion, debate and difference of opinion is very healthy. But I would not take it as far as voting on an issue. I stated my position. It is possible to elect people who espouse a view that you agree with, but it is not okay to ask people to vote on the issue itself. Opinions neither win nor lose by being voted on. The debate has to be incessant and cannot be settled with a vote.

I had already decided to step down as the president of the APCLC in the Kurnool meeting. The atmosphere was so charged and polarized that no formalities were maintained, although I was leaving after a fifteen-year tenure as president, during the most difficult period in the civil liberties movement in Andhra Pradesh. I left without even a goodbye. In the next meeting in Guntur, there was a split in the APCLC, which in my view was very unfortunate. I felt that after having built a movement against great odds, we did not have the right to split and weaken it.

Two years later, in 1995, I was elected the national president of the PUCL, a position I held till 2009. Although I was active at the national level, travelled extensively for PUCL work, and wrote frequently for the *PUCL Bulletin*, my work as a civil liberties lawyer continued as before, rooted in the state of Andhra Pradesh.

4

The Emergency

Challenging the Emergency in the Andhra Pradesh High Court

THE EMERGENCY ASSUMED frightening proportions in Andhra Pradesh. Illegal arrests spiralled uncontrolled—Naxalites, Opposition leaders, activists in mass organizations and student bodies—thousands of people were arrested. Illegal detention camps were set up in government buildings, schools, panchayat buildings, guest houses. Telugu writer 'Ampasayya' Naveen's novel *Cheekati Rojulu* ('Dark Days', 1979) provides us with a graphic account of that era of repression.[1] I started receiving phone calls from the night of 26 June. The first call was from Pattipati Venkateswarlu, who was the secretary of our Defence Committee and the general secretary of the APCLC. His house was raided, his books and APCLC documents were confiscated by the police, and he was arrested. The next caller was M.T. Khan. I got innumerable calls from poets, writers and their family members. By the morning, I had information of at least twenty to thirty people who had been arrested. I immediately studied the Emergency provision in the Constitution and picked up William L. Shirer's *The Rise and Fall of the Third Reich: A History of Nazi Germany* (1960) from the A.A. Hussain Bookstore in Abids. I saw close similarity between the methods of

1 Naveen. 1979. *Cheekati Rojulu* (Dark Days). Warangal: Pratyusha Prachuranalu.

Indira Gandhi and Shirer's description of Hitler in government. One part of this was the proclamation of Emergency.

I drafted a petition on behalf of Pattipati Venkateswarlu the very next day, 27 June 1975. I sent for his wife, Venkataseshamma, and included her details in the petition. I moved a lunch motion in Venkateswarlu's case the day after his arrest, challenging the legality of the Emergency, the validity of the MISA,[2] and the arrest of Pattipati Venkateswarlu. I think this was the first case to challenge the Emergency in the country. The lunch motion was heard by Justice K. Madhava Reddy. Commissioner of Police Sharanyan attended the hearing in his uniform. I knew that Sharanyan had been involved in the killing of the leader of the Srikakulam movement, Vempatapu Satyanarayana.

I argued before Justice Madhava Reddy that there were no grounds for Venkateswarlu's arrest. How could the secretary of the Defence Committee be arrested under the MISA? Justice Madhava Reddy immediately turned to public prosecutor Obulapathi Choudary and asked, 'Where are the grounds?' To which Obulapathi Choudary replied, 'The grounds are being typed, Milord.' I immediately insisted that this statement be recorded. Instead of grounds providing the logic for arrests, people were being arrested first and grounds fabricated later. Justice Madhava Reddy was in a quandary about how he should deal with this issue. If he followed my insistence and recorded the public prosecutor's statement, Obulapathi Choudary would lose his job. So he prolonged the discussion to buy time. In the meantime, the grounds were typed and delivered in the court hall. After that, they brought about an amendment in the law to the effect that it is not permissible to question the grounds of arrest. The circumvention of the rule of law by bringing about changes in laws and sections of laws became a common practice in Emergency cases. Prior to this, the Supreme Court had already ruled that the basic structure of the Constitution could not be changed through amendment.[3] I argued that it did not apply merely to the question of property rights but was immediately relevant to the protection of Fundamental Rights under the Constitution—and since the arrests were a derogation of Fundamental Rights, they could not be permitted under the Constitution. Justice Madhava

---

2 Maintenance of Internal Security (Amendment) Act, 1975 (No. 35 of 1975); Maintenance of Internal Security (Amendment) Act, 1976 (No. 14 of 1976); Maintenance of Internal Security (Amendment) Act, 1976 (No. 78 of 1976).

3 *Kesavananda Bharati vs State of Kerala* (1973) 4 SCC 225.

Reddy heard my arguments and immediately referred the matter to a full bench consisting of himself, Justice Gangadhara Rao and Justice Jayachandra Reddy.[4]

Defending Political Dissenters

Even while I was arguing this case, countless other arrests were made and detenus when produced in courts declared, 'Kannabiran is our lawyer.' I filed memos of appearance for all of them, and writ petitions.[5] I was overwhelmed with work. Jakka Venkaiah[6] and Y. Radhakrishna Murthy (YRK)[7] were members of the CPI (M). All CPI (ML) detenus named me. When in jail, the only breath of fresh air comes from court appearances. So on one pretext or another, the detenus would all file petitions, and I would argue their cases. I filed about 200 to 300 writ petitions during that time. I would file the same petition on behalf of four or five detenus. The court

---

4 *P. Venkateseshamma vs State Andhra Pradesh and Ors* (22.08.1975: APHC) Writ Petition Nos. 3306, 3361, 3374, 3381, 3444, 3445 and 3642 of 1975. AIR 1976 AP 1. Full bench: Justices K. Madhava Reddy, A. Gangadhara Rao, K. Jayachandra Reddy.

5 'One of the contentions raised in the writ petition by Sri Kannabiran, learned Counsel for the petitioners in some of the writ petitions was that Section 16-A (9) is ultra vires. It was however brought to our notice that a similar contention among others was raised in cases which were argued recently before the Supreme Court and the Supreme Court has reserved judgment in those cases. We therefore felt that it is desirable to. await the judgment of the Supreme Court so that we may be guided by that judgment.' *N. Venkat Ramani and Ors vs State of Andhra Pradesh and Ors* (08.04.1976 - APHC) : MANU/AP/0228/1976; 1977 CriLJ 1060, para 7.

6 Jakka Venkaiah (1930–2018) played a key role in building the communist party in Nellore district. After the formation of the CPI(M) he was mainly responsible for building the party organization and personally led many struggles of the agricultural labourers in the 1970s and the land struggles in the 1980s. He served as the district secretary, member of the party state secretariat and later the central committee; he was also an MLA for two terms from Allur constituency, Nellore district (1985 and 1994); https://cpim.org/pressbriefs/condolence-jakka-venkaiah; https://www.thehansindia.com/posts/index/Andhra-Pradesh/2018-05-29/CPM-veteran-leader-Jakka-Venkaiah-dies/385017. Accessed on 27 September 2021.

7 Y. Radhakrishna Murthy (1928–2013), of the CPI (M), based in Khammam, was jailed several times during the Emergency. He contested the 1977 Lok Sabha elections while in prison, and served as a member of the Rajya Sabha. https://www.thehindu.com/todays-paper/tp-national/tp-andhrapradesh/cpim-mourns-former-mp/article5256406.ece. Accessed on 27 September 2021.

dismissed this petition filed on behalf of Pattipati Venkateswarlu, and several other petitions as well.[8]

I could feel the drastic change in the court environment overnight—suspicion and fear was pervasive and visible in the way lawyers conducted themselves that day. The treasurer of our Defence Committee, Sreerama Rao, walked up to me and said, 'What is the use of the Defence Committee now? We can just as well shut it down.' I replied, 'Quite to the contrary, our work has just begun. Whether or not anyone joins me, I will continue to do this work, I must.' Even my lawyer friends began to avoid me. Only a few of my friends would join me for lunch.

There was heavy surveillance on my home. I often wondered why they did not arrest me. Perhaps they realized that I was the single lawyer doing these cases, so they let me be—they did not want the disrepute that might follow. Often, matters would come up for hearing simultaneously in two or three courts. I would sometimes seek adjournment, at other times, I would ask the detenus to present their own cases in court.

In one case I got conflicting decisions from the full bench and another bench. Justice Madhava Reddy and Justice K. Punnaiah were on the bench that heard a batch of writ petitions on behalf of Keshav Rao Jadhav, Narendra Shital Singh, Lashkari, P. Venkateswarlu and others.[9] Justice Madhava Reddy admitted the petition, Justice Punnaiah rejected it. The detenus shouted slogans in the court hall. Narendra Shital Singh and Lashkari threw slippers at the bench. That was wrong. Justice Punnaiah gave a ruling that he deemed fit. At a time when so many learned people had become Indira Gandhi's slaves, to react in that manner to Justice Punnaiah was

---

8 A second petition was filed on behalf of P. Venkateswarlu and others challenging their detention, where the bench consisting of Justice C. Kondaiah and Justice V. Madhava Rao ruled that: '… the orders of detention passed by the state government and the orders confirming detentions made by officers subordinate to it, as the case may be are declared to be invalid, illegal and liable to be quashed and are hereby quashed … [A]ll the detenu-petitioners before this Court in this batch of writ petitions except those in respect of whom the orders of detention have already been revoked, are hereby directed to be set at liberty forthwith in the Court itself.' The advocates who appeared in this case were R.R. Mooli, B.V. Subbarayudu (parties-in-person), R.V. Iyer, B. Tarakam, A.V. Koteswara Rao, A. Panduranga Rao, V. Venkataramaiah and C. Venkata Krishna, advocates. *P. Venkateswarlu and Ors. vs State of AP and Ors* (09.10.1975: APHC), WP No. 467/75, MANU/AP/0313/1975.

9 For discussion of this case see *N. Venkat Ramani and Ors vs State of Andhra Pradesh and Ors* (08.04.1976: APHC): MANU/AP/0228/1976; 1977 CriLJ 1060.

wrong. It is wrong to shout slogans in the court hall and fling slippers at judges. It is contempt of court. The judges summoned me to their chamber and said, 'How can you allow your clients to commit contempt of court? We will treat this as a contempt of court and impose punishments.' That would create a crisis. By then the detenus had already spent over six months in illegal custody. If they were punished again for contempt of court, they would be victims of further mistreatment. I was in a bind. On the one hand, I could not argue that they had not committed a wrong. On the other, I could not agree to their being punished for contempt of court. I appealed to Justice Punnaiah's humanitarian instincts: 'It is true that they were wrong and that they committed contempt of court. It is a denigration of the judge and the court. Yet, please consider that they have already been stuck in jail for six months without committing any crime, and without any investigation. Please try to understand their behaviour in that context. If you impose a fresh sentence on them for this offence, you will not gain anything. Please be benevolent and forgive them. Let them witness the grace with which you conduct yourself as a judge.' Justice Punnaiah accepted my appeal and forgave the conduct of the detenus.

The Nagi Reddy conspiracy case came to the high court during the Emergency in September–October 1975 before Justice Madhusudhan Rao.[10] The volumes of the statements of the accused were placed before him: Tarimela Nagi Reddy, 517 pages; another accused, 220 pages; a third accused, 330—I was ready to argue. The judge looked at the volumes and said, 'It is monotonous. I will post it before a division bench.' Then I smiled and said, 'This is not a case like ordinary murders. This is a case about people, who every one of them could be a chief minister of the state. They are very well-read, very well-informed, great intellectuals. And if we go through this case, I am sure you and I will emerge as better persons.'[11] Then immediately he said, 'What is the first document?' The first document was titled '*Takshana Karyakramam*' (Immediate Programme). So I told the judge, 'There is a sense of urgency in a communist but it is not meant literally. A revolution takes a long time to come. But a revolutionary will always say it's an immediate programme.

10 Aditya, M.K. 2016. 'Tarimela Nagi Reddy Remembered', countercurrents.org, 28 July, https://countercurrents.org/2016/07/tarimela-nagi-reddy-remembered. Accessed on 19 October 2021. See also, Harsh Thakor, 'Centenary of D.V. Rao and Nagi Reddy', *Frontier*, Vol. 50, No. 31, February 4–10, 2018, https://www.frontierweekly.com/articles/vol-50/50-31/50-31-Centenary%20of%20D%20V%20Rao%20and%20Nagi%20Reddy.html. Accessed on 19 October 2021.

11 See, for instance, T. Nagi Reddy's court statement, published as a book: Reddy, T. Nagi. 1978. *India Mortgaged*. Anantapuram: T. Nagi Reddy Memorial Trust.

If you read *The Communist Manifesto,* you will get the same feeling that they are in great urgency.' I had copies of *The Communist Manifesto.* I handed him a copy and read some passages from another copy. I talked about it and he got interested. He would wait every day for this post-lunch hearing of the case. He also had a desire to be known as a well-read man. This is the thing that saves this institution. And if you are not able to encourage this trend, and make it mechanical and boring instead, this institution will sink.

There was another Emergency matter that came up before the bench of Justice P. Chennakesava Reddy.[12] Radical Students' Union leader N. Venkat Ramani was among the detenus. He gave me details of the modalities of arrests in their case. Ordinarily, any person who is arrested must have a warrant in his name that specifies his offences and the sections under which he is charged. Ramani informed me that the police were taking blank warrants, making arbitrary arrests and then filling up the warrants. At that time Deputy Commissioner of Police (DCP) Ramakrishna Reddy was in the court hall. He too had blank warrants. Possessing blank warrants is against the law and may be punished. I informed Justice Chennakesava Reddy about this. Blank warrants were recovered from the DCP in the court hall. In a brimming court hall, Justice Chennakesava Reddy sharply reprimanded the police officer for violating the law. However, the atmosphere during the Emergency was such that despite knowing that blank warrants were used to arrest people, despite finding proof of this on the person of a senior police officer and reprimanding him publicly in court, and despite agreeing that it was an unlawful practice, Justice Chennakesava Reddy was unwilling to set aside the arrest. This was not unexpected. I had a strong hunch that no matter how strongly the judge felt that ours was a just demand, he would not set the detenus at liberty. This came true and the judge dismissed our petition. Although he knew it was an illegal arrest, he allowed it.

While hundreds were in prison, unable to secure release, thousands were confined in temporary detention camps and tortured by the police. The judges who ordered the release of some of the detenus in the cases I argued were few: Justice C. Kondaiah, Justice A. Sambasiva Rao, Justice K. Madhava Reddy, Justice Alladi Kuppuswamy, for instance. There is an irony here that cannot be missed. This was a government that claimed to be supportive of the left. And yet repression was at its most severe on left parties and their sympathizers. The CPI supported Indira Gandhi—S.A. Dange was followed by the party. I was in a dilemma. I had worked with advocate Ravi Subba Rao, who was with the CPI. Through him I met the living expenses of one

---

12 For discussion of this case see *N. Venkat Ramani and Ors vs State of Andhra Pradesh and Ors* (08.04.1976: APHC). 1977 CriLJ 1060; MANU/AP/0228/1976.

party full-timer for several years. But here I was arguing cases of state repression and challenging the Emergency, while the party I was providing monetary support to was supporting the Emergency. Tammareddy Lakshminarayana called for a meeting with us lawyers in the house of Kovvidi Narasimham, a lawyer who belonged to the CPI. Vadari Venkataramaiyya, a liberal lawyer who supported the CPI, posed a question: 'Should there not be a right to dissent?' Tammareddi Lakshminarayana retorted with, 'Whom should that right be for?' I was very uneasy. The question should be not for whom, but why. So I asked the question: 'Dissent against what should be the question. To ask the question "for whom" is very undemocratic.' With that, my stand became clear to them. They stopped taking my monetary contribution. I felt it was justified when there was a difference of opinion. At the same time, however, I was not antagonistic towards them. The circumstances of that time pushed them in that direction and they supported the Emergency. Even they admitted retrospectively that their stand on the Emergency was wrong.

In all the cases I argued, either my petition was dismissed or was referred to a full bench. I did not win any major victories, but what I did accomplish was an intense and long debate in courts in Andhra Pradesh on the Constitution and fundamental rights.

Arbitrary Arrests and Judicial Equivocation

Anyone who expressed dissent—even when the grounds of their dissent were valid—were thrown in jail. Countless others were detained without reason. Members of the Jamaat-e-Islami and RSS were arrested. There was a young boy, fifteen years of age, by the name Bhavani Shankarudu. My last writ petition in Emergency cases was filed on his behalf. He later became a leader of the Bharatiya Mazdoor Sangh.[13] One day, after arguing a habeas corpus case in the court of Justices Sambasiva Rao and Gangadhara Rao, I came out and lit a cigarette. This was soon after the Supreme Court ruled that the MISA was valid law.[14] Bhavani Shankarudu was produced in court. When the judges asked him who his lawyer was, the young boy said, 'Kannabiran.' He must have been instructed to do this in jail. The judges immediately said, 'Kannabiran has just left the court hall, call him back.' I went

13 https://timesofindia.indiatimes.com/city/visakhapatnam/bharatiya-mazdoor-sangh-slams-govt-ban-on-recruitment/articleshow/22860903.cms. Accessed on 27 September 2021.

14 *Additional District Magistrate, Jabalpur, vs Shivakant Shukla* (28.04.1976: SC) AIR 1976 SC 1207.

back in. Taking one look at the boy who had not yet grown a moustache, I said to the judges, 'If the law says that a boy like this poses a threat to internal security, it is a useless law.' The government pleader stood up and stated to the bench, even before he was asked his opinion, that these detentions should simply be confirmed in light of the Supreme Court judgment in the MISA case, and that there was no need to argue the cases. I turned to him with a repartee, 'I don't think you have become a judge yet.' I would be quick to respond in every situation like this before me in courts. While I was still there, VIRASAM leader K.V. Ramana Reddy was brought to the court.[15] He delivered a good speech which he ended with, 'Long live even bourgeois democracy.'

This spate of arbitrary and indefinite arrests reduced the families of several detenus to penury. Pattipati Venkateswarlu is an example. He was a young lawyer who was beginning to build a secure practice—how would his family support itself during his incarceration? I called for files pertaining to all the cases Venkateswarlu was handling, and asked his clerk Venkata Rao to inform all his clients that I would be taking care of their briefs. Every client had to first deposit their fees with his wife, Venkataseshamma, and then come to me. Only after she confirmed that she had received the fees would I argue the case in court. This was only one such instance.

Justice Thota Lakshmaiah wrote a long judgment praising the Emergency, perhaps in the hope that by that token he would be elevated to the Supreme Court.[16] Justice T.L.N. Reddy, then a district and sessions judge, wrote a judgment eulogizing

---

15 See Reddy, K.V. Ramana. 1977. *Detenu Diary* (Telugu). Kavali: Jhanjha Publications. K.V. Ramana Reddy (KVR; 1927–98) was a political scientist, biographer and editor. A teacher by profession, he was the founder–secretary of VIRASAM, editor of its journal *Arunatara*, general secretary of the All India League for Revolutionary Culture, and editor of its journal *Thunder*. He edited the complete works of legendary Telugu poet Sri. KVR faced sedition charges for editing the Telugu anthology *Jhanjha* and was imprisoned twice—during the Emergency, and as an accused in the Secunderabad conspiracy case.

16 *P. Hemalatha vs Govt of Andhra Pradesh* (23.04.1976: APHC); AIR 1976 AP 375; three-judge bench consisting of Justices A. Sambasiva Rao, Alladi Kuppuswami and T. Lakshmaiah. See judgment of Justice Lakshmaiah, paras 62–98: 'Emergency and Security of State'. Also, *B.V. Subbarayudu vs State of Andhra Pradesh, Andhra Weekly Reporter* 1975 (II) 437, in which Justice Lakshmaiah writes: 'Liberty itself is a gift of law ... There is no liberty above law or beyond law. It is a regulated liberty not an abstract one' (para 71) and 'How much is too much and how far is too far in times of emergency are all matters of policy with which Courts have nothing to do' (para 73). Bench: Justice C. Kondaiah and Justice T. Lakshmaiah.

the Emergency. What this points to is merely the fact that the intelligentsia that ought to have put social transformation at the forefront supported authoritarianism in pursuit of personal gain instead. This trend was in full public view.

V. Rama Rao, of the Jana Sangh (who later joined the Bharatiya Janata Party [BJP] and served as the governor of Sikkim), is a close friend of mine. He and CPI(M) leader Omkar filed a special writ petition. They were members of the Andhra Pradesh Legislative Council and the Andhra Pradesh Legislative Assembly respectively. 'Our involvement, as elected representatives, in the work of the Assembly cannot be construed as a threat to internal security. We attend the Assembly sessions to fulfil our public responsibility.' I argued for two days. It was before the bench of Justice Avula Sambasiva Rao. He asked how they should be sent. The petitioners suggested that they could be sent with an escort and after the session transported back to jail. The petition was struck down.

Advocate M.V. Ramamurthy's petition was even more unusual. He asserted that he had the right to have intimate relations with his wife. The Emergency had not struck down that right. Therefore, he argued that his right to sexual intimacy must be protected, and he must be permitted to be with his wife at intervals. When he filed this petition he was around sixty years old. He was a humorous person. This petition came before Justice P. Chennakesava Reddy. Vadari Venkataramaiah was the amicus curiae. Although his petition was also dismissed, it generated a lot of debate. I got acquainted with M.V. Ramamurthy through Emergency cases. Although we had differences of opinion on various matters, he was a very friendly and warm person, and a great conversationalist. The reason why the court struck down the petition was that it saw the right to intimacy as a private right, the protection of which was not the responsibility of the state.

Shaikh Meera, a secondary grade teacher in Bardipur village, Nizamabad district, detained in September 1976 under the MISA, petitioned the court seeking to be classified under Class B, rather than Class C, which was for prisoners, not detenus. The case came up before a bench consisting of Justice Ramachandra Raju and Justice A. Raghuvir. The public prosecutor opposed this on the grounds that in light of the Supreme Court judgment, the actions of the state could not be questioned under the Emergency, and that this matter should be resolved by the petitioner making a representation to the government. The court ruled in favour of Shaikh Meera and held that he should be treated as a detenu in Class B.[17]

---

17 Rule 20 of the Andhra Pradesh Preventive Detention (Regulation of Place and Conditions) Order, 1969, stipulates the procedure to be followed in the matter of representations to the government by detenus and prisoners. The court held

Detenus who secured release were rearrested in fresh cases. Jana Sangh leader Burra Subbarayudu was rearrested before he reached home after securing release from the court, and held in the police station. There were no lawyers to represent him. Advocate Babul Reddy, whose name he mentioned, was unwilling to represent him, so I did. In the process of detenus raining petitions on the courts, the latter became places of political assembly.[18] Since it was no longer possible to debate politics outside, courts now became the sites of such debates. People poured into them. As I walked from one court to another, a crowd would follow me. As I kept arguing cases, the case of senior advocate from Guntur, Jupudi Yagna Narayana,[19] was posted before the bench of Justice Chinnappa Reddy and Justice Jeevan Reddy. I had visited him and Gouthu Latchanna[20] in Osmania General Hospital. When detenus were unwell, they got admitted in hospitals outside. This also gave them an opportunity to meet their family and friends and breathe some fresh air. I had a MISA case hearing that was coming up before the full bench of Justice

---

that this is like an appeal 'from Caesar to Caesar'. 'An order which does not speak has the face of [an] inscrutable sphinx and we consider to exercise such right of "representation" against such an order is a vain exercise.' *Shaikh Meera vs Chief Secretary, Government of Andhra Pradesh, Andhra Weekly Reporter*, 1977 (II) 250, para 11. Bench: Justice Ramachandra Raju and Justice A. Raghuvir.

18 *Chalasami Prasad and 5 others vs State of Andhra Pradesh, Andhra Weekly Reporter* 1976 (II) 403, where the petitioners argued that 'by putting handcuffs to their hand, the police are infringing the freedom and liberty of the limbs of the detenus … [and] that handcuffing is un-civilised and un-cultured behaviour on the part of the State and Section 5 of MISA does not confer such a power' (para 11), but the court held that 'if handcuffing is found to be necessary in the interests of security … then certainly it cannot be said that it is an undue interference' (para 12) and dismissed the petition. Bench: Justice A. Sambasiva Rao and Justice K. Punnaiah. Chalasani Prasad (1932–2015) was at the time a lecturer of political science in Visakhapatnam, a well-known writer and a founder of the Revolutionary Writers' Association. Error in petitioner's name in case title.

19 Jupudi Yagna Narayana, an advocate from Guntur, was with the Jana Sangh and later the BJP, and a member of the Andhra Pradesh Legislative Council.

20 Gouthu Latchanna (1909–2006) was a freedom fighter and a leader of the backward classes and farmers from Srikakulam district. He was arrested during the Quit India movement and during the Emergency, and was an MLA representing Sompeta constituency of Srikakulam district, Andhra Pradesh, for thirty-five years from 1948–83. See https://en.wikipedia.org/wiki/Gouthu_Latchanna. Accessed on 27 September 2021.

Kuppuswamy, Justice A.V. Krishna Rao and Justice Ramachandra Raju[21] at the same time that Yagna Narayana's case was to be heard. I asked him if he would argue his case himself. He was ready to do it, and said the law would be struck down by the evening. He felt, rather innocently, that since his case was to be heard by two progressive judges, they would definitely strike the MISA down. I cautioned him that what would be struck down was not the law but his writ petition. 'Your assessment of persons, judges and the court are erroneous. It matters little whose bench it is. Striking down the law is something that will not happen,' I said to him. To take a decision of that kind, one needs extraordinary courage, and a very high ethical standard. That is rare in our country. The next day Yagna Narayana's writ petition was struck down. Progressive judges, without a thought, dismissed writ petitions of detenus from the Jamaat-e-Islami and the RSS. The question that was decided in these cases was: 'Whom is the right to free speech for?' Not 'why a right to free speech'.

Ranga Reddy of the Jana Sangh told me a very interesting story. Naxalite leader Neelam Ramachandraiah was arrested and shot dead by the police in November 1975. The police fabricated a story of an encounter. Since Neelam Ramachandraiah had earlier been a member of the legislative council, the leader of the assembly, Chief Minister Jalagam Vengal Rao, proposed a condolence resolution. Ranga Reddy objected: 'You ordered his killing, and you are proposing a condolence?'[22]

The Derogation of Due Process

In arguing about how arrests did not follow due process, I always stressed on the ways in which they derogated constitutional guarantees. However, even the Supreme Court ruled that in the matter of the deprivation of personal liberty, no basic feature of the Constitution was violated. The same court that ruled that in the matter of property there could be no law that altered the basic structure of the Constitution also ruled that personal liberty cannot be interpreted with reference

21 *N. Venkat Ramani and Ors vs State of Andhra Pradesh and Ors* (08.04.1976: APHC): MANU/AP/0228/1976; 1977 CriLJ 1060.

22 Andhra Pradesh Legislative Council. 'Condolence motion,' Dated 18 March 1976. In *Journal* (Twenty Fourth Session) (29 January–30 March 1976), p. 69. 'Sri V. Krishnamurthy Naidu, Leader of the House moved the following condolence motions and offered his condolences: "That this House places on record its deep sense of sorrow at the demise of Sri Neelam Ramachandraiah, former Member of the Andhra Pradesh Legislative Council and conveys its deep sense of sympathy to the members of the bereaved family.' Hyderabad: Andhra Pradesh Legislature.

to the basic structure doctrine. The basis of this interpretation was that since it is the state and the Constitution that confer rights, the same may be withdrawn. I am of the opinion that it is a grave error to interpret fundamental rights in this manner—any ruler, state, government or Constitution only confirms, respects and guarantees protection of the inherent rights of persons. Let us take the social contract theory in political philosophy. People enter into a conditional contract to vest certain authority in the ruler and government. A feminist philosopher has persuasively argued that the social contract is in fact a contract between men.[23] This is an argument I agree with.

With the Emergency, even the welfare provisions of the Constitution were adversely affected. The Emergency case came up in the Supreme Court. Even when I argued a case in the Andhra Pradesh High Court before a full bench, Justice Ramachandra Reddy said, 'If you file a petition that the police have shot and killed a boy in the street, it is not possible to admit it.' The attorney general of India, Niren De, said the same thing to Justice H.R. Khanna in the Supreme Court—that the right to life could be suspended during the Emergency. Justice Bhagwati was also on that bench. One judge wrote that the government was looking after detenus like a mother looked after her children.[24] Justice Y.V. Chandrachud said that he had 'lofty faith' in the government.[25] The Andhra Pradesh High Court full bench

---

23 The reference is to Pateman, Carole. 1988. *The Sexual Contract*. Stanford, CA: Stanford University Press.

24 Justice Hameedullah Beg: 'It seems to me that Courts can safely act on the presumption that powers of preventive detention are not being abused ... Furthermore we understand that the care and concern bestowed by the State authorities upon the welfare of detenus who are well housed, well fed and well treated, is almost maternal. Even parents have to take appropriate preventive action against these children who may threaten to burn down the house they live in.' *Additional District Magistrate, Jabalpur, vs Shivakant Shukla* (28.04.1976: SC): MANU/SC/0062/1976, para 396.

25 Justice Y.V. Chandrachud: 'The periodical reviews of detention orders, the checks and counter-checks which the law provides and above all the lofty faith in democracy which ushered the birth of the Nation will, I hope, eliminate all fear that great powers are capable of the greatest abuse. Ultimately, the object of depriving a few of their liberty for a temporary period has to be to give to many the perennial fruits of freedom.' *Additional District Magistrate, Jabalpur, vs Shivakant Shukla* (28.04.1976: SC) AIR 1976 SC 1207, para 490.

passed a judgment supporting the Emergency.[26] Even today, I am surprised when I read that judgment. If we look at Article 51A, which sets out the Fundamental Duties that purportedly derive from the values of the freedom struggle, these are values that apply uniformly to all: to the chief justice, to me and to the chief justice's stenographer. Justice H.R. Khanna was the lone dissenter who took a very principled stand on the Emergency and resigned. I have not come across another judge like him. In Andhra Pradesh, the court ruled in favour of preventive detention. The Supreme Court also cited the Andhra Pradesh decision favourably. Justice Bhagwati was part of this.

The Constitution of India prescribes the limits within which its institutions must function—in other words, even theoretically, the powers of the Constitution of India are not unlimited. The limits are prescribed in the Constitution—Articles 12-35 cover Fundamental Rights in Part III. The key parts of the constitution are the Preamble, Part III, Fundamental Rights, and Part IV, Directive Principles of State Policy. The Preamble speaks of political and social values. Indira Gandhi pushed aside these basic elements of the Constitution, and began to speak of duties. She introduced the 42nd Amendment to the Constitution in December 1976, that is, during the Emergency. Among others, it introduced two important changes. She included the words 'socialist' and 'secular' in the Preamble. Alongside this, she introduced Article 51A. P.M. Bhargava convened a conference, in which I presented a paper, where I argued that if on the one hand you introduce Fundamental Duties, and on the other hand you introduce socialism into the Constitution, this adds up to national socialism, that is, Nazism, a slogan that Hitler used. I didn't think it was a good sign that these words had been introduced in the Constitution. The discussion on fundamental rights comes up only when there is a violation of those rights. Even while enjoying fundamental rights, it is the duty of a citizen to protect the fundamental rights of others. This is the way in which we should understand the relationship between rights and duties. What I saw with Emergency cases was the gradual shrinking of rights guaranteed under the Constitution. The duty of social transformation was abdicated to the courts. I argued that the state could not subscribe to the values of the day, but must govern in accordance with the constitutional values that created it. Those are values that derive from the freedom struggle and respect for human dignity.

---

26 *P. Venkateseshamma vs State of Andhra Pradesh and Ors* (22.08.1975: APHC), Writ Petition Nos. 3306, 3361, 3374, 3381, 3444, 3445 and 3642 of 1975. Full bench decision. Justices K. Madhava Reddy, A. Gangadhara Rao, K. Jayachandra Reddy.

What is remarkable about this period, however, is that while the intelligentsia capitulated, ordinary people stood firm. They restored democracy.

1977 Elections and the Janata Government

The Janata government that came to power in 1977 made a few half-hearted attempts to investigate the wrongs committed during the Emergency. The Shah Commission inquiring into the excesses of the Emergency looked at the functioning of the executive and its manipulation by those in political power.[27] This was a golden opportunity for the Janata government to take a close look at and reform all political institutions and the executive, making them subservient to the Constitution. However, it did not make use of this opportunity. Jayaprakash Narayan (JP) was increasingly unwell by then. It was unreasonable to depend on him. The Janata government was voted to power in order to put an end to authoritarianism. The first step in this direction would be to define authoritarianism in this context. This was the key rationale for the setting up of the Shah Commission. There were other commissions set up to inquire into state atrocities. The task before these commissions was to point out where the governance systems had failed. Instead of making use of the commissions, the Janata government side-stepped them. Instead of restructuring institutions of governance, the government merely bided time.

Special courts were set up to hear cases of political offences during Indira Gandhi's reign.[28] This was a good move. It is necessary to separate ordinary crimes from political crimes. They sent the Special Courts Bill for presidential assent. It was passed as law. The Supreme Court also welcomed the Special Courts Act.[29] The judges expressed the hope that this would be an institutional mechanism that would curb the misuse of political power by governments. However, the special courts did not function as envisaged. There were four cases heard in the first round. Then, V.C. Shukla and a few others questioned the jurisdiction of these courts.

---

27 Report of the Shah Commission of Inquiry, appointed by the Government of India, under Section 3 of the Commissions of Inquiry Act, 1952, three volumes. 1978. Available at https://countercurrents.org/cc280615.htm. Accessed on 27 September 2021.

28 The Special Courts Act, 1979 (Act No. 22 of 1979), an act to provide for the speedy trial of a certain class of offences (16 May 1979) to deal with cases where 'there is prima facie evidence of the commission of an offence alleged to have been committed by a person who held high public or political office in India'. Section 5.

29 *In Re: Special Courts Bill*, 1978, Special Reference No. 1 of 1978 (01.12.1978: SC:) AIR 1979 SC 478; MANU/SC/0039/1978.

The Supreme Court ruled again that this was a permanent court and its work was not limited to Emergency cases alone. When Indira Gandhi returned to power, another judge of the Supreme Court raised the question of the limits of the Shah Commission. Immediately, Indira Gandhi repealed the Special Courts Act with one stroke of the pen.[30] This was not questioned by anyone in Parliament.

There was no deep reflection on the causes of the Emergency and the ways in which the institutions of democracy might be strengthened, or even on what the meanings of constitutional governance are. The quality of governance did not change even after the Emergency. It was into this vacuum that the fundamentalist mobilization got entrenched. Even after the Emergency, no regret was expressed by any judge for the large numbers of illegal detentions that were permitted to continue unchecked by courts during the Emergency. It has always been my view that any person, no matter how big, if he comes to know that a prior judgment or governmental action committed or condoned was wrong, a public apology must be tendered. Instead of admitting to wrongs, but realizing full well that public accountability is a necessity, public interest litigation provided a new opportunity. Take the example of Justice P.N. Bhagwati. He suddenly saw new meaning in Article 21 of the Constitution. The aspects of Article 21 that were invisible to him when he wrote supporting the Emergency were suddenly visible now. The court now recognized arbitrariness as an aspect proscribed by Article 14, that the right to equality was not restricted to class and social justice. The Constitution was being seen in a new light. Courts then recognized that equality was a value that suffused the Constitution. This was a journey from a bounded/narrow justice system to an innovative justice system. From Sunil Batra's case[31] to Auto Shankar's case,[32] the jurisprudence of human rights and constitutionalism was elaborated in cases of persons convicted of grave crimes, rowdies, goondas and anti-social elements. I wrote in one of my essays that the Supreme Court after 1978 had begun to recite eulogies for dacoits. Each time there was a stellar judgment on the right to liberty, it was not in a case pertaining to an ordinary citizen or a political dissenter; it was about the freedom of those who should be in jail. This was after the Emergency.

30 The Special Courts (Repeal) Act, 1982 (Act No. 34 of 1982), 17 August 1982. Statements of Objects and Reasons: (1) 'The Special Courts Act, 1979 was enacted with the primary object of providing for the speedy trial of a certain class of offences. The experience of the working of the Act has shown that it has not inspired public confidence. Further, it has failed to achieve its object of speedy trial. It is, therefore, proposed to repeal the Act.'

31 *Sunil Batra vs Delhi Administration*, AIR 1980 SC 1579.

32 *R. Rajagopal and Ors vs State of Tamil Nadu and Ors* (07.10.1994: SC): AIR 1995 SC 264.

5

Right to Work: Cherabanda Raju and Raja Lochan

Article 311 of the Constitution of India

THE JUDGMENT THAT struck down the government order dismissing revolutionary writers Cherabanda Raju and Raja Lochan is very important. This was a judgment delivered by Justice Konda Madhava Reddy and Justice K.A. Muktadar. The dismissal order was based on Article 311 of the Constitution of India:

> 311. Dismissal, removal or reduction in rank of persons employed in civil capacities under the Union or a State.
>
> (1) No person who is a member of a civil service of the Union or an all India service or a civil service of a State or holds a civil post under the Union or a State shall be dismissed or removed by a authority subordinate to that by which he was appointed.
>
> (2) No such person as aforesaid shall be dismissed or removed or reduced in rank except after an inquiry in which he has been informed of the charges against him and given a reasonable opportunity of being heard in respect of those charges. Provided that where it is proposed after such inquiry, to impose upon him any such penalty, such penalty may be imposed on the basis of the evidence adduced during such inquiry and it shall not be

> necessary to give such person any opportunity of making representation on the penalty proposed. Provided further that this clause shall not apply:
>
> (a) where a person is dismissed or removed or reduced in rank on the ground of conduct which has led to his conviction on a criminal charge; or
>
> (b) where the authority empowered to dismiss or remove a person or to reduce him in rank is satisfied that for some reason, to be recorded by that authority in writing, it is not reasonably practicable to hold such inquiry; or
>
> (c) where the President or the Governor, as the case may be, is satisfied that in the interest of the security of the State, it is not expedient to hold such inquiry.
>
> (3) If, in respect of any such person as aforesaid, a question arises whether it is reasonably practicable to hold such inquiry as is referred to in clause (2), the decision thereon of the authority empowered to dismiss or remove such person or to reduce him in rank shall be final.

It was argued that the order cannot be challenged as it was issued under Article 311. I went ahead and challenged it in the Andhra Pradesh High Court. I argued that the provisions of Article 311 cannot be applied to the present context. Justice Madhava Reddy and Justice Muktadar agreed with my view, and, striking down the order, directed the reinstatement of Cherabanda Raju and Raja Lochan. My primary argument was that the government does not have the authority to arbitrarily dismiss an employee in government service without furnishing reasons for the same—and that Article 311(2)(c) also does not confer that authority on the government. The judgment affirmed this argument.

Article 311(2) says, 'No such person as aforesaid shall be dismissed or removed or reduced in rank except after an inquiry in which he has been informed of the charges against him and given a reasonable opportunity of being heard in respect of those charges.' Proviso (c) of Clause 2 of this article states the exception: '… Where the President or the Governor, as the case may be, is satisfied that in the interest of the security of the State, it is not expedient to hold such inquiry.' What this means is that the government can arrogate to itself the authority to dismiss an employee without any inquiry or reasons. Since both Cherabanda Raju and Raja Lochan were both teachers in government service, they were dismissed under Article 311(2)(c). The Government Order (GO) No. Ms. 214 dated 18 March 1980 dismissing Cherabanda Raju and GO No. Ms. 215 dated 18 March 1980 dismissing G. Raja Lochan were passed. I appeared for them in two separate writ petitions filed in the high court, arguing that both the GOs are undemocratic and unconstitutional and therefore should be struck down. The bench heard my arguments and the arguments of the government pleader from 9 July to 15 July and delivered the judgment on 15 July 1980.

Cherabanda Raju

B. Bhaskara Reddy, well-known as Cherabanda Raju, a Digambara poet and a revolutionary poet, was working at the time at the Government Junior College in Malakpet, Hyderabad, as a Grade One Telugu Pandit. He was in a government job from 1965 and was widely known as one of the founding members of the Revolutionary Writers' Association or VIRASAM. The police had registered the Secunderabad conspiracy case against a group of revolutionary writers and activists in May 1974. Cherabanda Raju was arrested on 18 May 1974, and suspended from employment vide an order issued on 6 June 1974 by the Hyderabad district education officer (DEO). He was released on bail in 1975, but by then Emergency had been proclaimed. He was rearrested almost immediately and detained under the MISA. He remained in jail and under suspension from his job throughout the period of the Emergency.

After his release once Emergency was lifted, the DEO, in an order dated 19 April 1977, withdrew the earlier suspension and transferred him to the Government High School in Seetaphalmandi. In less than three days, on 22 April, another order was issued staying the order of 19 April. Cherabanda Raju challenged this order in the Andhra Pradesh Administrative Tribunal. The response by the DEO to the tribunal notice is very interesting. He stated that he had received a letter from the DIG on 20 April, which directed that since the Secunderabad conspiracy case would conclude in one year, the accused in the case should not be reinstated.

I had been asking for a long time whether this state is being ruled by elected representatives of the people, or the government, or the Intelligence Department or the (Intelligence) DIG. On what authority can a (Intelligence) DIG issue orders to a DEO? And why did the DEO have to comply with this order? Cherabanda Raju's health had declined drastically because of the long period spent in jail. He was diagnosed with a malignant brain tumour while he was incarcerated. His medical treatment had started and there were serious doubts about whether and for how long he would be able to fight the disease. His friends and well-wishers were petitioning the government to reinstate him on health grounds. He died two years later. Implicating writers in the Secunderabad conspiracy case was itself a conspiracy. Revolutionary writers had been bringing their Marxist views to bear on their writing about society. Unable to stomach this, the government began a series of moves to file false cases against them. I argued in court that their removal from employment was part of this conspiracy on the part of the government.

The government pleaders, in their counter-affidavit, vehemently opposed my arguments. To quote from the judgment of the Andhra Pradesh High Court, in Cherabanda Raju's case:

> It is asserted that he and his co-accused 'have been indulging in systematic propaganda through their writings and speeches inciting people and particularly the students to resort to violence to overthrow the Government by an armed revolution. They also joined hands with Naxalite cadres who were wedded to violence and who were planning murders and dacoities' … [and] asserted that the revolutionary writers have been lending their support to these Naxalite cadres with the slogan 'Kalam Madi Katti Midi'.[1]

Raja Lochan

G. Raja Lochan joined government employment in 1955 as an assistant (teacher) and was posted in Government High School, Pedda Mupparam, Warangal district, and transferred as assistant to the Government Upper Primary School, Waddepally, Hanamkonda, in 1957, where he remained till his dismissal from service. 'Lochan' was his pen name. He was a member of the Revolutionary Writers' Association. According to the DEO, Lochan's writings were 'providing important propaganda, and is an attempt to spread Naxalite ideas and is also critical of the present educational system in the country' and 'that he thereby violated sub-rule (1) of Rule 19 of the Andhra Pradesh Civil Services (Conduct) Rules 1964'. The DEO sent him a notice on 4 August 1975 to show cause why action should not be taken against him. Lochan sent his explanation, after which on 3 February1976, the DEO sent him a second notice asking him to show cause as to why he should not be reduced in rank. Lochan's explanation to the second notice was considered as 'sufficient to hold the charge levelled against him proved'[2] and he was reduced to a lower scale and his increments were withheld in the financial year 1976–77. Lochan did not

---

1 *B. Bhaskara Reddy vs Government of Andhra Pradesh* (Writ Petitions nos. 1267 and 1278 of 1980, dated 17 July 1980), 1981 LAB. I.C. 18, para 3. Unless otherwise stated, all citations in this chapter are from this case. The Telugu words quoted mean 'the pen is ours, the knife yours'.

2 Para 4.

challenge this order as Emergency had already been declared, and he did not want to invite further vindictive action on the part of the state.

Even as this was happening, like in all other places, in Warangal too, on 20 June 1976, fifty writers, poets, intellectuals and teachers were taken into custody and detained in a police camp where they were tortured for two to three weeks. Lochan was one of the people detained in this manner. After sixteen days of torture, he was detained under the MISA on 10 July 1976 and sent to jail, where he remained till Emergency was lifted. Although released once the Emergency ended, he was rearrested on 23 March 1977. The police pressed false charges that he was accused in the Secunderabad conspiracy case.[3] They alleged that he wrote for the literary magazine *Srujana* and observed Lenin Jayanthi and May Day in Hanamkonda. He was released from detention in a few days, but this time around he was dismissed from his job on 21 March 1980.

The counter-affidavit asserted that

> he has been writing 'highly inflammable' verses inciting people to resort to violence and also making speeches to the same effect. He is a staunch worker of the Communist Party of India's (Marxist–Leninist) COC [Central Organizing Committee] (Kondapalli Seeta Ramaiah Group), which is wedded to violence and annihilation of class enemies. He is the Convenor of the Warangal Branch of Revolutionary Writers' Association, and that he is also inciting students to take up arms and to overthrow the Government. He has been spreading violent ideas to overthrow educational institutions.[4]

I described to the court the vindictiveness of the government towards Lochan. I argued that the allegations against them cannot constitute valid grounds for their dismissal from service and was undemocratic and illegal. I also argued that one of the allegations against both Cherabanda Raju and Lochan was that they were accused in the Secunderabad conspiracy case. The departmental inquiry was dispensed with under Article 311(2)(c) as being in the interests of the security of the state. However, if the sessions case trial in which they were accused was being held in open court publicly, it cannot be argued that a departmental inquiry should

3 'The charge-sheet [in the Secunderabad Conspiracy Case] does not disclose Sri Raja Lochan, the petitioner in Writ Petition No. 1278/1980 as one of the accused in that case': para 9.

4 Para 5.

be dispensed with in the interests of the security of the state. The judges were in total agreement with me:

> ... when that very material and perhaps some more is placed before the Court in a public trial, it is beyond one's comprehension as to how it can ever be said that [it] is not expedient to hold a departmental enquiry and holding of such an inquiry is against the interest of the security of the State.[5]

Good Faith in the Governor's Decision?

The government pleader then argued that the court could not go into whether the governor's decision was tenable on whatever grounds—one being that the relevant material for him to make an informed decision was not placed before him. He relied for this argument on *Jagdish Dajiba vs The Accountant General of Bombay*,[6] where the Nagpur Bench of the Bombay High Court observed:

> If courts were to demand proof of such satisfaction and the evidence of material on which the satisfaction was reached, the Courts would be virtually depriving the President of the powers and confidence which the Constitution in its wisdom has reposed in the President.[7]

He also quoted the decision of the division bench in Andhra Pradesh in *Mohammed Azam vs State of Hyderabad*,[8] where the court observed:

> The state of person's mind cannot be determined by the objective test and as long as the President, Governor or the Rajpramukh acted in good faith, their satisfaction cannot be enquired into in a Court of Law.[9]

Justice Madhava Reddy and Justice Muktadar observed that both these judgments predate the Constitution (Fifteenth Amendment) Act, 1963, and that after the decision of the Supreme Court of India in *Samsher Singh vs State of Punjab*,[10] the

---

5 Para 12.

6 *Jagdish Dajiba vs Accountant General of Bombay* AIR 1958 Bom 283 at p. 289.

7 Ibid. Quoted in para 17.

8 *Mohammed Azam vs State of Hyderabad*, AIR 1958 AP 619.

9 Ibid. Quoted in para 18.

10 *Shamsher Singh v. State of Punjab*, 1974 AIR 2192.

precedents cited by the government pleader were no longer valid. The Supreme Court had held that 'the satisfaction required by the Constitution is not the personal satisfaction of the President or Governor but the satisfaction of the President or Governor in the constitutional sense in the Cabinet system of Government'.[11] Drawing on this, Justice Madhava Reddy and Justice Muktadar observed that

> ... it would certainly be open to the Court to find out if there was any material at all and whether that material was relevant and whether the Governor in reaching the conclusion he did, acted bona fide. A limited power of review is vested in the Court to find out whether the satisfaction of the Governor is not his personal satisfaction but a satisfaction based on the advice of his Council of Ministers.[12]

The government pleader then argued that there was 'other material', namely that Cherabanda Raju participated in some secret meetings. The court asked the government pleader to place the evidence before the court. The government pleader agreed on the condition that the record would not be disclosed to the petitioners. The court refused to look into this material and reach a conclusion without disclosing it to the petitioners as 'it would be violative of the well-known principles of natural justice'.[13] In Raja Lochan's case, since he was erroneously named as accused in the Secunderabad conspiracy case, the court held that 'The order of the Governor so far as Raja Lochan is concerned is ... vitiated by taking into consideration material which is wholly baseless'.[14]

The orders of dismissal were quashed and they were reinstated.

---

11 Ibid. Quoted in para 19.

12 Para 20.

13 Para 23.

14 Para 27.

6

Naxalite Conspiracy Trials in Andhra Pradesh

ANYBODY DESIROUS OF understanding the Naxalite movement in the state only needs to read the charge sheets filed by the government in the various conspiracy cases. The officers who write these charge sheets are the official historians of the movement. The conspiracy cases I have argued are:

Parvathipuram conspiracy case (1969–76); Nagi Reddy conspiracy case (1969–71); Secunderabad conspiracy case (1974–89); Chittoor conspiracy case (1979–85); Ramnagar conspiracy case (1986–2003); Bangalore conspiracy case (1992–99).

Of these, I appeared for the entire duration of the case (assisted by my juniors) in the Secunderabad, Ramnagar and Bangalore cases.[1] In the remaining ones I appeared to make specific interventions. The Secunderabad and Ramnagar cases dragged on for the longest time. I was forty-five years old when the trial in the Secunderabad conspiracy case commenced. When it reached a conclusion, I was sixty. I told the judge that it was time he relieved me of the case. I had spent three

1 Advocate K. Prakash (1946–2016) (who was with the BJP) assisted K.G. Kannabiran in the Secunderabad conspiracy case, and advocate R. Mahadevan assisted him in the Ramnagar and Bangalore cases.

decades of the five decades that I was in practice arguing conspiracy cases against Naxalites.[2]

The conspiracy cases were a central part of the government's strategy to destroy the Naxalite movement. I have always felt that if the government followed the rule of law and governed justly, there would have been very little space for the growth of the Naxalite movement. Adhering to the rule of law would mean taking political note of the questions the movement was raising and working out political resolutions to these questions. The Constitution itself recognizes the need for social transformation. Instead of focusing on the transformative aspect, governments take easy resort to eroding the rule of law. This is universally true of governments the world over.

Parvathipuram Conspiracy Case

Naxalbari reached Srikakulam and the movement cascaded and produced several great leaders. Puchalapalli Sundarayya used to visit me often in the days of the Bhargava Commission. One day, I asked him to think about his gains and losses, his rights and wrongs in the movement; I asked him what his balance sheet would look like. His eyes filled with tears: 'Leaders like Vempatapu Satyanarayana and Adibhatla Kailasam rise once in fifty or even hundred years.' The growth of the Naxalite movement in Srikakulam was fuelled by gross misgovernance and the callousness of successive governments towards the people. The Girijans of Srikakulam rose in large numbers to confront oppressive rule. Instead of responding to the questions the movement was asking, the government banned meetings, demonstrations and associational freedoms. Koranna and Manganna, Adivasi leaders of the Srikakulam movement, were among the first to be shot dead. What was their crime? They were part of an organization of Adivasis that was demonstrating against oppressions of landlords who had settled in the agency areas and moneylenders.

Mededi Satyam, a local landlord who had the support of the government, fired on the procession, killing them. Although the Adivasi movement had been building up, the deaths of Koranna and Manganna made the Adivasis rise up in arms. Seeing this, the Naxalites began mobilizing peasants in the surrounding areas, and took

2 For a detailed discussion of the law on conspiracy see Kannabiran, K.G. 2008. 'Conspiracies of Association: Associational Offences, Associational Freedoms and the Rule of Law'. In *Challenging the Rules of Law: Colonialism, Criminology and Human Rights in India*. Eds Kalpana Kannabiran and Ranbir Singh. New Delhi: Sage, pp. 382–408.

the position that the revolution could be hastened through individual annihilation of class enemies. The movement soon spread to the entire state. Hundreds of people were shot dead by the police. Thousands were detained—with and without recourse to law. When I think back, I feel that the government at that time was still reluctant to resort to mass illegal arrests and detentions. The Madras Suppression of Disturbances Act, 1948, was pressed into service—areas from Srikakulam in the north to Karimnagar in the south were declared 'disturbed areas', and people were arrested, taken to disturbed areas and shot. The entire family of Tabelu Nayudu, a Naxalite leader, was shot in this manner and the deaths passed off as occurring in an exchange of fire. We were suddenly confronted with indiscriminate killing by the police on the one side, and the framing of Naxalites and their sympathizers in conspiracy cases on the other.

Charu Majumdar in his political statement before the court stated that

> ... there was no conspiracy as such by the accused but there was an open fight by the girijans for their rights against the land lords and money lenders and other exploiters of the Srikakulam agency areas. The girijans of the agency area and Srikakulam district fought for the restoration of their lands in the hands of moneylenders and landlords, who exploited them and for occupying Banjar lands and for resisting the collection of boosted up loans. There was no secret in the agitation of the girijans against the exploitation by the landlords and the moneylenders and the atrocities committed on them when they fought for their rights ... In order to suppress the girijan struggle the Government conspired and foisted this case.[3]

All the accused stated before the court that when the Girijans were organizing themselves into a sangam (union) and for that purpose were holding a conference on 31 October 1967 at a place called Mondemkal, the landlords headed by Mededi Satyanarayana (Satyam), opened fire on them, killing two Girijans, Koranna and Manganna. This sparked off the Srikakulam Girijan revolt. Quite a few of the accused were lawyers, and the state was putting the Constitution, its values and governance to test. In containing the spread of the Naxalite movement, the state

---

3 Statement recorded before the court of the additional sessions judge, Visakhapatnam, in the Parvathipuram conspiracy case. Complaint in the court of J.F.C.M. [judicial magistrate, first class] Parvathipuram, PRC 8/70. *Sri. S. Veeranarayan Reddy, Deputy Superintendent of Police, Crime Branch, CID, Hyderabad vs Chowdary Tejeshwar Rao and 139 Others.*

embarked on the illegitimate use of the legal system and the Constitution as well. Mededi Satyanarayana, who sparked off the Srikakulam movement, was let out on bail; the protesting Girijans and their leaders were arrested and held in custody in various jails and were unable to furnish bail or produce sureties because they had no legal assistance immediately after arrest, and the sums stipulated by the courts were quite heavy and onerous.

While the people of Srikakulam, Visakhapatnam, East and West Godavari districts were involved in several cases for all the overt acts in the various areas of the state, an ingenious police officer thought out a method of prosecution which set the trend in dealing with Naxalites in the state. The conspiracy prosecution involved all the leaders of the movement by linking up the sum total of all the crimes registered under various police station jurisdictions in the state. The Parvathipuram conspiracy, as it is popularly known, was filed as a private complaint by police officer S. Veeranarayan Reddy. It was also registered as a crime under the IPC and a charge sheet filed in respect of the same 140 accused. The supplemental strategy was to use the Andhra Pradesh Suppression of Disturbances Act, 1967.

The charge was that twenty-three meetings were held between 23 October 1968 and 27 January 1970 in various places to reach an agreement on the commission of offences. The meetings listed by the investigating officer were: Boddapadu (Srikakulam district meeting); Guttikonda Bilam; Calcutta (All India Coordination Communist Revolutionaries); Chikkala Sudarshanarao's house (Visakhapatnam Provincial Committee meeting); Gangannadoravalasa; Gorapannaguda (near Sobba, Srikakulam district); District Committee meeting; Aviri; Polamguda (Bobbili workers meeting); Mahaboobabad (Warangal district); Lambadatanda, near Ankshapuram; Sobba (Srikakulam); Metturu (Srikakulam district conference of area organizing committee); Srikakulam Agency; Ethamanuguda (Dalam commanders' meeting); Calcutta (Central Organizing Committee meeting); Megada Hills (Conference of Dalam Commanders and Organizers); Chelluri forest in a hideout (Chittoor district); Voyagam hills (Somapeta area committee); Vaigam village (Sompeta area Dalam commanders' meeting); Kengarsingi (Sompeta area Dalam committee meeting); Hampi (Rayalaseema regional committee meeting; agency committee meeting).[4]

---

4 Excerpted from Justice K.A. Muktadar's judgment in *State represented by Deputy Superintendent of Police, Crime Branch, Hyderabad vs Chowdary Tejeshwar Rao and Ors.* Sessions Case No. 46 of 1973, Criminal Appeals Nos. 958/77, 542/77, 177/77, 141/77, 963/76, 572/77. High Court of Andhra Pradesh, Judgment delivered on 13 July 1979, pp. 4–5. Unreported judgment.

Further, that between October 1968 and July 1970, a 'number of dacoities, murders and encounters with the police took place in Srikakulam District ... and from the very manner in which these offences were committed, it could be safely inferred that such offences were committed in furtherance of the conspiracy because these specific offences for which some of the accused were convicted do not smack of personal rivalries or factions'.[5]

The charge sheet laid emphasis on the acceptance of Mao's philosophy of armed revolution as against faith in the Constitution and the parliamentary path. Along with the evidence, it also laid emphasis on their political beliefs which motivated the commission of offences. Party activities were criminalized and implicated as a matter of course. Almost all the twenty-three meetings were public meetings, which, if read as a conspiracy, would be a direct erosion of freedom of assembly. The existence of sedition as an offence implied that the audience of such meetings were culpable. Such understanding of law erodes the value of freedom of opinion.

There were initially 240 persons accused in the Parvathipuram conspiracy case. Even while the investigation was in progress, half of them were shot dead. Finally, charge sheets were filed only for seventy-five accused.[6] When the case was being deliberately delayed, we filed writ petitions in the high court. In Visakhapatnam, lawyers P.L. Naidu, Bhuvan Mohan Patnaik, Rachakonda Viswanatha Sastry, Achanta Lakshmana Rao and others were appearing in the special court.[7] Ravi Subba Rao would travel from Hyderabad for some of the hearings. The judgment of the special court came up for appeal in the high court. Around fifteen meetings were named in the Parvathipuram case charge sheet as being part of the conspiracy. Guttikonda Bilam was one of the places listed but the sessions judge did not consider it to be part of the conspiracy.

A close look at the case papers reveals to us the criminalization of Naxalite politics by the state. Jalagam Vengal Rao, the then home minister, had a two-pronged strategy: eliminate Naxalites and trap their sympathizers in the labyrinths of law by implicating them in conspiracy cases. At the time of the Parvathipuram

5 Quoting the public prosecutor, Obulapathi Chowdary, pp. 21–22. *State represented by Deputy Superintendent of Police, Crime Branch, Hyderabad vs Chowdary Tejeswara Rao and Ors.* Sessions Case No. 46 of 1973, Criminal Appeals Nos. 958/77, 542/77, 177/77, 141/77, 963/76, 572/77.

6 *State represented by Deputy Superintendent of Police, Crime Branch, Hyderabad v. Chowdary Tejeswara Rao and Others*. Sessions Case No. 46 of 1973.

7 See also *A. Lakshmanarao vs. Judicial Magistrate, First Class, Parvatipuram and Ors.* AIR 1971 SC 186.

conspiracy case, S. Veeranarayan Reddy was the deputy superintendent of police (DSP) in the Crime Branch CID. He was the investigating officer in this case. He had earlier filed a private complaint himself that was replete with his political views. He followed up his private complaint with filing the charge sheets as the investigating officer on behalf of the government. Both the private complaint and the charge sheet stated that the accused were planning to wage war against the state. My basic question was this: Did a police officer, either on his own behalf or on behalf of the government, have the right to allege that anyone is preparing to wage war against the state? Who is he representing? Did he seek prior sanction? At what level does he represent the government? Once he has filed a private complaint in a case, does he not need prior sanction to file a charge sheet in the same case? Did he seek such sanction? But our courts equivocate and prevaricate on the rule of law. They did not see my questions as material to the facts placed before them. The court held that sanction can be taken at any time. This was a fait accompli. By this token, the prosecution can begin even before the investigation is complete, and evidence can be gathered along the way. This completely subverts the essential elements of justice, namely that an accused person may only be prosecuted if the investigation points to his involvement in an offence.

In the Parvathipuram case, both Adibhatla Kailasam and Nagabhushan Patnaik escaped from jail while the trial was ongoing. Another charge sheet was filed that both of them had escaped from prison and committed murder. Since Adibhatla Kailasam was killed soon after in an encounter, he was not present in person either in the second case or in the Parvathipuram case. Nagabhushan Patnaik was rearrested and remanded to judicial custody. The court acquitted him of the charge of jailbreak because the prosecution was unable to prove that he had escaped from jail and had been rearrested.

In a parallel case, Nagabhushan Patnaik was awarded the death penalty for murder. The sessions judge who sentenced him to death was K.V.L. Narasimha Rao, who had been promoted from munsiff magistrate to district and sessions judge. That was the time when Naxalites were boycotting bourgeois courts, so Patnaik refused to defend himself. The judge awarded the death penalty ex parte. The sentence was not carried out for a very long time because Patnaik was quite ill.[8] Execution, after all, can only be carried out when the convict is in perfect health.

---

8 Refer to Lok Sabha Debate on Nagabhushan Patnaik's health in the Introduction. 'Re: Medical Treatment of Shri Nagabhushan Patnaik Detained in an Andhra Jail', *Lok Sabha Debates: Seventh Session* (Fifth Lok Sabha), 23 February 1973, pp. 236–40.

When the Parvathipuram trial resumed, this offence that Patnaik had been sentenced for came up again. There was a cross-examination, and the judge ruled that Patnaik was not a party to the crime of murder.[9]

By the time the Parvathipuram case came for appeal to the high court, the CPI (ML) had splintered. The accused wanted to ensure that lawyers sympathetic to their respective groups would appear for them. This created a lot of confusion. Finally, I just told them that they should leave decisions regarding legal representation to us lawyers, and we would decide how best to distribute the cases between us. Chowdary Tejeshwar Rao was an important leader then. He agreed to my proposal. Despite this, the splintering of the movement did interrupt our preparations for the case.

Finally, I called my friend, advocate C. Padmanabha Reddy, and said, 'Let us all argue the case together. You establish that there is no proof of conspiracy because there is no "agreement between the conspirators". I will follow that up with questions of law.' We proceeded in that manner.

In the Parvathipuram conspiracy case, the charge was that the accused intended to commit murders and dacoities, and to wage war against the state, and that they 'concealed the design to wage war against the government', aware that such concealment would facilitate the waging of war against the government (Section 123). They were charged with sedition (Section 124); criminal conspiracy (Section 120B); criminal conspiracy to overawe the government (Section 121A); and collecting arms and ammunition to accomplish this objective (Section 122).

The prosecution offered ridiculous arguments in support of their charge of concealment of design to wage war. For instance, the use of initials for names of persons in letters was said to be intended to conceal this plot: V.S.N. (Vempatapu Satya Narayana), C.T.R. (Chowdary Tejeshwar Rao), P.K. (Panchadi Krishnamoorthy), K.S. (Kondapalli Seetharamaiah).

I addressed Justice Muktadar, 'Milord, your peons refer to you by your initials when they talk to us. We too refer to you by your initials among ourselves. Can this conceal your identity?' Justice Muktadar saw my point.

It is possible to implicate any number of people in a conspiracy. It is almost impossible to assert their involvement in the conspiracy without their confessional statements on record, and yet the confessional statements are not admissible in a court. This is not because they are recorded before a police officer, but because they are recorded after the conspiratorial offence has been carried out. Evidence in a criminal trial is always examined in accordance with the Indian Evidence Act. According to Section 10 of the Indian Evidence Act, there must be evidence to prove

9 For a discussion on this case see Chapter 10.

that the conspirators were acting with common intention prior to the commission of the offence.[10] There must be evidence of unlawful acts, or of lawful acts carried out unlawfully. Once this is proved, the action of any one of the conspirators is deemed to be an action carried out by all of them. The agreement to conspire may be proved with circumstantial evidence. But the prosecution lacked the understanding or the capacity to use Section 10 to their advantage. Most importantly, when it is argued that there has been a conspiracy, or acts in furtherance of a conspiracy, there must be contemporaneous evidence that establishes this charge. Agreements reached after the act is carried out are inadmissible—even if such agreement is reached among co-conspirators. In every conspiracy case, the prosecution gathered countless agreements and statements of approvers, all of which were discounted in the course of the trial. This is a key element in the definition of the crime of conspiracy because it safeguards the indiscriminate use of the charge of conspiracy against all and sundry.

The second baffling aspect of the conspiracy cases was that although 'conspiracy' is a crime under the IPC, our state police pooled different cases together to construct the charge of criminal conspiracy. The prosecution in all these other cases was still ongoing. The evidence produced in those cases was again produced in the conspiracy cases.

Justice Seetharama Reddy decided that since there was no evidence of an 'agreement between the conspirators', it was not necessary to examine the witnesses

---

10 Section 10, Indian Evidence Act: 'Things said or done by conspirator in reference to common design.—Where there is reasonable ground to believe that two or more persons have conspired together to commit an offence or an actionable wrong, anything said, done or written by any one of such persons in reference to their common intention, after the time when such intention was first entertained by any one of them, is a relevant fact as against each of the persons believed to so conspiring, as well for the purpose of proving the existence of the conspiracy as for the purpose of showing that any such person was a party to it. Illustration: Reasonable ground exists for believing that A has joined in a conspiracy to wage war against the [Government of India]. The facts that B procured arms in Europe for the purpose of the conspiracy, C collected money in Calcutta for a like object, D persuaded persons to join the conspiracy in Bombay, E published writings advocating the object in view at Agra, and F transmitted from Delhi to G at Kabul the money which C had collected at Calcutta, and the contents of a letter written by H giving an account of the conspiracy, are each relevant, both to prove the existence of the conspiracy, and to prove A's complicity in it, although he may have been ignorant of all of them, and although the persons by whom they were done were strangers to him, and although they may have taken place before he joined the conspiracy or after he left it.'

on this point. The second judge, Justice Ramachandra Raju, held that guilt had been established in the case of fourteen persons, and convicted them. The two judges had reached opposite conclusions. The case was therefore referred to a third judge, Justice K.A. Muktadar. This was the time when he was appointed on the Commission of Inquiry into the custodial death of Ahmed Hussain and the rape of Rameeza Bee by policemen in Hyderabad. He brought his experience in the commission to bear on the Parvathipuram conspiracy case. He heard all our arguments. Although he was the only judge hearing our case at this stage, his judgment would be the final one. He decided that all the accused be acquitted. He ruled that the prosecution was unable to prove that there had been a conspiracy:

> I am fully satisfied that there is not enough evidence on behalf of the prosecution even to infer that there is prima facie evidence from which it could be gathered that there exist reasonable grounds to believe that two or more persons have conspired together to commit an offence. In these circumstances, with due respect, I am not in a position to agree either with the reasoning or the conclusions of my learned brother Ramachandra Raju J. On the other hand I am constrained to hold that the prosecution has not at all proved the case against the accused. Therefore the accused are entitled to be acquitted and I hereby acquit them all of all the charges levelled against them ... the accused are directed to be released forthwith unless they are required in any other case.[11]

After he delivered the judgment, he said to me, 'Kannabiran, you made me write a really lengthy report on the Rameeza Bee inquiry. Now you have made me write a long 200-page judgment on this case.'

Secunderabad and Ramnagar Conspiracy Cases

The famous Secunderabad conspiracy case proceeded in much the same way as the other conspiracy cases.[12] The FIR was registered in May 1974. As in the case

11 Justice K.A. Muktadar, *State represented by Deputy Superintendent of Police, Crime Branch, Hyderabad vs Chowdary Tejeswara Rao and Others*. Sessions Case No. 46 of 1973, Criminal Appeals Nos. 958/77, 542/77, 177/77, 141/77, 963/76, 572/77. High Court of Andhra Pradesh, Judgment delivered on 13 July 1979, pp. 146–7.

12 *State of Andhra Pradesh vs Inguva Mallikarjuna Sharma and Ors.* Sessions Case No. 10/75 in the court of the second additional metropolitan sessions judge, judgment delivered by Judge P.V. Rama Sarma, on 3 May 1988.

of police officer Veeranarayan Reddy in Parvathipuram, police officer Alfred was both the complainant and the investigating officer in this case. He made a list of meetings that had taken place in different places, and a list of offences committed before and after these meetings, and slapped them together in a conspiracy. Of the people accused in this case were Kondapalli Seetharamaiah, K.G. Satyamurthi, Inguva Mallikarjuna Sharma, Barla Yadagiri Raju, Mandadi Ravindra Reddy, K.V. Ramana Reddy, Tripuraneni Madhusudhan Rao, Cherabanda Raju, P. Varavara Rao, M.T. Khan and M. Ranganatham. Revolutionary writers were shown as accused along with revolutionary activists. The sessions court acquitted all the accused in a judgment delivered on 27 February 1989. Along with the Secunderabad conspiracy case, the revolutionary writers and accused were charged with conspiracy in the Chittoor conspiracy case. In that case as well, the sessions court acquitted all the accused.

Even as the trial for the Secunderabad conspiracy case was ongoing, a raid was conducted on a house in Ramnagar locality—Nalla Adi Reddy and others were arrested. It was claimed that the raid yielded arms and ammunition, revolutionary literature and explosive substances. Offences committed prior to this raid were put together to construct the Ramnagar conspiracy case, Crime No. 92/1986, in the Hyderabad City Crime Police Station.[13] The accused in this case were some of those in the Secunderabad conspiracy case: Kondapalli Seetharamaiah, K.G. Satyamurthi, Mukku Subba Reddy, Nalla Adi Reddy, Puli Anjaiah, Mallojula Koteswara Rao, K.V. Ramana Reddy, P. Varavara Rao, N. Sudhakar and Gaddar. The charge sheet initially named thirty accused. Of these, some Naxalites who surrendered were dropped, Kondapalli Seetharamaiah, owing to his failing health, was dropped, eleven were killed in encounters, and yet others went underground. Although 253 witnesses were named in the charge sheet, only thirteen were examined. Although the charge sheet stated that 300 weapons were recovered during the raid, not a single weapon was produced before the court. Finally, only Varavara Rao and Sudhakar faced trial in this case and were acquitted by the sessions court, eighteen years later, on 29 November 2003.

13 *Deputy Superintendent of Police, Special Task Force, Hyderabad vs Pendyala Varavara Rao and Anr.* Sessions Case 51/1987. In the court of the metropolitan sessions judge, Hyderabad. Decided on 25 September 2003.

Bangalore Conspiracy Case

The other case was the Bangalore conspiracy case in which I presented written arguments.[14] The charge was that there was a meeting of Naxalite leaders in Sravana Belagola in Karnataka in 1991, after which offences were committed. With the arrest of Naxalite leader Patel Sudhakar Reddy in Bangalore, the police claimed that a huge cache of arms and ammunition were recovered from his house on 6 April 1992. The strange claim about the Bangalore conspiracy case was that the first raid took place in Bangalore. Thereafter, there were raids in Chitradurga, Kolar, Bellary and Goa. All these raids were carried out by the Andhra Pradesh Police. They could not register a case in Bangalore as it was outside their jurisdiction. So they made an illegal arrest in Hyderabad and combined all the others with this. The police had made a habit of fabricating cases based on false allegations. In this case, on 20 April, roughly two weeks after the first raid in Bangalore, they claimed to have arrested a person called Gorla Kumaraswamy at Jubilee Bus Station in Hyderabad, and recovered a double-barrel gun and twenty-five bullets. After that, they raided other places in the city and claimed to have made arrests and registered a complaint in the Investigation Cell Police Station, in the Hyderabad Special Intelligence Branch (Crime No. 1/1992).

Between April 1992 and March 1993, they arrested twenty-four revolutionary activists and sympathizers, and showed them as well as some arms traders as accused in this case. In this case, police officer Venkat Reddy was complainant and investigating officer. By the time the charge sheet was filed on 19 April 1993, forty-seven persons were shown as accused. On 12 April 1994, the number of accused named in the charge sheet was amended to sixty-three. Although 236 witnesses were named, the prosecution produced only 104 witnesses in court. They said they had 611 exhibits. Since the police claimed that they had recovered arms and ammunition from different places, the court found the prosecution witnesses unreliable. It felt that Venkat Reddy had not adhered to procedure in conducting the panchnama and securing signatures of the panches. The court held that the investigating officer had acted in violation of the procedures set out in the IPC, the Arms Act and TADA.

The arms dealers admitted to selling arms in accordance with the law and denied the charge that they had violated the provisions of the Arms Act or that they had

14 *S. Appa Rao and Ors vs State of Andhra Pradesh*. Sessions Case No. 207/1993 (Cr. No. 1/1992). In the court of the second additional sessions judge. Date of judgment: 9 April 1999. *State of Andhra Pradesh vs S. Appa Rao and Ors*. Criminal Appeal No. 795 of 1999. JT 2001 (2) SC 13.

committed offences under TADA. The prosecution failed miserably in its attempt to show them as accused in the conspiracy. Similarly, the prosecution had lined up unlicenced arms dealers, brokers, middlemen—but could not point to a single piece of evidence that might establish the claim that all these accused were co-conspirators in a crime. The competence of the prosecution was evident from the fact that it could not identify the personnel of the Special Intelligence Branch (SIB) who accompanied Venkat Reddy when he went to conduct the arrests and raids in Karnataka. These personnel were not summoned to appear in the court. The prosecution also could not tell the court if any officers of the Karnataka Police who had jurisdiction over the area in which the Andhra Pradesh officers were carrying out arrests had accompanied Venkat Reddy or not. No officer of the Karnataka Police was summoned to the court. Venkat Reddy himself did not know whether Bangalore, Bellary, Kolar and Goa—the areas he conducted raids in—were areas notified under Section 5 of TADA or not.[15] He also did not state where and before which executive magistrate he had produced the arrested persons. He could not answer this question even during cross-examination. He did not hand over the items confiscated during the raids to the court at any stage, nor did he take the written permission of the court to retain these items in his custody. In my cross-examination, I asked Venkat Reddy whether the weapons he had listed as confiscated during the raids were not the same weapons that were claimed to have been retrieved by the police after the encounters that took place between 1987 and 1992. He answered that they were. This habit of circulating the same set of weapons between different encounter and raid sites, not surrendering them to the court in the course of investigation, was an old one. I was, in this case, able to establish that the claim of confiscation of arms and ammunition during raids was a false one. In the normal course all weapons that are confiscated should be sent for forensic examination and the forensic report must be produced before the court. This was not done.

The court did not place any reliance on the confessional statements of the accused. The prosecution showed eight surrendered Naxalites as the prosecution witnesses. They recorded their statements about Naxalite conspiracies and other

---

15 Terrorist and Disruptive Activities (Prevention) Act, 1987, Section 5: 'Possession of certain unauthorised arms, etc. in specified areas—Where any person is in possession of any arms and ammunition specified in Columns 2 and 3 of Category I or Category III (a) of Schedule I to the Arms Rules, 1962, or bombs, dynamite or other explosive substances unauthorisedly in a notified area, he shall, notwithstanding anything contained in any other law for the time being in force, be punishable with imprisonment for a term which shall not be less than five years but which may extend to imprisonment for life and shall also be liable to fine.'

Naxalite activities. The identities of these witnesses were kept secret. They were not brought to court. Neither the court nor the defence lawyers were given an opportunity to cross-examine them. In short, the famous Bangalore conspiracy case was a mess.

I reiterated my arguments on Section 10 of the Indian Evidence Act, detailed in the Parvathipuram case. I countered the implication of arms traders as co-conspirators in this case. Arms traders sell arms to anyone who pays for them regardless of political or other objectives behind the purchase. To construct an agreement between buyers and sellers of arms as proof of conspiracy was to extend the limits of 'agreement with common intention' beyond reasonable limits. American judge Billings Learned Hand uses his famous analogy of the 'traffic light' to illustrate this point:

> It is never permissible to enlarge the scope of the conspiracy itself by proving that some of the conspirators, unknown to the rest, have done what was beyond the reasonable intendment of the common understanding ... And this is equally true, when the crime which the conspirators have agreed upon, is one of which they severally might be guilty though they were ignorant of the existence of some of its constituent facts. While one may, for instance, be guilty of running past a traffic light of whose existence one is ignorant, one cannot be guilty of conspiring to run past such a light, for one cannot agree to run past a light unless one supposes that there is a light to run past.[16]

All the evidence and confessions furnished by the prosecution in the Bangalore conspiracy case were about the purchase of arms and ammunition outside Andhra Pradesh. The mere fact of buying arms and ammunition does not justify the charge of conspiring to commit crime with common intent. Further, all the incidents mentioned took place outside Andhra Pradesh. Therefore, I argued that the court did not have the jurisdiction to hear the case. On the charge of conspiracy, I cited the judgment of the US Supreme Court in *Krulewitch v. United States*:[17]

> The modern crime of conspiracy is so vague that it almost defies definition ... Despite certain elementary and essential elements, it also, chameleon-like, takes on a special coloration from each of the many independent offenses

16 *United States vs Crimmins* 123 F.2d 271 (2d Cir. 1941). Decided 3 November 1941.

17 *Krulewitch vs United States* 336 U.S. 440, 443–44 (1949). Para 10.

> on which it may be overlaid ... It is always 'predominantly mental in composition' because it consists primarily of a meeting of minds and an intent.

Further, the US Supreme Court invoked the Sixth Amendment, and stated as follows:

> An accused, under the *Sixth Amendment*, has the right to trial 'by an impartial jury of the State and district wherein the crime shall have been committed.' The leverage of a conspiracy charge lifts this limitation from the prosecution and reduces its protection to a phantom, for the crime is considered so vagrant as to have been committed in any district where any one of the conspirators did any one of the acts, however innocent, intended to accomplish its object. The Government may, and often does, compel one to defend at a great distance from any place he ever did any act because some accused confederate did some trivial and by itself innocent act in the chosen district. Circumstances may even enable the prosecution to fix the place of trial in Washington, D.C., where a defendant may lawfully be put to trial before a jury partly or even wholly made up of employees of the Government that accuses him.[18]

In any case, the prosecution must first establish the fact of conspiracy. It must identify the conspirators. It is only after this that involvement of each of the accused, and relevant evidence pointing to such involvement, may be examined. It also has to be established that evidence pointing to one of the accused is admissible for all. However, in such a sweeping charge, it is difficult for the judge to keep track of the sequence of evidence placed before the court. So basically, what happens is this: each accused is confronted with details of the actions of the other accused and the various statements; he has no idea which of these he was supposed to be part of, knew about, was not part of, intended. It is on this kind of evidence that the judge is expected to make a reasoned decision. In other words, the evidence of a conspiracy

---

18 Ibid., para 20. *US Constitution, Sixth Amendment*: 'In all criminal prosecutions, the accused shall enjoy the right to a speedy and public trial, by an impartial jury of the State and district wherein the crime shall have been committed, which district shall have been previously ascertained by law, and to be informed of the nature and cause of the accusation; to be confronted with the witnesses against him; to have compulsory process for obtaining witnesses in his favor, and to have the Assistance of Counsel for his defence', https://constitution.congress.gov/constitution/amendment-6. Accessed on 20 October 2021.

is ordinarily collected on the basis of the belief that there exists a conspiracy. Before the crime of conspiracy is proved, it is presumed that a conspiracy existed. It is true that it is an extremely difficult task for the prosecution to prove a conspiracy. But the burden on the accused is much heavier. So also the onus on the co-accused in a conspiracy. There is rarely firm proof of another person's crime. In this situation it becomes very difficult for him to convince the judge of his own innocence because the judge believes that all the accused are birds of a feather. I used different parts of the *Krulewitch* judgment to support my arguments.

The court of the second additional metropolitan sessions judge, which was a designated TADA court, acquitted all the seventeen accused of all charges on 4 April 1999. The prosecution filed a criminal appeal (No. 795/99) in the Supreme Court, but on 21 December 2000, the Supreme Court affirmed the judgment of the TADA court and declared the seventeen accused not guilty.

7

Tarkunde Committee, 1977–78

Naming 'Encounters' as 'Murders by the State'

A WORD ABOUT encounter killings. During the Emergency, while I was arguing writ petitions of detenus in court, I would often hear of the deaths of revolutionary activists in police firing. In a country that calls itself a democracy, this treacherous killing of citizens by the state is unacceptable by any standards. This was part of the larger project of wiping out political dissent—and was primarily used to decimate the Naxalite struggle. West Bengal and Andhra Pradesh first witnessed this trend. It then spread to other states. I got completely immersed in fighting this. As a human being, and as an advocate, I strongly felt that we could not be silent spectators to state violence. Condoning violence by the state is the first step to authoritarianism and state arbitrariness. These methods were similar to the methods deployed by Hitler. The difference was that Hitler killed entire groups of people and confined and tortured entire groups in camps with no accountability. The Universal Declaration of Human Rights was adopted in 1948 against that background. No law could give the government the right to kill. In our state, during the Telangana armed struggle, this method of killing political dissenters was used on a large scale. P. Sundarayya wrote that the Indian Army that came to Andhra to quell the communist resistance killed 2,500 people.[1] This points

1 Sundarayya, P. 1972. *Telangana People's Struggle and Its Lessons*. Calcutta: Communist Party of India (Marxist).

to the utter lawlessness and lack of restraint with which the government of that time conducted itself. In the first two decades after Independence, however, barring this, there was no major incident of killing people on this scale till the rise of the Naxalite movement. At this point we witnessed a turn to the murder of dissidents as a method of rule.

The first instance of this in Andhra Pradesh may be seen in the Srikakulam movement. Several people were killed in encounters and the police were given the responsibility of destroying revolutionary politics. The democratic spirit in the political leadership was being severely eroded by those in power. After the Emergency, during Indira Gandhi's reign, these authoritarian trends got more deeply entrenched. Chief Minister J. Vengal Rao's knowledge of politics was limited to winning elections—he did not understand any other form of politics. In those days, people used to say that he relied solely on intelligence reports to become the chief minister, that he owed his chief ministership to M.V. Narayana Rao, the DIG (intelligence) at the time, who gave him a clean chit.

We need to reflect on why fake encounters are a serious concern for civil liberties movements. Ordinarily, when there is a murder, there is a crime registered under Section 302 IPC. There is an investigation into the crime. A charge sheet is filed. A trial is conducted from the level of the trial court to the appellate courts. But when a police officer kills someone and calls it an encounter, it is never questioned. A right which is not granted to elected leaders is granted to a salaried policeman. Further, the procedure prescribed under Section 174 of the CrPC in the matter of post-mortem or inquest in any case of unnatural death is never followed.[2] This is a

2 Section 174, CrPC: Police to enquire and report on suicide, etc.

(1) When the officer in charge of a police station or some other police officer specially empowered by the State Government in that behalf receives information that a person has committed suicide, or has been killed by another or by an animal or by machinery or by an accident, or has died under circumstances raising a reasonable suspicion that some other person has committed an offence, he shall immediately give intimation thereof to the nearest Executive Magistrate empowered to hold inquests, and, unless otherwise directed by any rule prescribed by the State Government, or by any general or special order of the District or Subdivisional Magistrate, shall proceed to the place where the body of such deceased person is, and there, in the presence of two or more respectable inhabitants of the neighbourhood, shall make an investigation, and draw up a report of the apparent cause of death, describing such wounds, fractures, bruises, and other marks of injury as may be found on the body, and stating in what manner, or by what weapon or instrument (if any); such marks appear to have been inflicted.

distortion of laws that is rationalized by courts in different ways: that these actions do not come within the jurisdiction of laws; that it is not possible to define the limits of the law; that it is impossible to determine actions that violate the law. Courts use any number of excuses to turn a blind eye to this violation of the law. Encounter killings have continued seamlessly from the time of Alluri Seetarama Raju till today. Across different periods, the crime is the same. We could compare encounter murders to murders by religious fundamentalists. This has to do with the problem of intolerance.

Bhuvan Mohan Patnaik—a very good-natured, gentle lawyer—who was an accused in the Parvathipuram conspiracy case, for the first time, made an attempt to delegitimize this obnoxious practice which had appropriated the status of legitimacy in the Parvathipuram conspiracy case. He devoted a considerable part of his cross-examination of the police witnesses to an exposure of the hollowness of the claims of these encounters. This issue arose because within the period from registering of the crime to the filing of the charge sheet, and the trial, more than 100 accused had been shot in fake encounters, and police witnesses who were produced to speak of the events in the charge sheet also deposed with regard to these encounters. This method adopted by Bhuvan Mohan Patnaik enabled him to establish that the police practices to which the state acquiesced were wholly unlawful. He raised this issue during his own trial and tried to prove that they were not encounters, but murders. However, as a lawyer, he knew that he could not do anything more in a case where he himself stood accused of various charges along with the other accused. If it was established in the trial that there had been a murder misnamed as an encounter, the court would have to take cognizance of the murder. If it lacked the jurisdiction to try the case, it would have to refer the case to an appropriate court. The people alleged to have misused the law in this manner would have to face cross-examination. But there were procedural aspects in a criminal trial like the Parvathipuram conspiracy case that obstructed an accused person facing trial from leading evidence on murder by the state.

The Madras Suppression of Disturbances Act, 1948, which was operative in the Andhra area of the Madras Presidency, contained a provision enabling a police officer not below the rank of a sub-inspector of police to open fire, even to the extent of killing, for any assembly of more than five persons carrying what he considers to be lethal weapons, in any area in the state notified to be a 'disturbed area'. Various

---

(2) The report shall be signed by such police officer and other persons, or by so many of them as concur therein, and shall be forthwith forwarded to the District Magistrate or the Sub-divisional Magistrate.

offences under the IPC carry enhanced penalties under this Act. According to Section 3 of this Act, the government has the power to declare any area as a 'disturbed area'. Section 5 of the Act states:

> Any Magistrate, and any Police Officer not below the rank of Sub-Inspector, may, if in his opinion it is necessary so to do for restoring or maintaining public order, after giving such warning, if any, as he may consider necessary, fire upon, order fire to be opened or otherwise use force, even to the causing of death, against any person who in a disturbed area is acting in contravention of any law or order for the time being in force in such area, prohibiting the assembly of five or more persons or the carrying of weapons or of things capable of being used as weapons.

Under normal circumstances, if the police want to fire on an assembly of people, they must have the sanction of a magistrate. This provision does not apply to disturbed areas. It is originally under this Act that physical liquidation in the name of encounters was brought on to the agenda. This Act, which was applicable to the Madras Presidency, was adapted under Article 372 of the Constitution around 1967, and was made applicable to the entire state of Andhra Pradesh. Police officer M.V. Narayana Rao was one of those who used this provision most brazenly.[3] The provisions of this Act and the notifications were grossly abused by apprehending persons described to be Naxalites and transporting them to 'Disturbed Areas' where they were shot dead in cold blood.

Background to the Independent Investigation of 'Encounters'

Once Emergency was declared, it was no longer necessary to mask murder by the state with recourse to the 'Disturbed Areas' argument. People were indiscriminately shot just about anywhere. I heard of the Giraipalli encounter while I was in court arguing writ petitions of detenus. I also heard of the encounter killings of Neelam Ramachandraiah and Jampala Chandra Sekhar Prasad while I was in court. There was no stopping the rogue state. There were no legal hurdles that prevented the

3 Menon, Amarnath K. 1979. 'Despite police brutality, Andhra Pradesh government honours its police chief.' *India Today*. 31 December. https://www.indiatoday.in/magazine/indiascope/story/19791231-despite-police-brutality-andhra-pradesh-government-honours-its-police-chief-822321-2014-02-11 Accedssed on 6 May 2022.

police from resorting to brute force. Neither the IPC nor the CrPC permit the killing of persons in self-defence. And yet this massacre continued unchecked. There were three major aspects of illegal state action during the Emergency: first, arbitrary detentions; second, arrest and illegal confinement in detention camps (which were often eight to ten times more than the official arrests admitted to); and third, the selective killing of those in illegal detention in encounters. Tarimela Nagi Reddy, in *India Mortgaged*, spoke about these arbitrary killings.[4] He described how Battula Venkateswara Rao, the Naxalite leader, was killed in an encounter. That is only one instance—there were several like this.

A couple of months after Emergency was lifted in 1977, M.V. Ramamurthy called a meeting in the Young Men's Christian Association (YMCA), Narayanguda, under the aegis of Citizens for Democracy, founded by Jayaprakash Narayan. Ramamurthy chaired the meeting, and several people spoke. In the course of the discussion, Jwalamukhi made a suggestion that an independent committee be set up to investigate encounter deaths during the Emergency. Although the Shah Commission had already been set up by the government, it did not look at the cases in Andhra Pradesh. Several people therefore felt that an independent committee was a good idea, and decided that I should be convenor of this committee. My responsibilities included the difficult task of deciding who the members of the committee would be. I thought hard about the members who would constitute the committee. All those who spoke at that meeting were people who either represented or were close to Naxalite groups. I felt strongly that the committee would not move forward if I only had members who were communists, Naxalites and their sympathizers. Moreover, the internal conflicts between different communist groups would stall the work of the committee. I eventually sorted out this dilemma on my own and did not seek advice from anyone.

Jawahar Guha, a barrister based in Calcutta, was a friend of mine, and I used to argue his cases in Hyderabad. One day, after our work in court was done, he invited me for a drink to the Ritz Hotel, where he was staying. By then, I had been the legal counsel for Ritz Hotel for several years. I met Deepak Shourie, Arun Shourie's younger brother, at the Ritz—Deepak was working with a company called Metal Box. He had come to Hyderabad on work and was also staying there. As we sat talking about what had happened in Andhra Pradesh during the Emergency, Arun Shourie's name cropped up. By this time, Arun Shourie was the editor of the *Indian Express*, and was in the PUCLDR (People's Union for Civil Liberties

---

4 Reddy, T. Nagi. 1978. *India Mortgaged.* Anantapuram: Tarimela Nagi Reddy Memorial Trust.

and Democratic Rights) in Delhi. I told Deepak that I had work with Arun and requested an introduction. A couple of days later, I travelled to Delhi, met Arun Shourie and stayed with him.

When I described to him what had happened in Andhra Pradesh, he offered his unconditional support. The two of us then discussed the possible members of the committee. By then I had also heard V.M. Tarkunde speak at another meeting in the YMCA, Hyderabad—a good speaker, he was a leader of the Radical Humanist Movement, and was closely associated with JP in the civil liberties movement. A former judge of the Bombay High Court and a practising Supreme Court advocate, he represented Kuldip Nayar, who had been arrested during the Emergency, in the Supreme Court. Arun Shourie and I met Tarkunde in the Supreme Court. He took time out of his busy schedule and we discussed the formation of the committee with him in the Supreme Court Bar Association office. Tarkunde, by then, was a well-known figure, and very short-tempered. We both had an argument over something. That was the first time we were meeting. At the end of an animated meeting, I insisted he accept our request to chair the committee. He readily agreed. Arun Shourie and I then went to Connaught Place for lunch and discussed other possible members of the committee. We felt that constituting the committee in the broadest possible manner would be the best way. From Andhra Pradesh, we had Balwant Reddy, M.V. Ramamurthy, Kaloji Narayan Rao and K. Pratap Reddy. Around that time, Arun Shourie had become quite close to JP. He suggested B.G. Verghese and Nabakrishna Choudhury. I requested Arun to be the secretary of the committee. The committee was formally announced with eight members and V.M. Tarkunde as the president in April 1977.

Before I elaborate on the rest of the committee, I must speak about how K. Pratap Reddy became a member of the committee. As part of our inquiry into encounters, I travelled to Delhi often, carrying the statements of witnesses to the encounters. It was not easy for me to carry these records to Delhi and deposit them safely in Arun Shourie's custody. The police were making every attempt to confiscate the records and destroy them. On one of those trips, I met Pratap Reddy at the airport. Since he was at the time with the Janata Party, I felt I could avert this danger of losing the statements if he carried the papers. We then invited him to the committee. As a matter of fact, we had planned to have a medical doctor as a member, but since the person we approached was not willing, there was an empty position. The committee, once it was fully constituted, consisted of V.M. Tarkunde (former judge, Bombay High Court), B.G. Verghese (former editor, *Hindustan Times*), Nabakrishna Choudhury (former chief minister of Orissa), Arun Shourie (editor, the *Indian Express*), Balwant Reddy (professor, Administrative Staff College of India), Prajakavi Kaloji Narayan Rao, senior advocates M.V. Ramamurthy and K. Pratap Reddy and me. We then decided to discuss the work of the committee with Jayaprakash Narayan, who by then was very ill in Jaslok Hospital, Bombay. I met Swami Agnivesh for the first time in Jaslok Hospital during our visit to JP—we were introduced to each other by Arun Shourie.

JP was very frail. Arun and I sat on either side of his bed and answered his questions. Finally, we recorded JP formally announcing the constitution of the committee. The work of the committee was to investigate encounter killings in Andhra Pradesh. We received all the petitions, visited places where incidents were said to have occurred, recorded our findings, and released reports for the public. However, the matters investigated by this committee required strategizing. We had to deal with the possibility of threats from the state and the police—so it was of utmost importance to ensure complete confidentiality and secrecy in our work. These suggestions came from JP. We then began recording the incidents.

Fact-Finding by Tarkunde Committee

The Tarkunde Committee was the result of a collective reflection on how we might stop this scourge. On the whole, during the Emergency, seventy-seven persons were killed, and declared to have died in encounters by the government. Our task was to investigate each incident fully and arrive at a list of how many had died in fake encounters.

The first encounter we investigated was the Giraipalli encounter. On 15 July 1975, four young men, all active in the Naxalite movement led by Kondapalli Seetharamaiah (this was before the formation of the People's War Group), were shot dead close to the Giraipalli forest in Medak district. They were Surapaneni Janardhan (Regional Engineering College, Warangal), Lanka Muralimohan Reddy, P. Sudhakar and V. Ananda Rao (all residents of Warangal). Janardhan and the other three were arrested separately, tortured for over a week, and then tied to trees in Giraipalli and shot, according to information we received. On 22 June 1975, a moneylender called Donthula Anthaiah, known for his cruelty, was murdered in Sirisinagandla village near Giraipalli. There was an investigation into his murder, in the course of which these four young men were apprehended and interrogated for many days. After that they were shot and it was declared that they died in an armed encounter. My friend, advocate Challa Narasimha Reddy, then with the CPI (M), was Donthula Anthaiah's lawyer. After Anthaiah was killed, the police implicated him in the murder.

We travelled throughout the state in the months of May and June 1977 and examined three encounters thoroughly. Our first report, released in Delhi, listed ten persons who had been killed in fake encounters. In our second report released in June, there were details of nine more fake encounter killings. We presented our witness statements, evidence and reports to the then prime minister, Morarji Desai, and then home minister, Charan Singh.

Advocate Narasimha Reddy helped me a great deal in putting together the facts of the Giraipalli encounter. He was then practising in Siddipet. He knew all the facts pertaining to this case—and since we were friends he was willing to share the information with me. We discussed the incident at great length and Narasimha Reddy gave me the minute details of the encounter. I had first met Narasimha Reddy through my close friend, advocate Panchagnula Satyanarayana. He knew everyone who had been arrested in Anthaiah's case, and where they had been detained and interrogated. I was able to visit each of them and speak to them. I was able to convince them to speak the truth without fear. With Indira Gandhi's defeat, all these witnesses gathered the courage to testify to the encounter publicly. There was not a single person I cross-examined in the Giraipalli incident who was afraid of speaking the truth. My friends and I would go to different areas and record the statements of witnesses. Balwant Reddy was always ready to join me.

When I was inquiring into the Giraipalli incident, I came to know that the people who had been illegally arrested in connection with this incident had been detained in Nilagirithota Dak Bungalow in Mulugu, Medak district. This was a guest house that belonged either to the forest department or the public works department (PWD). A few SPs and DSPs had camped here for a few days. I went to the guest house and asked the watchman to bring me the guest register. On the precise dates of the encounter, there was an entry that showed that the district SP, Subhash Chandra Bose, had stayed in that guest house. I circled his name and put my signature: K.G. Kannabiran, Secretary, Tarkunde Committee. I called the watchman and took his signature on the register copy. I noted the names of guests before and after this entry and the dates of their stay. This would make it impossible for them to tear off the pages and destroy evidence.

Surprisingly, we did not face any hurdles from the police. I had expected that they would make every effort to derail our work. This did not happen, because the police had no clue about what we were doing, nor did they expect that we would visit villages, speak to the people and record the statements of witnesses. They assumed we were just doing something in Hyderabad and were best ignored. In the days when the committee was at work, countless friends supported us. Dozens of them would drop in at my home every evening. The one person who helped me more than anyone else was Ranganatham. He was detained during the Emergency because he edited the paper *Pilupu*. He worked with the APCLC for a short while after the Emergency and had a good understanding and interest in these issues. He felt strongly that we should do something to stop these killings in the future. He typed very well and would come every morning and work till late. We kept collecting any information we could find on encounters; he would type it all up and Vasanth would edit it—my office was running like a factory.

Our second inquiry was into the Chilakalagutta encounter. Chilakalagutta is the forest near Pakala, close to Narsampet in Warangal district. P. Ramanarasaiah of Old Malakpet, Hyderabad, and his associates, Janakirama Reddy, Narayana and Srihari, were arrested and transported in a van covered with tarpaulin to Chilakalagutta and shot dead on 31 October 1975. P. Ramanarasaiah was the state secretary of the CPI (ML) Chandra Pulla Reddy group. He was the tenant of a person called Pritam Singh who stayed in the government quarters. The police went to his house, caught Ramanarasaiah, tied him up and bundled him into a van. CPI(M) leader and MLA M. Omkar testified before the Bhargava Commission that he knew of this incident. In the course of our inquiry, we found that Ramanarasaiah and his associates had been brutally tortured and their fingers chopped off. I also heard that the then IGP, Ramachandra Reddy, had been informed about Ramanarasaiah's arrest. By then, Ramanarasaiah was a senior leader who had earned considerable respect. It was perhaps because of this that the police informed the senior officers of the arrest. We also heard that Ramachandra Reddy instructed his subordinate officers to produce Ramanarasaiah in court. We don't know what happened thereafter. He was not produced. Four of them were killed.

The third incident we inquired into was the Yellandu encounter that took place on the intervening night of 5–6 November, 1976. Two people were killed: Neelam Ramachandraiah and Jampala Chandra Sekhar Prasad. Neelam Ramachandraiah was a former MLC (member of the legislative council), a senior communist leader and part of the CPI (ML) Chandra Pulla Reddy group. Jampala Prasad was an engineering student and a Progressive Democratic Students' Union (PDSU) leader known throughout the state. And yet, the police announced this as an encounter in which two 'unidentified Naxalites' were killed. We found several leads that pointed to the possibility that both of them were arrested on the evening of 4 November 1976 in Vijayawada. They were transported that night to Yellandu, which was 100 kilometres away in Khammam district.

We continued inquiring into other encounters—in Guntur and in Prakasam. Nine persons were killed in these incidents. We began collecting evidence around the killing of Jaya Rao, Surya Varma, Sathyanandam and Mallikarjuna Rao. I think two of these four were Dalit. They were not all killed together. Each was killed separately on different days. I remember going to a village called Thettu in Chittoor district. We saw the location of the encounter. My taxi broke down there, so I got on to a lorry and reached Kavali in neighbouring Nellore district, and went to K.V. Ramana Reddy's (KVR) house. KVR saw me off in the station the next day. A big police platoon boarded my compartment. KVR was worried that they may harm me as I had the evidence of the Thettu encounter with me. I told KVR that I had no option—if they took away my records, I would just have to return to Thettu and do it all again. To complicate matters, an intelligence officer also boarded my compartment. But the ride was uneventful.

Reports of Civil Liberties (Tarkunde) Committee

The members of the committee were all based in different places. Tarkunde and Arun Shourie did not come on fact-finding missions as part of a deliberate strategy to keep a low profile during the fact-finding process. We made preparations to release an interim report nationally detailing these three incidents: ten activists in the revolutionary movement who were killed in Giraipalli, Chilakalagutta and Yellandu. I prepared the draft of the interim report and V.M. Tarkunde, Arun Shourie, B.G. Verghese and I studied the entire draft word by word to make sure it would be approved by all members. It was released on 16 May 1977 in Delhi.[5] The report shocked the country.

The second report was released in Delhi in June 1977. Arun Shourie has written at length about them in his book *Institutions in the Janata Phase*.[6] Our reports were printed in Telugu and distributed widely. The reports of the Tarkunde Committee were known across the country.[7]

Our reports were always sent to the Prime Minister's Office and to the home minister. We met Prime Minister Morarji Desai and Home Minister Charan Singh

5 'Police "Murdered" Alleged Naxalites in State'. 1977. *Indian Express*, 17 May, p. 1.

6 Shourie, Arun. 1980. *Institutions in the Janata Phase*. Bombay: Popular Prakashan, pp. 150–68. The reports of the committee are reprinted in this book.

7 A summary of the first interim report is also available in 'Encounters are Murders: Interim Report of the Civil Liberties Committee'. 1977. *Economic and Political Weekly*, Vol. 12, No. 21, 21 May, https://www.epw.in/journal/1977/21/our-correspondent-columns/political-prisoners.html#. Accessed on 29 September 2021. For a Telugu translation of this report, see Rao, Adhiraju Venkateswara. 1977. *Hantakulevaru?* (Who Are the Killers?). Hyderabad: Velugu Publications. For a summary of the second interim report of the Tarkunde Committee see 'Second Report of Civil Rights Panel: Cold-blooded Murder of 9 in Guntur'. 1977. *Indian Express*, 13 June, pp. 1, 9.

several times during this period.[8] I got to know Morarji Desai well. On one occasion we discussed what we could possibly do in this matter. We felt a judicial commission constituted under the Commissions of Inquiry Act, 1952, would be best. As soon as he read our report, Morarji Desai decided that it had to be a judicial inquiry and asked us to discuss the matter further with the home minister. We discussed the matter with Home Minister Charan Singh in great detail. Although he was also interested in an inquiry commission, he felt it could not be a commission constituted by the central government. Since law and order was a state subject, he felt that the authority to constitute such a commission rested with the state government. We argued with him: 'When there has been a gross violation of Article 21 of the Constitution and people have been brutally killed, how can you debate about whether this is within the jurisdiction of the state or centre? This is not a "law and order" matter that is limited to the state list. It is a premeditated murder of political dissenters. Therefore the central government must intervene.' After this debate, the central government decided that they would designate a judge and the state government would constitute the commission and ensure its smooth functioning. It was perhaps an understanding reached between the state and central governments.

8 The Report of the Civil Liberties (V.M. Tarkunde) Committee was discussed in the Lok Sabha on 15 June 1977, soon after the release of the second report. Samar Mukherjee, Satyendra Narayan Sinha, Ahalya Rangnekar and Gangadhar Appa Burande raised questions with Home Minister Charan Singh responding to them. See Introduction for a discussion of this debate.

8

Commissions of Inquiry against State Violence in Andhra Pradesh, 1977–83

Commissions of Inquiry

BEFORE GOING INTO the details of three of the earliest commissions of inquiry that I appeared in, it is important to reflect on the role of a commission constituted under the Commissions of Inquiry Act, 1952. Such a commission cannot be a substitute for a trial by a court, nor is it part of the formal courts of law. In instances where an inquiry is conducted by a sitting judge, according to law, the judge does not enjoy his powers as a judge while he sits on the commission. A commission of inquiry is only an instrument that a government may use to gather information on a particular matter. It is not empowered to take decisions on the matters it investigates in the manner in which a court of law can. Further, even the investigation, examination of witnesses and evidence gathered by the commission cannot be used by a court of law. We therefore cannot treat an inquiry as being in the nature of court proceedings.

It is the state's responsibility to investigate every crime and produce the accused before a court of law. The court in turn conducts the trial according to procedure established by law, and if it is proved that the accused persons are guilty, they may be deprived of life or personal liberty. When a crime is committed, it is not possible for a court to delegate the responsibility of ensuring justice to another body.

I took on the responsibility of presenting my arguments before every commission of inquiry, starting with the Bhargava Commission of Inquiry into encounters in Andhra Pradesh and the Muktadar Commission of Inquiry into the rape of Rameeza Bee and the death of Ahmed Hussain in police custody in Hyderabad. When there is a protest against the extraordinary use of force and violence on the people by the state, particularly the police, the government sets up commissions like these. The government sees protests as waging war against the state—and gives standing instructions to its police force to brutally suppress any protest. However, under the Indian Constitution, the right to protest is a fundamental right.

Justice Bhargava Commission, 1977–78

Prime Minister Morarji Desai and Home Minister Charan Singh announced the constitution of a one-man commission of inquiry, under the Commissions of Inquiry Act, 1952, headed by retired Supreme Court judge Justice Vashishtha Bhargava. Their proposal was agreed upon by Chief Minister J. Vengal Rao, who really had no option in the matter.[1] A most extraordinary commission in the history of the state, the Bhargava Commission, came into being.

During one of my trips to Delhi around this time, Arun Shourie and I went to Connaught Place for lunch. On reaching there, we found Naxalite leader Satyanarayan Singh waiting for us. He was a Naxalbari-era leader from Bihar who had founded a new party after differences with Charu Majumdar. He argued that Marxist–Leninist parties must enter electoral politics, and during 1977–79 made every effort to build bridges between Charan Singh and left revolutionaries. He died in the 1980s but by then he had risen to prominence. This was the first time I met him and at the time I think he may still have been underground. As soon as Arun Shourie introduced him to me, he rose, held my hand and said, 'Kannabiran, Prosecutor of Prosecutors.'

The notification announcing the Bhargava Commission was published on 21 July 1977. We had intense discussions on how best to go about our work with the commission. Justice Bhargava arrived in Hyderabad and the proceedings of the commission started in Dilkusha Guest House. Justice Tarkunde came to Hyderabad

1 'Vengal Rao had best of relations with Morarji Desai and Charan Singh. But in spite of that, the pressure of the socialists was so much and particularly Jayaprakashji was very particular that these matters must be gone into'. P. Shiv Shankar in *The Advocate* (documentary film on K.G. Kannabiran, D&N Productions, 2007), Part 2: https://www.youtube.com/watch?v=lrLStnOMP4s&t=10s at 4:16/39:50. Accessed on 13 October 2021.

for the first meeting with the commission. He was the first to record his statement before Justice Bhargava. After that, advocate Venkatakrishna of the OPDR made an announcement to Justice Bhargava that in a class society, justice is always subordinate to class and can never be classless. With this, the OPDR withdrew from the commission proceedings, and set up an independent committee to inquire into all the encounters that had taken place in the state with Mohan Ram, Rajni H. Desai and others. The inquiry based on the findings of that committee took place in Srikakulam.

The Bhargava Commission commenced its inquiry. B. Narsing Rao, a district and sessions judge, was named as the secretary of the commission. He was a sensitive judge who had written prolifically in Telugu under the pen name Beena Devi. As secretary, he released the first public announcement of the Bhargava Commission on 21 July 1977.[2] According to this announcement, the one-man commission of inquiry headed by Justice Vashishtha Bhargava would proceed on four terms of reference: (1) The situation created by Naxalite activities in the state of Andhra Pradesh or parts thereof, steps and instructions given by the state government to deal with such activities and the results thereof; (2) Complete details of every encounter between police and Naxalites in the state from 1968–77; (3) Allegations of murder and brutal torture of Naxalite detenus; (4) Policy measures to prevent such a situation in the future.

The inquiry by the Justice Bhargava Commission commenced. Advocate M.V. Ramamurthy and I appeared on behalf of the Tarkunde Committee and began our arguments. Advocate Panchagnula Satyanarayana also appeared with us. Advocate P. Shiv Shanker was appointed to represent the state.[3] His task was to present arguments on behalf of the police officers, for which a remuneration of Rs 1,500 per day was sanctioned to him from the state exchequer. In those days, that was a very high remuneration. The police department made a representation to the commission that they would like a lawyer to represent the department. IGP K. Ramachandra Reddy ensured that advocate T. Ananta Babu was appointed to that

---

2 'Bhargava Committee Appointment Notified'. 1977. *Indian Express*, 23 July, p. 3.

3 'I had a great regard for Mr Vengal Rao, the chief minister. He was a man of integrity and honesty. Very straightforward person. So it was he who requested me when the Janata Party government came and they appointed Bhargava Commission, he was keen that I should appear for him.' P. Shiv Shankar in *The Advocate* (documentary film on K.G. Kannabiran, D&N Productions, 2007). Part 2. https://www.youtube.com/watch?v=lrLStnOMP4s&t=10s at 4:16/39:50. Accessed on 13 October 2021.

position. He tried to appoint advocate K. Kulanda Reddy to assist Ananta Babu. When I look back now, what strikes me is the speed with which we responded to various situations arising during the commission's proceedings. The notification of the commission was released on 21 July 1977. Within ten days, several appointments had been made.

Of these, we contested the appointments of Ananta Babu and Kulanda Reddy on the grounds that they were malafide, with M.V. Ramamurthy filing a memorandum before the commission to this effect on 5 August 1977. We argued that the commission did not require the assistance of lawyers; that district and sessions judge B. Narsing Rao who had been appointed secretary to the commission would be adequate to the task. Further, we pointed out that Ananta Babu had served as IGP K. Ramachandra Reddy's legal adviser and was continuing to work in that capacity when he was appointed. A lawyer who was so closely associated with the IGP who was facing allegations of murder and torture of Naxalites, we argued, could not be permitted to assist the commission. Similarly, advocate Kulanda Reddy was the younger brother of IGP Ramachandra Reddy. We demanded that the appointment of these two lawyers be struck down. Secondly, we argued that since the people of the state had a keen interest in the commission's proceedings, the commission must release interim reports to the public after the inquiry into each incident was completed. Of these three demands, Justice Bhargava only conceded our demand to disallow advocate Kulanda Reddy from assisting the commission. Ananta Babu continued to assist the commission.

The Bhargava Commission was stalled even before it reached the stage of releasing an interim report. Between 5 and 9 August we submitted two more memorandums. The first had to do with the procedure to be followed by the commission, and the second sought an amendment in the order of the terms of reference of the commission. When I read the two memorandums thirty years later, I realize their historical significance. The memorandum of procedural matters submitted to Justice Bhargava on 9 August 1977 raised six important concerns. Primary was our contention that the work of the commission was likely to be derailed by the fact that the government in power was the government accused of perpetrating the alleged atrocities. Our doubts were justified over the next five to six months. We cautioned the commission that in order to continue to work without obstacles there were six areas of concern:

1. Good faith and instilling confidence,
2. Prioritizing the terms of reference,
3. Investigation of incidents of murders and torture,

4. Continuation in office of the present government and officers,
5. Necessity of interim reports,
6. Summoning of necessary official documents.

Good Faith and Instilling Confidence

By then, the commission, through a public notification, had invited statements from witnesses, but there was no assurance of any protection to the witnesses who might come forward to testify, nor any assurance that their statements would not be tampered with. Under these circumstances, disclosure of the names of witnesses or the details contained in their statements makes the intimidation of witnesses and tampering with evidence imminent. Attempts may be made to destroy records connected to the statements. Therefore, we argued, the commission must assure witnesses of protection and confidentiality. To support our argument we brought forward the case of E. Bhikshapathi. We recorded his statement on 30 July 1977. Arun Shourie and Kaloji Narayan Rao recorded his statement made in Telugu. The statement was signed by three witnesses: two advocates from Hanamkonda, Warangal—P. Vithal Rao and S. Shankaraiah—and revolutionary poet and teacher P. Varavara Rao.

Edulapuram Bhikshapathi, aged twenty-four, from Vadepalli village situated between Hanamkonda and Kazipet, was an eyewitness to the Giraipalli encounter. He stated that Janardhan, Murali Mohan, Ananda Rao and Sudhakar were tied to trees and shot in Giraipalli forest in front of him. Tarkunde filed this testimony as part of the preliminary inquiry of the committee. Anticipating that he was in danger after having recorded his testimony, the Tarkunde Committee provided him with a safe house in Hyderabad. But, Bhikshapathi, who worked as a daily-wage labourer, found it difficult to stay on in Hyderabad, and returned to Vadepalli. With help from Janata Party leader P. Shankaraiah, he met the district collector and stated that he feared for his life and requested protection from Shamim, a police officer who had earlier subjected him to torture. The collector, in consultation with the district SP, provided protection to Bhikshapathi. He was required to travel every day to the collector's office and sign in the presence of the revenue assistant—as a way of making sure he had not been harmed. This arrangement was made on 6 May 1977. Within a week, two police officers visited Bhikshapathi in his house and threatened him with dire consequences since he had testified before the Tarkunde Committee and had been collecting evidence on the Janardhan encounter case. This intimidation continued till 23 July, when the Bhargava Commission began its work. Then, on 26 July 1977, police officers went to Bhikshapathi's house and offered him

Rs 20,000 and a job if he refused to testify before the Bhargava Commission. They also warned him not to testify. Bhikshapathi stated all these facts in his statement recorded on 30 July 1977. This was his second statement. We handed this statement over to Justice Bhargava and urged him to provide protection to witnesses and assure confidentiality of statements.

Prioritizing the Terms of Reference

The second point had to do with the four terms of reference proposed by the state government which stretched from the growth and spread of Naxalite activities in the state to future policy directions. Although it may be a welcome move to understand the issue in the broadest possible terms, we contended that the commission was set up to inquire into the unlawful murder of persons in violation of the law, and to provide a measure of public confidence in the justice system at a time when people were agitated about this situation. Therefore, the murders, torture and terror that triggered this unrest must be investigated first. We needed to first determine whether these were murders, or armed encounters, or acts of self-defence. If they were murders, it was necessary to determine who the killers were. These were two immediate tasks before the commission. It was necessary, we argued, to prioritize the terms of reference of the commission.

Investigation of Incidents of Murders and Torture

The third point raised in our memorandum was very important. What would be the sequence in the investigation of murders and torture? According to information gathered by us, during 1969–76/77, at least 250 people had been killed in encounters. Of these, we had collected detailed evidence pertaining to nineteen deaths. We also had preliminary evidence pertaining to the deaths of seventy to eighty Naxalites. It was possible that other organizations also had some more information. We therefore felt that it would be easier for the commission to proceed with its inquiry incident-wise. This was necessary in view of the fact that there was no reliable government agency which could be entrusted with the task of gathering this evidence.

Continuation in Office of the Present Government and Officers

There are serious allegations of torture and murder against government officers. Facing such serious charges, the chances of the officers and the government itself disappearing witnesses and destroying evidence were high. If they continued in positions of authority and decision making, these chances would be even greater. Therefore, we demanded that the officers facing allegations of torture, murder and intimidation must be suspended from their jobs pending inquiry. If it was not possible to suspend them, such officers must be transferred to another state and junior-level personnel must be transferred to other districts pending inquiry. If the government was unwilling to take these steps, we cautioned the commission that the continuation of such government itself would be detrimental to the inquiry.

Necessity of Interim Reports

If the commission, in the course of its inquiry, arrived at findings on particular incidents, it would be advisable to release such findings to the public in the form of interim reports. It was our view that such public communication would give moral courage to the countless witnesses who were hesitant to come forward, and would convince them that this commission was committed to arriving at the truth in this matter.

Summoning of Necessary Official Documents

The commission had already started gathering evidence from witnesses through a public notification. However, that announcement did not mandate the submission of relevant documents and evidence from the central and state governments. We requested the commission to requisition specific documents from the central and state governments. In the event of the government not complying with the commission's direction, we demanded that the documents be officially seized by the commission. The official documents listed by us in the memorandum were as follows:

1. Official government documents pertaining to the Naxalite issue, and the specific directions and orders issued by the Andhra Pradesh government to the police department;
2. Details of programmes organized by the police on this issue;
3. Details of transfers of police officers and orders in the previous three years, and especially in the three preceding months;
4. Details of rewards given to police officers from 1969 to 1977 and the reasons for the rewards;

5. Details of travel logs and bills filed by police officers from 1967 to 1977 in areas designated as Naxalite-prone;
6. All post-mortem reports, panchnamas and inquest reports of persons said to have died in encounters during 1969–77;
7. Travel details and reports for the preceding two years of police officers who were part of teams involved in alleged encounters with Naxalites from 1968 to 1977;
8. Telephone bills of the chief minister, chief secretary, IGP and DIG for the period 1968–77;
9. Register of wireless messages transmitted between Mulugu–Gajwel–Siddipet–Hyderabad; Vijayawada–Khammam; Yellandu–Hyderabad; Srikakulam–Hyderabad, and all records pertaining to the same; and
10. Records pertaining to the travel and log books of police personnel travelling to Hyderabad city from Medak, Warangal, Khammam, Krishna and Guntur.

We demanded in our memorandum that these documents be immediately secured by the commission, and the departments concerned directed to hand the same over to it, and that these documents not be transmitted to the commission through the government of Andhra Pradesh. The commission only agreed to a couple of our demands: that witness protection shall be provided and the order of incidents inquired into need not be fixed. The police opposed our demand for the confiscation of official documents. The government counsel stated that it was not possible to comply with that demand. If we had managed to get hold of even one of these documents, the facts behind fake encounters and the misuse of public funds would have been revealed.

In its inquiry into the Giraipalli encounter, the Bhargava Commission nominated a few experts from different fields, a handwriting expert, Prakash Rao, who was to assist Shiv Shankar, and a few others. On the whole, there were twenty-five witnesses from our side and a few more from the government side. Our first witness was Challa Narasimha Reddy, an advocate from Siddipet, who gave us an excellent statement. The cross-examination was started by Prakash Rao. Narasimha Reddy tore him to pieces. When I think of it, the way Narasimha Reddy conducted himself that day was nothing short of brilliant. We were still confronted with a major issue: How should we ensure protection of witnesses? How should we bring them to appear before the commission, and how should we ensure that they reach back home safely without being abducted or harmed by the police? We did not tutor our witnesses to speak even a single untruth. Even ordinarily, I have always said in court that if you utter the truth, no matter how many times and before how many people you repeat it, and no matter how many times you are cross-examined, your statement will remain the same. It is only when you lie that your account changes from one recounting to another. This was not a practice generally followed by lawyers. They tended to tutor witnesses, which would lead to their faltering during cross-examination. The person who gathered the evidence pertaining to the Giraipalli incident was Rajkumar, a student of the Regional Engineering College, Warangal, and a leader of the Radical Students' Union. He would accompany witnesses to the commission and give us information about witnesses. He would bring the witnesses to our home in Domalguda after 9 p.m. A small house which doubled as my office, it was always bustling with relatives and children. The witnesses would also stay there with us. I conducted the preliminary examination of the witnesses in my home. When I spoke to them, I was confident that all of them were speaking the truth, and instructed them to truthfully state what they knew and had witnessed before the commission. We had to take utmost care, because if the police got scent of the details of any witness, his safety would be jeopardized. M. Omkar, an MLA belonging to the CPI(M), was also very supportive of our work and took a keen interest in the proceedings of the commission.

M.V. Ramamurthy and I would go directly to the commission. Shiv Shankar had no idea how to cross-examine witnesses. His cross-examination was limited to taking one sentence from the statement and putting a question to the witness: 'You have said this, I put it to you that you are not speaking the truth; what do you say to that?' It was in the course of this inquiry that I realized why prosecutions fail. Inspectors and prosecutors always think about how a statement can be made to sound rational and foolproof. They prepare a strategic plan, and get the witnesses to present their plan. But witnesses, or anyone for that matter, can only state what they see. If they have not witnessed an incident, they will not be able say anything about it. It matters little how famous the lawyer is. What happens in fact is this. This is also the reason why prosecution witnesses often contradict their statements or turn hostile.

It was precisely because we did not tutor our witnesses that Shiv Shankar was unable to unsettle any of them. In the inquiry into the Giraipalli encounter, Shiv Shankar cross-examined the witnesses a day after they recorded their statement. He would always seek permission to cross-examine them on the following day. I, on the other hand, would never ask for time.

We had almost completed the inquiry into the Giraipalli incident. The only witness to be examined was T. Kameshwara Rao, inspector of the Special Branch. In order to help me in the inquiry, senior journalist Adhiraju Venkateswara Rao met Kameshwara Rao over drinks, got him to talk and recorded the exchange. Kameshwara Rao did not know the conversation was being recorded. He blurted out all the details in a drunken state. I handed over the tapes given to me by Venkateswara Rao as evidence to the commission. Kameshwara Rao denied that the voice on the tape was his. This went on for a few days. Friends like K.S. Gopal and Sashi worked untiringly on the tapes—running them back and forth for hours and transcribing them. A lot of people attended the Bhargava Commission hearings. The Muktadar Commission that inquired into the rape of Rameeza Bee the following year had hundreds of people attending its hearings. In comparison, the Bhargava Commission had fewer people. But there is no doubt that it was a really good inquiry. Justice Bhargava was a very principled person—he had served as a district judge, high court judge and Supreme Court judge.

While the inquiry was in progress, a person by the name Kondaiah read the reports in the press and came forward to record his statement as a witness. The conduct of the police with respect to his statement is one that must be discussed. Vallabhaneni Kondaiah, a young man, worked as a fitter in Bajaj Automobiles in Pune. He was a student at the Central Institute of Tool Design in Hyderabad, and had rented a room to stay. Murali Mohan and Ananda Rao, who were killed in the Giraipalli encounter, were arrested from Kondaiah's room. Kondaiah was also arrested, detained for a few days and let off. He later took up the job in Pune. After reading about the Bhargava Commission proceedings, Kondaiah wanted to testify. He came directly to me. He was very concerned that two people apprehended from his room had been killed in what was alleged to be an encounter. He expressed regret at the fact that he was not able to do anything. He was a reliable witness to the arrest of Murali Mohan and Ananda Rao.

Before Kondaiah came to me, there were some witnesses staying with me. It was winter, I think. One of them had no shirt on. I gave him my shirt to wear. That night, when he walked out to smoke, he was abducted and taken away in a police jeep. The next day, Shiv Shankar stated before the commission, 'Kannabiran is holding witnesses in unlawful custody; here is one such witness', and he produced this person. He said I was forcing people to testify.

I asked the witness only one question: 'Did I ask you to say anything?'

'No, ayya. You asked me to state what I knew.'

'Did I tell you that I would give you a shirt or something else if you record your statement?'

'Wasn't it I who asked you for a shirt since it was cold and I did not have a shirt to wear, ayya?'

Justice Bhargava did not take serious note of this, but I am recalling this as an illustration of the way in which prosecution lawyers try to derail or mask facts by taking recourse to pettiness.

Even while cross-examining Challa Narasimha Reddy and Bhikshapathi, the prosecution lawyers focused all their attention on these kinds of petty, inconsequential details. The prosecution submitted a petition to the commission that I had confined Kondaiah and was forcing him to bear false witness, and that Kondaiah should be removed from my custody. As a matter of fact, when advocate A. Ramakrishna, who was Shiv Shankar's junior, filed this petition, Kondaiah was not in my home. I refused to file a counter-petition. The question was not whether I held Kondaiah in custody. The fact was that I only produced witnesses who of their own accord expressed the desire to testify. So I took a principled stand not to file a counter. I told the commission that they could arrive at the truth on their own. Then Justice Bhargava directed that the witness be brought to his chamber. He refused the police request to keep him in a hotel with his uncle. It is possible that the counsel of elders can be wrong, he said. The effort by the police to intimidate Kondaiah and his uncle rebounded in this manner. Kondaiah was made to sit in Justice Bhargava's chamber.

I requested Justice Bhargava to settle this matter first before I proceeded with my work, since there were unfair allegations against me. I told him that if it was found that I had confined this witness and forced him to give false testimony, I would withdraw from the commission's proceedings. I went out, and sat smoking a cigarette. Justice Bhargava questioned Kondaiah on the facts. Kondaiah told him that when he saw the news reports on the commission in the newspapers, he felt it was his responsibility to approach the commission and state what he knew about the incident: 'Two of my friends were taken away from my room in my presence. After that the police announced that they had been killed in an encounter. I feel I must say somewhere that this is a falsehood. I have just arrived from Poona after reading the news of your commission. Even yesterday I was not in Hyderabad. I found out who the lawyer was who was representing the victims, and went to Kannabiran garu's house this morning, and came here from there. Nobody has forced me to testify.' Kondaiah's statement was clear. Justice Bhargava dismissed the prosecution's petition and continued the inquiry in a very principled manner.

Several witnesses were examined. The witness statements, Bhargava's interventions and the cross-examinations were widely reported in the press. I was able to convince the people that what I was presenting before the commission was nothing but the truth. I was able to establish conclusively that the Giraipalli incident was not an armed encounter as the police were claiming; that the four people had been held in illegal custody, tortured for days, tied to trees and shot dead.

There are a couple of other points about this inquiry. The four people who were killed along with several others had been held in illegal custody in Nilagiri Rest

House and tortured. Because they had been held in custody for several days, the arrested persons got to know the names of the officers responsible. They were able to give us the names of intelligence and other officers who interrogated them, and were able to recognize them. It was then that I unexpectedly got some information. This was the time when the Secunderabad conspiracy case hearings were proceeding full steam. There was a prosecution witness called Pachipalu Venkulu in that case. The police told the court that he had participated in the offences being tried and had turned approver under police protection. He was housed in some police station, or office or guest house. Because he was from the working class, they would keep asking him to do odd jobs for them. They allotted to him the job of shredding some old papers and incinerating them. In those days, the police would retain some record of the work they did—even the most heinous acts were recorded somewhere.

A word on how police records are maintained. Earlier, FIRs were sequentially numbered in a book for FIRs—in order to write an FIR, a sheet would need to be torn from this book, so there was a record of the number in the counterfoil as well, like a bill book. But the police did not comply with procedure. In Chandra Pulla Reddy's case, for instance, we found that an FIR sheet had an earlier date than the FIR sheet with the previous number in the sequence. It was on that basis that we were able to argue effectively and win. After that the police stopped using sequential numbers for FIRs. On the whole, the police made no effort to maintain systematic records. And so they delegated the task of destroying old records to Pachipalu Venkulu.

Among those papers was a memorandum that announced rewards and promotions for police personnel who had participated in the Giraipalli encounter. Pachipalu Venkulu brought this paper to me. By then the examination of the witnesses had been completed. While I was thinking about how I should proceed, this memorandum was delivered to me. If I stated that I had a copy of this memorandum, I might be told that it was not authentic; they could say that I had fabricated this document; they could ask me how I got hold of the document—and thus derail the proceedings. Instead, I asked the commission to direct the police to produce the memorandum that stated who the officers were who participated in the encounter, and details of the rewards given. Shiv Shankar, arguing for the state, claimed privilege in respect of these lists. Justice Bhargava overruled this claim of privilege. I asked Panchagnula Satyanarayana to argue on this point. Justice Bhargava announced a change in procedure. He said that he would not share the list with us since it was a privileged document, but when the said police officers faced cross-examination, we could ask them, based on the information we had, whether they had received rewards or not. If they denied receiving the rewards, he would make a decision by referring to the list on his file and record false testimony. The list had names of several police officers. They could not deny that they had received rewards and promotions. After all, they could not lie before the commission. Further, they all knew that Justice Bhargava had the official list with him. Each one took the witness stand—one said he was given Rs 2,000, another that he received Rs 1,500, yet another that he had received Rs 1,000.

I had proved my point. The same officers I had named as the perpetrators of torture in Nilagiri Rest House were the ones listed in the memorandum to receive rewards and promotions. So there was a connection between Nilagiri Rest House, the Giraipalli encounter and the distribution of rewards. The prosecution brought an inspector named Sriramulu from central Intelligence. I examined him. There was a secretary in the home department at the centre called Srinivasan Varadarajan, who met Justice Bhargava and informed him that just as Shiv Shankar was being paid Rs 1,500 a day by the state government, Home Minister Charan Singh was of the opinion that Kannabiran should also be given the same remuneration. When Justice Bhargava informed me that the central government would like to pay a remuneration to one of the three lawyers representing the defence and sought our consent, we refused. He then asked me to meet him in his chambers. 'I received information from the central government. They had an inquiry conducted on you by a Central Intelligence officer. I know you have a good practice. But you are putting that aside and assisting the commission. So please accept some remuneration for this work,' he said. I replied that I did not want the remuneration; I was doing this work because of my political convictions, not in anticipation of rewards. If I had accepted, I would have got about Rs 80,000–90,000 by then—a huge amount in 1978. It did not make a difference to me. I declined the offer.

After that, on each day when the hearings were posted, Ananta Babu and Shiv Shankar kept expressing their inability to be present using one pretext or another. Finally, Justice Bhargava told them, 'Kannabiran is attending the hearings purely on personal commitment, taking no remuneration, so I can accept his request if he is unable to appear on a particular date. But the two of you have been hired for this job and are receiving remuneration for your work. You will have to be present on any day that I require your presence here.'

I filed a petition before the commission that we should go to Giraipalli and visit the forest where the encounter took place. The police filed a counter. They submitted an illustration of a forest to Justice Bhargava, which showed a dense green forest with reddish earth. They told him it was a dense forest and it would be difficult to go there. I insisted that Justice Bhargava must see the forest and that there would be no problem going there. We left for Giraipalli. Justice Bhargava and I were in an Ambassador car. Before we reached, the police said it would not be possible to go there in a car, that we must transfer to a jeep. I said we would go as far as the car could take us and walk from there or get into the jeep at that point depending on the distance. I asked our driver to proceed. Our car went right up to the trees to which Janardhan, Murali Mohan, Ananda Rao and Sudhakar had been tied and shot. We then went to the spot where they had been cremated. Janardhan's father gave his ashes to me, and I had them immersed in the Hussain Sagar. This is another illustration of the uncivilized, unlawful way in which the police conducted themselves.

Justice Bhargava was studying the proceedings very carefully. His copy of every statement was marked in red and blue during the cross-examination. He told me in no uncertain terms, 'You have proved your case.' I then requested him to release an interim report with his decision on the Giraipalli incident. He refused, saying that he would wait till the entire inquiry was completed before presenting his decision. I felt this approach of his was unreasonable and was upset by this.

At one stage, Justice Bhargava ordered the CBI officers who were with him to find out whether the police were interfering with witnesses. The officers wrote about how the police were interfering with and intimidating witnesses. Justice Bhargava sent his officer to record the statements of witnesses in Giraipalli, among whom there was a police witness. I think his name was Komarrayya. Half an hour before he reached there, the local Special Branch police visited the witnesses, got them drunk and induced them to give false testimonies. On his return, the officer saw some Special Branch personnel at the bus stand, and, suspicious that they might have intimidated the witnesses in Giraipalli, he went back and recorded fresh statements. He submitted these statements to Bhargava. There were so many incidents like this during the hearings of the Bhargava Commission. Even while we were engaged in arguments around Kameshwara Rao's tapes, we thought about which incident we should present for inquiry next.

When we got the report that the police were intimidating witnesses, I went to Giraipalli and sat in the open, smoking. The villagers were looking at me suspiciously. They would not speak their mind until they were sure they could trust me. I kept talking to them and did not ask any questions.

I casually said to them, 'After all, the police are saying the four Naxalites killed in Giraipalli were responsible for Donthula Anthaiah's murder. Then what is wrong with the police killing them?'

An uneducated shepherd was among the villagers gathered around me. He had probably never seen a school. He retorted, 'Then why do you have courts, ayya?'

I felt at the moment that the sense of the rule of law that this shepherd had was something the police lacked. Even our lawyers do not understand the rule of law. I went to court from Giraipalli. A few lawyers met me and we were chatting. This was at the time that the Justice Bhargava Commission was in full swing.

One lawyer came up to me and asked in impeccable English, 'Mr Kannabiran, why should Naxalites who have no faith in the Constitution or law be given the protection of the Constitution or law?'

He thought he had posed a profound question for which I would not have an answer. In response, I narrated the incident with the shepherd in Giraipalli, 'That shepherd has never been to school. Your parents have spent considerable resources on your education, and yet you have not the faintest idea of the rule of law. Your education has been a waste,' I said.

We decided to take the Chilakalagutta incident in which Ramanarasaiah was killed. Even as we were planning this, a key witness in that incident, Pritam Singh, was abducted by the police. Ramanarasaiah was staying in Pritam Singh's house in Old Malakpet at the time of his arrest. After the Bhargava Commission inquiry commenced, Pritam Singh decided to record his statement. He saw the board of public prosecutor K.V.N. Narasimha Rao and went in because it was a lawyers' office. The public prosecutor made Pritam Singh wait in his office and called the police, who apprehended him there and took him to Nagpur. As soon as I came to know of this, I filed a petition in the court against all three public prosecutors, and argued that all of them should be disqualified and removed from their positions since they were conducting themselves like salaried employees of the police department. As a result of my arguments in the Shadnagar court and the high court, all three public prosecutors were divested of their jobs. It was only after that case that the necessary qualifications for appointment as public prosecutors were specified through an amendment in the law. In Ramanarasaiah's case, Omkar brought some witnesses, but I did not have confidence in them. They would narrate how Ramanarasaiah and others were arrested and taken in vans to Warangal and Chilakalagutta. Hearing them, I felt that anybody could give statements like this, there was nothing that set them apart. The key witness was Pritam Singh, who alleged that Ramanarasaiah was arrested from his house. But for the inquiry on this incident to begin, his presence was necessary. Had Pritam Singh been able to record his statement before the commission, we would have had conclusive evidence on the Chilakalagutta case, like we did on the Giraipalli case.

I decided to defer the inquiry on Ramanarasaiah's case and suggested to my team that we should inquire into the Yellandu case where Neelam Ramachandraiah and Jampala Chandra Sekhar Prasad were killed. I had the post-mortem report in this case, a fact the police were not aware of. According to the report, the two had been shot in the chest from very close range. In an exchange of fire, these injuries were unlikely. Dr Y. Radhakrishna Murthy helped me get hold of these post-mortem reports. In those days, the CPI(M) members helped a great deal in securing evidence of the encounters involving Naxalites. The first witness in this encounter case was K. Lalita. She was earlier a PDSU leader, and had been an eyewitness to the arrest of Jampala Chandra Sekhar Prasad. At the time of the inquiry, IPS officer Roddam Prabhakar Rao was the managing director of the Andhra Pradesh State Road Transport Corporation. He was the officer who arrested Lalita during the Emergency, and subjected her to brutal torture. She narrated to Justice Bhargava the details of the torture she underwent. She identified Roddam Prabhakar Rao. Her statement was published widely in newspapers—readers now knew how brutally a woman had been tortured in police custody.

There was a psychiatrist in Hyderabad called Dr Majid Khan. He phoned me while the Bhargava Commission inquiry was in progress: 'I heard that you have made a representation to the central government regarding some police officers. Can you tell me the names of the officers listed in your representation?' We used to send the list of police officers named in the course of our investigation in the Tarkunde Committee to the central government in sealed covers. The officers were really scared that their names might be in the sealed covers. One of them consulted Dr Majid Khan for therapy. Dr Majid Khan asked me to read the names of the officers out to him, so that if the officer consulting him was on the list, he could treat him more effectively. I said to him, 'Doctor, you are a doctor by profession. Can I ask you who your patients are and what they are being treated for? You must protect their confidentiality. I too, like you, am in a profession. I will not ask you who the officer is who has been mentally disturbed by the Bhargava Commission and is seeking treatment from you. You don't ask me whose names are on my list.' Later, I got to know the names of the officers who had sought psychiatric treatment during the inquiry.

What the police do not realize is that when they torture a person in custody, that person will never forget them. In their dealings during torture, the police call out to each other by name. Therefore, the detenus remember the names of the officers. When they take the witness stand, they tell us what they remember. The police began to argue that if details were published in this manner it would be a blow to the morale of the police force. If the police say that this retelling of experiences of torture is a blow to their morale, we can understand how low and weak their moral standards are.

The police officers then went in a delegation to Chief Minister Chenna Reddy and created a ruckus.[4] They argued that it was difficult for them to work if their

4 J. Vengal Rao (Congress) was the chief minister when the Bhargava Commission commenced its proceedings in July 1977. After the assembly elections in March 1978, M. Chenna Reddy (Congress) became the chief minister, assuming office on 6 March 1978, and accomplished the task of winding up the commission of inquiry in July 1978.

dignity was assaulted in this manner. Chenna Reddy decided to stop the proceedings. He notified that the proceedings of the inquiry should be held in camera. As an in-camera proceeding would not ensure the safety of the witnesses, other members of the committee and I, after due deliberations, walked out of the inquiry. We informed Justice Tarkunde and Justice Bhargava that we would not participate in an in-camera inquiry and withdrew. Thus ended the effort to fight this dastardly habit of the state known as encounters.[5]

The Justice Bhargava Commission had to close down without completing any of the tasks before it. That was tragic. However, for the short period that it carried out its work, it revealed many important truths to the people. By July 1978, the Bhargava Commission could no longer continue its inquiry.[6]

Both the Shah Commission and the Bhargava Commission were really good commissions that did very good work. They would have provided a road map to the government to put in place policy measures for good governance. Yet, it was the government itself that derailed the Bhargava Commission, just in order to protect a few police officers. There was no report put out by the commission. Its proceedings revealed the vengefulness and cruelty with which the police could

---

5 'The police had been saying that they had not been doing any encounters. On the contrary, they were confronted with the encounters and therefore they have to fight. Well, how far it is true I cannot say. But later events – *later events* – give an impression to me – *give an impression to me* – that the encounters did not appear to be the real encounters. They were make-believe affairs and people were killed.' P. Shiv Shankar in *The Advocate*, a documentary film on K.G. Kannabiran, (D&N Productions, 2007). Repetitions with emphasis by the speaker. Part 2: at 11:34-12:15/39:50. https://www.youtube.com/watch?v=lrLStnOMP4s&t=10s. Accessed on 13 October 2021.

6 'I don't think it went off more than 8 days or a little more. I don't remember now.' 8:33/39:50; 'But the commission felt that, and *perhaps rightly so*, that it was sought to be scuttled.' 8: 49-8:52/39:50. P. Shiv Shankar in *The Advocate* (documentary film on K.G. Kannabiran, D&N Productions, 2007). Emphasis added. Part 2: https://www.youtube.com/watch?v=lrLStnOMP4s&t=10s. Accessed on 13 October 2021. Reports of the commission show that it heard the cases for eleven months, and that it was stalled by Chief Minister M. Chenna Reddy, who succeeded J. Vengal Rao and came to power in March 1978, by which time the Bhargava Commission had already completed eight months. See also 'Justice V. Bhargava: Disgusted with Andhra Pradesh Government'. 1978. *India Today*, 15 July, https://www.indiatoday.in/magazine/indiascope/story/19780715-justice-v.-bhargava-disgusted-with-andhra-pradesh-government-818432-2015-01-24. Accessed on 5 October 2021.

conduct themselves, and demonstrated the fact that they were capable of every kind of conspiracy to stall an inquiry. The worst part of this was that the state supported, encouraged and participated in this unlawful conduct by the police.

On the whole, the Bhargava Commission was a very rich experience.

Justice Muktadar Commission of Inquiry, 1978

Rameeza Bee was gangraped in a police station in Hyderabad on the intervening night of 29-30 March 1978. And her husband, Ahmed Hussain, beaten to death when he confronted the policemen about Rameeza's rape the following morning, on 30 March 1978. Rameeza Bee was less than twenty years of age. She and her husband were returning home after watching the second show of a film, when Rameeza was arrested on charges of practising prostitution.[7]

The custodial violence and murder of Ahmed Hussain in the Nallakunta police station and the rape of his wife in the same police station triggered widespread protests in the state, which soon grew into protests against the government. A one-man Commission of Inquiry was constituted by Chief Minister M. Chenna Reddy under the Commissions of Inquiry Act, 1952, with a sitting judge of the Andhra Pradesh High Court, Justice K.A. Muktadar, to inquire into the incidents of rape and custodial death. This Muktadar Commission was notified on 7 April 1978; it submitted its report to the government on 10 May 1978. Between April and May, both the Bhargava Commission and the Muktadar Commission were inquiring into deaths and violence in police custody in Andhra Pradesh. The Bhargava Commission wound up in July 1978 without being allowed to complete its task, and the report of the Muktadar Commission was tabled in the Andhra Pradesh Legislative Assembly in August 1978.

The police deliberately refused to cooperate with the Muktadar Commission and did not extend any support mandated by law. On the other hand, the police and the state openly provided support to the policemen accused in the case. The police, at different levels, were asserting themselves as an independent force. This made one wonder, even at that time, whether the government had even minimal control over the police, which was part of the government; and whether the political

7 The name of the victim–survivor is mentioned here, as all the public records, news reports, reports of the commission of inquiry conducted by a sitting high court judge, Justice K.A. Muktadar, legislative assembly debates and court judgments, dating back to 1978–82, identify her by name. The case itself is remembered as the Rameeza Bee case.

leaders who came to power had any commitment at all towards reining in the police and bringing them within the rule of law.

Justice Muktadar was a good judge. He was appointed to this commission of inquiry when he was a sitting judge of the high court. He took his task very seriously. Till that point he was not aware of the atrocities the police were committing routinely although he had practised for a long time as a lawyer. As soon as the commission was notified, Madhusudhan Raj of the Vimochana Party came to me and gave me the vakalatnama. The CPI(M) participated in the inquiry, while the CPI did not.

The Muktadar Commission hearings, conducted in the premises of the Andhra Pradesh High Court, were open to the public, and there would be 1,000–1,500 people attending the sessions every day.

In my view, a very significant fact that came to light in the course of the commission hearings was the links between the police, sex workers, brokers and others who provided related services. In fact, I stated this to Muktadar in a packed court—that there was a nexus between organized prostitution, the police and middlemen.

The post-mortem report of Rameeza Bee's husband, Ahmed Hussain, said that he died of heart attack. There was no reference whatsoever to the injuries and wounds on his body. There was no attempt to ascertain whether there may be any other cause of death. Forensic expert Dr Khandlikar wrote that report. In the matter of this crime, he shielded the police completely. I cross-examined him during the hearings of the commission. The problem in this country is that all the institutions that are meant to support the people or the justice system in inquiries of this kind are tilted completely in favour of the offenders. In the event of the offender being a policeman, the police, instead of investigating him, spend all their energies finding ways of extricating him from the investigation. The forensic department finds ways of falsifying/changing evidence so that the police officer escapes conviction. This was Khandlikar's work in the Rameeza Bee–Ahmed Husain case.

A doctor called Nagaraj conducted the post-mortem. He prevaricated so much during the cross-examination that the commission reprimanded him and made a note of this aspect as well. There was a circle inspector in the Kachiguda police station called Ramana Reddy. He made a strange announcement during the hearing. In response to a routine question from me during cross-examination, he said that the general diaries in police stations were printed by private printers. And that the diaries had the logo of the government. The general diary is extremely important in the law and order responsibilities of the police. It is a department book in which the police records details of crimes as they come to their notice. The crime entries must be made chronologically—there cannot be entries made randomly anywhere in the book. These diaries are printed by the government and distributed to police officers. But Ramana Reddy said they were available in the market and were printed by private printers.

In that commission, the only point that the government, police and their witnesses tried to establish was that Rameeza Bee was a prostitute. My argument was that even if she was a prostitute, the police had no right to do what they did to her and her husband.

There was another strange aspect that surfaced in the hearing. The police gathered all the pimps, brokers and prostitutes from all the police station limits and produced them as witnesses before the commission. All of them together tried to establish that Rameeza was a prostitute. This reminds me of an amusing incident. They brought a pimp from the Afzalganj police station. His statement made everyone burst into laughter.

Cross-examining him, I asked, '*Aapka dhanda kya hai?*' He said, '*Dhanda karta hun, saab.*' Meaning, he organized prostitution. This man was a key witness produced by the police. He said, '*Hamaare customer bade officer log hai, saab.*' [Our customers are all big officers, sir.] He said this openly, unhesitatingly. I asked him if police officers also went to him. '*Haan, aate, saab. Bade police officer aate, saab.*' [Yes, they come, sir, big police officers come, sir.] He said this much to the amusement of Justice Muktadar.

The police produced witnesses like this and tried to prove that Rameeza Bee was a prostitute. There was no connection between the proceedings and whether or not she was a prostitute. People may think it is a strategy to distract or divert the inquiry; it is in fact a stupid strategy.

After the inquiry concluded, Muktadar wrote a good report.[8] My regret is that even though the report was tabled in the legislative assembly, it did not result in the conviction of the perpetrators.[9] Even before the trial of the accused policemen began, they had the case transferred to Raichur in Karnataka through a petition in the Supreme Court, saying that a sessions judge in the state in which Justice Muktadar was a sitting high court judge would be biased against them. Advocate Sripati Rao was the public prosecutor and advocate Seethapathi was the defence

---

8 Report of the Commission of Inquiry (to enquire into the detention of Sri Ahmed Hussain and Smt. Rameeza Bee, death of Ahmed Hussain, etc. Constituted under Notification GO Ms. No. 263, General Administration (General–A) Department, dated 7 April 1978, by the Hon'ble Sri Justice K.A. Muktadar. Andhra Pradesh, Hyderabad.

9 'Discussion on the Report of Muktadar Inquiry Commission'. 1978. *Andhra Pradesh Legislative Assembly Debates*, Vol. 8, No. 2, 7 September, pp. 196–251.

lawyer.[10] The Raichur court held that there was no evidence against the accused and acquitted them. The appeal in the Bangalore High Court too went in favour of the accused.[11] All the evidence that was gathered by the commission went waste, and none of its findings came on record in the trial.

One day, many years later, when I was travelling to Delhi, a policeman saluted me at the airport. I wondered who he was. He said, '*Kya, saab, mai yaad nahi hai aapko? Aap mere khilaaf lade the naa, saab, woh Rameeza Bee case mein, main Surendar Singh, acquit ho gaya saab.*' [What, sir? Don't you remember me? You appeared against me in that Rameeza Bee case. I'm Surendar Singh, I got acquitted.]

Justice H.A. Iyer Commission of Inquiry, 1983

In March 1983, hundreds of tobacco farmers in Tangutur, fifteen kilometres from Ongole, Prakasam district, called for a rail and 'rasta roko' agitation to demand better prices that favoured tobacco growers instead of the burden they bore in a traders' market that depressed prices to the detriment of the farmers.[12] The demonstrators first went on a hunger strike. When the government did not respond to their demands or show any signs of opening up talks, their unrest grew. The police officers who went to break the demonstration took an executive magistrate along. Ordinarily, such an executive magistrate is a lower-level revenue authority. This was basically to sanction firing on the crowd. Three people died in the firing, and six were injured.[13]

Chief Minister N.T. Rama Rao was forced by the Opposition to constitute a judicial inquiry into the firing during a stormy debate in both the Houses on 15 March 1983, a day after the firing.[14]

---

10 Sessions Case No. 33/1980, *State of Andhra Pradesh vs T. Surendar Singh and Ors*, district and sessions court, Raichur.

11 Criminal Appeal No. 238/1981, *Sayeed Ahmed and Ors vs State of Andhra Pradesh* and Criminal Appeal No. 34/1982, *State of Andhra Pradesh vs T. Surendar Singh*. Decided during 7–8 March 1984, Karnataka High Court at Bangalore (unreported). The editor is grateful to Justice Goda Raghuram for a copy of this judgment.

12 Menon, Amarnath K. 1983. 'Deaths of Three Tobacco Growers in Andhra Bring into Focus the Plight of the Farmers'. *India Today*, 30 April.

13 'Tobacco Growers' Stir Turns Violent: 3 Dead in Firing at Tangutur'. 1983. *Indian Express*, 15 March, p. 1.

14 'Judge to Probe Tangutur Firing', *Indian Express*, 16 March 1983, p. 1.

Justice H.A. Iyer was appointed as the one-man commission under the Commissions of Inquiry Act, 1952, to inquire into the police firing in Ongole. On our way to the hearings in Ongole town one day, we saw a large number of policemen in mufti intimidating people and preventing them from attending the hearings. When we entered the hall where the hearings were to take place, the first five rows of chairs were occupied by policemen in mufti, according to information given to us by local people. We informed Justice Iyer of this immediately. On seeing that the judge had been informed of their presence, they left the hall.

This was not our first experience of such intimidation. When Justice Bhargava had commenced his inquiry in Lakeview Guest House a few years earlier in Hyderabad, a junior judge, Purushottam Reddy, was on his way there to testify before the commission. Although he was stopped at the gate and ordered to go back by a police officer, he went ahead and recorded his statement. When he reached home, the owner of the house he had rented, a police officer, asked him to vacate immediately.

Coming back to Ongole, although the hearing was completed, Justice Iyer—a good person with whom I had developed cordial relations during the inquiry—wrote a report that the police firing was unavoidable given the circumstances, and that none of the demonstrators/witnesses had been able to identify the policemen who had allegedly opened fire on them.

Conclusion

The police get away with murder in this country. Take the case of a lock-up death in the Chandrayangutta police station in Hyderabad. As soon as I heard of it, I filed a petition in the high court, and the court appointed a commissioner to inquire into the incident. When the commissioner visited the police station, the sub-inspector was not present, and there was only one sentry on duty. When asked for details of the incident, the sentry stated that the deceased person wandered around the police station for a bit, and then asked him to open the cell, which the sentry did. He then went in and consumed cyanide that he was carrying with him! After all, the police lock-up is the only place where a person who is vexed with life can safely commit suicide. These are the kind of cock-and-bull stories the police fabricate and we believe.

We expect that a government constituted by elected representatives will function with rectitude and diligence. We expect that such government will put in place the plans and policies that will further the effectiveness of laws and the Constitution. We expect that people's representatives will take the responsibility of disciplining the government and ensuring that it does not turn authoritarian. We expect that we will have a justice system in which judges are non-partisan and fair. We expect simplicity and honesty from our elected political leaders and judges. We expect that especially when they have been vested with the authority, they will act self-consciously and with humility. But all these expectations crumbled in the course of the first decade after Independence. The harsh reality of where we had arrived hit all of us in June 1975 with the declaration of Emergency. Even a court which ought to have firmly held its ground capitulated to authoritarian rule in June 1975.

Following this, when the Janata Party government was elected to power in 1977, several commissions of inquiry were set up under the Commissions of Inquiry Act, 1952. The primary purpose behind the setting up of these commissions was to understand the process of the erosion of governance. At that time, we felt that it was necessary to take stock of the situation. The purpose was to restructure governance, not to review the Constitution—and the reports of these commissions, it was believed, would aid the government in this task. However, this was not achieved. And yet, the demand for a judicial commission became a standard political demand every time there was a major irregularity in governance or administration.

Extraordinary tenacity is required to carry out long-term political struggles around issues. But in the short term, each struggle requires a point of resolution or conclusion. The demand for a judicial inquiry is one such resolution that struggles/movements arrive at. The most unresponsive government too cannot ordinarily refuse this demand. The purpose of commissions of inquiry is to make judicial processes transparent and accessible to common people, and open a route to formal justice. But our political system has perfected the art of subverting democratic processes. Commissions are now used to defer matters that require immediate resolution. We cannot of course change the entire system overnight. But it is our responsibility to keep chipping away at the system and bring in small reliefs from time to time. This is the work the civil liberties movement has been engaged in.

9

Encounters in the 1980s and 1990s

THE CONGRESS GOVERNMENT returned to power in the centre in 1980. In the month of September, ten persons were shot dead in two separate encounters in Warangal and Nalgonda, and from then on encounter killings continued as usual. During 1980–89, 203 people were killed in encounters, and twenty-one people taken into custody disappeared. When Mandadi Ravinder Reddy and Parsaiah, accused in the Secunderabad conspiracy case, were killed immediately after being produced for judicial remand before the judicial magistrate in the compound of the Suryapet magistrate, and when two more young persons were shot dead in the month of October in Suryapet, we filed a writ petition in the Supreme Court, which was numbered WP (Criminal) 68 of 1982. Before that, as part of our fact-finding mission, we met the Suryapet magistrate and asked him, 'They were in judicial custody and you allowed them to die?' George Fernandes was in the team that interviewed that magistrate in Suryapet. Our petition was kept pending in the Supreme Court till 26 March 1993 and it came up before Justice Kuldip Singh and Justice Yogeshwar Dayal who passed the following order:

> These writ petitions relate to the alleged fake encounters stated to have taken place during the period 1980–81. Due to the lapse of time no useful purpose will be served to continue with these petitions. We therefore dispose these petitions as having become infructuous.[1]

---

1 Cited in written arguments before the NHRC inquiry on encounters, 1997. On file. See NHRC, *Annual Reports 1995–96* and *1996–97* for details of the inquiry.

Before passing this order, the Supreme Court directed us to make a representation to the state government. Our other petitions on extrajudicial killings were dismissed by the Supreme Court on the grounds that we could file private complaints. Considering we petitioned the court that the police establishment was killing people as a matter of policy, we were surprised that an issue of such an endemic nature was disposed of so perfunctorily. We always held the view that every court, from the lowest to the highest, should be primarily a court of human rights. We never believed that violations of human rights should be inquired into by institutions other than courts. It was our conviction that if institutions of justice were able to take a firm stand on human rights, the rule of law would become a reality. But we were also acutely aware of the failings of courts at every level. They faltered in offering protection to life and liberty. And yet, there were notable exceptions.

Madhusudan Raj Yadav

Madhusudan Raj Yadav was a very quiet young man. I presided over his wedding. He must have been around forty-two years old when he died. His father was a government employee. I have so many happy memories with Madhusudan Raj. One day as I was walking from Golconda Crossroads to Gandhinagar, Madhu stopped his scooter next to me and said, 'Sir, why do you walk around alone like this? Anyone can do anything to you. Please don't walk around alone.'

He dropped me off at my friend's place on his pillion. Earlier, Madhusudan Raj was active in the PDSU. When Kaloji contested the assembly elections against Chief Minister Vengal Rao in 1978, Madhusudan Raj played a major role in the election campaign.

Madhu was shot dead by the police in a house in the Gandhinagar locality in Hyderabad on 26 July 1995. The next day's newspapers carried a report by the police that an unidentified Naxalite from the People's War Group had been killed in an encounter in the city.[2] By that time, these fabricated stories of the police had become common. While I was in the high court that day, one of my juniors came up to me and said, 'Sir, this looks like Madhusudan Raj. Apparently he has not been contactable since this encounter took place.' I felt that this should not happen to someone like him. Although my attitude to every encounter is the same, I had known Madhusudan Raj for over fifteen years and felt there was need for urgent intervention.

I walked into the court hall and made an oral application: 'There is a report of an encounter. The details raise suspicions, and the police are planning to dispose

2 *Indian Express*, 27 July 1995.

of the body before it is identified. I suspect that the person killed in the encounter is Madhusudan Raj Yadav. If it is him, I know him very well. I presided over his wedding. We must ensure that the body is not disposed of before it is identified. If it is him, the body should be handed over to his family.' I also informed the court that I would file a writ petition on the grounds that this was a fake encounter. The high court bench, in response to my oral application, gave interim orders that Madhusudan Raj's wife, Swarna, and his father, Neelakantha Yadav, should identify the body in my presence and prohibited the police from disposing of the body:

> It goes with the duty of the police and it needs no reiteration that every case of homicide in whatever circumstances it occurs has to be registered as a case for investigation and the police for the said reason is duty-bound to make all efforts to secure the identification of the victim of the homicide. Since no formal application has been made and there is no appearance before us of any person on behalf of the State, it is not possible for us to know whether police has registered a case and has taken steps to secure the identification of the victim of the homicide or not. We, however, see justification in the prayer made on behalf of Smt. Swarna and Sri T. Neelakantha Raj Yadav and the submissions of Sri K.G. Kannabiran for immediate order of the Court:
>
> (1) that the Director General of Police, Andhra Pradesh and the Commissioner of Police, City of Hyderabad, shall ensure that the body of the alleged Naxalite which is kept in the mortuary in Gandhi Medical Hospital, Secunderabad, is not interfered with and kept in the mortuary until Smt. Swarna and Sri T. Neelakantha Raj Yadav, the wife and father of Sri. T. Madhusudan Raj Yadav, are permitted to see the dead body and accordingly identify whether the dead body is of T. Madhusudan Raj Yadav or of some other person;
>
> (2) that the Superintendent, Gandhi Medical Hospital, Secunderabad, is directed to keep the dead body of the alleged naxalite in the mortuary and not to permit anyone to remove the body from the mortuary until further orders of the Court; and
>
> (3) Sri K.G. Kannabiran, Advocate, is permitted to accompany Smt. Swarna and Sri. T. Neelakantha Raj Yadav and be present at the time of the identification of the dead body by them.[3]

Two weeks later, after hearing the arguments and counter-arguments, and taking note of the investigation, the then chief justice, Justice Prabha Shankar Mishra,

---

3 *K.G. Kannabiran vs Chief Secretary, Government of Andhra Pradesh and Ors* (14.08.1995: APHC). 1995 (2) ALT (Cri) 490; MANU/AP/0710/1995, para 1.

and Justice C.V.N. Sastri delivered an important and far-reaching judgment on 14 August 1995. They held that

> We have good reasons to order that the case of assault by the police personnel upon Madhusudanraj Yadav should be registered and investigated by some independent agency and not by any person connected with the Andhra Pradesh Police. The main reason for our taking this view is the way the counter-affidavit has been filed to justify why a case has not been registered and why the police party which accomplished its task by arresting Lingamurthy decided to lie in wait to arrest Madhusudanraj Yadav. It is a fit case, in our opinion, in which a direction be issued to the Government of the State of Andhra Pradesh to give sanction and accordingly entrust the case to the Central Bureau of Investigation and direction is issued to the Central Bureau of Investigation through the Central Government, i.e., Union of India represented through the concerned Secretary in the Ministry of Home for registering and investigating the case of the alleged assault resulting in the death of Madhusudanraj Yadav. The Director General of the Central Bureau of Investigation is directed to appoint a team of officers, if necessary, to investigate the case. The State Government and the Director General of Police, Government of Andhra Pradesh, are directed to fully co-operate with the investigation. [4]

There are some important aspects of this judgment. The report on his death was registered in Mushirabad Police Station under 'Crime no. 150/95'.

> According to the First Information Report, it was he who committed the offence of interfering with the discharge of duty of the informant and others who had come to arrest him. He allegedly grappled with them, wriggled away, took out his revolver and fired at them with the intention to kill them and in self-defence they returned the fire resulting in his instantaneous death. In the scuffle one constable received injuries. In all these Madhusudanraj Yadav received several bullet injuries and one constable received some injury obviously not caused by a fire-arm. Do we have the law that a group of police personnel will report that they were making arrest of a person who attempted to evade the arrest and since in his attempt to evade the arrest he used force, they returned the force and caused his death and the law would accept the statement and sanctify the end of a life in accordance with the procedure

4 Ibid., para 12.

> prescribed by law? We have already noticed the guarantee under Article 21 of the Constitution of India and also the words 'procedure established by law' are not ineffective and lifeless but are expressions of the faith of the people who have sanctioned interference with the life of a person only by a procedure which is reasonable, fair and just. Indian Penal Code has defined 'culpable homicide' as follows: 'Whoever causes death by doing an act with the intention of causing death, or with the intention of causing such bodily injury as is likely to cause death, or with the knowledge that he is likely by such act to cause death, commits the offence of culpable homicide.'
>
> It is difficult even to imagine that Police Officers who used fire-arm to hit at the body of Madhusudan Raj Yadav were not aware that by such act they were likely to cause his death. Of course, what they did had a justification or not and, although falling within the definition of an offence, the act by them is excusable or not are matters which shall be dealt with but only when the truth or otherwise of their plea is tested in accordance with law. It will neither be correct nor proper at the outset to ignore altogether the act of the commission of the offence and not to register a case at all of a homicide at the hands of the police personnel who allegedly fired at Madhusudanraj Yadav. We have given our anxious consideration to the matter before us and we see good reasons to hold at this stage that on the statement of the same very police personnel who have alleged that Madhusudanraj Yadav fired at them but caused no injury by the fire-arm, and that they fired at him and as a result, Madhusudanraj Yadav got fatal injuries, a case should have been registered and investigated in accordance with law by the competent authorities.[5]

If this legal reasoning is to be translated into commonly understood terms, let us assume it was an encounter. Even so, the fact remains that the death of one person has been caused by another, and therefore, it must be registered as a case of murder. During the trial, the person responsible for causing death may explain the circumstances in which he acted in self-defence.

This important judgment was delivered exactly twenty years after the Bhargava Commission. The Andhra Pradesh High Court bench in this case repeated exactly what I had argued before the Bhargava Commission. For twenty-five years, we had been persistently arguing that these were fake encounters, murders by the state. In this case, the high court also held that these were murders which must be registered

---

5 Ibid, para 11.

as murders and investigated according to procedure established by law. We called the then chief minister, J. Vengal Rao, a killer. He was the architect of fake encounters in this state. He was the one who encouraged murder by encounters and converted it into a method of rule. Or we may say that IGP M.V. Narayana Rao scripted the method and Vengal Rao adopted it.[6]

Justice Prabha Shankar Mishra's judgment in the Andhra Pradesh High Court was historic. I felt that day that the high court judgment calling out this brutal method of murder by the state was the fruit of my arduous labour and struggle over decades. It was my personal victory, and the victory of the civil liberties movement that I had led.

NHRC and the Justice Ranganath Mishra Inquiry into Encounters in Andhra Pradesh

Alongside this, we undertook another task. K. Balagopal and I prepared a petition that was submitted to the National Human Rights Commission (NHRC). That petition emphasized the enormity of the problem of encounter killings in Andhra Pradesh, providing details of 250 deaths in encounters in the state.

Justice Ranganath Mishra was the chairman of the NHRC. Although there were divided opinions about him, he was among the best judges to have occupied that position. He had the courage of conviction to take a firm stand. While submitting the petition to him, we requested him to tour the state and familiarize himself with the situation on the ground, and he agreed. In this process I met him several times. The inquiry by the NHRC took place in 1994–95.[7]

---

6 Menon, Amarnath K. 1979. 'Despite police brutality, Andhra Pradesh government honours its police chief.' *India Today*. 31 December. https://www.indiatoday.in/magazine/indiascope/story/19791231-despite-police-brutality-andhra-pradesh-government-honours-its-police-chief-822321-2014-02-11. Accessed on 6 May 2022; Menon, Amarnath K. 2019. 'Judge, Jury and Executioner'. *India Today*, 10 December; Rao, N. Venugopal. 2007. Fake Encounters: Story from Andhra Pradesh. *Economic and Political Weekly*, Vol. 42, No. 41, 13 October, https://www.epw.in/journal/2007/41/commentary/fake-encounters-story-andhra-pradesh.html. Accessed on 6 May 2022.

7 See report on hearings 'Cops Rough up Kannabiran', *Deccan Chronicle*, 8 August 1994; National Human Rights Commission, *Annual Report 1995–96*, p. 11, para 3.11: 'Allegations of "fake encounter" continue to be heard, particularly from areas of armed militancy. The Commission views such charges with utmost seriousness and probes them thoroughly in exercise of the powers conferred on it by the Statute

Justice Ranganath Mishra came to Andhra Pradesh and held meetings at four or five places. Even while he was here, the police in Warangal and Anantapur attempted to physically attack Balagopal. I decided to attend the inquiry scheduled to be held in Nalgonda and informed Justice Mishra on the phone. I told him that we wanted to show him the true character of the Andhra Pradesh Police and that I would demonstrate this to him in Nalgonda. I was invited to the dais with Justice Mishra. The police brought a gang of rowdies to the meeting, who began to shout slogans and tried to disrupt the meeting. As I got off the dais and went towards them, Special Branch police in mufti surrounded me and began to push, jostle and manhandle me. I think Gopinath Reddy was the SP of Nalgonda—he just stood by and watched while I was being pushed around. After a while, pretending to intervene, he walked me to my car. Vasanth had accompanied me to Nalgonda. She drew Justice Mishra's attention to what was happening off stage. Till then, his attention was directed elsewhere. He had not seen what was happening to me. He was very angry. He cancelled lunch and the remaining programme, summoned the police, vented his anger on them and asked for an explanation. They cooked up some story.

---

to call for reports, conduct an investigation or hold a regular enquiry. For instance, in the course of 1995, a special Bench of the Commission was constituted to enquire into the allegations of false encounters made against the police in Andhra Pradesh by the Andhra Pradesh Civil Liberties Committee (APCLC). The Bench held public sittings in Hyderabad and recorded evidence. As important questions of law regarding proper procedure to be followed in the matter of registering the cases and conducting of investigation arose for consideration, the Commission notified the Solicitor General of India and the Advocate General for the State of Andhra Pradesh. On grounds of convenience, arguments were heard at the Headquarters of the Commission and final orders are expected to be pronounced shortly.' (Under the Chairmanship of Justice Ranganath Mishra.) In its *Annual Report, 1996–97*, under the chairmanship of Justice Venkatachalaiah, the NHRC issued procedural guidelines on the investigation of 'encounters': 'The Commission intends to monitor this matter most carefully, and it will, if necessary, designate specially selected representatives to assist it in this task. The Commission considers the practice of "fake encounters" to be unconscionable. It cannot permit the right to private defence, spelt out in Chapter IV of the IPC, to be manipulated to justify "fake encounters", or the procedures of Section 46(3) of the Code of Criminal Procedure to be subverted to serve such an end.' Para 3.17, p. 13. See especially letter of NHRC chairman Justice M.C. Venkatachalaiah to the chief ministers of all states dated 29 March 1997. NHRC, *Annual Report 1996–97*, Annexure VI, pp. 107–09, https://nhrc.nic.in/sites/default/files/Annual%20Report%201996-97.pdf. Accessed on 7 September 2021.

After this, Justice Ranganath Mishra returned to Hyderabad and commenced an inquiry into encounter deaths. Of the 250 cases we had placed before him, he asked us to select five or six cases on which he would conduct an inquiry. There was an unusual obstacle we faced. He said there was a limitation in that he could only inquire into encounters that had taken place one or two years prior. This surprised me because it did not make any sense. There can be no limitation of time for investigation or inquiry into crime, especially murder. Yet, there was a provision that remained in the law—any of our learned judges could at any time have struck it down, but this did not happen. Justice Mishra now pulled out that limitation. As a matter of fact, since an inquiry of this nature could not result in conviction, at least it would have had a disciplining effect on police lawlessness, and the facts could be made public.

Once the inquiry commenced in Dilkusha Guest House, the police bribed witnesses, and made sure key witnesses did not testify. They brought in witnesses to give false testimonies. In one word, the police conducted themselves exactly as ordinary criminals and murderers would.[8] While this inquiry was in progress, police officer Dinakar Prasad began to intimidate witnesses and threaten them. Justice Mishra summoned and censured him. Dinakar Prasad was the police officer who arrested Bangalore University professor Nagari Babaiah and interrogated him. He accused Babaiah of arranging rental accommodation for Kondapalli Seetharamaiah, and other such allegations. During the interrogation, Dinakar Prasad and Babaiah were seated on either side of a table—less than two feet between them. He picked up a paperweight from the table and threw it at Babaiah. His aim was so good that according to reports the paperweight missed Babaiah and hit the leg of an inspector sitting at the far end of the room, resulting in a fracture. That was how perfect his aim was. And they claimed that they fired from a distance but shot the target. Justice Mishra ordered Dinakar Prasad to leave the premises.

Once the inquiry was completed, Justice Ranganath Mishra said that all the incidents he inquired into were murders, and that they must be properly investigated and tried in a court of law. The following year, in 1997, the NHRC, under the chairmanship of Justice Venkatachalaiah, carried Justice Mishra's findings forward and issued directions to all chief ministers in the matter of

8 For a news report on the conduct of the police during the same proceedings in Warangal and Nalgonda see front page headline: 'Cops Rough up Kannabiran', *Deccan Chronicle*, Monday, 8 August 1994.

encounters, following directly from our petition to Justice Ranganath Mishra and the hearings of the NHRC.[9]

Conclusion

I am reminded of an old case of Syed Bin Ali, a mafia gang leader in Hyderabad who was shot in the post–Rameeza Bee riots in 1978. His wife saw him being shot and filed a writ petition in the high court. I saw a young man arguing and told him that I would argue this case. I started arguing thinking at least in the case of a rowdy the high court may hold that this encounter is a crime. I argued before Justice Muktadar and told him that the presumption is that killing in self-defence is murder, and it has to be registered as a murder. The person who claims he killed in self-defence has to establish it in a court. I showed him the Evidence Act and he referred it to a bench. When the matter went to the bench the public prosecutor asserted that he had a right. So I told the judge, 'Sir, I will rest for two to three hours. Let the public prosecutor search for the provision which enables a police officer to shoot to kill a person and place it before you. I will wait for him. Today, tomorrow, you can give him any number of days to search for the provision. I will wait.' It could not be found. Justice K. Ramachander Rao asked me, 'Why is it a police officer is given a firearm?' I replied that he was given a firearm to be used only in self-defence: 'While regulating peace, while regulating people, processions and maintaining peace and public tranquillity, there may be situations where he would have to defend himself. So he is given that gun. He is not given that gun to be trigger-happy and shoot everybody.' By and large what I found was that I was able to deal with the judges very effectively and they had very liberal values, a very sturdy common sense and a sense of justice.

In the case of Madhusudan Raj Yadav, the government filed an appeal in the Supreme Court, which was dismissed at the admission stage. And yet, before Justice Ranganath Mishra and on every possible occasion thereafter, the government would assert that this case could not be considered as its appeal was pending. The then DGP, H.J. Dora, kept repeating this and diverting the attention of the court, fully aware that his statement was false.

---

9 Letter of NHRC chairman, Justice M.C. Venkatachalaiah to the chief ministers of all states dated 29 March 1997. NHRC, *Annual Report 1996–97*, Annexure VI, pp. 107–09, https://nhrc.nic.in/sites/default/files/Annual%20Report%201996-97.pdf. Accessed on 7 September 2021.

In the case of another encounter, an advocate approached the court for another judgment of this nature. This was a misguided move since there was already a judgment in place, and all we needed to do was find ways of forcing its implementation. There are protocols that must be followed, especially by lawyers appearing in political cases. It is our responsibility not to cause any undue hardship to litigants; not to roll back political gains that have already been won; and to exercise duty of care to ensure we do not act in a manner prejudicial to progressive politics. With this new case before it, the three-judge bench decided that Prabha Shankar Mishra's judgment must be examined by a larger full bench to determine whether the judgment delivered by Justice Mishra was correct or not.[10] This is the stage we had reached in matters of encounters in courts.[11]

All through this period, murder by encounters became the method of governance.[12] It was only in the matters of right to life and liberty that there was a doubt about whether this right was worthy of protection. The problem with encounters is that there is indifference among the general public. There is no investigation according to procedure. Where an investigation is conducted, it is the murderers who investigate. Even judges with liberal values lacked empathy especially in cases of the right to life and liberty.

Encounters are not a complex matter. There is an international standard on extrajudicial murders by the state, and there are conventions that set out the norms. Today, we are also at the stage where we are demanding that revolutionary groups respect human rights and the rule of law. The tradition of respect for human rights renders political organizing more effective and meaningful. There is a universal consensus that limitations must be placed on the exercise of authority. Violence

---

10 *Andhra Pradesh Civil Liberties Committee & Ors vs State of Andhra Pradesh and Ors.* 2007 (5) ALT 639; MANU/AP/0488/2007. The three-judge full bench referred the case to a larger full bench.

11 The full bench consisting of five judges held that an independent FIR shall be registered on a specific complaint made alleging that any identified individual had caused death on account of bullet injuries in an encounter with the police and in the absence of such a specific complaint the police had to follow the procedure under Section 176 of the CrPC without prejudice to investigation. *Andhra Pradesh Civil Liberties Committee vs Government of Andhra Pradesh,* 2009 (2) ALD 1. This was the last case on 'encounters' in which K.G. Kannabiran appeared.

12 For a recent report, see, Asian Human Rights Commission (AHRC), 2018. *The State of Encounter Killings in India: Target, Detain, Torture, Execute.* New Delhi: ACHR, https://www.ecoi.net/en/file/local/1457651/1226_1549878602_encounterkillingsindia.pdf. Accessed on 7 October 2021.

erodes the ends of struggle and weakens them. Encounters target particular political groups and decimate political dissent. Some political groups target the Constitution and decimate its enemies in similar fashion. The murders of police officers in the state are examples of this. We have Hindu mythological stories that justify impunity. Take the example of Hiranyakashipu. He sought a boon of life with impunity—that he may not be killed by day or by night, by human or by animal, indoors or outdoors—putting him above punishment irrespective of his actions. What I have learnt from this story is that impunity multiplies danger. Every religion will have similar examples of the sanction of impunity. But these stories also tell us that impunity has its limits. There have been big leaders and police officers who thrived on impunity for a time, but were brought down by the power of peoples' resistance.

The photographs are from the Kannabiran family's personal collection. We are grateful to the photographers who documented K.G. Kannabiran's life and work at various stages.

L-R: Patel Sudhakar Reddy (killed in a police encounter in 2009), Shakamuri Appa Rao (killed in a police encounter in 2010) and Modem Balakrishna – co-accused in the Bangalore conspiracy case (A-14, A-8 and A-46, respectively), being led into court in chains. For a detailed account of this case see Chapter 6, 'Naxalite Conspiracy Trials in Andhra Pradesh.' See also Chapter 18: 'Peace Talks in Andhra Pradesh.'

Cricket Match between Chief Justice XI and Kannabiran XI in Lal Bahadur Stadium on Friday, 18 April 1997. Chief Justice Prabha Shankar Mishra hits a shot with well-known lawyer K.G. Kannabiran bowling. (Source: *Eenadu*, Saturday, 19 April 1997). In 1995, K.G. Kannabiran filed a writ petition in the Madhusudhan Raj Yadav encounter case, in which Justice Mishra wrote a landmark judgment (see Chapter 9, 'encounters in the 1980s and 1990s', especially section titled 'Madhusudhan Raj Yadav').

Dr A. Ramanadham sitting in a protest (third from left). On his right is the poet Varavara Rao. See Chapter 3, section on Andhra Pradesh Civil Liberties Committee for details of Dr Ramanadham's work and death.

Dr A. Ramanadham (1933–85), paediatrician and vice president, Andhra Pradesh Civil Liberties Committee, was shot by unidentified policemen in his clinic in Warangal on 3 September 1995.

At APCLC, 9th State Conference, 6–7 January 1996, Mahaboobnagar.

APCLC president M.T. Khan (in white), who was imprisoned during Emergency and a co-accused in the Secunderabad conspiracy case discussed in Chapter 6.

L-R: Civil liberties leader Professor G. Haragopal; K. G. Kannabiran; human rights advocate, Telugu writer, poet and Dalit leader Bojja Tharakam (1939-2016); and noted literary critic and scholar Professor Chekuri Rama Rao (1935-2014). Bojja Tharakam appeared for detenues in the Emergency cases (Chapter 4, 'The Emergency'), and represented the victims' families in the Karamchedu and Tsundur cases (Chapter 13, 'Dalits and the Rule of Law'). Prof. Haragopal and senior advocate Tharakam were and members of the Concerned Citizens' Committee which initiated the peace talks between Maoists and the government of Andhra Pradesh (Chapter 18, 'Peace Talks in Andhra Pradesh'). This photo was taken at the book release of Varavara Rao's *Sahacharulu* in 1990, published in the English as *Captive Imagination: Letters from Prison* (Penguin/Viking, New Delhi, 2010), republished in Telugu in 2019 while he was in custody.

With Swarnalatha, wife of Madhusudhan Raj Yadav, who was shot in an encounter in Hyderabad in 1995. For a discussion of this case, and the landmark judgment of Chief Justice Prabha Shankar Mishra on encounters, see Chapter 9, 'Encounters in the 1980s and 1990s', especially section titled 'Madhusudhan Raj Yadav'.

Early 1970s with advocate V. Venkataramanaiah, a close friend, who was later advocate general, Andhra Pradesh High Court.

Kannabiran with advocate B. Chandrasekhar (1966–2013) in Guntur, 1989. Chandrasekhar was the special public prosecutor in the Tsundur case of the massacre of Dalits.

Kannabiran, Vasanth and daughter Kalpana, 1969.

K.G. Kannabiran, Vasanth Kannabiran and grand-daughter Ramya with members of K.G. Kannabiran's office – lawyers and clerical staff, c. 1996/97.

Kannabiran and Chandrasekhar addressing the victims' families in Tsundur after the 2007 verdict of the special court convicting the accused in the Tsundur massacre case under the SC/ST Prevention of Atrocities Act, 1989.

K.G. Kannabiran and Vasanth being honoured at the 'siropao' ceremony held at Gurudwara Sri Nanak Jhira Sahib, Bidar, after KGK represented the victims' families in the Justice P.K. Shyamsunder Commission that enquired into the murder of Sikh Students in Bidar, Karnataka, in 1988.

Press briefing at a protest site, Hyderabad, 1984.
Photo credit: Navroze Contractor.

K.G. Kannabiran in 2008.

R-L: Nikhileswar, KGK, Jwalamukhi and Bojja Tarakam. Nikhileswar, who received the Kendra Sahitya Akademi award in 2021, and Jwalamukhi (1938-2008) were among the Digambara poets jailed for their writing (see the chapter on Emergency).

Second conference of All India Peoples' Resistance Forum, mid-1990s.

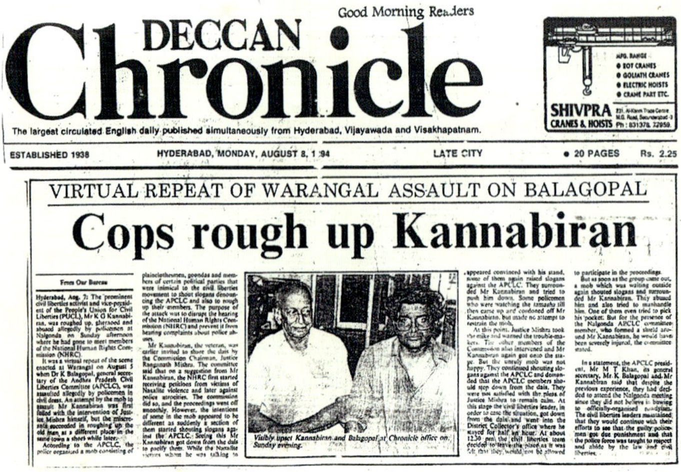

Good Morning Readers

DECCAN Chronicle

The largest circulated English daily published simultaneously from Hyderabad, Vijayawada and Visakhapatnam.

ESTABLISHED 1938 | HYDERABAD, MONDAY, AUGUST 8, 1994 | LATE CITY | • 20 PAGES | Rs. 2.25

VIRTUAL REPEAT OF WARANGAL ASSAULT ON BALAGOPAL

Cops rough up Kannabiran

From Our Bureau

Hyderabad, Aug. 7: The prominent civil liberties activist and vice-president of the People's Union for Civil Liberties (PUCL), Mr K G Kannabiran, was roughed up, gheraoed and abused allegedly by policemen at Nalgonda on Sunday afternoon where he had gone to meet members of the National Human Rights Commission (NHRC).

It was a virtual repeat of the scene enacted at Warangal on August 5 when Dr K Balagopal, general secretary of the Andhra Pradesh Civil Liberties Committee (APCLC), was assaulted allegedly by policemen in civil dress. An attempt by the mob to assault Mr Kannabiran was first foiled with the intervention of Justice Mishra himself, but the miscreants succeeded in roughing up the old man at a different place in the same town a short while later.

According to the APCLC, the police organised a mob consisting of plainclothesmen, goondas and members of certain political parties that were inimical to the civil liberties movement to shout slogans denouncing the APCLC and also to rough up their members. The purpose of the attack was to disrupt the hearing of the National Human Rights Commission (NHRC) and prevent it from hearing complaints about police abuses.

Mr Kannabiran, the veteran, was earlier invited to share the dais by the Commission Chairman, Justice Ranganath Mishra. The committee said that on a suggestion from Mr Kannabiran, the NHRC first started receiving petitions from victims of Naxalite violence and later against police atrocities. The commission did so, and the proceedings went off smoothly. However, the intentions of some in the mob appeared to be different as suddenly a section of them started shouting slogans against the APCLC. Seeing this Mr Kannabiran got down from the dais to pacify them. While the Naxalite victims whom he was talking to appeared convinced with his stand, some of them again raised slogans against the APCLC. They surrounded Mr Kannabiran and tried to push him down. Some policemen who were watching the *tamasha* till then came up and cordoned off Mr Kannabiran, but made no attempt to restrain the mob.

At this point, Justice Mishra took the mike and warned the trouble-makers. The other members of the Commission also intervened and Mr Kannabiran again got onto the stage. But the unruly mob was not happy. They continued shouting slogans against the APCLC and demanded that the APCLC members should step down from the dais. They were not satisfied with the pleas of Justice Mishra to remain calm. At this stage the civil liberties leader, in order to ease the situation, got down from the dais and went into the District Collector's office where he stayed for half an hour. At about 12.30 pm the civil liberties team decided to leave the place as it was felt that they would not be allowed to participate in the proceedings.

But as soon as the group came out, a mob which was waiting outside again shouted slogans and surrounded Mr Kannabiran. They abused him and also tried to manhandle him. One of them even tried to pick his pocket. But for the presence of the Nalgonda APCLC committee member, who formed a shield around Mr Kannabiran, he would have been severely injured, the committee stated.

In a statement, the APCLC president, Mr M T Khan, its general secretary, Mr K Balagopal and Mr Kannabiran said that despite the previous experience, they had decided to attend the Nalgonda meeting since they did not believe in bowing to officially-organised rowdyism. The civil liberties leaders maintained that they would continue with their efforts to see that the guilty policemen got due punishment and that the police force was taught to respect and abide by the law and civil liberties.

Visibly upset Kannabiran and Balagopal at Chronicle office on Sunday evening.

Deccan Chronicle, Monday, 8 August 1994. Report of assault by police during NHRC hearings on Encounters in AP. (See Chapter 9, 'Encounters in the 1980s and 1990', especially section on NHRC hearings). In photograph, K.G. Kannabiran and K. Balagopal (1952–2009).

At the conference of the Indian Association of Lawyers, Vijayawada, 1989.

Sidam Shambhu (1968–2018) with Kannabiran, Hyderabad 2010. Shambhu from Adilabad was a widely respected Adivasi leader from the Gond community, and was a co-founder of Adivasi Hakkula Porata Samithi – Tudum Debba (see Chapter 12, 'Tribes in Fifth Schedule Areas', especially the section on Arka Vasanth Rao and Gondwana Sangharsh Samithi).

10
The Death Penalty

Right to Life and Abolition of the Death Penalty

OSCAR WILDE'S *DE PROFUNDIS* always come to my mind when the state punishes people, more so when a person is sentenced to death:

> Society takes upon itself the right to inflict appalling punishment on the individual, but it also has the supreme vice of shallowness, and fails to realise what it has done. When the man's punishment is over, it leaves him to himself; that is to say, it abandons him at the very moment when its highest duty towards him begins.[1]

The latter half of the twentieth century saw a sea change the world over in the matter of the extreme penalty of death, with country after country outlawing it totally, or confining it to war crimes or putting a moratorium on its implementation as an experimental step. A total of 118 countries have taken one of these three steps, while India is among the seventy-six nations that have resisted reform in this matter. The abolitionists are not countries that do not know of acts of organized violence and terror such as India is witnessing. The most enthusiastic abolitionists are Latin American nations that are plagued by all the problems India is familiar with. Yet

1 Wilde, Oscar. (1905) 2007. *De Profundis.* https://www.gutenberg.org/files/921/921-h/921-h.htm. Accessed on 26 October 2021.

they have risen above the immediate context and seen that the death penalty is the last remnant of the uncivilized attitude to punishment that was widely though not exclusively prevalent the world over once upon a time. Namely, that the perpetrator of the offence must suffer what the victim has suffered, an attitude that is popularly and pithily described as 'the philosophy of an eye for an eye'.

It is my firm belief that if we recognize the rights of the people and restructure our institutions from the standpoint of people's rights, the positive values of our society will be enormously strengthened. If we only understand society through the barrel of the gun—whether on the side of the government or on the side of the revolutionaries—we only hurtle towards destruction of our society and its values. A true democracy is one in which rights and life are respected. It is for this reason that when we argue on the death penalty awarded by courts, one argument is: Why should this person be killed? Another argument is: Why should he not be killed? Hearing both sides, if the judges then conclude after due deliberation that the person facing trial should be executed, it is still murder in my view. Nothing less. The crime of murder is defined as the intentional, conscious, premeditated act of killing a person. All these ingredients of the crime of murder are present in the death penalty. Of course, historically, death has been the punishment for certain crimes. At all times, the kin of victims demand the death penalty for the perpetrator. However, what is silenced in the debate on the death penalty is the fact that the opponents of the death penalty do not for a moment argue that there should be no punishment. There are punishments worse than the death penalty—imprisonment for life, for instance. Those who insist that the perpetrator of a crime must die forget that there are other punishments. If it is argued that the wishes of the kin of victims must be honoured in sentencing, we could find ourselves in a situation where the only acceptable punishment for all crimes would be the death penalty.

However, the fundamental characteristic of a fair trial and humane sentencing is the non-partisan application of the rule of law, and the elimination of personal views, vengefulness and individual retribution. We have won significant victories in establishing these principles in institutions of justice. We have for the most part been able to eliminate the role of personal views in deliberations on justice—focusing instead on a dispassionate application of procedure established by law. It is for this reason that I always feel that the idea of the 'rule of law' is a precious gift of bourgeois society. Of course, the bourgeois classes themselves eroded it subsequently, especially when compliance was not in the interests of their class—yet, the value of that gift endures. It is irrelevant here to ask questions like 'whose rule of law' or 'whose justice'. The moment we ask the question 'for whom', the course of justice is derailed. It is only when the personal element enters the deliberation on law that justice is defeated. Handing over a case or a crime to an impartial body to investigate and thereby ensuring the elimination of personal considerations is of utmost importance.

There is an argument that there will be no fear of consequences if the death penalty is abolished; that there will be an increase in crime; and that it is the death penalty that keeps crime in check. Abolitionists have never argued that the perpetrator of a crime should be let off without punishment. In a trial that establishes beyond reasonable doubt that a person has committed a crime, and that he is guilty of murder and atrocity and must be punished, he will be awarded one of two punishments: either imprisonment for life or the death penalty. My point is simple: it is life imprisonment that should be awarded, and not the death penalty.

There is a convention followed in India that the death penalty should be awarded only in the rarest of the rare cases.[2] What do we mean by 'rarest of the rare'? How is it to be defined? It is impossible to define 'rarest of the rare'. We have no instrument or method to measure the rarest. Therefore, what comes into play in settling this dilemma and providing a means for 'measurement' is the personal prejudice of the judge. This has made judgments on the death penalty an expression of personal views. Once a judge determines and rules that a particular case comes within the meaning of the rarest of the rare, it cannot be changed by anyone. In such cases, there is no possibility to open up a deliberation on the attributes of the crime and contest its definition as rarest of the rare.

The option left in this scenario is to sidestep the definition of crime and show other reasons why the punishment may be amended. Even the parliament and the president can only consider mercy petitions without reference to the definition of the crime by the court. In this process, it becomes necessary to take into account the circumstances leading to the crime, the perpetrator's social location and his social and political values, since the court has already taken a decision on whether the crime constitutes the rarest of the rare. The president therefore cannot reopen that question—he can only think of the crime and the punishment outside of that definition, and without reference to it.

I must narrate the details of a few cases where I intervened before I discuss the political cases.

---

2 For a discussion on the Vijayavardhan Rao–Chalapathi case, see Kannabiran, K.G. 2004. *The Wages of Impunity: Power, Justice and Human Rights*. Hyderabad: Orient Longman, pp. 190–94.

Murder and the Death Penalty

The jailor in Secunderabad jail, Narasimha Reddy, called me to meet a prisoner on death row. The prisoner also wrote me a letter from the jail. The man from Medak district in Andhra Pradesh was awarded the death penalty in a case of rape and murder. He was a very poor man from a backward caste—with a wife and child and 1 acre of land. The district judge expressed an opinion that he must have committed the crime since he was poor. This is a view that is very common in our society—that the poor commit crimes and poverty drives people to commit crimes. The death penalty in this case was confirmed. I met him and asked him whether he had committed the crime. If so, why did he do it? He wailed that he had been falsely implicated in this case. There was no clear evidence pointing to his involvement in the crime. He had a conflict with the owner of the land next to his. That owner wanted him to give over his land, and to achieve this implicated him in this case of rape and murder. He was convicted to death by hanging by the judge on the basis of that suspicion on the basis of statements given to the police during a police investigation. The case was posted before the bench of Justice Ramanujulu Naidu. I entered appearance and argued that these statements were not admissible at all. I read out the judgment of the sessions court, pointed out that he had been awarded the death penalty on the basis of suspicion, and argued for ten minutes. Justice Ramanujulu Naidu agreed with my arguments and acquitted the man. I had no difficulty at all in getting him acquitted.

When K.C. Abraham was the governor of Andhra Pradesh, he sent me a referred trial pending in the high court for confirmation of death sentences, and requested me to represent the accused. They were two brothers, sons of a retired police constable who killed their father. I think they slit his throat. They were angry with their father for getting drunk every day and battering their mother. Not able to bear this brutality inflicted on their mother they decided to put an end to their father's life. They were arrested and one of them was sentenced to death by the sessions court. When the matter came up for confirmation to the high court, I argued and succeeded in having the sentence commuted. The advantage with this provision was that the entire case would be reheard and the evidence re-examined to find out whether evidence against the accused led to a conclusion beyond reasonable doubt that the accused were guilty. Such a procedure assures us that the system respects life as a very important value in our democratic set-up. A referred trial has a human rights facet. The other important step towards preserving life is the provision that makes the death sentence alternative to life imprisonment. By a series of decisions, the court has laid down that a death sentence can be imposed only in the rarest of the rare cases. This was on account of the relentless campaign carried on by the abolitionists. In the matter of terrorist laws, however, this referred trial procedure has been dispensed with.[3]

The Sheikh Mahboob Subhani case in Guntur in 1999 was a case of unpardonable violence against a young woman. Subhani inflicted fatal wounds on this young woman's face. There was a furore in various sections of society and a campaign demanding the imposition of the death sentence by a section of the public. There was a resolution of the Bar Association not to provide him any legal assistance. This was a trend I had witnessed in the Parliament attack case. In the case of Subhani, the one defence lawyer who appeared also withdrew, and an overzealous district judge who had no understanding of the theory of justice in courts and the role of a judge in the justice system sentenced him to death, literally playing to the gallery. In the referred trial, the bench of Justice R.M. Bapat and Justice D.S.R. Verma held that such judges should not be given sessions powers and insisted on a retrial. However, as there was some cross-examination of a few witnesses the case was remitted back for cross-examination of the rest of the witnesses and posted before a sessions judge in Vijayawada. I was appointed as state brief counsel to complete the task. I examined other witnesses and did not contest his conviction but canvassed for a life sentence. I was happy to argue before an understanding young judge who agreed with me and sentenced him for life.[4] I addressed a letter to the Bar Association, stating the reasons why advocates should not pass a resolution of this kind. Barring advocates from defending certain unpopular accused is a very uncivilized method of functioning in a society. It is often found to be very communal as well.

Once, I received a petition from a convict lodged in the death cell in the central prison in Belgaum, Karnataka, awaiting execution. He was a tailor living with his fairly rich sister. He had access to her jewellery, which he would remove periodically and pledge to borrow money for purchasing cloth for stitching ready-made garments. After making the garments, he sold the clothes in the market, redeemed the jewellery and put it back where it was stored. One does not know for how long he had been doing this. But one day, as he was removing the jewellery, his aunt walked in. It was at night and in the panic of being discovered, he picked up a *katthi peeta* (vegetable cutter with a base) and attacked her; when her daughter

3 For a detailed discussion on the implications of terrorist laws for deprivation of life in the case of the murder of General A.S. Vaidya, see Kannabiran, K.G. 2004. *The Wages of Impunity: Power, Justice and Human Rights*. Hyderabad: Orient Longman, pp. 102–06.

4 'College Girl Murderer gets Life Imprisonment', *Times of India*, 27 November 2001. https://timesofindia.indiatimes.com/city/hyderabad/college-girl-murderer-gets-life-imprisonment/articleshow/2062449136.cms. Accessed on 10 October 2021.

came in, he attacked her too and both died in the attack. He surrendered to the police. He was sentenced to death and was in the death cell in Belgaum. I did not believe this was a case where he merited a death sentence. The course of his conduct showed that he was fond of his sister. The breach of trust in his act of stealing his sister's property stares at us. But could the act of replacing the jewellery after redeeming it faithfully be called a breach of trust and theft and wrongful conversion? There were several grey areas like this which confronted us where we would always like to settle for lesser sentence. I managed to have his sentence commuted to life.

Of all my campaigns against the death penalty, one case of capital punishment imposed by the Government of Oman totally stumped me. There was a tennis coach, Bikshapathi, who had earlier worked in the Lady Hydari Club in Himayatnagar. He was taken to Muscat by a doctor and was staying with him. Bikshapathi was accused of killing the doctor's wife and daughter and he was tried according to the laws of Oman. The trial court sentenced him to death and it was confirmed in the appeal. Bikshapathi's wife and mother came to me because people had told them that I could pull this man back from the jaws of death. I have no such powers, and Islamic criminal law is quite different. I corresponded with our embassy in Muscat, and was told that the doctor was working in a hospital in Delhi. My first problem was: How would I request a man to forgive the killer of his wife and daughter? How would I persuade him, and what was the philosophical argument I would ground my request in? I requested Mr Tarkunde, Mr Chibbar, general secretary of the PUCL, and the ex-president of the PUCL, Mr Rajinder Sachar, to personally visit him and request for a pardon. They were not able to find him. The letters sent by me also came back. One day, I received a letter from the office of the envoy that the doctor was in Muscat to attend the reconciliation meeting where it would be open to the kin of the accused and the kin of the victims to arrive at some reconciliation. If the kin of the deceased agreed to a settlement, the accused would be acquitted; if the kin refused, the execution would be prompt and swift. Bikshapathi's family could not reach him, and he was executed. His mother informed me of this and pleaded for the return of his body. Could we have requested the doctor to forgive Bikshapathi for his crime?

Political Crimes and the Death Penalty

I cannot say that my views on the death penalty have always been so clear. The first time I worked on the death penalty and thought deeply about it was in the context of the Bhoomaiah and Kishta Goud case. At that time, I did not have a deep understanding of the question. It has deepened in the course of the past thirty years. However, I have always firmly believed that the death penalty cannot be a way to settle political differences or conflict.

The debate on the death penalty began in Andhra Pradesh with Bhoomaiah and Kishta Goud in the early 1970s. There are five instances of the death penalty being awarded in political cases in Andhra Pradesh. I was involved in all of them to varying degrees: K. Bhoomaiah, G. Kishta Goud, Nagabhushan Patnaik, Intha Ramana Reddy and Barla Yadagiri Raju. Of these, I argued the Barla Yadagiri Raju case fully. In the early 1980s, Barla Yadagiri Raju, a Naxalite, was sentenced by Judge Gogineni Radha Krishna Rao. He surmised that since the offence took place several years earlier and identification of the accused may be difficult, it was necessary to rely on the statements of witnesses given to the police during investigation. In the high court it came before a very conventional judge, Justice M. Ramachandra Raju. There was no case at all against Barla Yadagiri Raju, and yet the lower court awarded the death penalty. I narrated the case details and asked on what grounds the death penalty could be awarded in this case, arguing that it was a case of wrongful conviction and sentencing. The hearing concluded in fifteen minutes. Justice Ramachandra Raju asked the prosecution how they would defend the sessions court judgment. Even a judge like Justice Ramachandra Raju could not but strike down the conviction.

I argued Bhoomaiah and Kishta Goud's case after they had been awarded the death penalty and the matter came before the high court. They were both Naxalites.[5]

---

5 Varavara Rao's description of the 'peasant revolutionaries' K. Bhoomaiah and G. Kishta Goud merits recall: 'Bhoomaiah was from Muthunuru village of Peddapalli Taluq (now district, the place from where Kishanji and Vadkapuram Chandramouli also hail) of Karimnagar district on the banks of the Godavari. He comes from a 'Jangama'—a non-Brahmin priest community. Kishta Goud was from Kannaram village of Asifabad Taluq, Adilabad district, on the other side of the Godavari. Both were married. Bhoomaiah had children also. But most of their youthful life was spent in the Telangana Armed Struggle (1946–51) till it was withdrawn … Bhoomaiah and Kishta Goud shared the company of some … revolutionaries like I. Mallikarjuna Sharma, Mukku Subba Reddy (state secretary, CPI [ML], COC) and of course K.G. Satyamurthy who has influenced them and in turn was immensely influenced by them and wrote vivid memories in prose and poetry. Telugu literature is enriched with memories of Bhoomaiah and Kishta Goud and their martyrdom.' Rao, P. Varavara. 2017. 'Bhoomaiah, Kishta Goud, Bhabani Da and Sumanta'. *Frontier*, Vol. 49, No. 51, 25 June–1 July, https://www.frontierweekly.com/articles/vol-49/49-51/49-51-Bhoomaiah.html. Accessed on 31 October 2021.

G. Kishta Goud was accused of killing Bodekanti Mallaiah, the former police patel of Terkapalli village in Adilabad district; K. Bhoomaiah was accused of murdering Lachu Patel of Ginnedari village. The sessions judge, Vasudeva Rao, sentenced both of them to death in January 1972, confirmed by the high court. The sessions court judgment focused more on the Naxalite movement and the hazards it posed than on the individual crime for which the accused were being tried. The appeal was filed in the high court, with Pattipati Venkateswarlu and Ravi Subba Rao arguing. Justice Avula Sambasiva Rao heard the arguments and confirmed the judgment of the sessions court. That was the beginning of Bhoomaiah and Kishta Goud's solitary confinement on death row. The sentence was not carried out immediately as mercy petitions were pending before the president.

Nobody had any difference of opinion on the actions of Bhoomaiah and Kishta Goud. None of us argued that they did not commit the acts they were accused of. However, we argued that it must be recognized that they did not commit the murders for personal gain. We argued that their actions sprang from a strong political purpose and praxis to eliminate exploitation and oppression in society. They had an extreme political conviction that when the goals set out in the Indian Constitution were eroded, they could be restored through the use of force and violence. Therefore, we argued, although the murders were crimes without doubt, the political context within which they were located must be taken into consideration. We argued that they could not be considered ordinary criminals. There was widespread support for our views. Renowned American journalist Lawrence Lifschultz, film personalities K.A. Abbas, Mrinal Sen, Utpal Dutt, political leaders Bhupesh Gupta, Chandra Rajeshwar Rao, P. Sundarayya and George Fernandes led a movement to commute the death sentence awarded to Bhoomaiah and Kishta Goud. After the first mercy petition to the president failed, the execution was scheduled for the early hours of 26 November 1974. Pattipati Venkateswarlu managed to get a stay on 25 November by petitioning the court on some technical issue. From that moment the movement for the abolition of the death penalty gained ground rapidly. There were meetings and conferences across the state. Political parties, trade unions and student organizations campaigned for its abolition. Although the execution was deferred because of the strength of this campaign, the noose kept hanging over Bhoomaiah and Kishta Goud.

About a month before Emergency was declared, in May 1975, there were moves to carry out the execution again. Ordinarily, a person who is about to be executed is informed of this at least twenty-four hours in advance. On 10 May 1975, Bhoomaiah and Kishta Goud were informed that they would be hanged the following day. Although there are walls and cells within cells, word spreads very fast in jails. If a prisoner gets some information, in a very short while, all prisoners get to know it. All the prisoners learnt very soon that the two were to be executed. Mushirabad jail, located on the main road near Secunderabad railway station, was the only place with facilities for hanging. Madhusudan Raj Yadav and B. Pradeep happened to pass by the jail that day—since as student leaders they had been in and out of jail in those days, they stopped by to greet the jawans on sentry duty. One of the jawans quietly gave them this news. Pradeep immediately rushed to Pattipati Venkateswarlu, but he was out of town and the courts were on vacation. Pradeep then came to me. Justice O. Chinnappa Reddy and Justice Gangadhar Rao formed the vacation bench. I prepared a petition and sent my junior K. Narasimha Chari to the residence of Justice Chinnappa Reddy in Banjara Hills. Some of us tried to meet Chief Minister Jalagam Vengal Rao but he refused to meet us. We met the acting governor, Obul Reddy, who expressed his inability to help us. We gathered in front of Mushirabad jail and tried in vain to convince the jail superintendent that we had moved a house motion before the vacation judges, and he should defer the execution till the matter was decided.

Just as we were wondering what we might do, my junior Narasimha Chari, OPDR leader C. Venkatakrishna and Venkat Reddy brought the stay order from Justice Chinnappa Reddy. Justice P. Satyanarayana Raju's son, Srirama Raju, was then a registrar of the high court. He communicated the order to the jail authorities. On the whole, for a second time we managed to pull Bhoomaiah and Kishta Goud from the jaws of death. We stepped up the campaign against the death penalty and intensified our struggle for justice and made every effort to rescue them from the noose.

Exactly a month later, in June 1975, Emergency was declared. It was no longer possible to organize on any issue. So the only course left to us was the legal battle on the death penalty. The case was posted before the bench consisting of Justice K. Madhava Reddy and Justice Madhusudhan Rao. By then I had to limit my arguments to legal and technical/procedural issues. I argued that their offence must be considered as arising from their political beliefs if we were to do justice in this case. I argued for a whole day that it was unreasonable to execute them as a way of delegitimizing their political struggle. Justice Madhava Reddy was a judge who always patiently listened to the arguments of advocates. Justice Madhusudhan Rao was a very good man. He would keep asking questions and urging lawyers to think their arguments through. In the course of arguments he asked me, 'Why should Naxalites who do not believe in the Constitution take shelter under it?' I replied, 'When such issues come before the court, it is your values and not their values that are on trial. It is the values enshrined in the Constitution and the values of the state that are under test.' The lawyer for the centre, Subrahmanya Reddy, could not counter my argument.

The case came before Justice V.R. Krishna Iyer in the Supreme Court.[6] By this time, Bhoomaiah and Kishta Goud had spent four to five years on death row, uncertain of when they would be executed. That was the biggest punishment of all. Therefore, we argued that the death sentence in this case should be commuted to life. The arguments in the Supreme Court were presented by the CPI lawyer R.K. Garg. Krishna Iyer had a reputation for being a progressive judge, so we were hopeful that Bhoomaiah and Kishta Goud would not be executed. But we realized that once one is caught in that maze, it is very difficult to extricate oneself. Even a progressive judge must stay within a very narrowly defined rule of law. Justice Krishna Iyer, holding that the category of 'political offence' was not defined by the IPC, and that a crime is a crime, struck down our petition.[7] Yet, even on this question, there are widely divergent views among judges, as was evident from Justice Chinnappa Reddy's acceptance of this distinction in the case of Intha Ramana Reddy, discussed below.

A few days before Bhoomaiah and Kishta Goud were executed, I spoke to CPI leaders Mohit Sen and Chandra Rajeshwar Rao. Bhupesh Gupta attempted unsuccessfully to discuss the issue with Indira Gandhi. She was not willing to discuss the matter even with the CPI leaders who were her allies. During the Emergency, she was not in a mood to listen to anybody, nor was she ready to show mercy to anyone. Finally, on 1 December 1975, Bhoomaiah and Kishta Goud were hanged in Mushirabad jail.

After their execution in 1975, the death penalty in political cases declined sharply. It was not awarded by any court in cases in which I appeared thereafter. In other non-political cases where the death penalty was awarded, I intervened, argued, and made every attempt to have the sentence amended.

---

6 *G. Krishta Goud and Ors vs State of Andhra Pradesh and Ors* (03.10.1975: SC), (1976) 1 SCC 157. Justices A.C. Gupta and V.R. Krishna Iyer. The petitioner is also referred to as Kishta Goud.

7 'Patriots and others seeking of accomplish [sic] political goals or to attack the political order may commit acts which under municipal laws may be crimes ... and sometimes for purposes of reprieve as a class called political offences. But the Penal Code, which, by oath of office, we enforce, makes no such classification and in the cold stare of our criminal system, murder is murder ... As Judges, we cannot re-write the law whatever our views of urgent reforms, as citizens, may be ... and, however regrettable and irrevocable, taking of human life by the States' coercive apparatus, may be, our sympathies have no jural relevance. So the new and expanding trend towards abolition of capital penalty, while true, cannot help the hangman's rope in this case.' Ibid.

The case of the prosecution against Nagabhushan Patnaik[8] was that he escaped from jail and committed two murders in a Girijan hamlet. In those days, the activists in the Srikakulam movement boycotted 'bourgeois courts' and refused to defend themselves. As a result, the judge awarded the death penalty without hearing arguments from the defence.[9]

Nagabhushan Patnaik was in poor health—his wife approached a well-known lawyer, A.S.R. Chari, to appear in this case.[10] Chari went up in appeal. The court heard the arguments and the judge ruled that Nagabhushan Patnaik did not commit the crimes he was accused of, and that the evidence was not reliable. The police then foisted two new cases—escape from prison and two murders—and made this part of the Parvathipuram conspiracy case, by which time Naxalites had given up their boycott of courts (Chapter 6). After a 'not guilty' verdict had been given by one court, the same case was joined with another case. I placed these facts before the court and the two judges hearing the case gave two different judgments. One awarded the death penalty and the other held the accused not guilty. Had the death penalty been carried out, it would have been irreversible—could they have brought him back to life? I argued that as a matter of fact having held him in custody on the basis of such an erroneous judgment was itself a violation of the right to life and personal liberty guaranteed by Article 21 of the Constitution. I wrote down this entire process and sent it to the Supreme Court. I requested Mr Tarkunde to argue the case with me. It was probably around 1978. Justice Amarendranath Sen of the Supreme Court opined that this case must be heard. But the senior judge, Justice Murtaza Fazl Ali, felt there was no need to hear it. He felt that it would taint the judgment. What is to be done if there is ultimately a conflict between a judgment and the right to life?

---

8 1934–98, leader of the CPI (ML). For a related case during his prison term in Visakhapatnam, see *D. Bhuvan Mohan Patnaik and Ors vs State of Andhra Pradesh and Ors.* AIR 1974 SC 2092; MANU/SC/0038/1974.

9 Another case where the death penalty was awarded and the case referred by the sessions judge to the Andhra Pradesh High Court: *Sessions Judge Nellore Referring Officer vs Intha Ramana Reddy* on 12 February 1971. 1972 CriLJ 1485. Bench: Justice O. Chinnappa Reddy, Justice A. Reddy: 'The peculiar circumstances of the case were such that it was impossible to effectively protect the accused's right under Article 21 of the Constitution except by the appointment of a Counsel by Court, notwithstanding the refusal of the accused to have such counsel. The refusal of the accused to have Counsel was immaterial since a Fundamental Right could not be waived' (para 3).

10 A.S.R. Chari (1908–72), Supreme Court lawyer, author of *Memoirs of an Unrepentant Communist,* Hyderabad: Orient Longman, 1973.

We asked whether they would have considered the judgment final if he had been executed. Then Justice Murtaza Fazl Ali decided that the prisoner may be released on parole. Finally, clemency was granted by the President.[11] Even then, the prisoner was not released from jail. The ends of justice were not met in this case. Recognizing this, a series of minor adjustments were made, as if to compensate for the larger injustice.

Intha Ramana Reddy was a Naxalite who was convicted for the murder of one Venkata Reddy. When Intha Ramana Reddy's case come up for appeal before the high court, Justice Chinnappa Reddy summoned Ramana Reddy to court. He requested B.P. Jeevan Reddy and P.A. Choudary (former public prosecutor) to advise him, [12] and made an attempt to formulate a definition of political crime.

---

11 'More than 100 MPs belonging to all sections of this House had made a petition to the hon. President and to the Prime Minister and had pleaded for mercy and for commuting his death sentence.' Re: Medical treatment of Shri Nagabhushan Patnaik detained in an Andhra jail. *Lok Sabha Debates* (Fifth Lok Sabha), 23 February 1973. New Delhi: Lok Sabha Secretariat, pp. 236–40

12 Justice O. Chinnappa Reddy: '1. In this case we are presented with a difficult problem and faced with a strange situation, quite unprecedented, arising out of an unusual attitude adopted by the accused, who quite unmindful of the serious charge of murder made against them, refused to participate in the proceedings before the lower Court and persist in their refusal in this Court also. In the committal Court as well as in the Court of Session, when examined by the presiding magistrate and the judge respectively, they plainly and bluntly stated that they had no faith in the law Courts of the land, established according to them to protect the interests of the landlords, capitalists and the like. They professed to be "Naxalbarites". As they had not engaged any Counsel to defend them and as they had refused to answer the question whether they were possessed of sufficient means to engage a Counsel, the learned Sessions Judge thought it desirable to appoint a Counsel at the cost of the State to defend them. He requested a senior practitioner of the Court to defend them but the accused would have none of it and told the Sessions Judge that they did not want the services of a lawyer. The case therefore proceeded without the accused being defended by a lawyer. The prosecution examined twenty witnesses. At the end of the examination of each witness, the accused were asked by the Sessions Judge whether they wished to cross-examine the witness. They declined to cross-examine any witness. Instead they shouted slogans. When examined by the Sessions Judge at the conclusion of the evidence for the prosecution, they reaffirmed their lack of faith in Court and the present social system. At the close of the trial the learned Sessions Judge convicted the three accused under Section 302 read with Section 34 and sentenced A-l and A-2 to death and A-3 to imprisonment for life. While A-3 has preferred an appeal through Counsel, A-l and A-2, it is reported by the Jail Superintendent, have

In any crime, even if it involves a murder, if there was no personal motive to kill the other person, where there was no personal gain from committing the crime, where the crime is committed in pursuance of a broad-based ideology, such a crime may be defined as a political crime/offence. The Supreme Court in its judgment quoted an extract:

> We now come to the question of sentence. A-1 and A-2 (the respondents) were sentenced to death by the learned Sessions Judge. Both of them professed to be Naxalites. They appear to labour under the sincere belief that organised violence in rural areas directed against rich landlords labelled by them as enemies of the people will soon lead to an armed instruction [sic] and revolution and thereafter, to the abolition of all inequality and to the happiness, prosperity and peace of all the people of India. While it is true, on the one hand, that the accused killed an innocent person who had done them no harm. It must also be borne in mind, on the other hand, that they did not act out of any personal motive but out of what they conceived to be a public motive. They had no personal animosity against the deceased and they sought no personal gain. The means of murder employed by the accused as a step to achieve their ultimate goal was certainly blameworthy, but it cannot be said that their motive, according to their conception, was a low or mean motive. While it is necessary to recognise that the dictates of conscience which lead to injury to others may also merit severe punishment sometimes [sic]. It is also necessary to recognise that people acting out of genuine and passionate motives according to their conscience, do not merit extreme punishment. In that view to [sic] we think that the sentence of death passed on A-1 and A-2 must be set aside. Instead, we sentence each of them to suffer imprisonment for life.[13]

---

refused to prefer an appeal. Their case also is however before us in the reference made by the learned Sessions Judge under Section 374 CrPC for confirmation of the sentences of death. They have refused to be represented by any Counsel at the hearing of the reference. Having regard to the importance of the matter we requested three senior practitioners of this Court, Sri R. Ramalinga Reddy, Ex-Public Prosecutor of the State, Sri P.A. Chowdary and Sri B.P. Jeevan Reddy to assist us on the legal and constitutional questions involved.' *Sessions Judge Nellore Referring Officer vs Intha Ramana Reddy* on 12 February 1971. 1972 CriLJ 1485, para 1. Bench: Justice O. Chinnappa Reddy, Justice A. Reddy.

13 Extract of judgment of the Andhra Pradesh High Court quoted by the Supreme Court in *State of Andhra Pradesh vs Intha Ramana Reddy and Anr* on 16 November

This enunciation was presented before a bench which included Justice P.N. Bhagwati. The bench disagreed and struck it down, citing Justice Krishna Iyer's ruling in *G. Kishta Goud and Anr vs State of Andhra Pradesh.*[14]

The Offence of Rape and the Death Penalty

In 1999, the then chief minister of Andhra Pradesh, N. Chandrababu Naidu announced that he would lobby for the death penalty for rape. This argument in favour of the death penalty as most appropriate in cases of rape has gained increasing currency in the past couple of years. In a climate of increasing violence against women, this might seem to be the most appropriate solution, one that reflects a concern for justice and a genuine desire to prevent sexual crimes against women. Reports in the press have also generally been favourable to this demand, drawing up a balance sheet of crimes against women and the complete absence of convictions, inferring that it is only the fear of extreme punishment that can act as a deterrent. At the time, I wrote an article, with Vasanth and Kalpana, that was published in *The Hindu*, opposing this view.[15] Five years later in 2004, Dhananjay Chatterjee was sentenced to death for the rape and murder of a young girl in Calcutta. I have always been opposed to the death penalty. In this case, I wrote an open letter on 5 July 2004 to the President of India, asking him to commute the sentence to imprisonment for life. Chatterjee was executed on 15 August 2004.

There are four issues we need to look at in order to engage in an informed debate: the definition of rape; penal jurisprudence on the death penalty historically; the constitutional validity of the death penalty; and the exemption of rape by a husband of his wife from the definition of rape. To elaborate on this last issue first, incidents of extreme violence against women in the family are now commonplace. Torture by husbands leading to the death of wives is not uncommon, and it is reasonable to presume that this

---

1976, AIR 1977 SC 708. Author: Justice A.C. Gupta. Bench: A.C. Gupta, P.N. Bhagwati, P. Shinghal.

14 *State of Andhra Pradesh vs Intha Ramana Reddy and Anr* on 16 November 1976, AIR 1977 SC 708. Author: Justice A.C. Gupta. Bench: A.C. Gupta, P.N. Bhagwati, P. Shinghal.

15 K.G. Kannabiran, Kalpana Kannabiran, Vasanth Kannabiran, 'Death as Deterrent?' *The Hindu*, 28 November 1999.

torture includes sexual abuse, unreported because it is not a crime. If we look at the acts that are legally defined as rape, it can be seen that marital rape conforms to four of the six clauses. But it is outside the purview of the law. Consistency is a hallmark of justice. However, although men who murder their wives are punishable by the law, just as any person, man or woman, committing murder is punishable, men who rape their wives, can do so with impunity. It is only those who rape the wives, daughters, sisters, mothers of other men who are punishable. The demand for the death penalty for rape brings this stark reality of women's lives to the surface. Although we have been witness to the most gruesome violence against women in the family, we have not once heard a vociferous demand for the death penalty for men convicted in these cases.

The demand for the death penalty for rape, therefore, reflects the traditional patriarchal and reactionary view of women as property, and of rape being not an assault on the integrity of the women so assaulted alone, but more so of the community, of society, of the nation. Examining the penal framework of criminal jurisprudence in India and the position that the death penalty occupies will help us to better appreciate the applicability of the death penalty to rape.

Section 300 IPC defines 'murder', while Section 302 IPC prescribes the punishment for murder. Section 302 reads as follows: 'Whoever commits murder shall be punished with death, or imprisonment for life, and shall also be liable to fine.' Under 302 IPC, life imprisonment is the minimum punishment, the maximum sentence being death. Further, Section 354 (3) CrPC provides that, 'When a conviction is for an offence punishable with death or, in the alternative, with imprisonment for life or imprisonment for a term of years, the judgment shall state the reasons for the sentence awarded, and, in the case of sentence of death, the special reasons for such sentence.' Fifty-one sections in the IPC prescribe life imprisonment as the maximum punishment. The Constitution Bench of the Supreme Court, in *Bachan Singh v. State of Punjab*, held that the death sentence as a punishment should be awarded only in the 'rarest of rare' cases.[16]

Section 303 IPC prescribes the death penalty alone with no alternative in cases where a convict, serving a life sentence, commits murder. The court under this section cannot exercise its discretion and award a lesser sentence. The arguments of Justice Chandrachud in *Mithu v. State of Punjab*

16 *Bachan Singh v. State of Punjab*, (1982) 3 SCC 24.

on the constitutional validity of Section 303 are extremely relevant to our arguments. Citing several decisions by the Supreme Court which expanded the meaning and scope of Articles 14 (Right to Equality) and 21 (Right to Life and Personal Liberty), he argued that Article 21 could now be read after *Bachan Singh* as, 'No person shall be deprived of his right to life or personal liberty except according to fair, just and reasonable procedure established by valid law.' He further says, '... it is now too late in the day to contend that it is for the legislature to prescribe the procedure and for the courts to follow it; that it is for the legislature to provide the punishment and for the courts to impose it ... [T]he last word on the question of justness or fairness does not rest with the legislature ... [I]t is for the courts to decide whether the procedure prescribed by a law for depriving a person of his life or liberty is fair, just and reasonable".[17] This decision unequivocally advocates the striking down of Section 303 as unconstitutional.

In light of these arguments, we need to ask several questions. So far, the death penalty has been reserved for murder, with life imprisonment being the minimum sentence. This viewed in the light of *Bachan Singh* would mean that it is not every murder that would invite the sentence of death, but only those in which all the ingredients of the offence put together would come within the definition of the 'rarest of rare'. The decision of whether a particular murder constitutes a 'rarest of rare' offence is one that depends upon judicial discretion, not on the legislature. Within the judiciary itself, discretion will and must in the interests of a fair trial weigh heavily in favour of safeguarding the right to life and personal liberty, not against it.

By asking for the death penalty for rape, are we now saying that the death penalty should be prescribed as punishment for offences less serious than murder of the most gruesome kind? If the demand is for the death penalty as a maximum punishment, what is the minimum punishment being asked for? The existing rape law prescribes a minimum sentence of imprisonment of seven or ten years. Is the proposal being put forward now asking for death or life imprisonment, or is it asking for death or seven to ten years? Penal jurisprudence cannot rely on abstract notions of honour and chastity. It must be grounded in more real notions of quantifiable wrong, comparability and equivalence, because what is at risk is the taking of life (which is irreversible).

Finally, we come to the crucial question of whether the death penalty per se is constitutional. There has for several years now been a debate worldwide

17 *Mithu v. State of Punjab*, 1983 SCC (Cr) 404. Para ix.

and a campaign calling for the abolition of the death penalty. At this critical juncture, do we want to engage in the self-defeating exercise of adding to the catalogue?

Conclusion

On thinking back I feel that while there were several reasons behind our failure to secure commutation of the death penalty in the case of Bhoomaiah and Kishta Goud, the methods we adopted were also responsible. We projected them as heroic Naxalites. Although they were Naxalites and active in the movement, this alone was not enough to challenge their death penalty. Foregrounding that aspect resulted in a vengefulness on the part of the state. In one of the meetings during the campaign against the death penalty, while Bhoomaiah and Kishta Goud were on death row, Pattipati Venkateswarlu declared that armed struggle is our fundamental right. G.K. Reddy wrote an article that the courts were unclear and confused about their approach to revolutionary violence. These views certainly had an effect on judgments and judges. I feel on hindsight that perhaps if we had challenged the death penalty in more subdued tones, we may have succeeded in having the sentence commuted. In any case, after that execution in 1975, there were no more death penalties in political cases. The prosecution was unable to establish, even in a single case, that the defendants had committed the offence, and therefore the question of any penalty did not arise.

It is needless to reiterate that such exercise of clemency is not condonation of the crime committed. The executive's exercise of the prerogative of clemency is not a comment on the judiciary's appreciation of the case. It belongs to a different realm of authority altogether. It touches upon what the courts are not empowered to look into, namely the penal philosophy of the state.

If 'rarest of the rare' cases become frequent, we are slowly regressing to the position that the death penalty is mandatory where the present normal rule of 'life sentence' is becoming an exception. This regression, before it becomes a norm, needs a debate. If the state is allowed the role of an avenger in an iniquitous society like ours, death sentences, if allowed to stay, may be invoked against political dissent. The major articulate premise in the Indian Constitution is 'Justice' in the Preamble. Justice as per the constitutional value system is a moderating force of all human relationships as also of all institutions under the Constitution in their relationship with the people.

By executing the criminal, you are not curing the wrongdoer, for he is not there to be reformed. By executing him, the wrong in cases of capital punishment is not undone. It is retributive and is an instance of state terror to prevent others from following that course. This deterrence, history will tell us, never worked.

Another weighty reason for commuting the sentence is the principle, which was repeatedly laid down by the apex court, that when the convict spends long periods on death row awaiting execution, that is reason enough for commutation to life. The principle, which courts laid down for themselves, would also govern the discretion of the president while exercising his pardoning power.

Solitary confinement is frowned upon by the civilized world and the international body is of the view that such confinement cannot be for long periods. They are also of the view that solitary confinement as a form of punishment in prison discipline should be eliminated. What is happening in India is that petitions for pardon are left pending for disposal for long periods and the convicts are held in death cells. For whatever reason, such solitary imprisonment in a death cell would be violative of Article 21 and is arbitrary and violative of Article 14, even though they are confined in a death cell as per prison rules. It is possible for the government to relieve such persons from the horror of spending day after day for years in a death cell waiting for death or commutation. The mistake of the government in their failure to set up norms in respect of persons waiting for disposal of their mercy petition one way or another does not diminish the agony of waiting endlessly for impending death. That should be one of the factors to be taken into consideration for purposes of commutation.

Uninformed public pressure and public expectations have played their role in the sentencing policy in this case. In the words of Albert Camus:

> But beheading is not simply death. It is just as different, in essence, from the privation of life as a concentration camp is from prison. It is a murder, to be sure, and one that arithmetically pays for the murder committed. But it adds to death a rule, a public premeditation known to the future victim, an organization, in short, which is in itself a source of moral sufferings more terrible than death.[18]

There is no equivalence possible. Many laws consider a premeditated crime more serious than a crime of spontaneous violence. What then is capital punishment but the most premeditated of murders, to which no criminal's deed, however calculated it may be, can be compared?

18 Camus, Albert. 1961. 'Reflections on the Guillotine'. In *Resistance, Rebellion and Death*. New York: Alfred A. Knopf, pp. 173–234, p. 199.

11

The Afzal Guru Case

K.G. Kannabiran appeared for Shaukat Hussain Guru in the trial court in Delhi in the Parliament attack case. Briefly, the details of the case are as follows: on December 13, 2001, while Parliament was in session, a car carrying five men and loaded with explosives entered the compound of Parliament House. The attack was foiled by the security personnel but eight security men were killed in the shoot-out in which the five intruders were shot dead. Four people were arrested soon after and tried under POTA – Afzal Guru, Shaukat Hussain Guru, S.A.R. Gilani and Afsan Guru. Although the trial court convicted three of the accused and awarded the death penalty, it was only one of them, Afzal Guru, whose death sentence was confirmed by the Supreme Court of India. Two were acquitted by the high court and one was acquitted of terror charges by the Supreme Court and awarded a lesser sentence. Deeply invested in this case, Kannabiran was of the view (shared by a wide cross-section of human rights defenders) that Afzal Guru was denied the opportunity for a fair trial and saw his conviction as a travesty of justice – a view he elaborates on in this chapter.[1]

Questions Arising from the Trial of Afzal Guru

IF THE PROCEEDINGS of the trial of Afzal Guru and three others before the designated judge under the Prevention of Terrorism Act (POTA), 2002, were to be videographed, one would have understood the trivialization of the rule of

1 *State (NCT Delhi) vs Navjot Sandhu* (2005) 11 SCC 600. For a detailed account of Kannabiran's work as lawyer for the accused in the Parliament Attack case see Nitya Ramakrishnan, 2020. 'Trial Lessons from K.G. Kannabiran: Parliament Attack Case, *Livelaw*, 5 December. https://www.livelaw.in/columns/kannabiran-nitya-ramakrishnan-parliament-attack-case-pota-166860. Accessed on 8 September 2022.

law in this country. The case itself was a highly publicized affair, the investigation parading the accused before the print and electronic media in what can be described as a trial before the committal stage; the screaming headlines and news reports prevented any disinterested endeavour to understand the case and assess the evidence for and against the accused. The media attention the case received foreclosed any possibility of just conduct, and in such a case conformity to procedure is the only visible guarantee of justice. The attack on Parliament generated such hostility all around that nobody was willing to appear for the accused in the first instance. A relatively junior lawyer was appointed as amicus by order on 1 July 2002. The trial commenced on 8 July. On the same day, Afzal petitioned the court as follows:

> Hon'ble Sir, Respectfully I am not satisfied with state council (Counsel) appointed by the court. That I need a Competent Senior Advocate as Amicus Curiae to meet the ends of justice from this court. The way the Court is treating me I could not get justice. It is therefore requested to appoint one of the following lawyers: 1. Ashok Agarwal; 2. Pandit R.K. Naseem; 3. R.K. Dham; 4. Mr Taufil.

On 12 July 2002, after recording twenty prosecution witnesses and after another protest by Afzal, the learned judge passed the following order:

> Afzal states that he does not want the amicus curiae ... to represent him. He had earlier given the list of four advocates ... The judge ascertained their willingness to appear as amicus for Afzal when they happened to appear before him in another case, but [they] expressed their inability to become amicus curiae in this case.

The court further observed:

> I consider that if accused wants a lawyer of his choice, he is free to engage himself the lawyer of his choice, but if he has not engaged a lawyer of his choice and has asked the court to appoint amicus curiae, the court can appoint amicus curiae out of panel available with it or out of the willing advocates. Afzal has been given the liberty to cross-examine the witnesses.

Reminiscent of the Procurator of Judea, this ritualistic approach left Afzal undefended throughout, and vitiated the conviction and sentence. He understood the seriousness of the charge he was facing and so wanted the services of an experienced lawyer.

Two lawyers refused to appear and he did not ask the other two. After the young amicus was discharged from representing Afzal, there was no other advocate defending him. Although there were advocates engaged to defend the other three accused, they had no brief to defend Afzal, for he did not consent to such a course, as was evident from the representations made to the court. In these circumstances, it was impossible either to presume or infer that cross-examination was common. The designated judge who sentenced the three accused to death did not order the forfeiture of life of the wife of Shoukat Guru, Afsan Guru. Her newborn child was with her in prison.

These death sentences had to be confirmed by a bench of two judges under the provisions of the Code of Criminal Procedure. It was again a detailed retrial on the basis of recorded evidence with wide powers for courts to do justice. Every aspect of the case had to be and could be brought under scrutiny. In the final submissions filed on behalf of Afzal, this aspect of the case was brought into sharp focus. Articles 14, 21, 22 and 39A ensure that an accused is tried according to procedure established by law, where procedure means not any procedure but a fair and just procedure, including access to justice. The court giving Afzal the liberty to cross-examine is a vacuous liberty which implies a comprehensive understanding of the Evidence Act and the Criminal Procedure Code. This freedom given by the court without discharging its constitutional obligation is itself a total denial of his constitutional right to defend himself effectively. The high court in the referred case recorded these facts in paragraph 133 of its judgment, and proceeded to record that Afzal had in fact cross-examined eighty prosecution witnesses. The high court held, 'Mohd Afzal continued the trial without any objection or grievance.' This conclusion is not supported by the proceedings of the trial court. Afzal had more than once requested for a counsel to be appointed by the court. But the court at the trial stage gave Afzal a Hobson's choice. 'Either accept the lawyer appointed by the court or cross-examine the witnesses yourself.' The gravity of the case is writ large and such a case cannot be disposed of in the manner it was done both at the designated judge's level and the high court. This issue was not raised before the Supreme Court.

The Right to Legal Defence

When one waives the right to counsel, it should be a decision informed by competence and intelligence. The failure of the designated judge to appoint a counsel was on account of the self-imposed limitation that he could not traverse beyond the panel of lawyers available to the court. It was not that lawyers were not available, but that they were avoiding handling Afzal's brief. 'Non-availability' and 'declined to appear' are two different categories. The latter is outright denial of equal opportunity before law. This would amount to refusal of access to justice. The position taken by the high court was wholly untenable.

The right to be defended by a lawyer is not only a fundamental right but a right guaranteed under the International Covenant on Civil and Political Rights (ICCPR), which have become mandatory thanks to its recognition by the Protection of Human Rights Act, 1993. Article 9 of the ICCPR gives a person a right to an effective remedy for the enforcement of the fundamental rights recognized by the Constitution or by law and Article 14(3)(d) guarantees the right to the accused to be tried in his presence and to be defended by a competent lawyer. The Supreme Court has read these articles in the Covenant along with the articles in the Constitution of India dealing with equality and equal protection of laws (Article 14); right to be tried according to procedure established by law (Article 21); right to be assisted by counsel from the time of arrest and during the trial (Article 22 [1 and 2], and 39A which deals with equal justice and free legal aid). According to the court, Article 39A is interpretative of Article 21 and points out that courts cannot be inert in the face of these articles. In one of the decisions cited by the counsel, the Supreme Court approvingly quoted the opinion of Judge Douglas of the US Supreme Court in *Argersinger vs Hamlin:*

> The right to be heard would be, in many cases, of little avail if it did not comprehend the right to be heard by counsel. Even the intelligent and educated layman has small and sometimes no skill in the science of law. If charged with crime, he is incapable, generally, of determining for himself whether the indictment is good or bad. He is unfamiliar with the rules of evidence. Left without the aid of counsel he may be put on trial without a proper charge, and convicted upon incompetent evidence, or evidence irrelevant to the issue or otherwise inadmissible. He lacks both the skill and knowledge adequately to prepare his defense, even though he [may] have a perfect one. He requires the guiding hand of counsel at every step in the proceedings against him ... If that be true of men of intelligence, how much more true is it of the ignorant and illiterate, or those of feeble intellect.[2]

After quoting this passage, there was no discussion of this decision and its applicability to the facts of this case. Reference to the passage relied upon by the counsel did not consider the ratio of the case. Without deciding the denial of the

---

2 *Jon Richard Argersinger, Petitioner, vs Raymond Hamlin, Sheriff, Leon County, Florida.* 92 S.Ct. 2006, para 15.

right to be assisted and defended by a lawyer, the court proceeded to the issue of the performance of a counsel and pointed out the difficulties of lawyers in performing this task. While being mechanical in dealing with the fundamental obligation of the court to provide lawyer assistance for defending the accused, it proceeded on a short dilation into the competence of the defending counsel who was not there, and that was the major complaint.

It was grossly unfair to conclude that permitting Afzal to cross-examine the witnesses would constitute compliance with Articles 21, 22 and 39A of the Constitution and the related international covenants. In the great debate that took place in the decades starting with the 1970s, the one issue which had the consensus of all the contending groups and intellectuals was that the rule of law should inform our understanding of the Constitution and governance. Yet, within a matter of two decades, the rule of law stood discredited as never before, the likes of which had not happened even in the dark days of the Emergency in 1975. Political prejudices paraded as juridical principles and communal prejudices entered the decision-making processes of the justice system, sometimes disguised as judicial activism.

The failure of the criminal justice system to bring justice to victims of mass violence is evident: the victims of the Sikh massacres in 1984; the indifference to the crimes perpetrated by the majority community in the 1992 Mumbai riots, leading to the appointment of the Srikrishna Commission; the riots in Coimbatore where crores of rupees worth of property was consigned to flames and the massacre of around two scores of Muslims went unnoticed, while the sequential blasts a few days thereafter led to arrests and the pretrial incarceration of around 170 persons for a decade, followed by prosecution; the Gujarat riots where the killings led to no accountability.

At the same time, we have the strident assertion of partisan 'justice' in the death sentences on Kehar Singh and Afzal Guru. These are two instances of the operation of the 'rule of law' in its paranoid state. One became a victim of substantive injustice and the other of processual injustice.

This is a major reason why human rights activists campaign against the death penalty. In a death penalty case in the US in 1994, Justice Blackmun's dissent is to the point: 'It seems that a decision whether a human being should live or die is so inherently subjective—rife with all of life's understandings, experiences, prejudices and passions—that it inevitably defies the rationality and consistency required by the Constitution.'[3]

---

3 *Callins vs Collins*. 510 U.S. 1141 (1994). Decided 22 February 1994, https://www.law.cornell.edu/supct/html/93-7054.ZA1.html. Accessed on 26 October 2021.

12
Tribes in Fifth Schedule Areas

Constitutional Architecture for the Protection of Scheduled Tribes

THE CONSTITUTION, WHEN it replaced the Government of India Act, 1935, gave an entirely different mandate to the government. The earlier classification of tribal areas was given the new nomenclature of Schedule V Areas and Schedule VI Areas. The British occupation of the country did not lead to the integration of tribal India with so-called 'civilized India'. It isolated the tribal societies and any marginal interference was only to put down tribal revolts. The history of this experience has been that the isolation of tribes was taken advantage of by the non-tribals who subjected them to intense exploitation. There were several uprisings—from the Mal Paharia uprising in 1772 to Naxalbari in 1968 in independent India. In the Constituent Assembly, there were a few able representatives who focused on issues pertaining to the tribes quite effectively. With our hegemonic and indigenous apartheid caste culture we thought homogenization is integration. Our assumption of equality, which was more a patronizing sentiment than a well-thought-out conceptual understanding of reality, did not reflect correctly the majority community's relationship with the plurality of communities living within the Indian part of the subcontinent. The castes within the 'Hindu fold' were seen to be in different stages of development. This inequality was running parallel to the inequities prevailing within and between the plural societies living in the subcontinent.

The Constitution took notice of the fact that the people living in the subcontinent had never experienced equality in their history, despite the Buddhist emphasis on equality—perhaps the first religion to do so. The tribal societies lived in comparative autonomy and in isolation. In fact, there is a large body of recorded opinion that the problems of tribes multiplied not by their isolation but by their coming into contact with the main body of the non-tribal community. The British policy was to provide protection through a policy of non-interfering isolation, which resulted in and in fact allowed their exploitation at the hands of landlords, moneylenders, contractors and also missionaries who were close to the British administration. Pursuant to this isolationist policy it took care to demarcate the areas predominantly inhabited by the tribes and classified them into 'excluded areas and partially excluded areas'. Section 91 of the Government of India Act, 1935, sets out the constitutional character of these areas. What is of interest for the present purpose is the fact that no law made by either the federal or local legislature shall apply to these areas unless so notified by the governor. The governor also had the power to modify the laws made by the federal and provincial legislature in their application to these areas. The history of the legislative and constitutional scheme was taken into account by the Constituent Assembly while formulating provisions with reference to the tribes. The Constituent Assembly carefully listed out the Schedule of the Tribes living in these Excluded and Partially Excluded Areas, all the while aware of the fact that neither the tribes nor the castes so inventoried were a homogeneous group—the collective name SC (Scheduled Caste) and ST (Scheduled Tribe) was a convenient term of reference without meaning anything more. It would therefore be wrong to conclude that the various categories included therein are equal or similar. What is important to note is that the Constitution took cognizance of the situation, and at various levels issued directives and protective mandates to enable these scheduled communities to rise to the level of equality with the rest. Thus, one will find a constitutional scheme emerging, providing principles of governance of the tribes living in the Fifth Schedule Areas.

The various provisions which constitute the constitutional scheme for the Scheduled Tribes are as follows:

- Article 14 as interpreted by the court for over half a century now bans not only unreasonable classification but also arbitrariness and unfairness in the treatment of persons.
- Article 15(4) provides special provision for the advancement of any socially and educationally backward classes of citizens or for SCs and STs. This article comes into play principally in matters of education. This should be normally read as

ensuring equality within the tribe or caste but also as between castes and tribes. This should work for the elimination of oppression and structural violence against women within castes and tribes and as between castes and tribes as well.

- Article 19 gives them all the fundamental right to freedom and it also stipulates that the state may, only by law, impose restraints on the exercise of the right to move freely throughout the territory of India or the right to carry on any profession or any occupation, trade or business for the protection of any STs. This law-making power enables the state to prevent people from migrating in large numbers to tribal areas by restricting the right to movement covered by Article 19(d), and the right to reside and settle in any part of the country covered by Article 19(5) can by law restrain persons from settling down in Schedule or Tribal areas under the clause. The right to acquire property, which is no longer a fundamental right, is also one of the rights that could be restrained for the protection of any Schedule Tribe.
- Article 23 deals with forced and bonded labour. The major portion of this labour comes from STs and SCs. The type of migration that takes place has always been due to destruction of their natural habitat driving them to the plains and urban areas in search of right to life, and in the process forcing them into bondage.

Reinforcing these fundamental rights, the Constitution created a set of mandatory principles of governance, in the nature of fundamental obligations. The makers of the Constitution wanted to free governance from litigiousness and so declared that these cannot be enforced in a court of law. It was not realized for long that non-enforceability in a court of law meant that these principles were politically enforceable. Some even looked on Part III (Fundamental Rights) and Part IV (Directive Principles) of the Constitution as being in an adversarial relationship.

It is important to note that the state in Part III and Part IV is defined by the limitations imposed on its political conduct and governance. The state is not an abstract entity but is defined by the enumeration of instruments and instrumentalities of governance. It includes the government and the parliament of India, the government and the legislature of each state, and all local or other authorities within the territory of India or under the control of the Government of India. The power and authority of the state is defined by the limitations imposed by the fundamental rights and obligations enumerated in Part III and Part IV. The Indian state is defined in terms of its limitations and not in terms of its power.

After setting out in Article 37 that the state shall apply the principles set down in Part IV while making laws, the latter directs it to establish a just social order in which justice, social, economic and political, shall inform all its institutions. Article 39 inter alia directs the state to provide for all citizens, men and women, equally, the right to adequate means of livelihood. It provides that the control of material resources of the community be so distributed as to serve the common good; that the operation of the economic system does not lead to concentration of wealth and means of production to the common detriment. Article 40 mandates the state to take steps to organize village panchayats and endow them with such powers and authority as may be necessary to enable them to function as units of self-government. This was achieved by the 73rd Constitutional Amendment and the provisions of the Panchayats (Extension to Scheduled Areas) Act, 1996 (PESA). Article 46(A) requires the state to protect and improve the environment and to safeguard the forests and wildlife in the country.

To secure the constitutional purpose in certain states, the proviso to Article 164 lays down that the states of Bihar, Madhya Pradesh and Orissa shall have 'a minister in charge of tribal welfare, who shall in addition be responsible for the welfare of SCs and backward classes or any other work'. Article 164 could have easily laid down that in all states which have areas covered by Schedule V there shall be a minister in charge of tribal welfare. To increase administrative efficiency uniformly such an amendment could be thought about.

It is important to look at the unfailing attention paid to this issue by the Constitution. The following is from Part XII, Article 275(1), which deals with finance:

> Provided that there shall be paid out of the Consolidated Fund of India as grants in aid of the revenue of a state such capital and recurring sums as may be necessary to enable the state to meet the costs of such schemes of development as may be undertaken by the state with the approval of the Government of India for the purpose of promoting the welfare of the Scheduled Tribes in that state or raising the levels of the administration of the Scheduled Areas therein to that of the Administration of the rest of the areas of the state.

Throughout, there has been an emphasis on the special responsibility of the central government for the progressive development of the Scheduled Areas and the Scheduled Tribes. These provisions were enacted in the context of the history of tribal revolts and the indifferent and exclusionist attitude of the British. Despite such attention, our governments continue the colonial legacy. The Constitution made a definite departure from the Government of India Act, 1935. A more positive role is given to the governor. He is expected to examine every enactment of the legislature or Parliament and make modifications in its application to Scheduled Areas for ensuring progress towards equality and justice in all its facets.

Apart from these, there are certain provisions that deal specifically with the tribes and Scheduled Areas. As a step towards empowerment, representation at the state and national level was ensured by a system of reservation of seats (Article 330). It has been a continuing misfortune of this country that the upper castes and non-tribals saw these efforts as discrimination in favour of the undeserving, and with this attitude in mind the bureaucracy and political government paid only nominal attention to the issues raised by STs and SCs. Article 338, which was recast and introduced by the 65th Amendment Act, 1990, creates a standing supervisory commission with powers to safeguard the rights and interest of tribes with the right to participate and assist in the planning process of the socio-economic development of STs. The commission is the authority that reports to the president on all matters of safeguard for tribes for effective implementation of policy and other related matters.

What appears to be very necessary is that any legislation relating to forests, environment and wildlife, if they touch upon the rights of STs, whether in respect of their right to residence and their right to land or forest produce, or right of way and pasture in forests, should be sent to the special officer under Article 338 for review on the subject matter of legislation. The special officer, when he receives the bill, shall hold sittings inviting various organizations in the area, whether governmental, quasi-government or non-governmental. At a public hearing of the gram sabhas of the affected region, the voluntary organizations and human rights organizations working on tribal rights and issues should also be heard. The report of the special officer after such public hearing on the bill shall be placed before Parliament for a debate. The special officer has the duty to 'investigate all matters relating to the safeguards provided for the Scheduled Castes and Scheduled Tribes under this Constitution and report to the President upon the working of those safeguards at such intervals as the President may direct, and the President shall cause all such reports to be laid before each House of Parliament'.[1]

This provision in its present form came into existence in June 1990. A committee of special officers representing forest, environment and wildlife can strengthen the safeguards and protection legislated by the Constitution under its own provisions and laws made by Parliament. The Constitution further empowers the president to appoint a commission to report on the administration of Scheduled Areas (Article 339). Commissions have been appointed, and the last of such reports

1 Constitution of India, Article 338(2).

by a commission to the president under this article was by the distinguished and committed civil servant B.D. Sharma, IAS, commissioner appointed under this article.[2] As the various provisions in the Constitution make Scheduled Areas and Scheduled Tribes the responsibility of the president, should the states have any power to make laws in this regard?

Various provisions of the Constitution have been set out that show the exclusive concern of the Constitution towards SCs and STs. This concern is to see that justice, equality and human dignity in all their facets are secured to these tribes who still continue to be victims of oppression and exploitation. Keeping in mind the total failure of the administration to ensure equality to STs, it becomes necessary to bring about a new understanding by interpreting the existing provisions differently. In 1969, the Kerala High Court had to consider the Kerala Hillmen Rules, 1964, made under the Kerala Forest Act, 1961. The high court found that it was an attempt to hold the tribe tied down to the settlement and function as bonded labour to the forest department. The court found that many provisions were anachronistic and part of a feudal legacy. While dealing with the constitutional infirmities in the Rules, they went into the legislative competence of the state legislature to deal with tribes. According to the court, STs were not indicated as a subject matter of legislation in any of the lists in Schedule VII and therefore the court held that if a law had to be made with respect to tribes it could only be done by Parliament by its residuary power under 248(1) read with Entry 97 of List I of Schedule VII.[3]

When detailed provisions have been made for their protection and welfare, can it be said that laws of a general nature made by a legislature or even Parliament can be applied to Scheduled Areas by ignoring the mandatory requirement of the Constitution? These constitutional provisions have to be seen as having a transforming role and any interpretation by the executive or the judiciary should be informed by this dynamic purpose. Constitutional provisions and statutes to enforce the constitutional purposes were never understood in their transformative sense but were dealt with in terms of outmoded canons of interpretation of original intent, plain meaning, etc., as tools of interpretation. This statutory focus on traditional interpretation and the patronizing rhetoric of the court, firmly tethered to this statutory archaeology, have led to laxity of enforcement and administration

2 *Twenty-Ninth Report of the Commissioner for Scheduled Castes and Scheduled Tribes* (B.D. Sharma Report). New Delhi: Government of India, National Commission for Scheduled Castes and Scheduled Tribes, 1990.

3 *Eacharan Ittiathi vs State of Kerala*, O.P. No. 3373 of 1966. Decided on 22 December 1969. Kerala High Court.

of these laws, resulting in keeping the tribes where they were when we attained Independence.

The Schedule V Articles 338 and 339 and the 73rd Amendment authorizing Parliament seem to support the interpretation placed by the Kerala High Court. Whether such restructuring with a free hand to the governor and the Tribes Advisory Council (TAC) playing the role of a legislature within a legislature furthers the empowerment of tribes is a question which could be usefully debated. It may be plausible to agree with the view of the Kerala High Court that as Scheduled Areas and Scheduled Tribes are not mentioned in any of the lists in Schedule VII, the power to legislate with reference to tribes falls within Entry 97 of List I which enables Parliament to exercise powers over residuary matters and subjects—taking support from an entry with reference to nomadic and migratory tribes in Item 15, List III of Schedule VII of the Constitution. Basically, the very tenable argument for the proposition that Parliament alone has the legislative power with reference to Scheduled Areas and Scheduled Tribes is the very structure of Schedule V.

Article 244(1) deals with the administration of Scheduled Areas and Scheduled Tribes in the country except Assam, Mizoram, Meghalaya and Tripura, where the provisions of Schedule VI apply. Paragraph 5(1) of Schedule V reads as follows:

> 5. Law applicable to Scheduled Areas.—(1) Notwithstanding anything in this Constitution, the Governor … may by public notification direct that any particular Act of Parliament or of the Legislature of the State shall not apply to a Scheduled Area or any part thereof in the State or shall apply to a Scheduled Area or any part thereof in the State subject to such exceptions and modifications as he may specify in the notification and any direction given under this sub-paragraph may be given so as to have retrospective effect.[4]

Paragraph 5(2) authorizes the government to make regulations for peace and good governance in the Scheduled Areas of the state, particularly in respect of matters specified therein:

> 5 (2) The Governor … may make regulations for the peace and good government of any area in a State which is for the time being a Scheduled Area.

4 Constitution of India, 1950, Schedule V, para 5(1).

In particular and without prejudice to the generality of the foregoing power, such regulations may—

(a) prohibit or restrict the transfer of land by or among members of the Scheduled Tribes in such area;
(b) regulate the allotment of land to members of the Scheduled Tribes in such area;
(c) regulate the carrying on of business as money-lender by persons who lend money to members of the Scheduled Tribes in such area.[5]

The governor is empowered, while making such regulation, to repeal or amend any law made by Parliament or the state legislature operating in the Scheduled Area. One is a general power and the other is with reference to a regulation regarding specific subjects. All regulations so made shall be submitted forthwith to the president. The makers of the Constitution have also set up TACs, a consultative body to the governor. The non-tribes from whom politicians and bureaucrats emerge have patronizing attitudes to the disinherited and the disadvantaged, and they have held on to the view that they know what is good for the people they administer. The result has been that the constitutional provisions have never been used for bringing about a change in the lives of tribal communities.

The second wave of the Naxalite movement in Andhra Pradesh manifested in a revolt by Gonds in Indervelli, Adilabad district. On 20 April 1981, the police opened fire against unarmed Gonds who were protesting—the death toll was sixty.[6] The Andhra Pradesh Civil Liberties Committee conducted an inquiry into the eighteen deaths for which information was available and the report was a detailed one. I recollect having questioned Mr Srinivasan, IAS, as to how he ordered the disposal of dead bodies as if they were animal carcasses. The refusal to hand over the bodies of people shot in encounters to their kith and kin was an extension of state violence. These were dead bodies of Girijans and their customs stipulate the conduct of the last rites, which was violated.

Official and court interpretations of these provisions have held back the progress of the tribes in the country, probably by another hundred years. Litigation against tribal communities was shifted from agency courts to civil courts, and in a country

5 Constitution of India, 1950, Schedule V, para 5(2).

6 Official statements put the figure at thirteen. See Raghuram, M. 1981. 'Carnage at Indervelli: A Report. *Economic and Political Weekly*, Vol 16, No. 24, 13 June, pp. 1047–50.

where courts are governed by a distorted adversarial system, the tribal people were made to play a losing game. The havoc wrought by the non-tribal litigant on tribal rights never entered the assessment of the various reports by various commissions. The judiciary, from a junior civil judge to the judges of the apex court, must bear the responsibility for the continuing vulnerability of STs. When laws were made touching them, the interpretation was basically against the interests of the tribes. Judges and administrators, barring very few exceptions, did not see such interpretation as out of tune with the constitutional scheme.

The Case of Arka Vasanth Rao: Panchayat Raj in Schedule V Areas

After the 73rd Constitutional Amendment, which introduced constitutional democracy at the grassroot level, a separate enactment titled Panchayat (Extension to Scheduled Areas) Act, 1996, had to be passed by Parliament on the basis of the Bhuria Committee recommendations. A group of Girijans filed a writ petition questioning the competence of the government of Andhra Pradesh to enforce the Andhra Pradesh Panchayat Raj Act, 1994, to tribal areas covered by Schedule V of the Indian Constitution. I appeared for Arka Vasanth Rao, vice-president of the Gondwana Sangharsh Samithi, and three other tribal persons, and won this case in the Andhra Pradesh High Court in 1994.[7] The petitioners from the Scheduled Areas wanted protections to such areas to be in place, as otherwise the large-scale migration of non-tribals there put the tribes at a severe disadvantage in terms of relative population size. My primary argument was that after the enactment of the Constitution (73rd Amendment Act, 1992), by Parliament and the insertion of Part IX (Articles 243 and 243A to 243O), the legislature of the state of Andhra Pradesh had no power to make a law that extended the operation of panchayats to Scheduled Areas. There was a specific constitutional injunction to this effect in Article 243M:

> 243M. Part not to apply to certain areas:
>
> (1) Nothing in this Part shall apply to the Scheduled Areas referred to in clause (1), and the tribal areas referred to in clause (2), of article 244;
>
> ...
>
> (4) Notwithstanding anything in this Constitution;
>
> ...

7 *Arka Vasanth Rao vs Government of Andhra Pradesh*, AIR 1995 AP 274. Advocate B. Nalin Kumar assisted K.G. Kannabiran in this case.

> (b) Parliament may, by law, extend the provisions of this Part to the Scheduled Areas and the tribal areas referred to in clause (1) subject to such exceptions and modifications as may be specified in such law, and no such law shall be deemed to be an amendment of this Constitution for the purposes of Article 368.

I argued that the Panchayat Act can only be applied to Scheduled Areas after a specific law to this effect is passed in Parliament, and that any contrary move by the state government would only trivialize this important constitutional protection. After a detailed hearing, the Andhra Pradesh High Court held that:

> For these reasons we hold that the application of the Andhra Pradesh Panchayat Raj Act, 1994 (Act 13 of 1994) to the scheduled areas in the State is clearly unconstitutional. Accordingly, allowing the writ petition, we declare that the Andhra Pradesh Panchayat Raj Act, 1994 (Act 13 of 1994) has no application to the scheduled areas in the State of Andhra Pradesh and consequently, elections under the said Act could not be held in the scheduled areas.[8]

The matter was carried to the Supreme Court and I appeared in the matter there. After hearing the arguments, the judgment was reserved for over one year. In the meantime, B.D. Sharma, S.R. Sankaran and others had the matter attended to through Parliament, and PESA was passed followed by the state amendment on those lines.[9]

---

8 Ibid.

9 Report of MPs and experts to make recommendations on the salient features of the law for extending the provisions of the Constitution (73rd) Amendment Act, 1992, to Scheduled Areas (Bhuria Committee, 1994). Members of the committee: Dileep Singh Bhuria, MP, chairman of the committee; Khagapati Pradhani, MP; M. Kamson, MP; B.D. Sharma, expert; Bhupinder Singh, expert; Bandi Oraon, vice-chairman, SC/ST Commission; Sushma Singh, joint secretary (monitoring), convenor. Minister for Rural Areas and Employment Yerran Naidu makes specific mention of the Andhra Pradesh case challenging the application of the Andhra Pradesh Panchayat Act in the Rajya Sabha debate on the Bhuria Committee report: 'The extension of Part IX of the Constitution by the States of Andhra Pradesh and Bihar to Scheduled Areas was challenged in their respective High Courts.' https://rsdebate.nic.in/bitstream/123456789/144204/1/PD_179_12121996_16_p292_p342_8.pdf. Accessed on 22 October 2021. For a detailed discussion of this and

The Polavaram Project

The Government of Andhra Pradesh had been contemplating the construction of the Indira Sagar Project (Polavaram) from 1943. One does not know whether the project was christened now or even as early as 1943. It was a multipurpose project located at Ramayyapet village at Polavaram in West Godavari district. About 75,798 acres covering around 278 villages would be fully submerged: about 27,798 families, consisting of about 1,17,000 people, 55,000 of whom belong to the ST category. It was planned to be a power and irrigation project. The project area was likely to submerge a wildlife sanctuary and lead to massive displacement. I appeared for this case in 2005.[10]

My central point was this: The Scheduled Area available to STs gets reduced with the construction of the dam and the submergence of villages. Barring the president, nobody has the authority to reduce the area, and yet there is no notification to that effect. Out of the 275 villages facing submergence, all the villages except fifteen were tribal villages. Along with 275 villages, 275 gram sabhas and nine mandal parishads would disappear. These representative institutions were not summoned or included in any deliberate decision making. These grassroots representative institutions are more important than the other representative institutions at a higher level and they were completely ignored. Of course, the court did not attach any significance to this point. Till today, the project has not secured the necessary environmental clearance, or clearance under the Wildlife Act and the necessary nod from the Supreme Court. The problem in all these matters was the lack of public pressure. No political party was interested in the Girijans and their lives. The Girijans lacked a strong regional or national organization to act as a pressure group for protecting their rights. The chief

---

related cases see, Kannabiran, Kalpana. 2022. 'Constitution-as-Commons and Spatial Justice in Adivasi India: The Continuing Legacy of Three Legal Cases'. In *State, Law, and Adivasi: Shifting Terrains of Exclusion*. Eds, Antje Linkenbach and Vidhu Verma. New Delhi: Sage/Spectrum, pp. 129–152.

10 *Andhra Pradesh Girijana Sangam vs Union of India and Ors*. WP No. 19067 of 2005. Advocate V. Raghu requested K.G. Kannabiran on behalf of the Andhra Pradesh Girijana Sangham, to appear as senior counsel in this case. For a detailed account of the case see Raghu, V. 2021. 'The Constitution and Scheduled Tribes in the Composite State of AP'. K.G. Kannabiran Lectures, *Livelaw*, 3 January, https://www.livelaw.in/columns/kannabiran-memorial-lecture-the-constitution-and-scheduled-tribes-in-composite-state-of-ap-167869. Accessed 22 October 2021.

justice of Andhra Pradesh High Court and his colleague delivered the judgment after one year.

The governments, both at the centre and state level, are not even contemplating creating an alternative area that will be brought under Schedule V so that the governance designed constitutionally may be applicable there without diminishing the extent of the area.

STs are a reserved category. But the tribes in the Scheduled Areas have certain additional privileges, as outlined in the previous section. The land within these is not transferable to non-tribals. Any transfer can take place only between tribal people, and any other transfer is invalid. Despite legal and constitutional barriers, entry into forests without the authority of law, and acts of depradation, plunder of forest resources and wealth is taking place unhindered. In fact, the Srikakulam movement in the late 1960s was sparked off by the killing of two Girijans proceeding to a meeting of the tribes for the exercise of their right to free speech and association (Chapter 6). The attempt to use law insurgently was never undertaken. Schedule V in the Constitution has been described by B.D. Sharma as a 'Constitution within the Constitution'.[11] Nobody seems to have studied it to enforce tribal rights in the region.

---

11 Ministry of Tribal Affairs and UNDP (United Nations Development Programme). n.d. *Land and Governance under the Fifth Schedule*. Available at https://tribal.nic.in/FRA/data/LandandGovernanceunderFifthSchedule.pdf, p. 2. Accessed on 10 July 2021.

13

Dalits and the Rule of Law

Law and Caste

INDIA ASSERTS ITS sovereignty when confronted with questions by international bodies on the deeply discriminatory practices and structural violence in Indian society. This argument is fallacious. The Universal Declaration of Human Rights, 1948, authorizes the scrutiny of specific discriminatory practices and human rights violation in all member states. A comparative analysis of practices that derogate on human dignity is extremely important for the protection of human rights. It is common practice for member states to resist international scrutiny as this would disrupt the established structures of dominance in each country. The caste order in Indian society is an example of this. It is expressed primarily through the ascription of practices of untouchability. It is necessary to recognize crimes against Dalits as crimes against humanity under the Rome Statute of the International Criminal Court. We pay a very heavy price for the sharp and violent disjuncture between social values and the secular ideas and pluralism enshrined in the Constitution. The violence often raises a doubt whether it is at all possible to dismantle discrimination with recourse to the Constitution alone. In order to accomplish the annihilation of caste and strike at the root of the deeply discriminatory majoritarian order, we need a sustained campaign on constitutionalism and constitutional values, and a cultural revolution.

Despite the Constitution, the civil rights of Dalits are not respected. This is aggravated by their social and economic subjugation by the dominant castes. In order to trigger social transformation, delegitimize structural violence and affirm the right to human dignity, Article 17 of the Indian Constitution unequivocally bans untouchability and makes it a punishable offence. The adoption of this article was followed with shouts in the Constituent Assembly of 'Mahatma Gandhi Ki Jai'. That is probably the last tribute we paid to the old soul. But caste practices cannot be wiped out in a day. In order to abolish untouchability, Parliament passed the Protection of Civil Rights Act in 1955, 'An Act to prescribe punishment for the [preaching and practice of "Untouchability"] for the enforcement of any disability arising therefrom and for matters connected therewith.'[1] Till that point, Article 17 on its own did not result in any change. Every Indian knows the meaning of untouchability. The Scheduled Caste and Scheduled Tribes (Prevention of Atrocities) Act, 1989, did not define the offence of untouchability, but enumerated its specific practices and criminalized them. Although the punishments were not severe, it was believed that the Act would be a deterrent to the practices of untouchability and bring about social change as a result.

Our fact-finding on caste discrimination in Mahbubnagar as part of our work in the APCLC revealed that untouchability was widely prevalent in the district. Small tea stalls had separate glasses for Dalit customers. This was despite the proscription of such practices under the Protection of Civil Rights Act. There was never any action taken against perpetrators of untouchability.

Indians are not merely argumentative. They are also prone to cause disquiet by distorting issues and derailing them. An example of this is the animated debates on the fact that 'untouchability' has not been defined. There was a debate in an Orissa case, *Hadibandhu Behera vs Banamali Sahu*, on the practice of excommunication in Hindu society.[2] The court dwelt on divisions among Chandalas and that 'Jati Chandalas' were different from 'Karma Chandalas'. Jati Chandalas, by this argument, were Chandalas by birth while Karma Chandalas were people from other (including dominant) castes excommunicated for their conduct by caste panchayats. There was a discussion on the definition of untouchability. It is true that the 1955 Act did not define 'civil rights'. However, it did state quite clearly that under Article 17 of the Constitution, any practice of untouchability shall be a violation of civil rights.[3]

---

1 https://legislative.gov.in/sites/default/files/A1955-22_1.pdf. Accessed on 17 October 2021.

2 *Hadibandhu Behera vs Banamali Sahu* (15.01.1960: ORIHC) AIR 1961 Ori 33.

3 'In the Untouchability (Offences) Act of 1955 (Central Act 22 of 1955) the expressions "untouchable" or "untouchability" have not been defined. But Section 4(x) of the Act makes it penal if any person on the ground of untouchability is

The second contentious issue is reservations. One example of the skewed interpretation of reservations is the argument that reservations for scheduled communities result in decreased opportunities for Savarna castes. This has historically never been the case. Savarna castes have for centuries enjoyed unlimited access to and domination over the public realm. For the first time in history, after the Constitution came into force, there were measures towards the more equitable distribution of wealth and resources across castes. They had up to that point understood it as political equality alone, but did not anticipate that their dominance in Hindu society would be eroded, and that society itself would be radically restructured. After enjoying unquestioned monopoly in the political domain, sharing space equally with other castes created difficulties. Savarna intellectuals keep repeating one argument: How can they be held responsible for historical wrongs perpetrated on castes at the bottom of the hierarchy? They question the fairness of visiting penalties for the wrongs of their ancestors on them. They insist that these historical wrongs cannot be an impediment to their lives. This is their primary argument in opposing reservations. The historical indignity suffered by Adivasi, Dalit and backward caste communities does not enter their account. This argument in favour of discounting historical wrongs perpetrated on Dalits in a consideration of present privileges enjoyed by Savarnas is inverted in the case of Muslims. Whether in the case of the Somnath Temple or Babri Masjid, the 'invasions' by Muslim rulers centuries ago have become the basis of revenge in the present, which has often descended into genocidal violence against them. The Savarna argument therefore is that they are not responsible for the historical wrongs perpetrated on Dalits, but must avenge the wrongs allegedly perpetrated on their forefathers by Mughal rulers.

Dr Ambedkar was very clear in his view that social transformation is a necessary precondition to political change:

> On the 26th of January 1950, India would be a democratic country in the sense that India from that day would have a government of the people, by

---

subjected to any disability with regard to the observance of any social or religious custom, usage or ceremony, or taking part in any religious procession. The outcasting of a person from society in consequence of which all other members of his caste exclude him from joining in any social or religious ceremony or usage may as well come within the scope of this penal clause unless one can restrict the meaning of the word "untouchable" to persons who are born as untouchables. The question is indeed interesting but in view of my finding on facts it seems unnecessary to decide this matter finally here.' *Hadibandhu Behera vs Banamali Sahu* (15.01.1960: ORIHC) AIR 1961 Ori 33 (para 8).

> the people and for the people. The same thought comes to my mind. What would happen to her democratic Constitution? Will she be able to maintain it or will she lose it again. This is the second thought that comes to my mind and makes me as anxious as the first … We must make our political democracy a social democracy as well. Political democracy cannot last unless there lies at the base of it social democracy … a way of life which recognizes liberty, equality and fraternity as the principles of life … We must begin by acknowledging the fact that there is complete absence of two things in Indian Society. One of these is equality. On the social plane, we have in India a society based on the principle of graded inequality which means elevation for some and degradation for others. On the economic plane, we have a society in which there are some who have immense wealth as against many who live in abject poverty. On the 26th of January 1950, we are going to enter into a life of contradictions. In politics we will have equality and in social and economic life we will have inequality. In politics we will be recognizing the principle of one man, one vote, and one vote, one value. In our social and economic life, we shall, by reason of our social and economic structure, continue to deny the principle of one man, one value. How long shall we continue to live this life of contradictions? How long shall we continue to deny equality in our social and economic life? If we continue to deny it for long, we will do so only by putting our political democracy in peril. We must remove this contradiction at the earliest possible moment or else those who suffer from inequality will blow up the structure of political democracy which this Assembly has so laboriously built up.[4]

The Constitution has not made any significant impact on caste orders—whether in the matter of untouchability or in the matter of discrimination based on caste.

The Case of Lingampalli Village, Cuddapah District

In the late 1980s or early 1990s, I was sitting in Justice B.P. Jeevan Reddy's court waiting for an admission. My friend, advocate Ella Reddy, was also waiting for his case to be called. His was listed above mine. The facts narrated by him attracted my attention. He complained against a joint collector who prevented a Reddy landlord

4 *Constituent Assembly Debates*. 1949. Vol. XI (14–26 November). On 25 November 1949, pp. 978–79, https://eparlib.nic.in/bitstream/123456789/763285/1/cad_25-11-1949.pdf. Accessed on 4 November 2021.

from entering his land on a complaint by some Dalits who were dispossessed from their land. The joint collector was a Dalit and that was his complaint. It was an interim measure pending a final inquiry. The landlord, Obul Reddi, rushed to the high court. It is interesting and also educative to discuss the facts of the Obul Reddi case.

In Lingampalli village of Sidhout Mandal, Cuddappah, in the state of Andhra Pradesh, some persons belonging to the depressed classes were allotted certain government lands. These assigned lands were from lands set apart for assignment to the depressed classes. It was in accordance with the revised assignment policy in G.O. Ms. 1142 Revenue Department dated 18 June 1954. The particulars are as follows:

S. No.	Extent	Assignee
126	4.53 acres	Gali Ramaiah
127/2	2.92 acres	B. Palakondaiah
131/2	1.34acres	Gali Chinna Obaiah
131/4	1.32 acres	Jada Pedda Kishtaiah
131/5	1.40 acres	Jada Chinniah

These lands were assigned to these persons between March and August 1955.

B.C. Obul Reddi, a revenue inspector turned lawyer, approached these persons and assured them that he would develop these lands if the Dalits would lease out the land to him. He also assured them employment on the farms for a wage. By agreeing to this, the Dalits, while retaining ownership in land, turned into wage labourers on their own farms. This Obul Reddi, after having convinced them, obtained their thumb impression on certain papers, which turned out to be a sale deed. After thus securing a sale deed, Obul Reddi informed the authorities that contrary to the conditions in D Form Pattas, the assignees (the Dalits) had sold these lands. On the basis of this, he had the assignments cancelled. Allowing some time to pass, he set up his nominees—three in number (Buddana Pedda Venkata Subbaiah, Gummadi Rangaiah and Vorkam Obaiah)—and had those lands assigned to them in February 1975. The time lag was necessary to lull the Dalits into the belief that they were still the owners; if they ever realized this and decided to fight, it would be too late for them to assert their rights. The new allottees were said to be from a different village, viz., Kadapayapalli. The lands were mortgaged by the new allottees to the Sidhavattam (Sidhout) Agricultural Development Bank in the year 1976 and were brought to sale on 26 April 1979 by public auction where the properties were purchased by the said Obul Reddi. The Dalits came to know only a year after the purchase how effectively they were kept in the dark and their lands were taken away by using the legal process itself.

They were agitated by this. By the time they realized what has happened, the next generation grew into adulthood, and it was they who took up the fight. A representation was made to the joint collector, who, I was told, was a Dalit himself. After some inquiries, and obviously upset by the deceit, on 23 January 1984, he passed orders holding the sale of lands through public auction by the cooperative sub-registrar invalid and directed the resumption of the lands.

Obul Reddi filed a writ petition in the high court questioning the order passed by the joint collector. This writ petition was filed in the year 1984, admitted and the operation of the order of the joint collector was suspended. The original assignees who were displaced filed an application that they were the proper and necessary parties, and that they were likely to be affected by any order passed by the court. They also filed a petition to have the stay vacated. On these, the high court ordered that the joint collector may complete the inquiry after due notice to the affected parties. This final order was made on 21 January 1987. The court directed the mandal revenue officer (MRO) to hold the inquiry, as it was under the impression that the same joint collector continued in office.

The MRO found that the lands were resumed in the year 1975 and the Dalits started agitating only from 1983. They ought not to have stayed silent for eight years, in his opinion, trying to reopen the issue 'when much water has already flown [sic] under the bridge'. He also held that the sale in favour of Obul Reddi violated GO No. Ms. 1033 dated 21 May 1970 as no approval of the collector was obtained prior to sale and thus confirmed the resumption. Neither the original Dalit assignees nor these subsequent assignees were parties to this inquiry. These orders were passed on 3 September 1988. The Dalit assignees made a representation to the MRO on 1 March 1988 that they were seeking modification of the orders dated 21 December 1987 under which the MRO was acting. On 1 August 1988, the high court observed that the joint collector against whom complaints were made stood transferred and directed that the inquiry be conducted by the joint collector who succeeded the earlier person.

The joint collector found that in respect of 4.43 acres assigned to one Ellatur Narasaiah, a farm servant of this Obul Reddi, the latter secured a sale deed and these lands were resumed on that ground. The collector found that 'Shri C. Obul Reddi, Advocate and his sons have grabbed all lands of the innocent and illiterate Dalits and defeated the very objective of land assignment by the Government to help the poor. They filed writ petitions, and writ appeals to prolong the issue and to keep the land under their adverse and illegal possession.' But he did not allot lands in favour of Dalits despite the above observation. This order was adverse to both parties. This was an order of resumption of the land by the government.

As the order was adverse to both parties, technically one need not make the other a party in a fresh proceeding. That is what happened in the case. Immediately after the MRO passed his order, Obul Reddi filed another writ petition questioning the decision of the MRO, and the writ petition was allowed, holding the sale in public auction as valid. The judge did not find anything incongruous in allowing the writ petition without the Dalit assignees who were parties to the proceedings.

The MRO decided on the basis of G.O. Ms. 1033 dated 21 May 1970 which imposed restrictions on the hypothecation of lands assigned to the land mortgage banks. According to this GO, the sale of land for the recovery of a loan shall not be confirmed without prior approval of the collector concerned. If such sale becomes necessary and if from the date of assignment ten years have not elapsed, it can be sold to Scheduled Castes. This, according to the MRO, was violated by the public sale conducted by the cooperative sub-registrar. It was specifically brought to the notice of the MRO that the state legislature had enacted the Andhra Pradesh Assigned Lands (Prevention of Alienation) Act, 1977, which superseded all existing administrative orders. The Act imposed restrictions on alienation. But he said the Act escheated mortgages in favour of cooperative societies. In his subsequent inquiry, the joint collector neither supported the view of the MRO nor opposed it. The result was that Obul Reddi got a prima facie right to file another writ petition, which was later allowed. When the Dalit assignees filed a writ petition, the judgment of the high court delivered earlier in favour of Obul Reddi stared them in the face. Although it was technically not binding it would influence the course of the proceedings. The collector confirmed the finding of the MRO that the Dalits had slept over the matter for eight long years. Unless the court held the entire transaction as fraudulent, the Dalit assignees would have no chance.

Thus, from 1954 to 1975, the Dalits were nominally owners and were working as wage labour on their own land. From 1975 to 1983, they spent their lives to gather the facts and make representations to the collector. Their resource position was such that they could only go thus far. From 1984, they had been litigating over the land and the fight was carried on by the heirs of the original assignees while the law, administration and justice system was systematically subverted by Obul Reddi. The Dalits stood condemned to deprivation because there was an eight-year delay.

To skulduggery and subversion of legal processes there has always been only one answer. In such circumstances, revolution has an irresistible appeal.

Atrocities against Dalits in AP

In 1983, soon after the rise of the Telugu Desam Party (TDP), even as elections were under way, there was an attack on Dalits in Padirikuppam. We had not till then heard of this kind of attack on Dalits in the state. We knew of the Kilvenmani massacre in Tamil Nadu where a landlord Gopalakrishnama Naidu was accused of setting 40 Dalits on fire. The mass attacks on Dalits there started as soon as they laid claim to the constitutional guarantee of equality. I went to Padirikuppam in Chittoor district three days after the attack. The upper-caste landlords had destroyed the huts of Dalits. They looted whatever few assets they had. They poured kerosene on a cow that was tethered to a hut and set it on fire. This despite the fact that the cow is sacred in dominant Hindu society. The provocation was that Dalits would vote for the Congress. The free exercise of their voting rights by Dalits was intolerable for the upper castes. I did not come across any condemnation of the brutal attack by the upper castes. This only pointed to the deep-seated belief among caste Hindus that Dalits did not have the right to political expression. Justice and the rule of law in the caste society is partisan by definition. It only applies to some. In this kind of context, individuals take the law into their hands with ease. In Kilvenmani, the prosecution could not hold its ground against Gopalakrishnama Naidu who was accused of perpetrating gruesome atrocity on the Dalits, and he was found not guilty by the courts. The judge expressed dismay that a person as respectable as Naidu was accused in this manner.[5]

Several years later, Naidu was shot dead by a radical group. Walter Dewaram, a cruel police officer in Tamil Nadu, killed every member of this group. This is yet another tale of police brutality in this country. The anger of the Kammas, who were with the TDP, against the Dalits of Padirikuppam, who supported the Congress, led to assaults there. The Justice Y. Venkateswara Rao Commission of Inquiry held

---

5 'Gentlemen Killers of Kilvenmani'. *Economic and Political Weekly*, Vol 8, No. 21, 26 May 1973. https://www.epw.in/system/files/pdf/1973_8/21/tamil_nadu_gentlemen_killers_of_kilvenmani.pdf. Accessed on 6 May 2022.

hearings on this incident and submitted its report.[6] This was repeated two years later in Karamchedu.

Karamchedu village near Chirala in Prakasam district witnessed a gruesome massacre on 17 July 1985. Kammas were the dominant landowning caste in this village—like in Padirikuppam—and owed allegiance to the TDP, while the Dalits supported the Congress. N.T. Rama Rao's son-in-law, Daggubati Venkateswara Rao who won the election on a TDP ticket, was a big landlord in this village. On 16 July 1985, two Kamma men led their cows to the drinking water tank in the Madiga hamlet and washed their dirty buckets in the tank. Munnangi Suvaarthamma, a Dalit woman, intervened and chastised them, and a minor altercation followed. The next morning, on 17 July, a horde of Kammas from surrounding villages raided the Dalit hamlet and murderously assaulted Dalits. Six Dalits were killed in the massacre, which led to the other Dalits fleeing the village and taking shelter in a church in Chirala. This was the second mass assault on Dalits in the first few years after the TDP came to power, and led to large-scale protests.[7] A commission of inquiry was constituted to investigate the Karamchedu massacre.[8] The violence

---

6 For a legislative debate on Padirikuppam, Karamchedu and Neerukonda caste atrocities, see 'Statement placed on the Table by Chief Minister [N.T. Rama Rao] re: Allegations against C.M., Allegations and responses nos. 113 & 114.' On Padirikuppam, CM's response: 'Government had instituted a Judicial Inquiry into the incident by appointing Sri Y. Venkateswara Rao, retired Judge of High Court as Commission of Inquiry. The Commission held that the local political rivalry accumulating over years between two groups … which gained momentum with the issue of Notification for General Elections on 16th December, 1982, was generally responsible for the fire mishap that occurred on 5th January, 1983, the polling day at Padirikuppam. The Commission has held that the incident has no caste or communal colour,' *The Andhra Pradesh Legislative Assembly Debates: Official Report* (Second Day of the Ninth Session of the Andhra Pradesh Legislative Assembly), Monday, 14 December 1987, p. 232, Q. no. 113.

7 Balagopal, K. 1985. 'The Karamchedu Massacre: A Report'. Guntur: Andhra Pradesh Civil Liberties Committee, 22 July, http://www.unipune.ac.in/snc/cssh/humanrights/05%20STATE%20AGRICULTURE%20FOREST%20DALITS%20AND%20TRIBALS/08.pdf. Accessed on 28 November 2021.

8 Menon, Amarnath K. 1985. 'Karamchedu in Andhra Pradesh Set to Become an Important Landmark in Harijan History'. *India Today*, 30 September, where Menon reports that the 'Harijans of Karamchedu in Andhra Pradesh, five of whom were killed by Kamma landlords two months ago, are bent on proving that hypocritical commiseration by political parties will not be their only legacy. Even the farcical fate of the state government's attempt to set up a judicial

in Karamchedu gave birth to the Dalit Mahasabha in Andhra Pradesh and signalled the rise of the Dalit movement in the state. I examined witnesses in a private complaint filed by the Dalits of Karamchedu. There was no response from the state. The private complaint became part of the case registered by the state after widespread protests. Bojja Tarakam appeared in this case. Some of the accused were found guilty by the district court in Guntur. Perhaps if the conviction and punishment had been awarded, Tsundur might not have happened. If only Justice Reddeppa Reddy had been conscious of the enormous social responsibility that rested on him as a judge in this case, we might have had different results.[9] Here, as in Kilvenmani, when the Dalits of Karamchedu could not secure justice from courts, Daggubati Chenchuramaiah, a Kamma elder from the village, was killed by a radical group. And yet, this retaliatory violence is no answer at all for holding in place the rule of law.

Tsundur

Four years after Karamchedu, there was an attack on Dalits again, this time in Tsundur village, Guntur district. This was the worst of the three attacks in terms of magnitude and barbarity. The massacre took place on Hiroshima Day, 6 August 1991. A mob of around 400 Reddis and Telagas attacked the Dalits in the village. Eight Dalits were chased and hacked to death. Two bodies were found stuffed in gunny sacks; one body was found with eyes gouged out. The gunny sacks with the bodies were thrown into the Tungabhadra canal and into the canal that runs parallel to the Madras–Howrah railway line. Three days after the massacre, probably on 10 August, Dalit leader Katti Padma Rao took the bodies in a procession through the village. A primary justification for the violence was that Mala youth

---

inquiry commission—last fortnight the second of the judges named to head the commission turned down the job—has not deterred them.' '[R]elying on the court to bring the culprits to book, [t]hey boycotted the enquiry commission of retired judge D.P. Desai after the state government's earlier attempts to start the inquiry failed (two judges had turned down the job in 1985).' Menon, Amarnath K. 1987. 'Harijans in Karamchedu Village in Andhra Pradesh Fight Doggedly for Justice'. *India Today*, 31 July.

9 Karamchedu Massacre Cases: In the court of the sessions judge, Guntur, Sessions Case Nos 80/86, 80/87, 22/88, SC No. 114/88; in the Andhra Pradesh High Court, Criminal Appeal Nos 1112/94, 1113/94 and 33/98; in the Supreme Court of India, Criminal Appeal Nos 356-8/1998, Special Leave Petition (CrL Nos 3788-90 of 1998).

had misbehaved with upper-caste women. We see this pattern replaying in other episodes of caste/majoritarian violence as well (See Chapter 16 on the Bidar riots).[10]

I went to the village with G. Haragopal and advocate B. Chandrasekhar. As we could not enter the village in our car, we walked through the crowds. When we reached the colony, huts had been set afire and it was not possible for us to reach the place where the last rites of the deceased were being performed. They were buried at 6 p.m. at the burial site called Rakta Kshetram. Owing to P.S. Krishnan's efforts, a new law had been enacted to recognize crimes against Dalits as 'atrocities', the massacre in Tsundur was registered under the Scheduled Castes and Scheduled Tribes (Prevention of Atrocities) Act, 1989 as an atrocity. This law, enacted towards the end of the twentieth century defines by law the extreme cruelty of Hindu caste society. Section 3 of the Act, which lists atrocities, tells us how inhuman the caste order is, and how dehumanized our society is.

Police officer R.P. Meena was designated as the special officer on this incident. The police opened fire on the protestors gathered in a camp set up for the Tsundur victims by Katti Padma Rao, killing one Dalit activist, Anil Kumar. I returned to Tsundur a second time then. The people believed that the investigating officer, Rayalaiah, who had recorded Anil Kumar's eyewitness account, had intentionally shot and killed Anil Kumar. They also believed that Special Officer R.P. Meena had a role. As a matter of fact, in incidents like this, if there is no proper investigation, it

---

10 See the 'evidence' placed before the Justice Gangadhar Rao Commission of Inquiry: 'It seems to be simply the obnoxious behavior of the Mala youth towards women of other castes. Their attitude to women of the weakest castes seems to [be] exploitative and violent, to the point of abduction and rape. Eve-teasing and harassment of women seem to have been a regular feature. While it was confined to the weaker castes no violent reaction resulted; however, when this behavior was extended to the Telega and Reddy women their men reacted violently. This was enough to confuse the issue as far as the Commissioner was concerned. This sole cause that he identified did not seem to merit the type of violent reaction leading to a massacre of 8 people ... It will be noted that as far as Tsundur is concerned, no Mala woman has been reported to have been so treated by any other caste person. Yet to put the emphasis on the primary or fundamental cause is a useful one. The Commissioner himself, in the course of fulfilling his mandated task ... *while admitting the validity of the view that it was the Mala youths misbehavior with women as the cause*, was not prepared to subscribe that it was the only cause.' Pingle, Gautam. 1999. 'Breakdown of Law and Order in Tsundur, Guntur: A Case Study for Department of Training, Government of India'. Hyderabad: Administrative Staff College of India, p. 19. Unpublished study. Emphasis added. The editor is grateful to Gautam Pingle for a copy of this document.

gets seared as a doubt into the collective memory of the survivors. What begins as a suspicion changes into a conviction over time. That is perhaps the reason why they say the wrongs committed by a person live beyond his lifetime.

There was a sense of national outrage over the Tsundur massacre.[11] A one-man commission was set up with Justice A. Gangadhara Rao to inquire into the incident.[12] After the killing of Anil Kumar, I met Meena immediately on arrival in Guntur. I told him that I was just paying him a courtesy call, and that I did not require his permission to visit Tsundur. I travelled to Tsundur from there but the police did not permit us to enter the village till Anil Kumar's last rites had been completed. As far as I can remember, among the people who walked with me to Tsundur were the poet Vimala, the cultural activist Arunodaya Rama Rao, advocate Bojja Tarakam and political scientist Kancha Ilaiah. The atmosphere in the village was very tense. Fearing further attacks, several people had fled.

I went to the village a third time when the trial for the case opened in the Guntur district court. My relationship with Tsundur, and the trial on the atrocities grew. The Dalits of Tsundur demanded that the trial be held in their village. Chief Minister Nedurumalli Janardhana Reddy agreed to the demand. A special court was notified and set up in Tsundur. Objections were raised regarding the completion of investigation by the prosecution. There is one truth that speakers in public meetings do not recognize in the matter of courts and trials. This is an inherent problem in the system of justice which a litigant who engages a lawyer knows well. Once an interim order is obtained, the trial can be indefinitely delayed. If the opposite party is the government, it is no problem at all to obtain the compliance of the state counsel. A client can tell his lawyer to prolong the case for as long as possible; and lawyers are taught to follow the instructions of their clients in this matter. This is evident in the number of interim orders secured by lawyers in any case. Ethics, for a lawyer, are limited to the ethics of the client. I was a member of the Bar Council twice. I was also a part of the Disciplinary Committee of the Bar Council. The volume of unethical practices by lawyers that came before me was shocking. If we were to look for parallels of legal representation for Dalits in India, we could look at the work of

---

11 See 'Re. Brutal Killing of Harijans in Tsundur Village of Guntur District, 1991. *Lok Sabha Debates*, 9 August 1991, pp. 287–97, https://eparlib.nic.in/bitstream/123456789/8774/1/10_I_09081991_p148_p153_T227.pdf. Accessed on 17 October 2021.

12 Justice A. Gangadhar Rao, 'Report of the Commission of Inquiry', General Administration (General B) Department, Government of Andhra Pradesh, Hyderabad,1992.

lawyers who defended African-Americans in the United States. They faced several hardships for the professional courage and commitment they displayed.

The first obstacle in the Tsundur case was the objection raised in holding the trial in the village. A criminal appeal was filed to challenge the government decision to locate the special court in Tsundur. It came for hearing before Justice Reddeppa Reddy. He said that it was not necessary to comply with that administrative decision. I had a very heated argument with him. Finally, he summoned the file with the notification. He could not strike down the notification and sent it back to the district court. This was aimed at delaying the trial. Even a delay of a couple of weeks would make it possible to buy out the witnesses. After the high court ruled that the trial should be conducted in Tsundur, the accused moved the court a second time. This time the petition came before Justice Somayajulu. It took time for it to be examined and decided. The defence lawyer argued very vociferously on how the Tsundur Dalits were dictating terms on the way the court should conduct itself. How can we allow Dalits in this country to dictate how a court should function? This was his question. His arguments were in the same vein. Justice Somayajulu struck down the petition filed on behalf of the accused. The accused then petitioned the high court a third time. This time they argued that a Dalit judge was appointed to the special court in Tsundur, compromising the possibility of a fair trial, and demanded that the judge be transferred. As a matter of fact, that judge was appointed to the special court as part of the routine transfers of judges. If one examines the accusations of the accused in this petition, it comes firmly within the meaning of atrocity as defined in the Scheduled Castes and Scheduled Tribes (Prevention of Atrocities) Act, 1989. I argued on these petitions in the high court. The accused also sent a similar appeal to the high court registry. The Dalit judge was eventually transferred—it was in my view an erroneous order issued by the high court.

After all the objections had been dealt with and settled, the trial began in the special court in Tsundur on 21 January 2004. There were 200 persons named as accused by the prosecution. Thirty-three of them died while the trial was ongoing. Seven had escaped arrest and were at large—so they were separated and the trial commenced with the remaining accused persons. The prosecution examined seventy witnesses. Nine witnesses were examined from the side of the accused. The court also examined 261 objects from the prosecution side and 287 objects on the accused's side. The prosecutor argued for twenty hours and the defence counsel argued for fifty hours. My young friend, advocate B. Chandrasekhar, who practises in Guntur, kept me informed of these developments in the trial. He was appointed the special public prosecutor in this case after the Dalits of Tsundur made a written appeal to the government. It was a trial that required tremendous courage of conviction. It is very rare for a lawyer to get an opportunity to argue a case like this. The request by the victims' families that they wanted a particular lawyer to represent them is a sign of the deep faith they have in the lawyer. He fully validated that act of faith. Twenty-one accused were awarded life imprisonment. Thirty-five were convicted for lesser offences and sentenced to one-year imprisonment or fines.[13]

Conclusion

What do we mean by civil rights? These are rights that are inherent in every person. The right to schools, water sources, places of public resort are all civil rights, among others. These are set out in Article 15(2) and Article 17. However, temple entry is not part of these provisions. The government has been given the authority to take appropriate steps to ensure equal access to places of worship. The guarantee against untouchability, against discrimination and the guarantee of equality in the Constitution made possible reservations in education and employment. These were some preliminary steps to ensure equality for scheduled communities. The philosophical wisdom and dissenting traditions in Hinduism have had no enduring impact on deeply discriminatory social practices. As a matter of fact, the orthodoxy and obscurantism that we thought we had left behind has returned with renewed power, making for increased levels of violence and brute force. All the arguments being presented today had already been debated in the Constituent Assembly and led to the constitutional consensus on untouchability, child labour, exploitation, bonded labour and slavery and so on. The Constitution in its foundational deliberations recognized these as offences. It was recognized that if education and employment are to be meaningful, they must be based on equality of opportunity—and this is only possible through reservations. Although there was a deliberation and debate on the need for special protections, what we witness today is an unrelenting attack on these very protections. Irrespective of what the legislatures and the Constitution

13 *State (Sub Divisional Police Officer, Tenali) vs Modugula Sambi Reddi and 218 Others*: Sessions Case No. 36/1993, in the court of the special sessions judge-cum-IV additional sessions judge, Guntur, 31 July 2007. For details, see Venugopal, N. 2014. 'Killing the Dead All Over Again'. *India Together*, 26 May, https://indiatogether.org/court-verdict-on-tsundur-massacre-human-rights. Accessed on 17 October 2021.

say, however, the interpretation of these provisions is dependent on the arguments of lawyers and the reasoning of judges in courts.

Even six decades after the Constitution came into force, the dominant castes in this country have not given up their claim to hegemony. Historical discrimination continues even today but under the garb of a claim to equality. This contest is taking place in the context of globalization against the backdrop of the Constitution.

14

The Murder of Shankar Guha Niyogi

I HAD A long association with Shankar Guha Niyogi, a very compassionate person, friendly, and a very good activist.[1] He once even asked me to contest the elections from any Chhattisgarh parliamentary constituency—I refused. That was the time when Chhattisgarh was part of Madhya Pradesh; Arjun Singh was chief minister. Niyogi introduced some unique traditions in the movement of the working classes in our country. He mobilized the workers to take an oath of abstinence from liquor. There was total prohibition in the areas, and workers regulated this themselves by imposing fines on anyone who defaulted on the oath. The businesses of the excise contractors came to a grinding halt. Since states are dependent on liquor, Niyogi was arrested under the National Security Act. Our governments are like that.

The Constitutional Promise and Niyogi

The murder of Shankar Guha Niyogi, a trade union leader, undermines the constitutional promise of an egalitarian social transformation.[2] The key words delineating the constitutional promise are socialism, equality and political and

---

1 This chapter interweaves K.G. Kannabiran's account of the Niyogi case in *24 Gantalu* and the section titled 'The Assassination of Shankar Guha Niyogi' (pp. 394–401) from the chapter titled 'Conspiracies of Association: Associational Offences, Associational Freedoms and the Rule of Law' originally published in *Challenging the Rules(s) of Law: Colonialism, Criminology and Human Rights in India*. Eds Kalpana Kannabiran and Ranbir Singh. New Delhi: Sage, 2008. Included with the permission of the publishers, SAGE Publications India Pvt. Ltd, New Delhi.

2 *CBI vs Chandrakant Shah and Ors,* Sessions Case no. 233/92, the court of the second additional sessions judge, Durg, Madhya Pradesh, and *State of Madhya*

economic justice set out in the Preamble. The fundamental obligations of the state are enumerated in Part IV of the Constitution by which the goals specified in the Preamble are to be secured. The Constitution has an economic philosophy which shall inform all the institutions of national life, and the state is mandated to structure a social order which secures to its citizens and others resident in its territory all facets of justice. It does not say that expropriators should be expropriated. Its aim is modest and not beset with incomprehensible jargon. It states that the ownership and control of the material resources of the community are so distributed as to best subserve the common good; that the operation of the economic system does not result in the concentration of wealth and means of production to the common detriment. This restraint on avaricious appropriation of material resources and on acquisition of opulence is necessary to transform India into an egalitarian society. Contemporary Indian society should ensure to all working men and women adequate means of livelihood; there shall be equal pay for equal work for both men and women; the health and strength of workers and the tender age of children are not to be abused and no one is to be driven to avocations unsuited to one's age and strength. Children should be allowed to develop in health, freedom and dignity and not suffer moral abandonment and exploitation. These mandatory obligations are politically enforceable by citizens through the exercise of associational freedoms, which the Constitution recognizes as inhering in the people.

Shankar Guha Niyogi, a very popular trade union leader, was organizing workers for around two decades in the Rajhara mines, which supplied iron ore to the Bhilai steel plant in Madhya Pradesh. He formed a central trade union organization, the Chhattisgarh Mukti Morcha (CMM). The diligence that our trade unions show towards mobilizing organized workers does not extend to unorganized workers. Niyogi had decided upon organizing the unorganized labour in that area, and so took up residence in Bhilai in 1990, and set up an office as well. His family lived in Rajhara. The settlement he brought about with the ACC cement factory in Jamul, Bhilai, in respect of the contract labour employed by them was an unprecedented success and increased his following among the working class in the industrially developing Durg district. He focused his attention on the plight of the working class in the emerging corporate tigers in Bhilai, of which the Simplex Group was one. These corporate tigers ran their fledgling capitalist enterprises as a feudal lord would his fiefdom.

Pradesh through CBI, etc. vs Paltan Malla, etc., Criminal Appeal No. 98 of 1999, Supreme Court of India.

Shankar Guha Niyogi took the Constitution and the rights guaranteed therein seriously. His entire struggle after he entered Bhilai was for improving the lot of the workers employed by the Simplex Group. The struggle he carried on there and the Gandhian tenacity he displayed during that period made him a legend in his own lifetime. His faith in the constitutional promise tenaciously drove him to enforce that promise in the Durg area of Madhya Pradesh. In fact, during 11–12 September 1991, Niyogi submitted a representation to the president of India to intervene and resolve 'long standing problem of workers and their (i) Right to life and bodily security as per Article 21 of the Constitution; (ii) Right to form Trade Unions as per Article 19 (1) (a) (b) & (c)'. He brought to the notice of the president two basic demands of the workers. His concern was that the workers be regularized when work is of a permanent nature in the industry—as per Section 10(a) of the Contract Labour (Regulation and Abolition) Act. He presented this memorandum, perhaps his last one, personally to the then president, R. Venkataraman, who had entered politics as a labour leader. Legally, the memorandum may have relevance as a statement made by a dead person, on the basis of which an investigation could be started. If the central government had taken serious note of it, this representation might have been the basis for protecting the right to life of a trade union leader. Neither happened.

Conditions of Workers in the Bhilai–Durg Industrial Sector

The labour in the organized sector unionization would broadly be around 8 per cent, and the labour in the unorganized sector at 92 per cent. While the Bhilai steel plant had an organized trade union, the labour working in small industries around it were left unorganized by the central trade unions. These small units also needed trade unions for effective collective bargaining. A law legislated to abolish contract labour and to regulate the labour in the meantime through a subverted interpretation by courts became a law for the perpetuation of contract labour with no security of tenure. No more than 10 per cent of workers in the entire Bhilai–Durg industrial sector were under permanent status. The rest were employed as 'contract labour'. The adversarial system of the courts reduced the adjudication of issues to battles of attrition between capital and labour extended over tiresomely long periods of time. After four decades of the Constitution, during which every principle of equality was defeated, Niyogi entered to fight for principles, which were comprehensively routed. The important thing to note is that all the time Niyogi was engaged in a struggle to enforce constitutional obligations made available to him through legislation, while the Simplex Group was using unlawful methods to suppress the rights of the workers and Niyogi's right to head the trade union of which they were members.

The Simplex Group of industries—around five in all—removed 973 workmen. There were protests and demonstrations on a day-to-day basis. The charter of demands would be raised; the service of these demand letters were refused and disputes were raised. The conciliation officer would enter into conciliation under the Industrial Disputes Act and invite the parties to solve the dispute. The management of the Simplex Group never attended these meetings, while the workmen did.[3] There was a total defiance of law by the Simplex Group. This behaviour of Simplex towards conciliation is not unique—it is the standard behaviour of all managements. This stubbornness to not abide by the law by managements very often intimidates the working class triggering violence, and this violence is extrapolated from a chain of events of which strike by employees is the consequence.

Niyogi decided to wrest the guaranteed rights politically. In response, the employers engaged goons to disrupt the protests by beating up the workers, and in fact two members were murdered by the employer's hirelings. Section 144 of the CrPC was promulgated, suspending associational freedoms. Injunction orders, which had the effect of imposing prohibitory orders, were obtained from the civil courts against the protesting workers. Several criminal prosecutions were launched in a number of jurisdictions against Niyogi and his men. This has been the way labour is fought through courts. This subversion is accepted as part of the rule of law, and so these methods do not amount to committing unlawful acts to paralyse the functioning of a trade union leader. They may not fit into the definition of the crime of conspiracy. When a dispute is referred to the tribunal, the employer challenges the jurisdiction of the tribunal in a matter that he does not consider to be an industrial dispute in appellate courts, so that by the time the matter is taken up for trial decades will pass. All these efforts by the Simplex Group to break the back of the movement led by Niyogi did not succeed. The unrelenting pursuit of their movement by the workers affected the Simplex Group financially. My observations are based on evidence from the trial. There was cogent evidence of every aspect of organization of the workers by Niyogi from the time he took up the issue of the Simplex Group workers; the various prosecutions launched against and about his detention and externment by the government; the details of police interventions at the behest of the industrialists in the course of his movement for a living wage. There is also evidence of advice via a confidential note (Ex P-261) as to how Niyogi

3 Based on the evidence of the assistant labour commissioner in the trial of those accused of murdering Niyogi.

should be handled, which was recovered in Moolchand's (A-5) residence. This action plan was very religiously followed. The events corroborate the advice.

What were the salient aspects of the Simplex management's views on Niyogi?

- Niyogi's increasing influence is due to the failure of the district administration in dealing with him;
- There should not be any hasty action for dealing with Niyogi;
- Rival trade unions should be given more importance;
- Niyogi's shortcomings must be written about daily in the newspapers;
- The subordinate police officers who give him information and sympathize with him should be transferred;
- Niyogi must be compelled to appear in all the criminal cases pending against him in Balod, Durg, Rajnandgaon and Bilaspur where there are arrest warrants against him, so that he will have no time to strengthen his position;
- His legitimacy with political parties and the district administration in the region must be undermined systematically, and his financial sources sealed.

These Kautilyan guidelines failed. On 27 September 1991, around midnight, Niyogi returned to his residence in Bhilai and went to bed around 2 or 2.30 a.m. Bahel Ram, who was also asleep in the quarters, woke up to a loud explosion and found Niyogi writhing in his bed. By the time he was taken to the hospital he was dead. The murder of Niyogi, according to the prosecution, was a consequence of organizing workers and starting a struggle for better wages and work conditions, especially of contract and other workers in the unorganized sector.

The Shankar Guha Niyogi Murder Case

The trial was conducted in the court of the second additional judge of the sessions court in Durg.[4] Deferring to the wishes of the CMM, the CBI requested me to join the prosecution in the high court at Jabalpur. I agreed to this request because it was a historic case where industrialists were the primary accused.[5] Special public prosecutor Y.K. Saksena appeared for the CBI. We stayed in a Methodist missionary

4 Sessions Case No. 233/92, *Central Bureau of Investigation, New Delhi vs Chandrakant Shah and Ors.* Court of second additional sessions judge, Durg, Madhya Pradesh.

5 Advocate V. Suresh assisted K.G. Kannabiran in the Madhya Pradesh High Court at Jabalpur.

guest house for a month while the hearing was in progress. The bishop's wife told me one day that two unknown persons were following me on a motorcycle. I just told her not to be surprised if she heard the news that the lawyer appearing in the Niyogi case, Kannabiran, was killed by unknown persons.

There was no relationship between Moolchand Shah and his brothers and Shankar Guha Niyogi excepting that of employer and trade union leader of the workmen of the former. The tenacious movement by the workers for securing the demands and the employer's refusal to abide by the law relating to the settlement of wage disputes can form a powerful motive for the crime. The trial judge, Mr T.K. Jha, did not extrapolate the crime from its setting. He studied the evidence in context and the inferences drawn were convincing. In fact, the sequential events dovetail into a conspiracy to commit a capital crime. One hundred and ninety-two witnesses were examined and the prosecution produced 455 documents. The investigation was detailed and every aspect was subjected to scrutiny. The trial judge dealt with evidence brought on record very meticulously and came to the conclusion that the documents recovered from his residence showed that Moolchand Shah, head of the Simplex Group, targeted Niyogi, and this was confirmed by the entries in his diary and the cassette he recorded prior to Niyogi's death. The hireling murderer, till then a small time history-sheeter, in his extrajudicial confession mentioned the names of the accused and also stated that there was an open conspiracy to malign and attack Niyogi and the workers, and that his gang had been hired for the purpose.

'Movement by Niyogi and the motive for the crime:' From the evidence gathered by the CBI, Judge T.K. Jha came to the compelling conclusion that Simplex Group was the most affected by the workers' agitation production-wise and prestige-wise that led to the decision to eliminate Niyogi.

'Beginning of conspiracy and its apprehensions:' While the Simplex Group was openly defying the law and the Constitution, they did not realize that committing a capital crime pursuant to that defiance is another matter. The first intimation of the conspiracy was an anonymous letter received by Niyogi at Dalli Rajhara, which he photocopied before handing over the original letter to the police station at Rajhara. The anonymous letter was a piece of credible information to set the ball rolling. It gave details about Chandrakant Shah's trip to Nepal. Chandrakanth Shah (A-1) did go to Nepal along with A-2 to A-4 and the investigation recovered documents and recorded oral evidence on this aspect of the conspiracy. The entire Nepal trip was covered by almost unrebutted evidence. The trip to Nepal was not disputed. The plea that Chandrakant Shah, brother of Moolchand Shah, went on a pilgrimage to Kathmandu was rejected by the trial court for very convincing reasons. This,

according to the sessions judge, was part of the conspiracy, and not a pilgrimage, as the first accused had not gone with members of his family.

This very fact was not taken note of seriously by the high court—that he visited Kathmandu in the company of co-conspirators and the accused in this case. The visit to Nepal by these accused persons and the recovery of a bill in the court's view did not advance the prosecution case to prove the criminal conspiracy alleged against them. The reasoning of the Supreme Court regarding the conspiracy charge is not very different from the reasoning of the high court. The organization of labour by Niyogi and the evidence of opposition to the agitation were wholly ignored by both the courts. The sum and substance of the appreciation of evidence by the Supreme Court is extracted:

> Several witnesses were examined to prove that Simplex and Kedia Distilleries were acting against the interests of the workers and there were series of agitations by the workers against the factory owners. Evidence was also adduced to show that some workers were retrenched from Simplex and the agitating workers wanted the reinstatement of the retrenched workers. Some of the witnesses examined by the prosecution turned hostile and did not support this version. The overall evidence given by the prosecution would only show that some agitation had been going on against the management of these industries and the deceased Niyogi was spearheading many of these agitations. This by itself would not prove the prosecution case of conspiracy.[6]

The prosecution, by cogent evidence, established that the struggle carried on by the workers led by Niyogi was to secure rights granted to the workers by various laws, and that the employer–accused has been systematically flouting all these laws and in addition employing violence, both overt and covert. Barring the trial court, which convicted the employer–accused, both the high court and the Supreme Court would not take into account the systematic flouting of the labour laws applicable to the establishments of the accused as a conspiracy leading to the conspiracy to kill Niyogi. The prosecution built the conspiracy charge based on the entire period of the assumption of leadership of the workers, the demonstrations, the injunctions by civil courts in the matter governed by the Industrial Disputes Act, the refusal to attend conciliation meetings, the attack on workers and various other issues.

6 *State of Madhya Pradesh through CBI, etc. vs Paltan Malla etc.*, Criminal Appeal No. 98 of 1999.

> A combination to violate without just cause, private rights contractual or other, in which the public has a sufficient interest is wrong. It is not necessary, in order to constitute a conspiracy, that the acts agreed to be done should be acts, which if done, would be criminal … A combination without justification to insult, annoy, injure or impoverish another is criminal conspiracy.[7]

The judge held five owners of the Simplex Group—Chandrakant Shah, Gyanprakash Mishra, Avadesh Roy, Abhaykumar Singh and Moolchand Shah—guilty and convicted them to rigorous imprisonment for life. The hired assassin, Paltan Malla, was sentenced to death. The judgment of the sessions court was delivered on 23 June 1997.

In my arguments in the Madhya Pradesh High Court at Jabalpur, I placed the conspiracy cases before the court and argued that, having pulled apart conspiracy cases for over three decades, I had finally now found a conspiracy case where there was strong evidence of conspiracy: the trips by the assassins to Nepal to purchase arms, and the details of their purchases; the string of false criminal cases in which Niyogi was implicated, forcing him to shuttle between different courts in the state; correspondence from the industrialist brothers that pointed to their association with Paltan Malla, the hired assassin; their multiple confrontations with Niyogi on labour disputes. The case that the trial court believed was extremely strong, awarding stringent punishment to all the accused on the basis of evidence, was struck down by the high court as lacking in evidence. The judge, by his own admission in the course of the hearing, had appeared for employers in trade union cases in his career as a lawyer. The CBI appealed in the Supreme Court against the judgment of the high court. The Supreme Court bench, consisting of Justices K.G. Balakrishnan and A.R. Lakshmanan, on 20 January 2005 disagreed with the high court in the matter of Paltan Malla. It concurred with the high court's decision on the industrialists. They held that Paltan Malla was guilty, but considering the fact that a long time had elapsed since the crime, they commuted his death sentence to rigorous life imprisonment.[8]

---

7 Russel, William O. *Russel on Crime.* 1964. London: Stevens and Sons, p. 1,490.

8 In the Supreme Court of India: *State of Madhya Pradesh through CBI and Ors vs Paltan Malla and Ors.* Criminal Appeal Nos. 98, 99, 100–02, 103–08 and 109–14 of 1999; AIR 2005 SC 733. Decided on 20 January 2005 (Justice K.G. Balakrishnan and Justice A.R. Lakshmanan).

The high court bench was from the very beginning hostile to the prosecution. The corporate lawyer-turned-judge, Justice Dubey asked me at the commencement of the hearing how long I would take. I said I would take more than a week. He retorted, 'Why one week? One or two days should be sufficient.' Dubey was taken by surprise when the court hall filled up with people from all over Chhattisgarh. He said suddenly: 'Turn towards them and argue in Hindi, so that the people you have brought here appreciate what you say.' I replied curtly that I was not in the habit of taking my audience along to listen to my arguments and that all those present were members of Niyogi's trade union and that his remarks were in poor taste. The high court struck down the trial court judgment in its entirety and acquitted all the accused on 26 June 1998.[9]

The Supreme Court held that

> The entries in the diary and the representation Niyogi had submitted to the President of India were in general terms. He apprehended some danger at the hands of some industrialists as the agitation of the workers had been going on and in some instances the henchmen of the industrialists had unleashed physical violence on the workers. Even though he had mentioned the names of some of the accused persons in the diary and in the cassette, that by itself may not be of any assistance to the prosecution to prove the case as the entries in the diary and cassette do not refer to any event, which ultimately was the cause of his death.[10]

Admittedly, like all conspiracy charges, a ruling would be arrived at on the basis of circumstantial evidence, where every link in the chain of evidence has to be established. But this does not mean discrediting the links in their severalty individually first and then rejecting the evidence established by circumstance. On the basis of these and other material the CBI carried on the investigation which revealed that the Simplex Group was the most affected by the agitation carried on

---

9 In the Madhya Pradesh High Court at Jabalpur: *State of Madhya Pradesh vs Paltan Malla @ Ravi* Cr. Ref. No. 5/97; *Moolchand Shah vs State of Madhya Pradesh*, Cr. A. No. 1278/97; *Paltan Malla @ Ravi vs State of Madhya Pradesh*, Cr. A. No. 1371/97; *Chandrakant Shah vs State of Madhya Pradesh*, Cr. A. No. 1441/97; *State of Madhya Pradesh vs Naveen Shah and 2 Ors*, Cr. A. No. 1863/97. Judgment delivered on 26 June 1998. Judges: Justice S.K. Dubey and Justice Usha Shukla.

10 *State of Madhya Pradesh through CBI, etc. vs Paltan Malla, etc.*, Criminal Appeal No. 98 of 1999.

by Niyogi and uncovered and discovered evidence of the role of each of the brothers and the hirelings. In fact, Paltan Malla filed a petition to include Kedia as one of the accused in the murder of Niyogi. On this application, evidence was led in and arguments advanced and the application rejected. This fact was adverted to in the judgment of the trial court.

The other items relied on by the prosecution to prove the case against the accused were the various recoveries effected by the investigating agency, but none of these items would prove the involvement of these accused in the conspiracy. These items would include Ex. P-239 recovered from the office of the first accused. This was a slip on which the registration number of the car being used by the deceased, Niyogi, and also the registration number of a jeep registered in the name of the CMM were written. This, according to the prosecution, would show that the accused were watching the movements of the deceased. We were not able to attach any further importance to these documents.

Another document is Ex. P-298, which is a letter alleged to have been written by the second accused to the sixth accused, indicating that he had received Rs 20,000 for the work he had done.

> The recovery of this letter by the investigating officer is surrounded in mystery. It is alleged that it was found in torn pieces and this letter is alleged to have been recovered on 15.12.1991 by the investigating officer when a search was conducted in the office of the first accused. The case of the prosecution is that the money transaction indicated in Ex. P-298 is the consideration given to the second accused for having caused the death of deceased Niyogi. PW-158 Devendra Jain was alleged to be the person who delivered this letter to the first accused, but he turned hostile and did not support the prosecution. Even if the letter is assumed to be true, it would only show that there was some money transaction between the second accused and the sixth accused and in no way it is proved that the amount of Rs 20,000/- alleged to have passed between the parties was in consideration of the illegal act carried out at the instance of the second accused. The High Court was justified in not relying on this document.[11]

The prosecution relied on the arrangement of granting the contract for a cycle stand in a cinema theatre by the name Maurya Talkies. PW-102 Kamaluddin was examined to prove this fact. He deposed that the contract was taken in the name

11 Ibid.

of A-3 Avdhesh Rai and the income from the cycle stand was deposited in the Syndicate Bank in the account of the second accused.

This, according to the prosecution, was an arrangement made at the instance of A-8, Baldev Singh Sandhu. PW-102 does not know anything about the nature of this transaction and there was no other evidence, oral or documentary, to show that the contract of the cycle stand at Maurya Talkies had anything to do with the murder of the deceased Shankar Guha Niyogi.

The evidence appreciated in this manner would certainly lead to acquittal. This case points to a gap in the understanding of the rule of law as woven into the constitutional scheme by the judiciary. In the grammar of the Constitution the thrust is on economic and political justice; the interpretation of criminal law and procedure should in no way serve to sustain and perpetuate the status quo.

The Investigation into Niyogi's Murder

In the case of the trial for the murder of Niyogi, the investigation did not provide any room for the court to reject the theory of conspiracy presented by the prosecution and found to be proved by the trial judge, unless there was reliable evidence to dislodge the prosecution evidence. This was the first case perhaps in the world where employers along with their hirelings were convicted on charges of conspiracy and murder of a trade union leader. The judgment in the sessions court was a very analytical appreciation of evidence keeping in view the rights that flow out of labour laws and the constitutional promise. The sessions judge viewed the events from the commencement of the workers' movement to the murder of the leader as a continuum, and in that view no link in the chain of circumstances supported the postulate of the innocence of the accused. It is my argument that unless the crime is contextualized in the employer–employee dispute in these cases, justice can never be done.

The police investigated the murder well. The sessions court awarded life sentences to the industrialists. The assassin, Paltan Malla, was awarded the death penalty. As long as the trial progressed, advocate Nandita Haksar stayed there, making sure there were no unnecessary adjournments or delays that derailed the trial. The CBI also fulfilled its responsibilities fully, and ensured that an environment was created where a prosecutor could actually conduct the trial and witnesses could testify before the court. Surprisingly, there were no discrepancies in the witness testimonies in court and their prior statements before the police. This entire process ensured that the guilty were punished. This is perhaps the only case in our country where industry owners were convicted for the murder of a union leader.

I wrote to the CBI after that judgment and said that in the matter of conspiracy and murder, the CBI had investigated the matter competently. Since the trial court judge was someone who had not yet capitulated to the distortions of the system, he delivered a good judgment. If he was someone who was subservient to the system, he would only have convicted the hired assassin. But as you climb up the justice system, you find that courts are unwilling to hold the powerful to account, convict them and send them to prison for murdering a person who led oppressed workers in their struggle for dignity.

Gaps between Courts of Different Jurisdictions

When we examine the Shankar Guha Niyogi judgments in the trial court, high court and Supreme Court, what we begin to understand is that in the same case with the same evidence on record, different courts can give vastly different judgments. Here, the trial court examined the evidence on record and convicted five persons. Looking at the same evidence, the high court found them not guilty and acquitted them. On that very same evidence, the Supreme Court decided that A-1 to A-8 should be acquitted as not guilty, but A-9 was guilty although there was no requirement for the death penalty as the lower court decided, but life imprisonment would be adequate.

The murder happened on 28 September 1991. The second additional sessions judge, Durg, delivered his judgment on 23 June 1997. I concluded my arguments in the high court on 6 March 1998. The high court delivered its judgment on 26 June 1998.

The question that arises before us is: How is it possible to arrive at such different conclusions based on the same evidence? However, there is an intelligible interpretation for each judgment. A key principle of jurisprudence is that if there are two ways of interpreting an issue, the interpretation that must be adopted is the one that gives the benefit of doubt to the accused. This is a very good principle. However, the problem is that courts do not deploy this principle in all cases. It is only when the accused are powerful, rich and influential that they remember this principle. When the accused are poor people or people who oppose the state, our courts never ever remember this principle. In those cases they only consider interpretations that are stacked against the accused.

There is a second problem. As the case moved up, the Supreme Court did not even attempt to analyse and understand the decision of the lower court. It only examined the judgment of the high court. As a matter of fact however, it is only the trial court that hears arguments on both sides, and evaluates the evidence before pronouncing a verdict. However, the Supreme Court assumed that if it went up in appeal to the high court, it obviously meant that there was some error in the trial judgment. The high court attempted to set that error right by pronouncing another judgment. Proceeding on this basis, the Supreme Court restricted itself to the high court judgment. The objective was not to arrive at the truth. If the trial judge came to a decision that was completely at odds with the high court, there must certainly have been reasons for that. The Supreme Court ought to have examined the reasons why he arrived at his decision.

15

Swami Premananda's Terror

The Crimes of Swami Premananda

PREMANANDA WAS THE founder of the Premananda Ashram in Pudukottai district of Tamil Nadu, set up in 1989. Originally, till 1984, he was carrying on his avocation in Sri Lanka. The ethnic conflict brought him to Tamil Nadu with his camp followers, and within a few years of practising his god–man's profession he was able to secure land, presumably from the government and a considerable following who were freely donating a part of their ill-gotten wealth to enrich the life of this 'saint'. Since Independence, there has been a proliferation of these god–persons. Their calling is unregulated. Even when regulated it may be merely formal, with authorities wielding regulatory control being apologetic while exercising lawful authority. They may even ultimately become their disciples and cover up their misdemeanours and thus perform useful services to these god–persons. Abraham Kovoor ran a campaign against these godmen in India and Sri Lanka. In Tamil Nadu, E.V. Ramasamy Naicker, or Periyar, took on the intellectual onslaught against these obscurantist religious practices foisted by the Brahmins on the population and the caste hegemony they set up by launching the self-respect movement. It is the survival of this strong tradition that was responsible for the prosecution of Premananda and the Sankaracharya.

This case is the among few of its kind where a trial was concluded by clearing all obstacles in the process. The facts were not complicated. Premananda was one of several god–persons who vended spirituality to the middle classes, whose lives were beset with uncertainty and insecurity. Traditional religion and orthodox mathas have failed to offer any solace to this population. Other missions like the Ramakrishna Mission, Swami Dayananda and the Chinmaya Mission have been attempting to cultivate in their following a philosophic approach to life by holding discourses on various aspects of Hindu philosophy. Developing a philosophic attitude to life is beyond the ken of ordinary men. It is a long, time-consuming process, and in the long run we are all dead. Short-term and instant remedies, cures and revelations, if possible, are what the people demand. Such an urgent religious need can only produce charlatans and mountebanks. In response to such a need there has been an unregulated proliferation of spiritual centres presided over by several god–men, and all these centres run to full houses. Devotees throng these spiritual centres and donate wealth, through which these centres develop organized infrastructure to carry on their activities. They absorb the services of doctors and other professional people who regularly donate their skills in exchange for a modicum of spiritual solace. These centres also absorb a large section of non-literate, semi-literate, educated, unemployed and unemployable people on payment, and with the offer of shelter and food to attend to daily chores.

All these centres and similar organizations in other communities in the country owe their origin and continuance to the rights of free speech and expression of their respective religious beliefs, and the freedom of association and assembly, and are legislatively subjected to morality, among other aspects which govern our society. It is needless to point out that civil and criminal laws are applicable to these religious institutions and centres, although they appear to be immune to law and authority. That is because of the tremendous clout the centres and heads wield in the political and administrative wings of the state. Internally, these centres and their heads command complete obedience from their followers and the people who work for them.

When extreme injustices and cruelties are perpetrated by these institutions, and when these come to the knowledge of the people, governments are compelled to bring them under the ordinary laws, and courts are compelled to correct or invalidate or treat them as crimes. Normally, they enjoy tremendous immunities, for these god–men are confidants of chief ministers, prime ministers, state governors and judges from the trial courts, right up to the apex court, and presidents.

On account of the spiritual eminence claimed by spiritual heads, there comes into existence a fiduciary relationship between the inmates of the centre and the spiritual head of the centre. As pointed out in *Kerr on Fraud and Mistake*:

> Whenever two persons stand in such a relation that, while it continues, confidence is necessarily reposed by the one and the influence which naturally grows out of that confidence is possessed by the other, and the confidence is abused or the influence is exerted to obtain an advantage at the expense of the confiding party, the person so availing himself of his position will not be permitted to retain the advantage, although the transaction could not have been impeached if no such confidential relation subsisted.[1]

The same text goes on to point out that such fiduciary relationships are created between a doctor and a patient and a spiritual or religious adviser and a follower of the faith.[2]

Prosecuting Swami Premananda

Courts proceed on the footing that these are unequal relations, and on the presumption that all acts done and transactions entered into are vitiated by undue influence, unless proved otherwise. One of the early precedents very close to the case against Premananda, but on the civil side, is *Allcard vs Skinner*,[3] a very old authority which still holds the field on undue influence despite the passage of two centuries. Cotton LJ (Lord Justice), dealing with the question of undue influence, held that such relationships called for strict judicial scrutiny and interference on grounds of public policy, and to prevent the relations existing between the parties and the influence arising there from being abused.[4] It was on this ground that he set aside the impugned transaction. Even the delay did not affect the claim by Ms Allcard. Dealing with the issue of undue influence, Lindley LJ pointed out: 'The principle must be examined. What then is the principle? Is it that it is right and expedient to save persons from the consequences of their own folly, or is it right and expedient to save them from being victimized by other people?' Lindley LJ held the view that people should be protected from being tricked or misled into situations on account of such unequal fiduciary relationships.[5]

---

1 McDonnell, D.L., and J.G. Monroe. 1952. *Kerr on Fraud and Mistake* (seventh edition). London: Sweet & Maxwell, p. 185.

2 Ibid., p. 232.

3 *Allcard vs Skinner* (1857) 36 Chancery Division 145.

4 Ibid., p. 171.

5 Ibid., p. 182.

The unequal relationships existing in institutions like the one run by Premananda did not receive the recognition they deserved. This is more so in the case of women participants in these institutions. The ashram was shelter to around 200 young men and 'grown-up girls' of Sri Lankan origin. The Pudukottai sessions court was presided over by a woman judge, Tmt R. Banumathi, who was later elevated to the high court.[6] The atrocious happenings inside the ashram were leaked out and it was the All India Democratic Women's Association (AIDWA) that brought out these crimes into the open and pursued the police to properly investigate and file a charge sheet.[7] Premananda maintained two levels of relationships in the ashram. He maintained a 'civilized relationship' with the devotees, both foreign and local, so that they were impressed with his saintliness and moral rectitude. For the orphaned and other disadvantaged girls and young women, he revealed his carnal desire. The former never witnessed the latter, but provided the character evidence for Premananda. This was a case which was pre-eminently fit for drawing the presumption of the operation of undue influence in the ashram. The ashram workers could not be voluntarily subjecting themselves to disadvantages of whatever nature. Despite the running presumption that the accused is, until proved otherwise, not guilty, in the course of the trial the burden of proof of facts keeps shifting, and the moment a fiduciary relationship is established the presumption of undue influence arises. If this presumption is not rebutted the voluntary character of the sexual relationship with the victims stands disproved. Section 111 of the Evidence Act, which has recognized the existence of undue influence in fiduciary relationships and such other relationships of confidence, reads as follows:

> Where there is a question as to the good faith of a transaction between parties, one of whom stands to the other in the position of active confidence, the burden of proving the good faith of the transaction is on the party who is in a position of active confidence.

The rule was founded on consideration of the difficulty, which must, from the condition of the parties, generally exist in obtaining positive evidence as to the fairness of transactions which are peculiarly open to fraud and undue influence:

---

6 Justice R. Banumathi retired from the Supreme Court of India in 2020, and was the first woman from Tamil Nadu to be elevated as a judge of the Supreme Court.

7 PUCL, lawyers from Tamil Nadu, Sudha Ramalingam (also with the AIDWA), D. Nagasaila and V. Suresh provided victim support and assisted in the prosecution.

> Wherever two persons stand in such a relation that, while it continues, confidence is necessarily reposed by the one and the influence which naturally grows out of that confidence is possessed by the other, and this confidence is abused or the influence is exerted to obtain an advantage at the expense of the confiding party, the person so availing himself of his position will not be permitted to retain the advantage, although the transaction could not have been impeached if no such confidential relation had subsisted.[8]

Julius Stone referred to an English decision of 1917 where the court of appeal was constrained to point out that there was no absolute doctrine that an 'adult man, as to whom undue pressure is not shown to have been exercised, ought to be allowed to enter into any contract he thinks fit affecting his own liberty of action'.[9] This was a case where it was held that a contract of loan executed by a workman, which assigned his wages and imposed among other restraints prevention of the borrower from changing his job, or his residence, was against public policy: 'No one has a right to so to deal with a man's liberty of action as well as his property, and the law says it is contrary to public policy.'[10] The possibility of undue influence coming into play in the whole episode cannot be ruled out. Such a possibility was recognized by the Criminal Law (Amendment Act), 1983, in a big way in institutions where women and young girls were offered shelter, and suitable provision was made in this behalf in Section 376(2)(d) of the IPC.[11] The provision defines a women and children's institution widely and would include the ashram run by Premananda. The claim that the ashram did not bear the character of a women's institution would be a very disingenuous way of placing the case. These religious institutions have multifaceted activities and any adjudication of the activities of these institutions must recognize and sever these activities for the purposes of breaches of law or otherwise.

---

8 McDonnell, D.L., and J.G. Monroe. 1952. *Kerr on Fraud and Mistake* (seventh edition). London: Sweet & Maxwell, p. 185.

9 Quoted in Stone, Julius. 2000. *The Province and Function of Law: A Study in Jurisprudence*. Delhi: Universal Law Publishing Co. (First Indian Reprint), p. 256.

10 Ibid.

11 Section 372(2)(d): 'Whoever … being on the management or on the staff of a jail, remand home or other place of custody established by or under any law for the time being in force or of a woman's or children's institution takes advantage of his official position and commits rape on any inmate of such jail, remand home, place or institution … shall be punished …'

Looked at from this perspective, which is the right one, the ashram would be comprehended by Section 376(2)(d) of the IPC. The consent used in this provision was supplemental to the definition of consent in Section 90 of the IPC.[12] These provisions enumerate various facets of facts which vitiate consent. The second clause in Section 375 says 'without her consent'. However, consent in situations where the man holds a dominant position is left unaddressed. This, in short, is the principle of undue influence. If we look at amended provisions of Section 376C(a), (c) and (d), my argument in this case was clear. Whoever uses his position to induce or seduce a woman will be committing an offence, but not rape. The area of undue influence is taken note of as the main ingredient to define the offences of rape or seduction. Both of these are not voluntary and therefore are offences. If for any reason it is held that it does not fall under Section 376C(c), the general characteristics set out in Section 376(2)(d) were very much present in the ashram run by Premananda and the case for conviction was clear.

The law on 'rape' as an offence and the trial that took place appeared like a parody of the former by the latter. It took a very long time to separate the rapist from the victim. The rapist was the criminal and the victim was the accomplice. The accomplice had to establish that she was a victim of sexual assault. Sidheshwar Ganguly was the honorary secretary of the Nari Kalyan Ashram, a large institution set up for receiving and looking after young girls and women who had no homes and those who had 'gone astray'. He used to come to the ashram at 7 p.m. daily and stay till midnight. Between January and April 1954 he was accused of committing rape on three girls (specifically identified) and others. An investigation into the complaint led to prosecution and conviction only with reference to one girl who was held to be a minor. It was a jury trial and the accused was convicted. The court rejected the contention that the victim was an accomplice and her evidence needed corroboration.[13] It was pointed out that it was only a rule of prudence and that nothing prevented the court from basing the conviction on the victim's

12 Section 90, IPC. 'Consent known to be given under fear or misconception.—A consent is not such a consent as is intended by any section of this Code, if the consent is given by a person under fear of injury, or under a misconception of fact, and if the person doing the act knows, or has reason to believe, that the consent was given in consequence of such fear or misconception; or consent of insane person.—if the consent is given by a person who, from unsoundness of mind, or intoxication, is unable to understand the nature and consequence of that to which he gives his consent; or consent of child.—unless the contrary appears from the context, if the consent is given by a person who is under twelve years of age.'

13 *Sidheshwar Ganguly vs State of West Bengal* (24.10.1957: SC): AIR 1958 SC 143.

testimony. In *Bharwada Bhoginbhai Hirjibhai vs State of Gujarat*,[14] the court took an unequivocal position on the requirement of corroboration when it said:

> In the Indian setting, refusal to act on the testimony of a victim of sexual assault in the absence of corroboration as a rule, is adding insult to injury. Why should the evidence of the girl or the woman who complains of rape or sexual molestation be viewed with the aid of spectacles fitted with lenses tinged with doubt, disbelief or suspicion? To do so is to justify the charge of male chauvinism in a male dominated society … Corroboration may be considered essential to establish a sexual offence in the backdrop of the social ecology of the Western World. It is wholly unnecessary to import the said concept on a turn-key basis and to translate it on the Indian soil regardless of the altogether different atmosphere, attitudes, mores, responses of the Indian Society, and its profile.[15]

The learned judges, thereafter, elaborated the various factors that would inhibit a girl or woman from making a full and almost immediate disclosure of sexual assault to others and the investigating agency. The enumeration by the judges was not exhaustive of the problems faced by a woman. Superimposed on the unequal position suffered by the woman in a male-dominated society were factors like inequality of class, wealth and status. In the case on hand, the girls who were admitted into the ashram were poor with no place to go back to. Complaining against Premananda therefore required enormous courage, particularly when he put on the act of giving solace to a large number of people. It was a relationship which was wholly unequal, where dominion over the mind and body of the victims was complete. It was not just abuse of his official position but the total abuse of the position he held in society as the spiritual head of a large, floating following. This position was again reiterated in *State of Maharashtra vs Chandraprakash Kewalchand Jain.*[16]

The case reported in *State of Maharashtra vs Priyasharan Maharaj* was the other case about the conduct of the spiritual head with the girl inmates of his ashram.[17] Kripalu Maharaj was accused of forced sexual intercourse with the pracharaks of his cult. At the time of framing charges, Kripalu Maharaj argued for discharge. As against the decision to frame charges, the matter was taken to the high court, and

14 *Bharwada Bhoginbhai Hirjibhai vs State of Gujarat*, AIR 1983 SC 753.

15 Ibid.

16 *State of Maharashtra vs Chandraprakash Kewalchand Jain*, 1990 AIR 658.

17 *State of Maharashtra vs Priyasharan Maharaj*, AIR 1997 SC 2041.

the latter discharged the accused on the grounds of delay and was influenced by the submission made that Kripalu Maharaj was a saintly old man who had renounced the world, and who was engrossed in spiritual activities and had a large following in India. The Supreme Court, repelling these submissions, pointed out that the High Court

> ... failed to appreciate that it is not unusual to come across cases where the so-called spiritual heads exploit young girls and women who become their disciples and come under their spell ... The High Court gave too much importance to the conduct of the three victims and the delay in disclosing those illegal acts to their parents and the police. What the High Court has failed to appreciate is how a victim of such an offence will behave would depend upon the circumstances in which she is placed. It often happens that such victims do not complain against such illegal acts immediately because of factors like fear or shame or uncertainties about the reactions of their parents or husbands in case of married girls or women and the adverse consequences which, they apprehend, would follow because of disclosure of such acts.[18]

The ratio laid down in the previous cases was again reiterated in *State of Punjab vs Gurmit Singh*.[19]

Rape is a physical assault on the dignity of the individual, unlike other offences, and it is also a violation of Article 21, the right to life. A criminal trial in this instance more importantly than in others is not a game of hide-and-seek but an attempt to restore dignity to its rightful place and the mores of the society as well. That, we believe, is the end result of such adjudications. Judge Banumathi found Premananda and his six associates guilty of deceiving believers, of cheating by claiming supernatural powers, misusing the faith reposed in him by his disciples, sexually assaulting several young women residents of the ashram, assaulting and murdering a young male inmate of the ashram and causing disappearance of the body by burying it within ashram premises, and arranging forced abortions of several women after such sexual assaults on them between the years 1990 and 1994. One of the seven accused was a woman, the rest were men. The eighth, a woman, absconded, and two men turned approvers. Seven charges were framed against Premananda: committing rape (thirteen counts), outraging the modesty of

---

18 Ibid., para 11.

19 *State of Punjab vs Gurmit Singh*, 1996 AIR 1393.

a woman (four counts), wrongful confinement and murder of the young ashramite Ravi, criminal intimidation and threat to cause death, and cheating.

The defence set out to prove the spiritual powers of Premananda, and this enterprise was undertaken by no less a lawyer than Ram Jethmalani. The judge said: 'In view of the spate of evidence let in by the defence of the alleged spiritual orientation of the first Accused and his spiritual powers, at first, it has become necessary to explode such myth.' With all these god-men, sleight of hand and a capacity to hypnotize are translated into spiritual powers. That is what Premananda was capable of. His great feat was regurgitating a Sivalinga on Mahasivarathri (*lingodhbhavam*) and materializing of *vibhooti* (sacred ash). We in Andhra Pradesh have been witnessing these being performed by the presiding god-man of this state for the past four or five decades. What is important is to demonstrate in a court of law that such a claim is a false claim. Judge Banumathi did this effectively at the trial:

> In any religion, empty rituals cannot change the human behaviour for the better. Most of the self-styled god men instead of advocating spirituality … [t]hey tend to hijack the minds of the disciples by external manifestation, like materializing vibhooti and other material objects … when the mind believes the same, the mental slits are closed to accept any new ideas or thinking.[20]

This is the traditional method of running down competitors, one of the survival techniques. The website maintained by him described him as a 'spiritual master' who 'removes clouds of ignorance from the mind'.

Characterizing the Premananda ashram as one that propagates a dark and despairing philosophy at a time when traditional religion has failed and material conditions are stressful for even seemingly rational people to lose their moorings, Judge Banumathi set about debunking the god-man's claim to spiritual powers by inviting one Marudhamuthu, a magician, to demonstrate lingodhbhavam in the court. Marudhamuthu, in an open court, regurgitated the linga and produced vibhooti from his empty palms. How did he do this? Marudhamuthu swallowed two capsules filled with kumkum and swallowed a banana after placing a 3 inch lingam in the centre. After resting for half an hour, he brought out the lingam with the kumkum. This was performed in front of those present in court. But

---

20 *Inspector of Police, C.B.; C.I.D., Pukukottai, Crime No. 1183/94 of Viralimalai Police Station vs. Premananda and Others*. Sessions Case No. 7/1996, Court of Sessions at Pudukottai, 20th August 1997, para 79.

for this very unique step of demonstrating the falsity of the claim to spiritual powers in the open court, the trial would not have been quite as successful. The debunking was necessary for the other witnesses to stand firm and depose. Very few judges would have thought about it and even fewer would have dared to perform this experiment or permit it inside the court. The demonstration of the deceptive potential of empty ritualism is derived from the self-respecters' critique of religion—a major aspect of which was the critique of religious practices, festivals, rituals and happenings. Without attacking spiritualism per se or religion per se in court proceedings, what was in effect brought into the courtroom was a creative engagement with matters of faith, linking the delegitimization of spiritual power to the commission of crime.

The young girls, seven of them of Sri Lankan origin and the rest from Tamil Nadu, entered the ashram very young—before they attained puberty. They were confined at the time of their first menstruation, immediately after which they were sent to Premananda. There were older women working in the ashram, but the complaints came from the younger ones, who were orphaned and totally dependent on the ashram. They resisted, despite their age and vulnerability. One girl was stripped and assaulted in front of the other girls; another was confined in a kennel without food and water; yet another was battered in the dining hall; one victim was tied to a calf and made to run across the ashram when she attempted to escape. When one of them objected to his use of force, the god-man told her: 'I am like your father. If I have sexual intercourse with you, you will not beget a child.' To another victim, he said, 'I am an incarnation of God. My touching you means you have earned merit (*punyam*) in a previous birth.' 'Other exhibitionist facts are not elaborated in the judgment for fear of vulgarization,' said Justice Banumathi. Ravi, a Sri Lankan youth, was wrongfully confined and beaten to death. There was a woman doctor, also an accused in the case, whose job it was to monitor the menstrual cycles of the girls and carry out abortions when necessary. After the girls were moved out of the ashram into the protective custody of a women's organization, one of them was found pregnant. Her pregnancy was terminated with her consent, and a sample from the aborted foetus along with the blood samples of the girl and Premananda were sent to the Centre for Cellular and Molecular Biology, Hyderabad, where the DNA test confirmed beyond reasonable doubt that Premananda was the father.

The Conviction of Premananda and His Associates

Judge Banumathi convicted all the accused to various terms but what is important is the conviction and sentence imposed on Premananda. He was sentenced to two life sentences which would run consecutively, that is, one after another, and the court held after the demonstration by Marudhamuthu, the magician witness, that god-men who claim spiritual powers on the basis of producing kumkum, vibhooti and small objects out of nowhere are committing the offences of cheating and are practitioners of fraud. *This finding was confirmed by the Supreme Court and is accepted as a principle to judge god-men in the future.*

During pendency of the trial, the case was carried to the high court thrice to seek bail and have the matter delayed—the attempts were unsuccessful each time and bail was refused.[21] When the matter was brought to the high court, the problem of steering through the case and getting the court to confirm the judgment became a Herculean effort. The judges in the high court were from different backgrounds. At that stage, I was approached by advocates Sudha and Nagasaila to appear for them, as on the other side Ram Jethmalani represented the god-man. In an unequal contest like this, I knew that some judges tend to be protective towards junior lawyers and I told them that they should go ahead and gave them detailed instructions on how to proceed. This proved successful and the decision went against the god-man. However, a full-fledged appeal is another matter. A criminal appeal is a retrial on facts, and particularly so when the trial judge had courageously convicted the spiritual hoax and sentenced him severely so as to deter god-men from fooling the innocent. AIDWA and PUCL lawyers at Chennai wanted me to appear for the victims. It meant staying away for long periods from Hyderabad. Advocate U.R. Lalit appeared for the god-man. Victims normally have no locus standi to intervene in criminal matters, although there have been exceptions to this rule. I was prepared with the arguments and wanted to intervene if the public prosecutor did a shoddy job. My being heard was at the discretion of the court. U.R. Lalit argued the case in three stretches, and that gave me a chance to be there when required. When his turn came, the public prosecutor argued the case for around ten to fifteen days. He covered every aspect of the case, and so I told the court I had nothing to add after the excellent work done by him. The matter was heard at length by Justice P. Shanmugam and Justice M. Chockalingam.

There were Herculean efforts to fix a bench. It was posted before a bench where the senior judge did not enjoy a good reputation, and the junior judge sitting with

---

21 *Swami Premananda vs Inspector of Police, C.B., C.I.D.* (29.09.1995: MADHC): MANU/TN/1057/1995 and I (1996) CCR 63 (Mad.) (seeking bail); *Swami Premananda vs C.B., C.I.D. Pudukottai* (28.05.1996: MADHC): MANU/TN/1175/1996 (seeking bail); *Swami Premananda vs the State* (24.05.1996: MADHC): MANU/TN/0214/1996 and 1996 CriLJ 3884 (seeking bail).

him was known to be a disciple of Premananda. With Swamis, this is a problem. The lawyers of the victims met the chief justice and requested that the matter be posted before another bench. On 13 December 2001, the Madras High Court confirmed the conviction and sentence without altering or reducing it, except for reducing the fine from Rs 66 lakh to Rs 61 lakh; they did not alter the sentence of thirty-two years on failure to pay the fine.[22] The Supreme Court confirmed the sentence without any reduction or alteration of sentences imposed by the trial judge.[23] The fine amount was directed to be distributed equally between the eleven girls who were the victims.

The sentence imposed by Judge Banumathi is a deterrent as no judgment has ever been. The crime of Premananda may even qualify as the rarest of rare cases for the death penalty. But the death penalty is so swift that the memory of this man may die with him. A life sentence one after another however, has a quality of deterrence, which practitioners of similar trade and avocation shall take notice of.[24] If punishments of deterrence are to have any effect at all, the principles of deterrence in the decision has to be broadcast and campaigned for. What is important is not the crime of rape alone, but the fact that the shield used to commit these crimes becomes suspect and thereby teaches people to make a distinction between religion and its obscurantist practices. For it is the latter that gives birth to mountebanks and charlatans and all the god-persons roaming about in the country who are commercial vendors of 'spiritual peace', a non-existent commodity.

22 *Chandradevi and Ors vs State of Tamil Nadu* (12.12.2002: MADHC): MANU/TN/2335/2002. See also *Sri Premananda Trust, Premananda Ashram vs District Collector, Pudukkottai and Ors* (07.03.2003: MADHC): MANU/TN/0282/2003—where the trust unsuccessfully sought a mandamus to prevent the fine imposed on Premananda being taken from the account of the trust.

23 *Kamalanantha and Ors vs State of Tamil Nadu* (05.04.2005: SC) AIR 2005 SC 2132.

24 Premananda died in 2011 in Cuddalore Central Prison aged 59 years.

16

The Rights of Religious Minorities

I SHALL EXAMINE the rights of religious minorities in two sections: (a) violence against religious minorities and (b) reservations, both areas in which I have intervened through courts and commissions of inquiry.

51A. Fundamental Duties. It shall be the duty of every citizen of India

…

(b) to cherish and follow the noble ideals which inspired our national struggle for freedom;

…

(e) to promote harmony and the spirit of common brotherhood amongst all the people of India transcending religious, linguistic and regional or sectional diversities; to renounce practices derogatory to the dignity of women;

(f) to value and preserve the rich heritage of our composite culture;

(g) to protect and improve the natural environment including forests, lakes, rivers and wild life, and to have compassion for living creatures.

Violence against Religious Minorities

In the various stages in the development of the struggle for human rights, we first concentrated on interrogating the state and government through our participation in commissions of inquiry, believing that we could effectively campaign for the protection of human rights by focusing on human rights violations. In a short while, we realized that our engagement with these commissions was not really contributing to strengthening the movement. That was when we felt we should inquire into human rights violations by involving people in the inquiry—through setting up public tribunals with public intellectuals, retired judges, etc. Among the first major episodes of mass violence against a religious minority in the post-Emergency period was against Sikhs, following the assassination of Indira Gandhi in 1984, and the targeting of Sikhs in the years that followed.

The work of building a Hindu *rashtra* commenced after the National Democratic Alliance (NDA) came into power. The National Commission to Review the Working of the Indian Constitution was part of this effort. Since it did not yield the desired results, the BJP quietly buried its report. Later, the same government constituted the Malimath Committee. Headed by former chief justice of the Karnataka and Kerala High Courts, Justice V.S. Malimath, the task of the committee was to review the criminal laws operative in the country and recommend reforms. It was to examine the constitutionality of core principles of criminal laws, and suggest any amendments that were felt to be necessary. It was also tasked with recommending amendments in the IPC and the Indian Evidence Act. It observed that the justice system in the country was very lax and must be more stringent and tough. On the whole, the recommendations of the Malimath Committee derogated the fundamental rights and freedoms protected under the Constitution. There was widespread discussion and criticism of the Malimath Committee report across the country. As a result, rather than expose the report to public debate, efforts began to insidiously amend laws and bring in these provisions through the back door.

It is important to understand the political context in which the Malimath Committee was constituted. The mass violence against Sikhs in the 1980s, especially after 1984, rise of Hindutva forces, the *rath yatra*, the demolition of the Babri Masjid and the battle cry for Ayodhya—all these firmly entrenched majoritarianism in Indian politics.

I will reflect briefly on my experience with challenging this anti-minority politics and upholding the rights of minorities in courts and with commissions of inquiry under different political regimes in different places—Bidar, Ayodhya, Coimbatore and Karnataka—between 1988 and 2009 to inquire into majoritarian violence against Sikhs, Muslims and Christians in India.

The Justice Somasekhara Commission of Inquiry was appointed by the Government of Karnataka to inquire into the attacks on churches in Karnataka in

2008–09.[1] I appeared before the commission on behalf of the PUCL and presented a written statement, which I recapitulate here.

> Orissa and Karnataka witnessed attacks on Christian communities. This could be said to have commenced from Stein's murder in Orissa. This was also followed by attacks on churches in Gujarat. We need to go back to a discussion on justice in plural societies and the meaning of secularism in India.

The Massacre of Sikh Students in Bidar

The year was 1988.[2] The growth of capitation colleges and profiteering through setting up of educational institutions had resulted quite inevitably in fierce competition. This soon turned into an attack on minority educational institutions. There is a gurudwara in Bidar, Karnataka, and a few capitation institutions, one of which was run by an A-class contractor, an influential man called Joga Singh, the head of the Guru Nanak Jhira Prabandhak Committee and the Guru Nanak Jhira Sahib Educational Foundation, which set up educational institutions. He wanted to set up a medical college in addition to the institutions already functioning under the trust—which were quite popular and had students coming in from across the country, including from Punjab, where the situation was tense. Joga Singh's closeness to Ramakrishna Hegde made it easy for him to secure recognition for the medical college in Bidar, but the anti-Sikh forces found the college to be a provocation. It fuelled their rage, in keeping with the recent history of violence

1 Justice B.K. Somasekhara Commission of Inquiry in Attacks on Churches in Karnataka. 'Set up in September 2008, the commission, headed by former High Court Judge B.K. Somasekhara, had 300 sittings and examined 754 witnesses during its inquiry into the series of attacks on churches across the State. The commission had submitted its interim report in September 2009 and final report in January 2011.' Kumar, B.S. Satish. 2014. 'Cabinet Rejects Somasekhara Commission Report on Church Attacks'. *The Hindu*, 16 October, https://www.thehindu.com/news/national/karnataka/cabinet-rejects-somasekhara-commission-report-on-church-attacks/article6507724.ece. Accessed on 18 October 2021. A copy of the report is available at https://www.thehindu.com/multimedia/archive/00376/Justice_B_K__Somase_376775a.pdf. Accessed on 18 October 2021.

2 *A Warning from Bidar: A Report on the Anti-Sikh Disturbances*. 1988. Delhi: Nagrik Ekta Manch.

and massacres of Sikhs across the country. Till the violence against Sikhs in 1984, the word 'minority' in public discourse referred only to Muslims and all religious and communal conflict was normalized as Hindu–Muslim conflict. With the influx of Sikh students, Bidar's economic situation had improved significantly. Better hotels, more vehicles, increase in rent for residential accommodation had made the students very visible in the town.

On 16–17 September 1988, there was a planned attack on Sikh students in Bidar, in which six students died and several were injured.[3] Justice P.K. Shyamsunder, a sitting judge in the Karnataka High Court, was appointed to inquire into the Bidar massacre by Chief Minister Bommai.[4] Joga Singh requested me to appear on his behalf before the commission. Advocate Chaman Singh and I argued before it.

On Vinayak Chathurthi, a group of Sikh students had eaten at the gurudwara langar and were on their way to their rooms. When they passed by a Ganesh mandap, Hindu men lounging around there shouted out foul abuses at them. The Sikh students did not respond immediately. They went to their rooms, got together with other Sikh students and went to the mandap with hockey sticks to beat up the Hindu men there. We got to know this because a DIG who appeared before the commission, S.S. Pavate, stated that he had sent a telex message that detailed how this trouble started. The message stated clearly that the Sikh students were provoked by the men sitting in the Ganesh mandap.[5]

At the time, the Sikh student population in Bidar was about 1,500. During the inquiry, we cross-examined the SP, a well-educated man with a PhD in anthropology.[6] His contention was that the Sikh students in the town attacked the mandap in a mob from three sides. By his account, the Sikh student population in Bidar would have to be around 7,000 to 8,000. Then I put a question to him: 'How many Sikh students do you think there are in Bidar? Did some people join them from outside the town?' The SP's story came apart.

---

3 'Clash Toll Rises to 6 in Bidar'. 1988. *Indian Express* (Bangalore), 19 September, p. 1.

4 'Shyamsunder to Probe Bidar Riots'. 1988. *Indian Express* (Bangalore), 28 September, p. 1.

5 'Bidar Riots: Police Force Inadequate'. 1989. *Indian Express* (Bangalore), 22 August, p. 5. This report details the questions put by K.G. Kannabiran to the DIG, Pavate, and the SP: 'To a question by Sikh counsel Kannabiran he said that he had not prevented Joga Singh entering Bidar on September 16.'

6 'Bidar Probe: Many Top Officers File Papers'. 1989. *Indian Express* (Bangalore), 26 February, p. 5.

The massacre was one of the most brutal ever. A seventeen-year-old boy, Bunty, recounted his experience. They stripped him down to his underwear, made him lie on the road and tried to run over him with a scooter, and when that did not work, a motorcycle. They then used a threshing machine, intending to dismember him, but the power went off and he survived. He appeared before the Justice P.K. Shyamsunder Commission. I argued that witnessing this violence would be a lifelong curse for this young boy, something he could never forget. The fact that four bodies were thrown into the well in the house of the SP showed how public this massacre was. Neither the SP nor the executive magistrate came to their rescue. All these facts were placed before the commission. One of the witnesses, a Sikh professor, criticized capitation colleges in his statement. Justice P.K. Shyamsunder was very displeased with this criticism and held forth on how Karnataka had served the country through its capitation colleges and praised the state's policy on this matter. I just listened quietly. After that, the Sikh professor, speaking about public security in Bidar, said that he had written to his state government that there was no public safety in Bidar, but it did not act. Justice P.K. Shyamsunder asked him which his state government was. He replied that it was the Punjab government. The judge laughed. At that point I got up and said to the judge:

> Please do not laugh. It is because he has no faith in your government that he decided to write to his government. This is the state of affairs of governance in this country. According to the Constitution, anybody can settle anywhere in the country. The government of the state to which they have moved are responsible for their security. But things have come to such a pass that this professor believes that his state by birth is responsible for his security. You got angry with his criticism of capitation colleges, and despite being a judge, you are unable to tolerate any criticism of your state government.

Ordinarily, when there is a violent confrontation of this kind, it is necessary as per the law for the executive magistrate to be present either to declare Section 144 or to authorize firing. But he showed up after everything was over and the massacre had been completed. When he was asked to explain his absence, he said he was busy with Ganesh puja, and by the time the puja was over, it was too late. He said this before the commission. 'Nero fiddles while Rome is burning,' I told the commission.

Justice P.K. Shyamsunder repeated my observations verbatim in the report of the Commission of Inquiry. He wrote that the district officials had failed to perform their duty. He did not find fault with the Hindu fundamentalists. That is another story. Even the officer, Pavate, who sent the teleprinter message, did not reach the scene or attempt to stop the violence. There are no gradations in injustice. If we recognize certain acts as unjust, it must be so irrespective of the class, caste, religion or social location of the victims. But we have got accustomed to looking at everything in graded terms. The witnesses who testified were scrambled together in such a disorganized fashion that it was difficult to make any conclusive statements based on their testimonies.

Five rowdies belonging to a gang called Neni were responsible for the entire violence. None of them were arrested. One of them testified before the commission and the prosecution cross-examined him. He held forth on how objectionable the conduct of Sikh students was on the streets, and how they would try to forcibly kiss Hindu girls. But not one of his statements was supported by evidence. I asked him one question: 'You are such a responsible citizen. Did you chastise the Sikh students who were misbehaving even once? Did you ask them to explain their behaviour? Did you ask for their names?' He had no answers. Basically, you don't need evidence to make wild allegations against minority communities. One of the things he said was that when a Hindu girl stopped at a traffic signal, a Sikh youth misbehaved with her. 'Who is the victim? Who are the witnesses? Did you register a complaint?' Again, no answers. 'Did Hindu boys never misbehave with girls on the roads? Did Hindu boys never harass girls? How come you did not kill them?' I asked. Justice P.K. Shyamsunder refused to bring my question on record. I objected, 'He said that they resorted to violence as retaliation for objectionable behaviour on the part of the Sikh students. I only asked him whether he had reacted similarly to objectionable behaviour by Hindu men. I don't see anything wrong with my question.' Justice P.K. Shyamsunder said, 'You can ask him if they behaved similarly with anyone else. That would suffice.' I told him that there were many people who were only too willing to believe these baseless allegations.

Ramakrishna Hegde himself held this view. We requested him to appear before the commission and record his statement, but he expressed his inability to do so. So I went to meet him, at which time he repeated these allegations. Karnataka PUCL member S. R. Hiremath published a report on the Bidar massacre, in which he wrote that the Sikh students were killed because they misbehaved with women. I confronted him and asked him to show me the basis on which he had made this statement. He had no reply.[7] Let us concede for a moment that the behaviour

---

7 See Chapter 13, Section 4 for a similar justification for the massacre of Dalits in Tsundur placed as 'evidence' before the Justice Gangadhar Rao Commission of Inquiry.

of the Sikh students towards women was inappropriate. Did that justify their massacre? Did they know who among the dead students had misbehaved? Did they only kill students who they knew had misbehaved? Or did they indiscriminately kill anyone they found from that community? This equivocation has silenced our protest against injustice. It is this tendency that strikes at the root of solidarity in movements against injustice.

If we believe that anyone who misbehaves with women must be killed, then men as a class must be killed. We must always emphasize the universality of certain values and ideals. Justice P.K. Shyamsunder concluded his inquiry and submitted a seventy- to eighty-page report in January 1990. There was nothing in the report that established responsibility for the crime. There were no recommendations regarding the action to be initiated against the officials involved. When the commission was sitting in Bangalore, Chandramouli, a reporter from the *Indian Express*, covered the proceedings every day. In the hearings that took place in Bidar, the people who attended were mainly Sikhs. Hindu rowdies would come too, but nobody else was really interested. Justice P.K. Shyamsunder warned me once: 'You are asking them uncomfortable questions. Please be careful.' I brushed it aside with, 'I am accustomed to this. It does not bother me.'

The violence against minorities in fact has its beginnings in the targeted violence against Sikhs after the assassination of Indira Gandhi. It was during the anti-Sikh violence that people of this country realized that it was not only Muslims who were religious minorities, but also Sikhs. When the brutal massacre of Sikhs, the assaults on Sikh women and the destruction of property was taking place, Indira Gandhi's son, and later prime minister of India, Rajiv Gandhi said in a speech: 'When a big tree falls, the earth shakes.'[8] Although many were taken in by this description, the fact is that those who were crushed were not the ones who lived in the shade of that tree. It is those that lived in the shade of that tree who perpetrated the massacre of innocent people from the Sikh community. Our institutions of justice do not know how to investigate or deal with massacres of this kind. Our governments are ill-equipped to do justice or take preventive measures.

---

8 Baweja, Harinder. 2009. 'When a Big Tree Falls, the Earth Shakes'. *Tehelka*, 25 April. Also, 'Watch Rajiv Gandhi Make His Infamous "Big Tree Falls" Speech Justifying the 1984 Anti-Sikh Riots'. 2015. Scroll.in, 20 November, https://scroll.in/video/1558/watch-rajiv-gandhi-make-his-infamous-big-tree-falls-speech-justifying-the-1984-anti-sikh-riots. Accessed on 28 November 2021.

The Citizens' Tribunal on Ayodhya, 1993

It is in this historical context that the Babri Masjid was demolished on 6 December 1992. This had a trigger effect on communal conflict in different parts of the country.

Muslims across the country expressed their dismay and opposition to the demolition. In Mumbai, the Shiv Sena led an unprecedented attack on Muslims, killing hundreds and rendering thousands homeless. Muslims who had for generations lived in this city were overnight turned into refugees in camps. The Justice Srikrishna Commission inquired into the massacre of Muslims in the Mumbai riots of 1992.[9] However, there were no actions taken on the basis of the findings of the commission. There was no compensation for victims and no trial or punishment for those responsible for perpetrating grave crimes. The rule of law and constitutional protections, especially Articles 14 and 21, were suspended at that moment. When there is a suspension of the rule of law at key moments like this, it is what makes way for people to take the law into their hands—and we label this extremism or terrorism. If we keep shrinking the space of the rule of law, it is an unequal application of the law. If this is not rectified from time to time, we make a mockery of law and justice.

After 6 December 1992, Ayodhya came to occupy centre stage. The demolition of the Babri Masjid was an unprecedented assault on the Constitution, and on the institutions of justice in this country. It is a symbol of genocidal massacre, like Jallianwala Bagh. There was widespread protest against this violence and a demand for a people's tribunal on Ayodhya. It was decided that an unofficial inquiry commission be constituted to inquire into the Babri Masjid–Ayodhya violence. The independent commission so set up in 1993 had Kamala Prasad as chair, and Kamal Mitra Chenoy, Kirti Singh, Dinesh Mohan, Sagari Chhabra and Suresh C. Shukla as members, with a large support team. They collected information, recorded statements and submitted a detailed report in July 1993. The Citizens' Tribunal was held in the Constitution Club in Delhi, with Justice D.A. Desai, Justice O. Chinnappa Reddy and Justice D.S. Tewatia as judges. Advocate A.G. Noorani, Professor Lotika Sarkar and I were amici curiae tasked with assisting the tribunal. The full report of the Citizens' Tribunal was published in May 1994.[10] How would we fix responsibility—

---

9 Report of Justice B.N. Srikrishna Commission of Inquiry in Mumbai Riots, 1992. https://www.sabrang.com/srikrish/sri%20main.html. Accessed on 6 May 2022.

10 *Citizens' Tribunal on Ayodhya: Investigation, Hearings and Judgment, January–December 1993.* 1994. New Delhi: Citizens' Tribunal on Ayodhya. The editor is

even on elected leaders—in a situation like this? This was a critical concern. After hearing all the witnesses and submissions, the judges concluded that

> … the politicisation of the Ram Janmabhoomi–Babri Masjid issue on a large scale by the entry of national political parties was the primary cause for all that happened. A local dispute was transformed into a national dispute and two leading political parties vied with each other to use the dispute to further their own political interests … These political parties and their leaders either diluted or poisoned the stream of secularism.[11]

The first necessary step towards separating religion from politics, the judges observed, 'should be a total ban on political parties subscribing to a communal credo directly or indirectly', with 'strong, stringent and swift action … against all communal political parties … and candidates resorting to communalisation'.[12] Holding that 'secularism is the weapon bequeathed to us to fight communalism',[13] the judges drew up a blueprint for reforming the media, institutions of the state, the educational system and social life—apart from compensation and legal redress to victims of the violence in Ayodhya—making the dignity of minorities the test of the strength of our democracy.

Less than a decade after this report warned of the consequences of impunity in the matter of Ayodhya, we saw the rise of genocidal violence against Muslims in Gujarat (Chapter 17).

The Coimbatore Bomb Blasts Case, 2006

The Coimbatore bomb blasts took place in 1998,[14] and were preceded by Hindu–Muslim confrontation. Properties worth a few crores of rupees belonging to Muslims were destroyed and twenty-two Muslims killed. I visited Coimbatore

---

indebted to Nirmala Karunan and Teesta Setalvad for a copy of this report.

11 Ibid., p. 305.

12 Ibid., p. 306.

13 Ibid., p. 308.

14 *Abdul Nazar Madani vs State of Tamil Nadu and Anr*, AIR 2000 SC 2293; (2000) 6 SCC 204, 2000 SCC (Cri) 1048. For an account of K.G. Kannabiran's involvement in this case, see B.B. Mohan. 2020. 'Criminal Law and Human Rights: "Distinctive Discrimination" and Article 21 Rights to Fair Trial'. K.G. Kannabiran Lectures on Law, Justice and Human Rights *Livelaw*, 25 December, https://www.livelaw.in/

immediately after this violence. There was no investigation into the gruesome killings, nor was any action taken against the accused. The serial bomb blasts took place when L.K. Advani visited Coimbatore soon after. The persons accused in the blasts were tried, but to date there has been no trial or investigation in the matter of the murder of the twenty-two Muslims.[15] This fact was admitted by the investigating officer himself in the bomb blasts case trial, for which a court was built inside the jail premises. The judge sat on a platform raised 10 feet above the ground. The others were down below. A small room was built for the judges to retire to. In the rear of the court hall, the authorities constructed a cage. In this way, offences under the IPC were tried in a court set up inside the jail and a jail set up inside the court. The 167 accused would be brought from the jail into this cage. Nobody else was permitted to enter the court, so the travesty of justice in this case was not known to the outside world. There was no protest against this atrocious state of affairs. I was appalled when I saw this in 2006 and immediately convened a press conference in Coimbatore and assailed the incarceration of the accused in this manner—in a democratic polity, this ought to have been a trial open to the public. On my insistence, news reporters were permitted to come into the makeshift court after I commenced my arguments. The families of the accused also asked to meet me—around a thousand people, all kin of the 167 accused, met me in person.

I had earlier argued cases in Tamil Nadu. I got to know one of the accused, Basha. When the blasts took place in Coimbatore, I anticipated that Muslims would become the target of attack yet again, and began to inquire into the details. After the initial stages of the trial in the sessions court were completed, advocate Mohan from Bhavani and advocate Tirumalairajan from Erode requested me to appear in the sessions court. I told them that I did not have the energy to participate in the entire proceedings, but would appear at the stage of arguments. This was in 2005. They organized a meeting in Coimbatore and invited me. During that visit, I also met the accused who were in jail. That was the time I saw the court set-up in the jail premises. Till then nobody from Coimbatore had seen that court. I visited the court

---

columns/criminal-law-and-human-rights-distinctive-discrimination-and-article-21-rights-to-fair-trial-167651. Accessed on 9 August 2022.

15 B.B. Mohan. 2020. 'Criminal Law and Human Rights: "Distinctive Discrimination" and Article 21 Rights to Fair Trial', KG Kannabiran Lectures on Law, Justice and Human Rights. *Livelaw*, 25 December. https://www.livelaw.in/columns/criminal-law-and-human-rights-distinctive-discrimination-and-article-21-rights-to-fair-trial-167651. Accessed on 9 August 2022.

after seeking permission from the judge as the defence counsel, and later called for a press conference, so that the world outside could learn of the injustice meted out to the undertrial prisoners who had by then been in judicial custody for eight years. I stayed in Coimbatore for a week in August 2006 and presented my arguments on behalf of the accused.

The key points I wish to bring to the notice of readers is this: There are times in the life of a nation when the rule of law is maintained strictly. There are other times when the rule of law is suspended. The principle of equality before the law has no room for inequality of this order. The bomb blasts in Coimbatore took place on the evening of 14 February 1998 in which fifty-seven innocent people were killed. The blasts were condemnable, and there is no doubt that the persons responsible must be punished. However, there is a difference between investigating a crime and bringing the culprits to book and rounding up the entire Muslim population and putting the community through a trial. What happened in the Coimbatore case was state retribution against an entire community. It was similar to the massacre of Sikhs after the assassination of Indira Gandhi in 1984.

Some of the 167 persons accused in the Coimbatore case remanded to judicial custody were able to muster legal support to apply for bail, but the district court and the high court dismissed the bail petitions. Some of them were also able to go to the Supreme Court, but met with no success there either. Being in remand for nine years was unheard of—and not part of any law in force. It was a case of punishment before conviction. In this context, the summary rejection of bail applications by courts at every level was nothing but state/judicial violence in the name of law. We must remember that the *Maneka Gandhi* judgment held that arbitrariness is a violation of the right to equality before law.[16] Article 21 of the Constitution of India protects us against such violence. Judicial arbitrariness is far worse than executive arbitrariness. If courts condemn persons to indefinite custody even before conviction, it paves the way for large-scale violation of the right to life by custodians of the Constitution. A majority of the 167 did not file bail petitions. Over a thousand witnesses were examined during the trial. A point to note about this case is that the offences under which the accused persons were charged were offences under the IPC, the Explosive Substances Act and the Arms Act—not POTA. The Unlawful Activities Prevention Act, 1967, which was amended in 2004 to bring it on par with POTA by the UPA government, was not the law under which they were charged. Put simply, the Coimbatore bomb blasts trial paved the way for the arraignment of Muslims as Islamic terrorists. Political militants like Maoists were killed without any inquiry

16 *Maneka Gandhi vs Union of India*, 1978 AIR 597.

or investigation. The method adopted for those labelled as 'Islamic terrorists' was different, as the Coimbatore case showed us.

The Importance of an Open Trial

The Coimbatore trial raises the question of the open trial, which was discussed in the Indira Gandhi assassination case. The Criminal Procedure Code 1973 has a specific provision for courts to be open. Section 327 reads as follows:

> 327. Court to be open.—3[(1)] The place in which any Criminal Court is held for the purpose of inquiring into or trying any offence shall be deemed to be an open Court, to which the public generally may have access, so far as the same can conveniently contain them:
>
> Provided that the presiding Judge or Magistrate may, if he thinks fit, order at any stage of any inquiry into, or trial of, any particular case, that the public generally, or any particular person, shall not have access to, or be or remain in, the room or building used by the Court.

All legal philosophers and experts have written about the significance of an open court. Justice K. Jagannath Shetty's views on an open trial in the case of *Kehar Singh* is extremely important.[17] The accused challenged their trial and conviction on the following grounds, among others:

> (i) Whether the High Court has power to direct the trial of the case at a place other than the normal seat of the Court of Session? (ii) Whether the trial inside the jail premises is the very antithesis of an open trial? (iii) Whether the trial proceedings were devoid of sufficient safeguards to constitute a public trial?

Justice Shetty reflected at length on the question of an 'open trial' or a 'public trial', drawing on Judge Cooley's views:

> It is also requisite that the trial be public. By this is not meant that every person who seeks fit shall in all cases be permitted to attend criminal trials; because there are many cases where, from the character of the charge and the

17 *Kehar Singh and Ors vs State (Delhi Administration)* (03.08.1988: SC): MANU/SC/0241/1988; AIR 1988 SC 1883.

> nature of the evidence by which it is to be supported, the motives to attend the trial on the part of portions of the community would be of the worst character, and where regard for public morals and public decency would require that at least the young be excluded from hearing and witnessing the evidences of human depravity which the trial must necessarily bring to light. The requirement of a trial is for the benefit of the accused; that the public may see he is fairly dealt with and not unjustly condemned, and that the presence of interested spectators may keep his triers keenly alive to a sense of their responsibility into the importance of their functions and the requirement is fairly observed if, without partiality of favouritism, a reasonable proportion of the public is suffered to attend, notwithstanding that those persons whose presence could be of no service to the accused, and who would only be drawn thither by a prurient curiosity, are excluded altogether.[18]

After a long rumination on the importance of an open trial that must also be open to the press, Justice Shetty concluded by saying, 'There can, therefore, be no doubt or dispute as to the adequacy of safeguards provided to constitute an open trial. Indeed, the steps taken by learned trial Judge are more than adequate to ensure fair trial as well as public trial.'[19] So the court inside the prison complex was deemed appropriate for an 'open trial'.

The Coimbatore blasts court was built on this logic. However much the facilities for a court inside a jail may conform to Cooley's views, can a court within a jail ever be an open court? Can people freely enter and attend court sessions inside a jail? Can it be assumed that persons attending the trial inside a jail will not be surveilled? Is it possible for reporters to report freely on a trial located within the premises of a jail? It is by this mockery of interpretation that the provisions for an open trial in the CrPC, read with Articles 19 and 21, were violated in several cases thereafter, especially in the laws relating to terrorist activities.

---

18 *Cooley's Constitutional Law, Vol. I, 8, Ed. 647, quoted in Kehar Singh and Ors vs State (Delhi Administration)* (03.08.1988: SC): MANU/SC/0241/1988; AIR 1988 SC 1883, para 189.

19 *Kehar Singh and Ors vs State (Delhi Administration)* (03.08.1988: SC): MANU/SC/0241/1988; AIR 1988 SC 1883, para 199.

Reservations for Muslims

The state of Andhra Pradesh has recognized marginalized Muslim communities as backward classes since 1970.[20] The multi-member commission constituted by the government of Andhra Pradesh under GO Ms. No. 870, Education Department, dated 12 April 1968, recommended the caste of Dudekula (also known as Laddaf or Noorbash) among the ninety-two castes recommended for inclusion in the list. Later, the government added the Mehtar caste, through an order that was upheld by the Hon'ble Supreme Court of India.

Subsequent to the recommendations of the Mandal Commission, and the direction of the Supreme Court of India in the Indra Sawhney case,[21] the Andhra Pradesh Commission for Backward Classes Act came into force in 1993. The Muslim community was one of fourteen communities included in the list of backward classes through GO Ms. No. 30 dated 25 August 1994. This order was challenged in the Andhra Pradesh High Court and was not given effect in pursuance of a direction to that effect from the court.

In 2004, the Commissioner of Minorities Welfare under directions from the government of Andhra Pradesh through GO Ms. No. 15 dated 4 June 2004 examined the social, economic and educational backwardness of the Muslim community in the state and recommended reservation of 5 per cent in employment and education under a fifth category, 'E'.[22] The Andhra Pradesh High Court struck down this order in 2004 and directed the government to reconstitute the Backward Classes Commission.[23] This reconstituted commission, headed by Justice Dalava Subrahmanyam, once again recommended the inclusion of the Muslim community in the list after due inquiry.[24]

20 The notes and references in this section of the chapter are part of the original unpublished essay written by K.G. Kannabiran: Ed.

21 p. 226

22 Government of Andhra Pradesh (2007). *Report on Identification of Socially and Educationally Backward Classes in the Muslim Community of Andhra Pradesh* (P.S. Krishnan Committee), Government of Andhra Pradesh, Hyderabad.

23 *T. Muralidhar Rao vs State of Andhra Pradesh* and *Ors,* 2004 (6) ALD 1. Bench consisting of B. Sudershan Reddy, Jasti Chelameswar, Ghulam Mohammed, A. Gopal Reddy and K.C. Bhanu, JJ. K.G. Kannabiran appeared in this case.

24 Government of Andhra Pradesh (2007b). *Report on Inclusion of Socially and Educationally Backward Classes among Muslim Community in the List of Backward*

The enumeration of Muslims within the category of backward classes in Andhra Pradesh has a history that goes back to 1970, based on the factual assessment of the socio-economic status of poor Muslim communities which form the overwhelming majority of the Muslim community as a whole in the state of Andhra Pradesh.

As the report of the Backward Classes Commission stated, 'social backwardness, which is crucial in the identification of backward classes ... is the outcome of socio-historical processes. There were various aspects to these processes. One important aspect related to traditional occupations'.[25] Inequality among social groups based on occupations is something that is found in all communities—among Hindu and Christian groups as well as among Muslim groups. For instance, the Ranganath Mishra Commission has noted that Ajlafs comprise occupational groups like carpenters, artisans, painters, graziers, tanners, milkmen, etc., and Arzals, the most underprivileged among Muslims, comprise the Halalkhor, Lalbegi, Abdal and Bediya.

Further, the word 'class' in Article 15(4) is wider than 'caste' and was meant to include backward classes in other groups where caste origins may not be clearly discernible, but which may yet be socially backward. The term 'backward classes' was defined in Section 2(a) of the Andhra Pradesh Commission for Backward Classes Act, 1993 (Act 20 of 1993), as 'such backward classes of citizens of Andhra Pradesh other than the Scheduled Castes and Scheduled Tribes as may be specified by the State Government in the lists'. Section 2(d) of the Act specified that lists were

---

Classes in the State of Andhra Pradesh (Dalava Subrahmanyam Commission), Andhra Pradesh Backward Classes Commission, Government of Andhra Pradesh, Hyderabad. Consequent to this, the Backward Classes Commission recommended a reservation of 4 per cent in education and employment for these fourteen groups, leading to the Andhra Pradesh Reservation in Favour of Socially and Educationally Backward Classes of Muslims Act, 2007 (Act 26 of 2007). In *T. Muralidhar Rao vs Government of Andhra Pradesh*, 2010 (2) ALD 492, a seven-judge bench of the Andhra Pradesh High Court decided that this enactment was ultra vires of Article 14 and therefore unconstitutional. K.G. Kannabiran appeared in this case as well, representing a private respondent, Dokka Manikya Vara Prasad, at that time an MLA belonging to the Indian National Congress. For a detailed discussion on this decision: Kannabiran, Kalpana. 2012. *Tools of Justice: Non-Discrimination and the Indian Constitution*. New Delhi: Routledge, pp. 285–94.

25 Government of Andhra Pradesh. 2007a. *Report on identification of socially and educationally backward classes in the Muslim community of Andhra Pradesh and recommendations* (P.S. Krishnan report). Hyderabad: Government of Andhra Pradesh, p. 12.

prepared by the government from time to time in order to provide reservation to classes the government found inadequately represented in educational institutions and in the services under the government.

The index of social backwardness is the inability to access equal opportunity in education and employment. The statistics provided by the Andhra Pradesh Backward Classes Commission in its report pointed to the fact that between the years 2002 and 2007, a mere 2.7 per cent of seats in professional education went to Muslim students and 3.49 per cent of government jobs went to them at the state level in a random survey of recruitments from 1999 to 2006. But even more shocking were the figures for the seven Muslim groups that were later identified as socially backward, namely, Fakeer, Pakeerla, Labbi, Qureshi, Muslim Rajakas, Turaka Kasha and Achukatlavandlu. In seventy-six departments of the state government, only 3.5 per cent of Muslims employed belonged to these classes. Muslims belonging to groups other than those listed as backward occupied 96.5 per cent of the jobs.[26] After due inquiry, the commission recommended that these seven groups and eight other groups—Guddi Eluguvallu, Siddi, Garadi Muslim, Attar Saibulu, Gosangi Muslim, Sheik, Hajam—which made it a total of fifteen groups, be included in the list of backward classes in the state of Andhra Pradesh and recommended a 4 per cent reservation for persons belonging to these groups in education and employment. This list was drawn up after careful consideration of data of various indices relating to social backwardness.

Historical Background to Reservation for Muslims

The Constituent Assembly ensured that religion would have no role to play in the governance of society. The right to freedom of religion and conscience contained in the Fundamental Rights chapter ensures equality to all religions, whether of minorities or the majority. Propagation of secular values would undoubtedly propel the forces of social transformation forward. The Haripura Congress session in February 1938 declared that it was its

> … primary duty as well as its fundamental policy to protect the religious, linguistic, cultural and the other rights of the minorities in India so as to assure for them in any scheme of government to which the Congress would be a party, the widest scope for their development and their participation

26 Ibid.

> in the fullest measure in the political, economic and the cultural life of the nation.[27]

Pandit Gobind Ballabh Pant, moving a resolution for setting up an advisory committee on fundamental rights, minorities and tribal and excluded and partially excluded areas, stressed the importance of the issue of minorities when he told the members of the Constituent Assembly:

> The question of minorities everywhere looms large in constitutional discussions. Many a constitution has foundered on this rock. A satisfactory solution of questions pertaining to minorities will ensure the health, vitality and strength of the free state of India that will come into existence as a result of our discussions here. The question of minorities cannot possibly be overrated. It has been used so far for creating strife, distrust and cleavage between the different sections of the Indian Nation. Imperialism thrives on such strife. It is interested in fomenting such tendencies. So far, the minorities have been incited and have been influenced in a manner which has hampered the growth of cohesion and unity. But now it is necessary that a new chapter should start and we should all realise our responsibility. Unless the minorities are fully satisfied, we cannot make any progress: we cannot even maintain peace in an undisturbed manner.[28]

While the members of the majority community were always alive to the Indian reality, the perception has generally been that the minority community can always be incited to misbehave and undo the effort of the majority community to build a cohesive society, breaking up all possibility of maintaining lasting peace.

Ambedkar pointed out that 'a communal majority will be free to run the administration according to its own ideas of what is good for the minorities'.[29] Such a state of affairs, he pointed out, could not be called democracy. It will have to be called imperialism.

Muslim members of the Constituent Assembly were asking for separate electorates or for proportional representation. Mohammed Ismail Saheb from

---

27 Cf. Rao, B. Shiva. 1968. *The Framing of India's Constitution: A Study*. New Delhi: IIPA, p. 746.

28 Ibid.

29 Ibid.

Madras argued for a system of separate electorates, arguing that they would, instead of acting as a divisive device, really bring about harmony among the people:

> The Muslims as well as the other communities want to contribute effectively and efficiently towards the harmony, prosperity and happiness of the country which is their motherland and for that purpose, they want to have equal opportunities with other people. They want to be an honourable section of the people of the land, as honourable as any other section; in the days of freedom they also want to have freedom of expressing their views. Sir, it may be said that they may express their views through the representatives elected by all the people put together. Supposing there is a difference of opinion between the minority community and the majority community, then will the representative of the majority community represent the different views of the minority, Sir?[30]

Z.H. Lari, a Muslim member from the United Provinces, proposed proportional representation to safeguard the interests of minorities. Taking the case of the United Provinces, he said the 10 per cent of Muslims could easily be ignored.

> The test of a system is to be made at critical times, at a time when passions are running high—not when things are smooth. Therefore my submission is that you should coolly consider the question whether apart from reservations of seats, apart from separate electorates, is there any democratic method which can ensure due rights to minorities—be it political, social or religious.[31]

Referring to the spirit of accommodation displayed by the House, he pointed out:

> Only the other day by endorsing the London decision you accepted the King as the link—a King whom you previously regarded as a symbol of Imperialism and oppression of our rights ... Should you not display that spirit of accommodation when you are dealing with a section of your own, whom you have agreed you cannot but have as an integral part of the nation?'[32]

30 *Constituent Assembly Debates: Official Report*. 1989. Book No. 3, Vol. 8, New Delhi: Lok Sabha Secretariat, p. 280.

31 Ibid., p. 287.

32 Ibid.

Vallabhbhai Patel, while introducing the Report of the Advisory Committee on Minorities, etc., for consideration of the Constituent Assembly prospectively overruled the issues that were later raised by the representatives of the minorities when he said:

> It is not our intention to commit the minorities to a particular position in a hurry. If they really have come honestly to the conclusion that in the changed conditions of this country, it is in the interests of all to lay down real and genuine foundations of a secular state, then nothing is better for the minorities than to trust the good-sense and sense of fairness of the majority, and to place confidence in them. So also it is for us who happen to be in a majority to think about what the minorities feel, and how we in their position would feel if we were treated in the manner in which they are treated.[33]

Sardar Ujjal Singh of Punjab, a Sikh, brought to the notice of the Constituent Assembly the Congress Resolution of December 1929 relating to Sikhs and minorities, which read:

> No solution thereof (i.e., the communal problem) in any future constitution of India will be acceptable to the Congress which does not give full satisfaction to the Muslims, Sikhs, other minorities.[34]

He pointed out that a resolution was passed by the Sikhs to boycott participation in the Constituent Assembly initially and that thanks to the efforts of Sardar Patel the Sikh community rescinded its earlier decision. He informed the Assembly that the Sikhs wanted their separate entity and position to be maintained and strengthened so that they could contribute their full quota to the service of the country.

Hansa Mehta of Bombay pointed out how the average woman for centuries has suffered from the inequalities heaped upon her by laws, custom and religious practices, and been denied ordinary human rights. She did not press for a separate electorate, reservations or quotas, but argued for equality:

> What we have asked for is social justice, economic justice, and political justice. We have asked for that equality which can alone be the basis of

33 Ibid., p. 272.

34 *Constituent Assembly Debates: Official Report*. 1989. Book No. 1, Vols 1–6, New Delhi: Lok Sabha Secretariat, p. 105.

> mutual respect and understanding and without which real co-operation is not possible between man and woman. Women form one half of the population of this country and, therefore, men cannot go very far without the co-operation of women.[35]

Jaipal Singh of Bihar, general, representing more than thirty million Adivasis, pointed out that for over 6,000 years his people had been treated disgracefully and neglected.

> The whole history of my people is one of continuous exploitation and dispossession by the non-aboriginals of India punctuated by rebellions and disorder …
>
> If history had to teach me anything at all, I should distrust this Resolution, but I do not. Now we are on a new road. Now we have simply got to learn to trust each other.[36]

These extracts from the debates are illustrative of the anxieties, doubts and fears which haunted the minorities and the response of the leaders of the majority community. The Preamble, the Fundamental Rights chapter, the chapter on Directive Principles, and the provisions to ensure autonomy and governance free from exploitation to the tribal areas really cover the issues raised, and these form the core of the Constitution. Most of these provisions reflect social conditions prevalent in the country which need urgent and continuing attention. Certain social evils had to be banished and be unequivocally declared unconstitutional. The attempt was to have a Constitution which would enable the people to cope with and transform Indian social reality within a liberal framework. The concepts of social, economic and political justice are not only the objectives of the Preamble but also the fundamental obligations in the governance of the country. Further, the Constitution represents the majority's assurance to the minorities that their claims to equality and dignity will be respected. Implied in this claim for equality are the right to treatment as an equal and the right to equal treatment. The latter deals with the formal aspect of equality, like the right to vote, equal access to opportunities, and is generally an assertion that other things being equal there shall be no discrimination between similarly placed persons, nor should there be a grouping of unequal or dissimilar categories of persons while dealing with distributive justice.

35 Ibid., p. 138.

36 Ibid., p. 144.

The right to treatment as an equal has in it the transformative potential necessary to realize the objectives set out in the Preamble. Equality has been the major premise in all written arrangements of governance of societies and this, when extended to minorities, would not only mean one person, one value, it would also include the rights of minorities as collectives to maintain their identity in dignity and extend to them a sense of participation in the management of the affairs of the society, by integrating them as equals in reality, not merely in form. This, in brief, is the history of the constitutional debate on minorities, and to contend that they gave up this identity or the Constituent Assembly intended at any time to deprive them of their identity would be ahistorical and merely be a majoritarian assertion which should not find acceptance in courts even as a legalistic argument.

While the first clause in Article 15 declares equal treatment for all, sub-clauses (a) and (b) reflect the existing social practices that had to be banished. While these provisions should normally aid our understanding of equality while interpreting clause (1) of Article 15, courts have been blind to this possibility, leading to an avoidable amendment of the Constitution. Sub-clause (2) of Article 15 reads:

> No citizen on ground only of religion, race, caste, sex, place of birth or any of them, be subject to any disability, liability, restriction or condition with regard to:
> (a) access to shops, public restaurants, hotels, and places of public entertainment; or
> (b) the use of well, tanks, bathing ghats, roads, and places of public resort maintained wholly or partly out of state funds or dedicated to the use of the general public.

Reservations in educational institutions and in government services are another aspect of the principle of equality. As already argued, one need not always go via Articles 15(4) and 16(4) for reservation, and one can directly access Articles 15(1) and 16(1) for justifications for reservation. In fact, even before the National Commission to Review the Working of the Constitution, a plea was made by representatives of minority communities for reservation under Articles 15 and 16, and the commission felt that

> ... under the existing provisions of articles 14, 15 and 16, it is open for the State to make reservation if it is of the opinion that such reservation is necessary and justified. The Commission noted that the ultimate aim of affirmative action of reservation should be to raise the levels of capabilities of

> people of the disadvantaged sections and to bring them at par with the other sections of society.[37]

In this background, to supersede minorities' identities under the caption 'occupation' is to mistake the import of the entire discussion on caste and occupation in *Indra Sawhney*.[38] To obfuscate the issue by bringing in 'creamy layer' and insisting that until that is determined the GO cannot be passed is not, in my view, a tenable legal argument. The question whether the GO was passed under Article 15(4) or 16(4) is irrelevant. It is this recognition of minority as an entity that led Parliament to constitute the National Minorities Commission by a statute in 1992 and correspondingly enact the Andhra Pradesh State Minorities Commission Act in 1998. The disadvantages of putting Muslim community members in the general Hindu category of social backwardness under Articles 15(4) and 16(4) are that the exercise would only be formal without any real benefit to such members of the minority community who are identified by the castes which they take along with them on conversion. Such an inclusion may further reinforce their minority status even within the backward class category. This exercise would also exclude the majority of the minority community who do not carry over any caste identity. Identification by minority status cannot be communal. The religion of the minority is only one index with the other indicia of social and educational backwardness growing out of poverty that is a consequence of unequal treatment of the minority. Even otherwise, minority identity is safeguarded and protected by several international covenants and United Nations resolutions. Identifying minorities by occupation will lead to an argument that the identification is on the basis of economic backwardness and thus the claim to reservation will be defeated.

Arguing for Reservation

Muslims as a minority in India are entitled to reservation under the equality code of the Constitution, as embodied in Articles 15(1), 16(1) and 16(2). The claim to affirmative action by Muslims need not be routed through Articles 15(4) and 16(4). That 'minority' is different from 'backward class' is evident from the National Commission on Minorities Act, 1992, and the Andhra Pradesh State Minorities Commission Act , 1998. As a consequence of our formulation, *M.R. Balaji vs State*

37 Report of the National Commission to Review the Working of the Constitution, para 3.7.

38 *Indra Sawhney vs Union of India*, AIR 1993 SC 477.

of Mysore[39] liberally or strictly defined would not apply. Article 15(1) asserts that the state shall not discriminate against any citizen on grounds only of 'religion, race, caste, sex, place of birth or any of them.' Article 16(1) further elaborates on it: 'There shall be equality of opportunity for all citizens in matters relating to employment or appointment to any office under the state.' Article 16(2) continues, 'No citizen shall on grounds only of religion, race, caste, sex, descent, place of birth, residence or any of them, be ineligible for, or discriminated against in respect of, any employment or office under the state.' This must be interpreted not in the restrictive sense that the state shall not discriminate, but must be interpreted to mean that the state has the responsibility for preventing discrimination against minorities by other groups in society and that the state is responsible for providing substantive equality of opportunity through affirmative action in favour of Muslim minorities.

Deliberating on the reach of Articles 14, 15 and 16, in *N.M. Thomas vs State of Kerala*, Chief Justice A.N. Ray observed as follows:

> Articles 14, 15 and 16 form part of a string of constitutionally guaranteed rights. These rights supplement each other. Article 16 which ensures to all citizens equality of opportunity in matters relating to equality of opportunity in employment is an incident of guarantee of equality contained in Article 14. Article 16(1) gives effect to Article 14. Both Articles 14 and 16(1) permit reasonable classification having nexus to the objects achieved.
>
> Discrimination is the essence of classification … Classification … is to be founded on substantial differences which distinguish persons grouped together from those left out of the groups and such differential attributes must bear a just and rational relation to the object sought to be achieved.[40]

Justice K.M. Mathew, in the same case, observed,

> The principle of proportional equality is attained only when equals are treated equally and unequals unequally. The principle of proportional equality involves an appeal to some criterion in terms of which differential treatment is justified … Article 16(1) is only a part of the comprehensive scheme to ensure equality in all spheres … Though complete identity of equality of opportunity is impossible in this world, measures compensatory in character and which are calculated to mitigate surmountable obstacles to ensure

39 *M.R. Balaji vs State of Mysore*, 1963 Supp 1 SCR 439.

40 *N.M. Thomas vs State of Kerala*, (1976) 2 SCC 310, para 21, 24.

> equality of opportunity can never incur the wrath of Article 16(1) … To give X and Y equality of opportunity involves regarding their conditions, where curable, as themselves part of what is done to X and Y and not part of X and Y themselves. Their identity for this purpose does not include their curable environment which is itself unequal and a contributor to inequality …
>
> Whether there is equality of opportunity can be gauged only by the equality attained in the result. Formal equality of opportunity simply enables people with more education and intelligence to capture all the posts and to win over the less fortunate in education and talent even when the competition is fair. Equality of result is the test of equality of opportunity.[41]

Justice V.R. Krishna Iyer, in the same case observes,

> In a spacious sense, "equal opportunity" for members of a hierarchical society makes sense only if a strategy by which the underprivileged have environmental facilities for developing their full human potential. This consummation is accomplished only when the utterly depressed groups can claim a fair share in public life and economic activity including employment under the state, or when a classless and casteless society blossoms as a result of positive state action. To help the lagging social segments, by special case, is a step towards and not against a larger and stabler equality.'[42]

Justice B.P. Jeevan Reddy, in *Indra Sawhney vs Union of India*,[43] dealt with all the relevant cases in his deliberations on the concept of equality, bringing in an unprecedented clarity on the concept of substantive equality. Examining the decisions of the Supreme Court on Articles 15 and 16, he traced the shift in the understanding of the court from a position that backwardness may be identified without reference to caste and with reference to social and economic backwardness alone[44] to a position that 'caste is a class of citizens and that if caste as a whole is socially and educationally backward, reservation can be made in favour of such caste on the ground that it is a socially and educationally backward class of citizens',

---

41 Ibid., para 75.

42 Ibid., para 141.

43 *Indra Sawhney vs Union of India*, AIR 1993 SC 477.

44 *Chitralekha vs State of Mysore*, AIR 1964 SC 1823.

referring to *P. Rajendran vs State of Madras*.[45] However, this matter was reviewed in *State of UP vs Pradip Tandon*,[46] where Article 15(1) was invoked by Chief Justice Ray to assert that backwardness cannot be assessed on the basis of caste or religion. The view in *Rajendran*, however, prevailed subsequently and was reiterated by Justice O. Chinnappa Reddy in *Vasanth Kumar vs State of Karnataka*.[47] By the same analogy, a minority is a social community that can lay claim to equality under Article 15(1), religion being the main index for the identification of minorities. Reiterating the decision in *N.M. Thomas*, Justice Jeevan Reddy, underscored Justice Murtaza Fazal Ali's opinion that 'the rule of 50% evolved in *Balaji* is a mere rule of caution and was not meant to be exhaustive of all categories' (para 713). Justice Jeevan Reddy also drew upon various decisions of the US Supreme Court in support of his opinion on the scope of substantive equality. Clarifying a particularly relevant aspect of this argument, he observed, in Indira Sawhney: 'Article 16(1) is a facet of Article 14. Just as Article 14 permits reasonable classification, so does 16(1). A classification may involve reservation of seats or vacancies as the case may be. In other words, under clause (1) of Article 16, appointments and/or posts can be reserved in favour of a class.' As per the same analogy, seats in educational institutions can be reserved in favour of a class under clause (1) of Article 15.

Statistics are available, and so long as the veracity of the statistics is not disputed, there is nothing wrong with placing reliance on the data made available. In fact such an argument was advanced in *State of Andhra Pradesh vs U.S.V. Balram*:

> 'If the Commission has only to go on doing the work of collecting particulars and materials, it will be a never ending matter. In spite of best efforts that any commission may make in collecting materials and datas, its conclusions cannot be always scientifically accurate in such matters. Therefore the proper approach should be to see whether the relevant data and materials referred to in the report of the Commission justify its conclusions.'[48]

The contention that Muslims as a minority must have access to avenues of affirmative action and equality of opportunity is supported by international law on various aspects of minority rights. A contemporary definition of the term 'minority' has been proposed by Professor Francesco Capotorti, special rapporteur of the

45 *P. Rajendran vs State of Madras*, AIR 1968 SC 1012, para 706.

46 *State of Uttar Pradesh vs Pradip Tandon*, (1975) 2 SCR 761.

47 *Vasanth Kumar vs State of Karnataka*, 1985 SuppSCC 714.

48 *State of Andhra Pradesh vs U.S.V. Balram* (1972) 1 SCC 660. This was quoted with approval in *Indra Sawhney*, para 709, when a similar contention was advanced.

United Nations Sub-Commission on Prevention of Discrimination and Protection of Minorities:

> [T]he term 'minority' may be taken to refer to: a group numerically inferior to the rest of the population of a State, in a non-dominant position, whose members—being nationals of the State—possess ethnic, religious or linguistic characteristics differing from those of the rest of the population and show, if only implicitly, a sense of solidarity, directed towards preserving their culture, traditions, religion or language.[49]

Under international law, religious minority groups were the first to be protected by treaty, as an adjunct to peace treaties in the aftermath of the First World War. Despite international instruments, however, it has been found all over the world that minority children face several barriers in accessing education—development deficits, geographical location, historical discrimination and stigmatization and practices of segregated settlements are a few of the several factors that impede opportunities. Minority rights in education and employment are based primarily on two desiderata which are usually complementary but which may occasionally conflict with each other. In this context, the guarantee of equal opportunity is only assured when along with the provision of educational and employment opportunities that aim at building on their talents, minority identity is sought to be safeguarded from erosion through appropriate measures in society and public institutions.[50]

It is only equality of opportunity through affirmative action that can transform majority–minority differences into more healthy forms of diversity and pluralism and pave the way for the values enshrined in Article 51A of the Indian Constitution.

Conclusion: Enlarging the Constituency of the Secular-Minded

The Constitution, which was debated in the background of Partition and the violence that followed, designedly gave us a secular system of governance, making no reference to either Hindu or Muslim or any other religion or faith.

Secularism was, until the 42nd Amendment to the Constitution, the inarticulate major premise of our governance. After the amendment, secularism was explicitly made one of the major premises of our constitutional arrangement. Nonetheless,

49 Capotorti, Francesco. 1979. *Study on the Rights of Persons Belonging to Ethnic, Religious and Linguistic Minorities*. New York: United Nations, p. 96, para 568.

50 Hodgson, Douglas. 1998. *The Human Right to Education*. Dartmouth: Ashgate, pp. 85–114.

communal politics and violence were present in some part of the country or the other and were slowly becoming a defining part of our political practice. Its entry into political practice spelt dangerous forebodings for the plural character of our society. This was not realized until religion in the guise of politics, leading a subterranean existence with less than nominal presence in representative bodies, surfaced in a big way as a major contending factor in the last decade and a half of the twentieth century.

The degeneration of electoral politics reduced secularism and the protection of minorities into the treatment of minorities as vote banks. Electoral politics devoid of social purpose and a movement towards bringing about equality and justice can only be for power and will therefore be violent.

In such circumstances, democratic governance will be the first casualty. Parties with a single-point anti-Muslim and anti-minority agenda will resort not only to ruthlessly quelling rebellion but will also reduce minorities living in the country to the status of second-class citizens. Shocking atrocities such as the Mumbai and Gujarat riots will be used to subdue the minorities by the terror such atrocities create. It is necessary to confront such atrocities by waging an incessant and unremitting struggle against these trends.

17

The Citizens' Tribunal on Gujarat, 2002

A Brief History of Communal Violence in Gujarat

IN THE HISTORY of public tribunals, the citizens' tribunal set up to inquire into the violence in Gujarat in 2002 is an important milestone.[1] On 27 February 2002, the Sabarmati Express carrying *kar sevaks* to Ahmedabad stopped at the Godhra railway station. There was reportedly an altercation with Muslim vendors on the railway platform that escalated, leading to one bogie, S6, getting engulfed in flames. Fifty-eight travellers were killed. Instead of setting the criminal justice machinery in the state rolling, the state government declared an official bandh, which was then used as a smokescreen to carry out the most gruesome attacks on Muslims across the state. Shocked at the scale of violence, human rights groups decided to constitute a citizens' tribunal on Gujarat. The Citizens for Justice and Peace movement constituted the tribunal and tasked it with inquiring into the various incidents of violence and submit a report. As the national president of the PUCL, I was part of this tribunal along with former Supreme Court judges Justice V.R. Krishna Iyer and Justice P.B. Sawant; former judge of the Bombay High Court

1 This chapter is a revised version of the chapter titled 'Narendra Modi's Hindutva Laboratory' (pp. 173–85) in *The Wages of Impunity: Power, Justice and Human Rights in India* (Copyright © Orient BlackSwan Pvt. Ltd, 2004). Reproduced with the permission of the publishers, Orient BlackSwan Pvt. Ltd.

Justice Hosbet Suresh; Mazdoor Kisan Shakti Sangathan (MKSS) leader Aruna Roy; former DGP, Tripura, Dr K.S. Subramanian; professor of social sciences at Jawaharlal Nehru University, Ghanshyam Shah; and professor of history at JNU, Tanika Sarkar. I stayed in Gujarat for twenty-two to twenty-three days while the tribunal was at work. We examined 2,400 witnesses and recorded their statements. The inescapable conclusion we reached was that there was a total breakdown of constitutional governance in the state during that period—the Constitution and democratic governance had been suspended and replaced by the machinery of a Hindutva laboratory. This account draws upon my experience as a member of the tribunal.[2]

It was in the fall of 1944 that Heinrich Himmler realized that the war was coming to a close; the game was up and the extermination facilities at Auschwitz and the other concentration camps had to be dismantled. He told Adolf Eichmann around this time, 'If up to now you have been busy liquidating Jews, you will from now on, since I order it, take good care of Jews, act as their nursemaid.'[3] That echoes Vajpayee's approach to the violence, and his act of sending K.P.S. Gill to broker peace in the state instead of setting Article 355 of the Constitution in motion.[4] This peace process was, like all such initiatives, as loosely structured as possible, promising no redress, no justice, but an abundance of pity for the plight of the victims of the macabre events of February, March, April and May 2002.

From the time BJP came to power in Gujarat, it has made every attempt to build a Hindu rashtra. It began its rule in the state by removing a ban imposed earlier on public servants being members of the RSS.[5] This adroit move became possible

2 Concerned Citizens' Tribunal. 2002. *Crime Against Humanity*, 3 vols. Mumbai: Citizens for Justice and Peace.

3 Arendt, Hannah. 1992. *Eichmann in Jerusalem: A Report on the Banality of Evil.* New York: Penguin, p. 138.

4 Article 355. Duty of the Union to protect states against external aggression and internal disturbance: 'It shall be the duty of the Union to protect every State against external aggression and internal disturbance and to ensure that the government of every State is carried on in accordance with the provisions of this Constitution.'

5 L.K. Advani, Union home minister: 'I would say that this decision of the Gujarat Government has been taken by the Gujarat Government in its own wisdom. We see no reason why any Constitutional directive should be given to the State Government in this regard (Interruptions) ... We have no power to give (Interruptions) ... So far even earlier circular used the word "advised". In this case I can only leave it to the judgment of the State Government. Whatever they do in their own wisdom after taking congnizanze of what [sic] has happened

because all our institutions had been destroyed by Mrs Gandhi's experiment in authoritarian rule. Also, none of her successors were leaders; they were plagued with one desire, and that was to be the prime minister of this country, whatever it took to get there. With this kind of leadership, the voters returned one hung Parliament after another.

In its previous incarnation as the Jana Sangh, the BJP had no presence in Parliament. Only after the 1975 Emergency did they join the movement led by Jayaprakash Narayan. They rode into parliamentary politics after the defeat of the Congress (I) in the elections held immediately after the revocation of Emergency, gaining some seats, but as part of the Janata Party headed by Morarji Desai. The latter was a motley crowd of politicians who paved the way for the BJP to enter the power structure.

There was a systematic assault on the Constitution and democratic values in the form of the anti-reservation stir and the Ayodhya rath yatra. In the context of failing welfare and democratic politics, with no threat from leftist movements, concerted attempts were made by the religious majority to wrest power in order to ensure governance at the centre. Successive prime ministers after V.P. Singh facilitated this capture of power by the theocratic forces led by the BJP. The first ten years of this period, however, did not see the vulgar display of religiosity by public functionaries across the spectrum that is commonplace today. In the context of these practices, secular values have lost their relevance. Every caste and religious division has become grist for the electoral mill. As the commitment to social transformation has diminished, the electoral process is becoming distanced from the people. What remains as campaign material are caste and communal factors, used as strategies in adversarial politics—the beginning of degeneration. The resounding success of the Dalit movement has not helped strengthen the democratic and secular content of our politics. Earlier, social reforms were used to bring about homogeneity by attempting to abolish caste divisions. These were attempts to rid society of its

---

and all that has been said, it would be for them to decide. That is all that I can say.' Proceedings other than Questions and Answers: 'SHORT DURATION DISCUSSION: Failure of Government of India to discharge its Constitutional responsibility to protect secularism by not prevailing upon the State Government of Gujarat to withdraw the circular removing the ban imposed on the State Government employees in participating in the activities of R.S.S.', *Rajya Sabha Debates*, 2 March 2000, p. 301. For a detailed parliamentary debate on this issue, see pp. 209–301, https://www.rsdebate.nic.in/bitstream/123456789/109648/1/PD_189_02032000_7_p209_p301_9.pdf. Accessed on 15 October 2021.

long-standing aberrations, which treated a sizeable majority within its fold as non-persons. Such noble aspirations are outdated in present-day politics.

Communal politics has not emerged suddenly. It has been with us for a long time, growing steadily after Partition. The contours of communal politics are now clearly defined. Representatives of the Visva Samvad Kendra, the RSS media cell, found fault with the presentation of the Gujarat riots in the media. They said that the media examined one person in a district and drew inferences about the entire episode. They gave us a copy of a magazine they had brought out which highlighted Godhra but not the subsequent anti-Muslim violence, although the issue had been printed much later. It traced the roots of India's communal violence to 1947. Their stand blocked further discussions.

We are taken back in time to Nathuram Godse, who, in his statement to the court, explained without remorse his reasons for killing Gandhi. His reasons were neither noble nor profound; they were limited to the communal ideology (if communal politics can at all be called ideology, that is) he was wedded to. It is impossible to understand Gandhi and the vision of society he had within a limited thought frame such as Godse's. During the course of his epic tour of riot-torn Noakhali, Gandhi was informed of the retaliatory violence in Bihar. He said: 'But, for a thousand Hindus to fall upon a handful of Muslims—men, women and children—living in their midst, is no retaliation, but just brutality. It is the privilege of arms to protect the weak and helpless. The best succour that Bihar could have given to the Hindus of East Bengal would have been to guarantee with their own lives the absolute safety of the Muslim population living in their midst. Their example would have told.'[6]

Gandhi hailed from Gujarat. What happened in Gujarat on 28 February 2002 is not just a negation of what he stood and died for, but equally a negation of the values we all fought for in the course of a long struggle for Independence.

Post-Independence India has not known a leader of sufficient moral stature to effectively intervene in periods of acute political violence. We are still to hone our institutions to respond quickly and justly, which alone will discipline people to respect law and authority. The judges, administrators, lawyers, the entire quill-wielding class, the doctors and others who run this nation, as also its population – each group has its' own agendas and philosophies, and these inform their decisions and attitudes, whether in normal times or in times of crisis.

There have been excellent analyses and interpretations of India's recurring communal riots. They have helped our understanding. The point, however is

6 Tendulkar, D.C. *Mahatma: Life of Mohandas Karamchand Gandhi*, Vol. 7. Delhi: Government of India, p. 258.

and has always been to change what happens. The politics of secularism has been ineffective.

The Massacre of Muslims in Gujarat, 2002

A closer look at the violence in Gujarat shows that even while the *shilanyas* was being debated inside the courts, preparations were under way outside to test the Hindu parties' strength, despite their precariousness within the electoral system.

Godhra is in the Panchmahal district of Gujarat. *The Sabarmati Express*, having carried the Ram sevaks to Ayodhya earlier, was bringing them back to Ahmedabad. They returned without expending their energies, as the shilanyas did not take place. The Ram sevaks, or a majority of them, must have been quite young, energetic and unemployed, because these are the recruiting bases for the Vishwa Hindu Parishad (VHP) and the Bajrang Dal. Gathering regularly gives these foot soldiers of Hindutva not only a sense of belonging but also an occasion for proximity and gregariousness with upper-caste Hindus.

The train was carrying around 1,200 passengers and was obviously overcrowded. Passengers with reserved seats had to allow heavy entry of Ram sevaks into their compartments. These people had all gone to Ayodhya to work for the party. There were complaints against these Ram sevaks both to and from Ayodhya on 27 February. They had inconvenienced even Hindu passengers in the reserved compartments. There were complaints by Muslim vendors on the platforms with regard to how much tea and eatables they had consumed. They had also misbehaved with the women assisting the Muslim vendors. By all accounts, there was an altercation between the Muslim vendors and the Ram sevaks at the Godhra station. There is no evidence that the other Hindus present on the platform participated in this altercation. But as the train pulled out, the chain was pulled, stopping it at the Falia signal, which was a Muslim area. There was an attack on S6, a reserved compartment. It can be inferred that antisocial elements among the Muslims living there converted an altercation into a communal riot. That it was spontaneous to start with cannot be ruled out. There was stone-pelting from outside. A few seconds thereafter, the compartment was in flames. The stones would have made the passengers bring down the shutters, but it is asserted that flaming cloth balls were thrown in from the outside. At Falia, the rail track is at a height of around twelve feet. The compartments have the added protection of three to four cross-bars running through all the windows to prevent miscreants and thieves entering. Once set on fire and flung in from ground level, the cloth balls must have found their way into the compartment. However, the outside of the bogey did not bear any marks of large-scale charring. Burn marks were found only on the outer fringes of the windows, but these could be due to tongues of flame from the inside. The fire totally destroyed the inside of S6, twisting the steel and other metal in the compartment. The tragedy is that the fire also consumed around fifty to sixty human beings, including a large number of passengers who had nothing to do with the goings-on in Ayodhya or the rest of the country. Such crimes should never go unpunished.

The train fire raises several questions. The home minister was personally aware of what had happened in the country after the Babri Masjid was brought down. What security measures were taken to prevent a flare-up of communal violence following the shilanyas? It is not a responsible reply to say that law and order is a state subject. The Ayodhya shilanyas had all the possibilities of a breakdown of public order, but the sensitivity the government should exhibit towards terrorist violence was absent in the face of a possibility of violence by the majority community.

After the Godhra tragedy, but independent of it, genocide was unleashed on the Muslim population of Gujarat. The day after the train fire, that is, on 28 February 2002, attacks on the Muslim population began in various parts of the state—almost at the same time. This simultaneity showed they had been planned long before Godhra. The chief minister described the first incident as communal violence and the consequence as secular violence. The latter was independent of Godhra because of various facts that have come to light. Those who were victims and others who were around but did not share the communal politics of the state government confirmed the plan to enact violence. There had already been preparations to support the shilanyas. The build-up of the theocratic agenda was very open. The statements of Praveen Togadia, general secretary of VHP International, Acharya Giriraj Kishore, senior vice president of the VHP, S.K. Jain, national convener of the Bajrang Dal, and others in the month of February were instructive. They are provocative; although made with reference to temple construction, the message was very clear. Take Praveen Togadia's statement to the *Asian Age* on 7 February:

> It will have to be Pakistan or the mandir. The mosque constructed by Babar at Ayodhya 450 years ago by destroying the Ram temple there and the September 11 attack on the World Trade Centre are symbols of Islamic Jihad. It is necessary for India, the Jews and the Western world to get together and fight Islamic militants.

Such statements always lead to the massacre of the Muslim minorities living in our midst. In one statement, the Bajrang Dal leader said that if Muslim organizations prevented the construction of the temple, the Dal would chant the Hanuman Chalisa at Delhi's Jama Masjid. Earlier, this outfit had assured the Supreme Court that the kar sevaks were a peaceful lot and would merely sing religious hymns at the Babri mosque. So they were allowed into it, but what happened there is a continuing story! What preparations were under way in other parts of the country can only be guessed at from what happened in Gujarat. The scale of these preparations came to light when the spark of communal violence was lit in Godhra.

A Docile Bureaucracy and Complicit Government

There was a BJP government in power in the state and the centre. During this time inspectors were carefully chosen to man certain police stations, also officers in key positions. Muslim police officers were not given executive posts, but were transferred to administrative posts. The Sangh Parivar had already spread out throughout the state. Cadres, now armed, were meeting regularly in various centres. Godhra has always had a communal history. This fact should have led the administration to effectively use its preventive detention laws. That course was not open because several ministers were reported to have actually participated in the violence and/or monitored the mobs they had organized. The tribunal had reliable information that ministers sat in the police control rooms at Gandhinagar and Ahmedabad and directed the mayhem; victims testified that a minister led one of the mobs that attacked Muslims and their property. A former chief justice of the state emphatically confirmed the people's version by declaring that the Constitution and the laws stood suspended from 28 February onwards. All the attacks in different parts of Gujarat commenced almost simultaneously. The killings also did not vary in pattern. Victims were killed, in the most gruesome ways and set on fire. A *tola* or a mob of ten thousand chased the Muslims till they were blocked by the police from fleeing to safety. The mob then fell upon them and killed them. A child victim told us that he saw ten members of his family being slaughtered. The manner in which Ehsan Jafri, Kausar Bibi and Geetha Ben were killed are too well-known to be recounted.

The violence that was enacted did not stop with just killing. There was also an effort to destroy the identity of those killed. Rich Muslims were killed too. The mobs had lists of the Muslims in each mohalla (neighbourhood), and also a list of their properties. Two high court judges, one of them sitting, were attacked and their houses destroyed. They had to flee Judges' Colony and take shelter in a Muslim locality. Women were raped in the presence of murderous tolas. Mob leaders identified mixed couples and killed both. Children were not spared. The properties and businesses of Muslims were systematically destroyed, including those where one of the partners was Muslim. A countless number of Muslim places of worship were destroyed. How does one explain this all-encompassing violence and destruction?

How does one explain the inaction by the state that drew a sharp comment from the NHRC? Or the systematic destruction of evidence on which testimonies were recorded by our Tribunal?[7] This was a crime that has all the elements of genocide. It was not the first time. The massacre of Sikhs in 1984 organized by the leaders of the Congress party was by no means a riot. The killing of students belonging to the Sikh community in Bidar in September 1988 was also not a riot. These were the deliberate targeting of particular religious groups.

Defining the Violence in Gujarat as Genocide

Talking about Hitler's 'final solution', genocide, in the words of Hannah Arendt, 'is an attack on human diversity as such, that is, upon a characteristic of the "human

---

7 Proceedings of the Concerned Citizens' Tribunal on Gujarat, headed by Justice V.R. Krishna Iyer of which K.G. Kannabiran was a member. The full report of the committee detailing all these assertions: *Crime against Humanity* (3 Volumes) may be accessed at https://www.sabrang.com/tribunal/ Accessed on 6 May 2022; Preliminary Report of NHRC headed by Justice J.S. Verma on Gujarat, 1 April 2002: 'NHRC makes preliminary comments and recommendations to the Government of Gujarat and Government of India.' https://nhrc.nic.in/press-release/nhrc-makes-preliminary-comments-and-recommendations-government-gujarat-and-government, Accessed on 7 May 2022; Confidential Report on NHRC visit to Gujarat in April 2002. https://www.outlookindia.com/website/story/annexure-i-confidential-report/215843 Accessed on 7 May 2022; *Threatened Existence: A Feminist Analysis of the Genocide in Gujarat.* Report by the International Initiative for Justice (IIJ), December 2003. https://www.onlinevolunteers.org/gujarat/reports/iijg/2003, Accessed on 7 May 2022. On anti–Sikh riots in Delhi 1984: 'Who are the Guilty? Report of a Joint Inquiry into the Causes and Impact of the Riots in Delhi from 31 October to 10 November 1984. People's Union for Democratic Rights and People's Union for Civil Liberties. http://www.unipune.ac.in/snc/cssh/humanrights/04%20COMMUNAL%20RIOTS/B%20-%20ANTI%20-%20SIKH%20RIOTS/01%20-%20DELHI/a.pdf. Accessed on 6 May 2022. Also Harsh Mander. 2010. 'Conflict and Suffering: Survivors of Carnages in 1984 and 2002'. *Economic and Political Weekly*, Vol. 45, No. 32, 7 August, pp. 57–65. https://www.epw.in/system/files/pdf/2010_45/32/Conflict_and_Suffering_Survivors_of_Carnages_in_1984_and_2002.pdf, Accessed on 7 May 2022.

status" without which the very words "mankind" or "humanity" would be devoid of meaning.'[8]

After the Second World War, an international covenant was brought into existence on 9 December 1948 'to prevent and punish the crime of genocide'. It has a total of nineteen articles, of which Articles 2 and 3 are important. Based on the German decimation of Jews, Article 2 defines the crime of genocide thus:

> Genocide means any of the following acts committed with the intent to destroy, in whole or in part, a national, ethnic, racial, or religious group, as such:
> (a) Killing members of the group;
> (b) Causing serious bodily or mental harm to the members of the group;
> (c) Deliberately inflicting on the group conditions of life calculated to bring about its physical destruction in whole or in part;
> (d) Imposing measures intended to prevent births within the group;
> (e) Forcibly transferring children of one group to another group.
> The covenant has also enumerated those offences that are punishable, and they are:
> (a) Genocide;
> (b) Conspiracy to commit genocide;
> (c) Direct and public incitement to commit genocide;
> (d) Attempt to commit genocide;
> (e) Complicity in genocide.

There is no law on genocide at present, nor if one were to exist could it have retrospective operation. I do believe, however, that the covenant on genocide has become part of customary law, as it does not conflict with any other existing law. Such an interpretation might have helped our National Human Rights Commission to conduct a detailed investigation into the Gujarat crimes. The facts narrated in its summary report on Gujarat added up to a prima facie accusation of genocide, but there was no detailed report. The commission had a present obligation to the people and a mandatory obligation to posterity to inquire into the violence in Gujarat and record its findings so that no political party or government would resort in the future to such brutal practices. As part of this obligation, the NHRC is under obligation to prepare a 'Model Statute on Genocide', including provisions for taking effective

8 Arendt, Hannah. 1992. *Eichmann in Jerusalem: A Report on the Banality of Evil.* New York: Penguin, p. 269.

preventive measures to protect religious, ethnic and linguistic minorities from being attacked. This action, in my view, was mandatory, because under the International Criminal Court, genocide and crimes against humanity are declared as offences. Political parties may not obey them, but the human rights commissions set up by various countries must enforce them, however limited their jurisdiction might be.

After the collapse of the socialist states of central and eastern Europe in 1989, violent ethnic conflicts erupted involving minorities in Europe. By 1993, war in the former Yugoslavia—in Croatia, Bosnia and Serbia along with Vojvodina and Kosovo—had taken a toll of several thousand lives and two million displaced. The violence spread to the Caucasus and Moldavia and threatened to engulf the former Soviet Union. It was during this period that a resolution declaring the rights of persons belonging to national or ethnic, religious or linguistic minorities was passed by the UN General Assembly on 12 December 1992. Genocide is the forfeiture of minority rights. The protection of minorities is expansively spelt out by this resolution, all of which is implied in our Constitution.

The persons who met in the Constituent Assembly knew only too well that they had to deal with a conflict-ridden diversified society. So they provided for secularism as a value which includes the objectives set out in the Preamble, the article pertaining to abolition of untouchability, bonded and child labour, and almost all of the Directive Principles of the Constitution. This is how the Supreme Court defined secularism in *S.R Bommai,*[9] in a decision made in the backdrop of the Ayodhya controversy. Now that all over the world ethnic claims and conflicts abound, there is a necessity for the world body to bring forth an international covenant on secularism in plural societies within states. The argument that secularism cannot be internalized and will therefore remain a problem appears to be wholly misconceived, as also our definition that it means 'all religions are equal'.

What is to be done? In this country, courts are not geared to deal with mass violence. In registering the Gujarat crimes, the first information reports, which are basic and important documents, are flawed because the state's police departments are associates in the crime. How can one ensure a fair and independent investigation? Is it possible for the NHRC to get together a special investigation team under the Protection of Human Rights Act to file charge sheets in all the cases in Gujarat? The Muslims of Gujarat needed justice in all the facets mentioned in the Preamble, and that is their right. Political justice by prosecuting the criminals is imperative, for that alone will ensure the dignity of the victims, survivors, their families, and the

9 *S.R. Bommai and Ors vs Union of India*, AIR 1994 SC 1918.

community that was targeted, and restore their faith in the system, by assuring them that their individual and collective rights as a minority will be protected.

A formal compliance with the law, a routine engagement with justice will not keep justice alive. The Constitution says that justice—political, social and economic—should inform all the institutions of the state. Our campaign for a secular democracy should commence from this statement in the Preamble. For, as Lord Griffich said: Oppression does not stand on the doorstep with a toothbrush moustache and a swastika arm band.[10]

10 Griffich, J.A.G. 1992. *House of Lords Debates*, Vol. 505, c. 1331, quoted in *Constitutional Studies: Contemporary Issues and Controversies*. Robert Blackburn. Ed. London: Mansell, p. 150.

18

Peace Talks in Andhra Pradesh

Early Beginnings of the Peace Talks

WHEN TDP LEADER N.T. Rama Rao returned to power in 1984 after a short derailment by Governor Ram Lal, he was prepared for talks with Naxalites and proposals for abatement of violence on both sides. I was then the president of the APCLC. He sent his sons-in-law Narra Chandrababu Naidu and Daggubati Venkateswara Rao to me, inviting us for discussions for what can be broadly termed as 'peace talks'. At that time, we had never contemplated bilateral talks between the ruling party in the state and the CPI(ML) (PWG). In the preliminary talks, we suggested to NTR that land should be distributed to the landless on an emergency basis. I recollect having suggested a committee consisting of B.D. Sharma, S.R. Sankaran and B.N. Yugandhar to ascertain the extent of land available and for monitoring distribution.

This course, we were confident, would lead to an abatement of violence. Instead, NTR followed the short-term measure of withdrawing cases against some of them. Almost all the major cases only served the purpose of setting on record the history of the Naxalite movement and thus held them on a short leash, rather than for securing conviction. Impunity was enacted as the rule of law. Right from the Parvathipuram conspiracy case to the Bangalore conspiracy case, they were reframing a conspiracy charge after prosecuting the offenders for overt acts. As the investigating officer of the Secunderabad conspiracy case, Alfred deposed before the court, he studied the old records pertaining to the Naxalites, and wrote out the FIR running into around forty pages. The technique was for the investigating officer to draw up a complaint and address it to himself. This tradition was set up by S. Veeranarayan Reddy, a police officer who investigated the Parvathipuram conspiracy case. Venkat Reddy, the investigating officer, admitted to framing a conspiracy case quinquennially so as to cover the period in which they were making arrests.

All of them, including the police officers who supervised the policy of encounters and participated in these killings, were handsomely rewarded from the state exchequer and awarded promotions. The Ramnagar conspiracy case, 1985, was the last to terminate and was the first case under TADA. In this case, I was sought to be implicated and the investigating officer was good enough to fix an appointment to interrogate me. If my memory is correct, he came with one Krishnamurthy. It would have been foolish to implicate me. I told them in so many words, and they were good enough to respect my advice.

When NTR assumed power, the police had already become a lawless force and a law unto itself. The CPI(ML) (PWG) unleashed violence even against the police. There were abductions added to this sullied atmosphere. The state abducted K. Balagopal of the APCLC and released him two days later. Our proposal for land distribution was obviously opposed internally and so nothing was done.

In 1989, the Congress party returned to power and Chief Minister Marri Chenna Reddy kept alive the decision to hold talks for peace. He lifted the ban and suspended the operation of police impunity for a while. We carried on our dialogue, and he also appointed a cabinet subcommittee to go into the issues raised by Naxalites. G. Haragopal and I appeared before the subcommittee. Lakhs of people attended the meetings held at Warangal and in the Nizam College grounds. Freedoms guaranteed under the Constitution were in full bloom for around three months, before impunity was brought into force in full vigour and constitutional provisions recognizing fundamental rights again stood suspended.

Judgment of Andhra Pradesh High Court in *S. Appa Rao vs State of Andhra Pradesh*, 1996

While arguing the case of Shakamuri Appa Rao, a member of CPI(ML) (PWG) who was prosecuted under TADA, a detailed discussion of the movement, the issues taken up by the movement and the brutal response by the state were narrated before the judge and our complaint on encounters was filed. We also produced socio-economic analyses by senior scholars in the field. During the period 1981 to May 1996, the police killed 1,140 Naxalites and casualties among the civilian population numbered 1,805, while 242 policemen were killed. Justice M.N. Rao was the presiding judge of the court along with Justice S.R. Nayak. They heard the case and felt that something should be done. This is reflected in the following excerpt from the judgment:

> 24. We can neither take up the study of competing value choices the society should adopt, other than the objectives enshrined in the Constitution, nor exhibit inclination to any particular value choice without racking up theoretical values—political, economic and social—and engendering controversies as to the contours of the judicial power of the State. Despite its magnitude and menacing dimensions, the problem, we think, does not admit of no solutions. A peace commission, with a representative character inspiring confidence in all sections of the society including the Naxalites and the police and backed by the State power and consent, we believe, can bring about immediate cessation of police encounters and violence by Naxalites and then only, in the resultant peaceful atmosphere, a meaningful search for permanent solutions is possible.
>
> 25. Both Sri K.G. Kannabhiran, the learned senior counsel for the petitioners, and Sri Chalameshwar, the learned Additional Advocate-General, are at one with us that the present situation demands immediate action akin to this—a saner and safer course. We gratefully acknowledge and appreciate their candour and concern.[1]

There cannot be a debate at a theoretical level between an exploitative order and the political forces fighting for its overthrow. This judgment triggered a debate—there were some who were apprehensive of such a prospect and put forth objections about its possibility. An insistence on constitutional beliefs and laying down arms were being aired in all these debates.

Committee of Concerned Citizens and the Peace Process

Around the same time, some of us met at S.R. Sankaran's residence and discussed the increasing trend of diminishing democracy in the state and discussed ways and means of restoring and widening the democratic space so that people may freely debate public issues without being branded as extremist supporters. All of us were in

1 *Shakamuri Apparao and Ors vs Government of Andhra Pradesh and Ors* (01.07.1996: APHC), 1996 (3) ALD 493.

search of democratic space and in the process we thought that our main agenda was to reduce political and state violence. We found that the search for democratic space had to confront the endemic violence in the state, which had effectively suspended governance in accordance with the constitutional value system. We formed ourselves into the Committee of Concerned Citizens (CCC).

Thereafter, the entire work of the committee and their interventions with the government and the CPI(ML) (PWG) were systematically recorded, covering the period from 1997 to 2002, which included the talks held during TDP rule.[2] The government had no interest in carrying on with the talks. As the PWG representatives were struggling to formulate the agenda with two ministers—one of whom was the retired CBI director representing the government—the police and Chief Minister Naidu made it plain that they were not interested in talks. The CPI(ML) (PWG) stuck to their unilateral declaration of ceasefire despite continuous violence by the police. Gaddar and Varavara Rao withdrew officially from the talks, making it abundantly clear that as the government did not create a conducive atmosphere they were withdrawing.

The talks between the PWG representatives and the government on the modalities took place on 5 June 2002, 9 June 2002 and 30 June 2002. The CCC thereafter called for a meeting of all political parties on 30 August 2002 at the New Press Club, Hyderabad. At that meeting, all the political parties gathered there unanimously resolved that in order to achieve permanent peace and tranquillity in the state, the process of talks between the government and the PWG, which was abruptly terminated due to failure of creation of a conducive atmosphere, should be resumed and both parties should respond with greater sincerity for this purpose. The Congress, CPI, CPI(M), BJP and Telangana Rashtra Samithi (TRS) were present, and were parties to this resolution. The TDP and AIMIM, though invited, did not attend.

Chandrababu Naidu was committed to putting down the Naxalite movement by granting enormous impunity to the police. This was also a time when private gangs consisting of surrendered Naxalites, who were generally under the surveillance of the police, were spreading a reign of terror. These forces targeted human rights activists of APCLC, and terrorized the rest of the people who then became silent spectators. The TDP, in its nine years in power, killed over 1,000 people in encounters, and around nine civil liberties' activists, four of whom were brutally

2 Committee of Concerned Citizens, 2002. *Third Report: 1997–2002*. Hyderabad: Committee of Concerned Citizens.

done to death by the vigilante groups who were under state surveillance.[3] With this record, the TDP passed a resolution that the elimination of Naxalites would be an election issue. Naidu justified the World Bank running the government, and therefore globalization also became an election issue. Thus, the World Bank credit card and total impunity in the exercise of power were his election issues. Emulating US president George W. Bush's stance on the 'war on terror', he also repeated the vacuous slogan: 'If you are not with us you are with Naxalites.'[4]

In the run-up to the 2004 assembly elections. several parliamentary parties made peace talks part of their election campaign, and the Congress party won an unprecedented victory, winning 185 out of 294 seats. To fulfil his election promise, Chief Minister Y.S. Rajasekhara Reddy started the peace process in May 2004. Home Minister Jana Reddy set about his business earnestly, making phone calls to human rights activists and starting a discussion. CPI(ML) (PWG) talked about setting up a monitoring committee whose job would be to check on complaints about the violation of the ceasefire agreement. The home minister identified a few civil liberties' organizations including the state PUCL to take up the job of identifying people in these organizations region- or district-wise. The CPI(ML) (PWG) nominated S.R. Sankaran, convener, CCC; Pothuri Venkateswara Rao, renowned journalist and former chairman of the Press Academy, also a member of the CCC; G. Haragopal, political scientist, also of the CCC; B. Tarakam, a well-known Dalit leader and senior advocate practising in the high court, also a member of the CCC; and me. Apart from the CCC, they nominated G. Seshaiah, general secretary, APCLC.

The CPI(ML) Janasakthi nominated Keshav Rao Jadhav, a well-known socialist and the president of the PUCL Andhra Pradesh state unit. They requested P. Varavara Rao, a well-known revolutionary writer, Gaddar, the famous balladeer,

---

3 According to the list of encounter deaths year-wise with different chief ministers in office from 1968 to 2021 collated by S. Jeevan Kumar, President of Human Rights Forum, from *Sveccha,* monthly magazine published by APCLC and from Reports of APCLC on Encounter Deaths, the number of deaths in the nine years between 1995 and 2004 (Naidu's term in office) is around 1,500. Unpublished list on file provided by S. Jeevan Kumar. See also Ramana, P.V. 2003. 'Surrendered Naxalites: A Menace'. Institute of Peace and Conflict Studies. 11 August. http://www.ipcs.org/comm_select.php?articleNo=1094. Accessed on 12 May 2022.

4 K.C. Suri, 2004. 'Andhra Pradesh: Fall of the CEO in Arena of Democracy'. *Economic and Political Weekly*, Vol. 39, No. 51, 18 December, pp. 5493–97. https://www.epw.in/journal/2004/51/special-articles/andhra-pradesh-fall-ceo-arena-democracy.html, Accessed on 7 May 2022.

and Kalyan Rao, a fine writer and the president of the Revolutionary Writers' Association (VIRASAM) to represent the party for settling the terms of the ceasefire, the modalities and the agenda. The government also nominated S.R. Sankaran as their mediator.

We spent around two weeks finalizing the terms of the ceasefire, which consisted of eight key points:

1. Neither party should act in a way leading to loss of life. They should not fire arms against each other.
2. The PWG or their squads or cadres or PGA (Peoples Guerrilla Army) in the areas where they have their presence should not harm the police. They should not harass official police and other politicians and should not assault them. They should not collect explosives or lay mines. The police shall not embark on combing operations for the arrest of squads, party leaders or sympathizers.
3. The PWG shall not harm the person or life of the informers. Similarly, the police should not indulge in any act causing harm to Naxalites, sympathizers or persons called militants.
4. Covert operations by introducing coverts into the parry should be stopped forthwith.
5. The government shall not encourage deployment of violence against the PWG, their sympathizers or their people's organizations. The government shall control antisocial armed gangs and the government and the police shall be solely responsible for lawful maintenance of a peaceful (violence-free) environment during the peace talks.
6. The CPI(ML) (PWG) shall not indulge in destruction of either private or public property.
7. With a view to ensure the peaceful progress of talks, political campaigning can be carried out but any political party members campaigning during the period shall carry no arms.
8. The police forces should not dog the steps of people who would like to meet the PWG leaders in connection with the talks. They should also not prevent or harass people for meeting or attempting to meet them.

We were stuck for several days trying to convince the PWG to accept the condition that during the peace talks they should not go about armed while addressing meetings. Their point of view was also understandable. They needed to protect themselves from ambush. There was also a resistance from the police with reference to the eighth point. In any case, this was our proposal.

We also demanded the lifting of the ban on CPI(ML) (PWG) and its affiliated organizations. It was banned under the Andhra Pradesh Public Safety Act, 1992. All the while we, including the government, were ignoring the ban for holding talks. It was due to expire on 22 July 2004, and we pre-empted its reimposition. On 21 July, there was a four-hour meeting with us all and ultimately the government announced its decision not to reimpose the ban. Ultimately, the talks failed because the government did not intend it to succeed. But the lessons we learnt were valuable.

The question before us as civil libertarians is, what is the social outlook of the civil liberties movement? In stating a perspective, the objective is never to support or condemn different sides, or even to take sides. The core concern is how we see and understand the issues before us. The Naxalite issue is an example. We formed the CCC which consisted of people with diverse views on issues—some were committed to viewing peace as an ultimate good that must be established; my view was that while peace must be a larger goal, would it be possible under the present circumstances? Especially with respect to the peace talks, I was certain that the talks would fail and it would be a wasted effort—because conflict between the two sides we were trying to bring together was inevitable. I kept repeating this view throughout the duration of the talks, although I also did see the importance of attempting to negotiate peace with the others. We did need to open out some new effort. It was necessary to stem the distortions both in governance and in movement politics—a necessary step in democratization. We were in a very difficult situation. The one person who showed a great interest in the talks right from the beginning was Pothuri Venkateswara Rao. He believed firmly that if both parties sat together and talked, it was possible to bring about peace. My view was that it was ideologically untenable. How would it be possible to reach a consensus between two opposed classes in an exploitative society? The only way we could move forward would be when the dominant class surrendered its power and hegemony. A 'change of heart' may be a possible for an individual, but can it be conceived at the systemic level? G. Haragopal was of the opinion that it marked a new turn. I was not convinced. But we embarked on the process. Some members of our committee who met the Maoist leaders returned stunned by their clarity and understanding. I have experienced this clarity in leaders, right from Kondapalli Seetharamaiah to the present leaders. Yet, at some point they take decisions that dismantle their clarity of purpose. Similarly, the government too falters towards impunity and loses ground in the efforts at bringing peace. When I think back, I feel it was easier for me to speak to someone like N.T. Rama Rao, who had no understanding of politics. It is far more difficult to speak to the leaders of today who have been in politics for decades. NTR had a basic humaneness and could draw a line between justice and injustice. Leaders today know no such distinction.

There was a good response to the peace talks from both sides. On the first day of the talks I realized that the government representatives had done no preparatory work prior to the commencement of the talks. They had no understanding of the issue. They had not studied the problem. They only came in order to demonstrate that they were fulfilling their election promises. I confronted them very sharply and told them in no uncertain terms that this was no way to go about the peace talks. Despite this, I felt there was scope for negotiations, and still a possibility for both sides to engage in talks. We could by this process get some clarity at least on a few issues.

The other fact we must recognize is that the talks were not the result of the need perceived by the two parties locked in conflict alone. It happened because the people wanted it—the people wanted deliberations around peace that would ease their lives. This wish was understood and conceded by the revolutionary groups, which is why they came to the negotiating table. The Congress party too, recognizing this popular demand, made it part of its election manifesto.

Peace is the collective right of the people. And civil liberties movements must address the peace question effectively. The peace talks were an important turning point keenly watched all over the country. It was the first time that a political resolution of this kind was attempted in independent India—people were given an opportunity to participate in deliberations around peace.

I have full confidence that someday the fruits of this effort will be realized. I am sure even Sisyphus must have dreamt that he would roll the stone to the hilltop someday, and I too believe that.

References

Cases Cited

A.K. Gopalan vs State of Madras 1950, AIR (SC) 27.

A. Lakshmanarao vs. Judicial Magistrate, First Class, Parvatipuram and Ors. AIR 1971 SC 186

Abubucker Siqqique and Ors vs State Represented by the Deputy Superintendent of Police, CBI/SCB/Chennai, Tamil Nadu, AIR 2011 SC 91.

Additional District Magistrate, Jabalpur vs Shivakant Shukla (28.04.1976: SC), AIR 1976 SC 1207.

Andhra Pradesh Civil Liberties Committee & Ors vs State of Andhra Pradesh & Ors. 2007 (5) ALT 639.

Andhra Pradesh Civil Liberties Committee vs Government of Andhra Pradesh, 2009 (2) ALD 1.

Andhra Pradesh Girijana Sangam vs Union of India & Ors. WP No. 19,067 of 2005.

Arka Vasanth Rao vs Government of Andhra Pradesh, AIR 1995 AP 274.

Bachan Singh v. State of Punjab, (1982) 3 SCC 24.

B. Bhaskara Reddy vs Government of Andhra Pradesh. (Writ Petitions Nos. 1,267 and 1,278 of 1980, dated 17.7.1980), 1981 LAB. I.C. 18.

B.V. Subbarayudu vs State of Andhra Pradesh, Andhra Weekly Reporter, 1975 (II) 437.

Bharwada Bhoginbhai Hirjibhai vs State of Gujarat, AIR 1983 SC 753.

Central Bureau of Investigation, New Delhi vs Chandrakant Shah and Ors. Sessions Case No. 233/92, court of second additional sessions judge, Durg, Madhya Pradesh.

Callins vs Collins. 510 US 1141 (1994), decided 22 February 1994, https://www.law.cornell.edu/supct/html/93-7054.ZA1.html. Accessed on 26 October 2021.

Chalasami Prasad and Five others vs State of Andhra Pradesh, *Andhra Weekly Reporter*, 1976 (II) 403.

Chandradevi and Ors vs State of Tamil Nadu. MANU/TN/2335/2002.

Chitralekha vs State of Mysore, AIR 1964 SC 1823.

D. Bhuvan Mohan Patnaik and Ors vs State of Andhra Pradesh and Ors, AIR 1974 SC 2092.

D. Parasuram Choudary and Ors vs Mandal Revenue Officer, Palasa, Srikakulam district, WP No. 17,494/2002 and WP No. 14,008/2002, dated 4 July 2002.

Deputy Superintendent of Police, Special Task Force, Hyderabad vs Pendyala Varavara Rao and Anr. Sessions Case 51/1987. In the court of the metropolitan sessions judge, Hyderabad. Decided on 25 September 2003.

Dr Bathula Sivarama Reddy and Ors vs State of Andhra Pradesh, Cr. A. Nos. 814, 843, 847, 848, 953, 957, 958, 962, 963, 964, 965, 966 of 1976; Cr. A. Nos. 141, 177, 369, 542, 572 of 1977; and 807 of 1978.

Duvvada Parasuram Choudary vs Santha Dalayya, 2014 (4) ALT 71.

Eacharan Ittiathi vs State of Kerala, O.P. No. 3373 of 1966. Decided on 22 December 1969. Kerala High Court.

G. Krishta Goud and Ors vs State of Andhra Pradesh and Ors. (03.10.1975: SC), (1976) 1 SCC 157.

Hadibandhu Behera vs Banamali Sahu (15.01.1960: ORIHC), AIR 1961 Ori. 33.

I. Mallikarjuna Sarma and Ors vs State of Andhra Pradesh (26.04.1985: APHC): 1986 (1) APLJ (HC) 126.

In Re: Special Courts Bill, 1978, Special Reference No. 1 of 1978 (01.12.1978: SC) AIR 1979 SC 478.

Indra Sawhney vs Union of India, AIR 1993 SC 477.

Inguva Mallikarjuna Sharma vs State of Andhra Pradesh, 1977 (1) ALT 638.

Inspector of Police, C.B.; C.I.D., Pukukottai, Crime No. 1183/94 of Viralimalai Police Station vs. Premananda and Others. Sessions Case No. 7/1996, Court of Sessions at Pudukottai, 20th August 1997.

Jagdish Dajiba vs the Accountant General of Bombay, AIR 1958 Bom. 283.

Jayendra Saraswathy Swamigal, Tamil Nadu vs State of Tamil Nadu and Ors (26.10.2005: SC), AIR 2006 SC 6.

Jon Richard Argersinger, petitioner vs Raymond Hamlin, sheriff, Leon County, Florida. 92 S. Ct. 2006.

Jwalamukhi alias A.V. Raghavachary vs State of Andhra Pradesh. ILR (1973) AP 114.

K. Yadava Reddy, B. Bhaskara Reddy, A.V. Raghavachary vs Commissioner of Police, Andhra Pradesh and State of Andhra Pradesh. WP Nos. 3115, 3116 & 3117 of 1971. High Court of Judicature at Hyderabad, 20 September 1971.

K.G. Kannabiran vs Chief Secretary, Government of Andhra Pradesh and Ors (14.08.1995:APHC): 1995 (2) ALT (Cri) 490.

K. Premkumar vs the Revenue Divisional Officer, Usilampatti, Madurai District (16.11.1987: MADHC): MANU/TN/0399/1987. Justice G. Maheswaran.

K. Premkumar vs the Revenue Divisional Officer, Madurai and Ors (06.06.2002: MADHC): MANU/TN/0905/2002. Justice M. Karpaga Vinayagam.

Kamalanantha and Ors vs State of Tamil Nadu, AIR 2005 SC 2132.

Karamchedu Massacre Cases: In the court of the sessions judge, Guntur, Sessions Case No. 80/86, 80/87, 22/88, SC No. 114/88; in the Andhra Pradesh High Court, Criminal Appeal. Nos. 1112/94, 1113/94 and 33/98; in the Supreme Court of India, Criminal Appeal Nos. 356–58/1998, Special Leave Petition (CrL Nos. 3788–3790 of 1998).

Kesavananda Bharati vs State of Kerala (1973) 4 SCC 225.

Krulewitch v. United States, 336 US 440, 443–44 (1949).

M. Baga Reddy vs Sonia Gandhi and Ors, 2001 (3) ALD 636.

Mithu v. State of Punjab, 1983 SCC (Cr) 404. Para ix.

M.R. Balaji vs State of Mysore, 1963 Supp. 1 SCR 439.

Mohammed Azam vs State of Hyderabad, AIR 1958 AP 619.

N. Venkat Ramani and Ors vs State of Andhra Pradesh and Ors (08.04.1976: APHC): MANU/AP/0228/1976; 1977 CriLJ 1060.

N.M. Thomas vs State of Kerala (1976) 2 SCC 310.

Nandini Satpathy vs P.L. Dani and Ors (07.04.1978: SC): MANU/SC/0139/1978; AIR 1978 SC 1025.

P. Hemalatha vs Government of Andhra Pradesh (23.04.1976: APHC); AIR 1976 AP 375.

P. Rajendran vs State of Madras, AIR 1968 SC 1012.

P. Santhanarajan vs State of Tamil Nadu and Ors (23.11.2005: MADHC): MANU/TN/2429/2005. Justice P.D. Dinakaran.

P. Venkateseshamma vs State of Andhra Pradesh and Ors (22.08.1975: APHC) Writ Petition Nos. 3306, 3361, 3374, 3381, 3444, 3445 and 3642 of 1975. AIR 1976 AP 1.

P. Venkateswarlu and Ors vs State of Andhra Pradesh and Ors (09.10.1975: APHC), WP Nos. 467/75, MANU/AP/0313/1975.

Peoples' Union for Civil Liberties vs State of Uttar Pradesh and Ors, 2000 (1) AWC 729.

Pinninti Kistamma and Ors vs Duvvada Parsuram Chowdary and Ors (08.01.2010: SC) (2010) 2 SCC 452.

R. Rajagopal and Ors vs State of Tamil Nadu and Ors (07.10.1994: SC): AIR 1995 SC 264.

S. Appa Rao and Ors vs State of Andhra Pradesh, Sessions Case No. 207/1993 (Cr. No. 1/1992). In the Court of the second additional sessions judge. Date of judgment, 9 April 1999.

State of Andhra Pradesh vs S. Appa Rao and Ors. Criminal Appeal No. 795 of 1999. JT 2001 (2) SC 13 (Supreme Court).

S.R. Bommai and Ors vs Union of India, AIR 1994 SC 1918.

Samsher Singh vs State of Punjab, 1974 SC 2192.

Sayeed Ahmed and Ors vs State of Andhra Pradesh and Criminal Appeal No. 34/1982, *State of Andhra Pradesh vs T. Surendar Singh*. Criminal Appeal No. 238/1981. Decided on 7–8 March 1984, Karnataka High Court at Bangalore (unreported).

Sessions Judge Nellore Referring Officer vs Intha Ramana Reddy on 12 February 1971. 1972 CriLJ 1485.

Shaikh Meera vs the Chief Secretary, Government of Andhra Pradesh, Andhra Weekly Reporter 1977 (II) 250.

Shakamuri Apparao and Ors vs Government of Andhra Pradesh and Ors (01.07.1996: APHC): 1996 (3) ALD 493.

Sidheshwar Ganguly vs State of West Bengal (24.10.1957: SC): AIR 1958 SC 143.

Sri Premananda Trust, Premananda Ashram vs District Collector, Pudukkottai, and Ors. MANU/TN/0282/2003.

State (NCT Delhi) vs Navjot Sandhu (2005) 11 SCC 600.

State (Sub-Divisional Police Officer, Tenali) vs Modugula Sambi Reddi and 218 Ors. Sessions Case No. 36/1993, in the court of the special sessions judge-cum-IV additional sessions judge, Guntur, 31 July 2007.

State of Andhra Pradesh vs T. Surendar Singh and Ors. Sessions Case No. 33/1980 district and sessions court, Raichur.

State of Andhra Pradesh vs Inguva Mallikarjuna Sharma and Ors. Sessions Case No. 10/75 in the court of the second additional metropolitan sessions judge, judgment delivered by Justice P.V. Rama Sarma on 3 May 1988.

State of Andhra Pradesh vs Intha Ramana Reddy and Anr on 16 November 1976, AIR 1977 SC 708.

State of Andhra Pradesh vs U.S.V. Balram (1972) 1 SCC 660.

State of Madhya Pradesh through C.B.I., and Ors vs Paltan Malla and Ors. Criminal Appeal Nos. 98, 99, 100–02, 103–08 and 109-114 of 1999; AIR 2005 SC 733.

State of Madras vs Champakam Dorairajan, AIR 1951 SC 226.

State of Maharashtra vs Chandraprakash Kewalchand Jain, 1990 AIR 658.

State of Maharashtra vs Priyasharan Maharaj, AIR 1997 SC 2041.

State of Madhya Pradesh vs Paltan Malla @ Ravi Cr. Ref. No. 5/97; *Moolchand Shah vs State of Madhya Pradesh,* Cr. A. No. 1278/97; *Paltan Malla @ Ravi vs State of Madhya Pradesh,* Cr. A. No. 1371/97; *Chandrakanth Shah vs State of MP* Cr. A. No. 1441/97; *State of Madhya Pradesh vs Naveen Shah and 2 Ors.* Cr. A. No.

1863/97. Judgment delivered on 26 June 1998. Judges: Justice S.K. Dubey and Justice Usha Shukla.

State of Punjab vs Gurmit Singh, 1996 AIR 1393.

State of Uttar Pradesh v Pradip Tandon (1975) 2 SCR 761.

State represented by Deputy Superintendent of Police, Crime Branch, Hyderabad vs. Chowdary Tejeswara Rao and Ors. Sessions Case No. 46 of 1973, Criminal Appeals Nos. 958/77, 542/77, 177/77, 141/77, 963/76, 572/77. Andhra Pradesh High Court, judgment delivered on 13 July 1979, pp. 4–5. Unpublished judgment.

State represented by Deputy Superintendent of Police, Crime Branch, Hyderabad v. Chowdary Tejeswara Rao and Others. Sessions Case No. 46 of 1973.

State represented by Deputy Superintendent of Police, Crime Branch, Hyderabad vs Chowdary Tejeswara Rao and Ors. Sessions Case No. 46 of 1973, Criminal Appeals Nos. 958/77, 542/77, 177/77, 141/77, 963/76, 572/77. Andhra Pradesh High Court, judgment delivered on 13 July 1979.

State represented by DSP, Crime Branch CID, Hyderabad vs Choudary Tejeswara Rao and 74 Ors. Sessions Case No. 46/1973. In the court of additional sessions judge, Visakhapatnam, judgment delivered on 30 August 1976.

Sujato Bhadra and Abhijit Mazumdar vs State of West Bengal. Writ Petition in the matter of indiscriminate and widespread genocide of Naxalites in West Bengal between 1968 and 1972 including prominent leaders of the Naxal movement by the police administration of the state in utter violation of their human rights and fundamental rights enshrined in the Constitution of India. In the High Court at Calcutta, 1997–98. Draft petition on file.

Sunil Batra vs Delhi Administration, AIR 1980 SC 1579.

Swami Premananda vs C.B., C.I.D. Pudukottai MANU/TN/1175/1996.

Swami Premananda vs Inspector of Police, C.B., C.I.D. I (1996) CCR 63 (Mad.).

Swami Premananda vs the State, 1996 CriLJ 3884.

T. Muralidhar Rao vs Government of Andhra Pradesh, 2010 (2) ALD 492 (LB).

T. Muralidhar Rao vs State of Andhra Pradesh and Ors, 2004 (6) ALD 1.

State of Uttar Pradesh vs Lalai Singh Yadav, 1976 SCC (Cri) 556.

United States vs Crimmins, 123 F.2d 271 (2d Cir. 1941). Decided 3 November 1941.

Vasanth Kumar vs State of Karnataka, 1985 Supp. SCC 714.

Official Reports and Parliamentary/Legislative Debates

Andhra Pradesh Commission for Backward Classes, *B.C. Commission Report on the Inclusion of Socially and Educationally Backward Classes among Muslim Community in the List of Backward Classes in the State of Andhra Pradesh*.

'Arrest of Ryots in Kambarigam Village'. 1985. *The Andhra Pradesh Legislative Assembly Debates: Official Report*, 13 September, pp. 511–15.

Constituent Assembly Debates, Vol. 11, 14–26 November 1949. On 25 November 1949, pp. 978–79, https://eparlib.nic.in/bitstream/123456789/763285/1/cad_25-11-1949.pdf. Accessed on 4 November 2021.

Constituent Assembly Debates: Official Report, Book No. 1, Vols 1–6, New Delhi: Lok Sabha Secretariat, 1989.

Constituent Assembly Debates: Official Report, Book no. 3, Vol. 8, New Delhi: Lok Sabha Secretariat, 1989.

'Discussion on the Report of Muktadar Inquiry Commission', *The Andhra Pradesh Legislative Assembly Debates*, Vol. 8, No. 2, 7 September 1978, 196–251.

Government of Andhra Pradesh (2007a). *Report on Identification of Socially and Educationally Backward Classes in the Muslim Community of Andhra Pradesh* (P.S. Krishnan Committee), Government of Andhra Pradesh, Hyderabad.

Government of Andhra Pradesh (2007b). *Report on Inclusion of Socially and Educationally Backward Classes among Muslim Community in the List of Backward Classes in the State of Andhra Pradesh* (Dalava Subrahmanyam Commission), Andhra Pradesh.

Backward Classes Commission, Government of Andhra Pradesh, Hyderabad, https://www.rsdebate.nic.in/bitstream/123456789/109648/1/PD_189_02032000_7_p209_p301_9.pdf. Accessed on 15 October 2021.

Justice A. Gangadhar Rao, 'Report of the Commission of Inquiry', General Administration (General-B) Department, Government of Andhra Pradesh, Hyderabad,1992.

Justice B.K. Somasekhara Commission of Inquiry. January 2011, https://www.thehindu.com/multimedia/archive/00376/Justice_B_K__Somase_376775a.pdf. Accessed on 18 October 2021.

Ministry of Tribal Affairs and UNDP. n.d. *Land and Governance under the Fifth Schedule*, https://tribal.nic.in/FRA/data/LandandGovernanceunderFifthSchedule.pdf, p. 2. Accessed on 10 July 2021.

National Human Rights Commission, *Annual Reports, 1995–6 and 1996–97* for details of the inquiry.

'Re: Medical Treatment of Shri Nagabhushan Patnaik Detained in an Andhra Jail'. 1973. p. 236. *Lok Sabha Debates* (Fifth Lok Sabha), 23 February. New Delhi: Lok Sabha Secretariat, pp. 236–40.

'Re. Brutal Killing of Harijans in Tsundur Village of Guntur District', 1991. *Lok Sabha Debates*, 9 August 1991, pp. 287–97, https://eparlib.nic.in/bitstream/123456789/8774/1/10_I_09081991_p148_p153_T227.pdf. Accessed on 17 October 2021.

Report of the Commission of Inquiry (to Inquire into the Detention of Sri Ahmed Hussain and Smt. Rameeza Bee, Death of Ahmed Hussain, etc. Constituted under Notification GO Ms. No. 263, General Administration (General A) Department, dated 7 April 1978, by the Hon'ble Sri Justice K.A. Muktadar. Andhra Pradesh, Hyderabad.

Report of the Shah Commission of Inquiry, appointed by the Government of India, under Section 3 of the Commissions of Inquiry Act, 1952, three volumes. 1978. Available at https://countercurrents.org/cc280615.htm. Accessed on 27 September 2021.

The Andhra Pradesh Legislative Assembly Debates: Official Report (Second Day of the Ninth Session of the Andhra Pradesh Legislative Assembly, Monday, 14 December 1987, p. 232, Q no. 113. (Commission of Inquiry on Padirikuppam, Andhra Pradesh.)

Twenty-Ninth Report of the Commissioner for Scheduled Castes and Scheduled Tribes (B. D. Sharma Report). 1990. New Delhi: Government of India, National Commission for Scheduled Castes and Scheduled Tribes.

Withdrawal of the circular by the government of Gujarat removing the ban imposed on state government employees in participating in the activities of the RSS. *Rajya Sabha Debates*, 2 March 2000, pp. 209–301.

Books and Articles Cited

A Warning from Bidar: A Report on the Anti-Sikh Disturbances. 1988. Delhi: Nagrik Ekta Manch.

Aditya, M.K. 2016. 'Tarimela Nagi Reddy Remembered', CounterCurrents.org, 28 July, https://countercurrents.org/2016/07/tarimela-nagi-reddy-remembered. Accessed on 19 October 2021.

'Andhra Detention Clause Quashed; Poets Freed'. 1971. *Hindustan Times*, 21 September .

Arendt, Hannah. 1992. *Eichmann in Jerusalem: A Report on the Banality of Evil*. New York: Penguin.

Asian Human Rights Council. 2018. 'The State of Encounter Killings in India: Target, Detain, Torture, Execute'. New Delhi: ACHR, https://www.ecoi.net/en/file/local/1457651/1226_1549878602_encounterkillingsindia.pdf. Accessed on 7 October 2021.

Balagopal, K. 1985. 'The Karamchedu Massacre: A Report'. Guntur: Andhra Pradesh Civil Liberties Committee, 22 July, http://www.unipune.ac.in/snc/cssh/humanrights/05%20STATE%20AGRICULTURE%20FOREST%20DALITS%20AND%20TRIBALS/08.pdf. Accessed on 28 November 2021.

Balagopal, K. 1991. 'Two Missing Women of Karimnagar'. *Economic and Political Weekly*, Vol. 26, No. 5, 2 February, pp. 201–05.

Banerjee, Sumanta. 1980. *In the Wake of Naxalbari: A History of the Naxalite Movement in India*. Calcutta: Subarnarekha.

Baweja, Harinder. 2009. 'When a Big Tree Falls, the Earth Shakes'. *Tehelka*, April 25.

'Bhargava Committee Appointment Notified'. 1977. *Indian Express*, 23 July, p. 3.

'Bidar Probe: Many Top Officers File Papers.' 1989. *Indian Express* (Bangalore), 26 February.

'Bidar Riots: Police Force Inadequate'. 1989. *Indian Express* (Bangalore), 22 August.

Blackburn, Robert, ed. 1992. *Constitutional Studies: Contemporary Issues and Controversies*. London: Mansell.

Camus, Albert. 1961. 'Reflections on the Guillotine', in A. Camus, *Resistance, Rebellion and Death*. New York: Alfred A. Knopf, pp. 173–234.

Capotorti, Francesco. 1979. *Study on the Rights of Persons Belonging to Ethnic, Religious and Linguistic Minorities*. New York: United Nations, p. 96, para 568. Accessed on 18 October 2021.

Chari, A.S.R.. 1973. *Memoirs of an Unrepentant Communist*. Hyderabad: Orient Longman.

Citizens' Tribunal on Ayodhya: Investigation, Hearings and Judgment, January—December 1993. 1994. New Delhi: Citizens' Tribunal on Ayodhya.

'Clash Toll Rises to 6 in Bidar'. 1988. *Indian Express* (Bangalore), 19 September.

Concerned Citizens' Tribunal. 2002. *Crime against Humanity*, three volumes. Mumbai: Citizens for Justice and Peace.

'Encounters Are Murders: Interim Report of the Civil Liberties Committee'. 1977. *Economic and Political Weekly*, Vol. 12, No. 21, 21 May, https://www.epw.in/journal/1977/21/our-correspondent-columns/political-prisoners.html#. Accessed on 29 September 2021.

France, Anatole. 1892. *Le Procurateur de Judée* (The Procurator of Judea), https://www.gutenberg.org/ebooks/58967. Accessed on 31 October 2021.

Hodgson, Douglas. 1998. *The Human Right to Education*. Dartmouth: Ashgate.

'Judge to Probe Tangutur Firing'. 1983. *Indian Express*, 16 March.

'Justice V. Bhargava: Disgusted with Andhra Pradesh Government'. 1978. *India Today*, 15 July, https://www.indiatoday.in/magazine/indiascope/story/19780715-justice-v.-bhargava-disgusted-with-andhra-pradesh-government-818432-2015-01-24. Accessed on 5 October 2021.

Kannabiran, K.G. 2004. *The Wages of Impunity: Power, Justice and Human Rights*. Hyderabad: Orient Longman.

Kannabiran, K.G. 1990. 'State of Civil Liberties in AP: An Open Letter to Chief Minister'. Also published in 'Legal Resources for Social Action', *Legal Perspectives*, Documentation File No. 18, pp. 13–23, http://www.unipune.ac.in/snc/cssh/HumanRights/01%20STATE%20DEMOCRACY%20AND%20LAW/51.%20Legal%20Perspectives%20Legal%20Resources%20for%20Social%20Action%20(LRSA),%20Documentation%20File%20No.%2018,%20Tamil.pdf. Accessed on 25 October 2021.

Kannabiran, K.G.. 2009. *24 Gantalu: Atmakadhatmaka Samajika Chitram* (Telugu. 24 Hours: A Personalised Social History). As told to and recorded by N. Venugopal. Hyderabad: Devulapalli Publications.

Kannabiran, K.G., Kalpana and Vasanth. 'Death as Deterrent?' *The Hindu*. 28 November 1999.

Kannabiran, Kalpana. 2012. *Tools of Justice: Non-Discrimination and the Indian Constitution*. New Delhi: Routledge.

Kannabiran, Kalpana. 2022. 'Constitution-as-Commons and Spatial Justice in Adivasi India: The Continuing Legacy of Three Legal Cases', in *State, Law, and Adivasi: Shifting Terrains of Exclusion*, Antje Linkenbach and Vidhu Verma, eds. New Delhi: Sage/Spectrum.

Kannabiran, Kalpana and Ramya K. Tella. 2022. 'Migration and "Intimate Citizenship": The "Small Voice" of Ansari Begum.' *Social Change*, 52 (2). June.

Kannabiran, Vasanth. 2020. *Taken at the Flood: A Memoir of a Political Life*. New Delhi: Women Unlimited.

Krishnan, P.S. 2019. *Social Exclusion and Justice in India*. New Delhi: Routledge.

Kumar, B.S. Satish. 2014. 'Cabinet Rejects Somasekhara Commission Report on Church Attacks'. *The Hindu*, 16 October 2014, https://www.thehindu.com/news/national/karnataka/cabinet-rejects-somasekhara-commission-report-on-church-attacks/article6507724.ece. Accessed on 18 October 2021.

McDonnell, D.L., J.G. Monroe. 1952. *Kerr on Fraud and Mistake* (7th Edition) London: Sweet & Maxwell.

Menon, Amarnath K. 1983. 'Deaths of Three Tobacco Growers in Andhra Bring into Focus the Plight of the Farmers'. *India Today*, 30 April.

Menon, Amarnath K. 1985. 'Karamchedu in Andhra Pradesh Set to Become an Important Landmark in Harijan history'. *India Today*, 30 September.

Menon, Amarnath K. 1985. 'Secunderabad Conspiracy Case: Special Court Faces Uphill Task'. *India Today*, 15 July, https://www.indiatoday.in/magazine/nation/story/19850715-secunderabad-conspiracy-case-special-court-faces-uphill-task-770200-2013-12-23. Accessed on 19 October 2021.

Menon, Amarnath K. 1987. 'Harijans in Karamchedu Village in Andhra Pradesh Fight Doggedly for Justice'. *India Today*, 31 July.

Naveen. 1979. *Cheekati Rojulu* (*Dark Days*). Warangal: Pratyusha Prachuranalu.

Orwell, George. 1937. *The Road to Wigan Pier*. London: Victor Gollancz.

Pateman, Carole. 1988. *The Sexual Contract*. Stanford University Press.

Pingle, Gautam. 1999. 'Breakdown of Law and Order in Tsundur, Guntur: A Case Study for Department of Training, Government of India'. Hyderabad: Administrative Staff College of India, p. 19. Unpublished study.

'Police "Murdered" Alleged Naxalites in State'. 1977. *Indian Express*, 17 May, p. 1.

Raghuram, M. 1981. 'Carnage at Indervelli: A Report. *Economic and Political Weekly*, Vol 16, No. 24, 13 June, pp. 1047–50.

Ramakrishnan, Nitya. 2020. 'Trial Lessons from K.G. Kannabiran'. *Livelaw*, 5 December, https://www.livelaw.in/columns/kannabiran-nitya-ramakrishnan-parliament-attack-case-pota-166860. Accessed on 21 September 2021.

Rao, Adhiraju Venkateswara. 1977. *Hantakulevaru?* (Who are the Killers?). Hyderabad: Velugu Publications.

Rao, B. Shiva. 1968. *The Framing of India's Constitution: A Study*. New Delhi: IIPA.

Rao, T. Madhusudana. 1982. 'Fief Which Survives by Law'. Sunday edition, *Indian Express*, 7 February.

Rao, T. Madhusudana. 1982. 'Litigation Overwhelms Legislation'. *Indian Express*, 8 February.

Rao, T. Madhusudana. 1982. 'Tillers Termed Trespassers'. *Indian Express*, 9 February.

Rao, T. Madhusudana. 1982. 'Lone Crusader'. *Indian Express*, 10 February.

Rao, P. Varavara. 2017. 'Bhoomaiah, Kishta Goud, Bhabani Da and Sumanta'. *Frontier*, Vol. 49, No.51, June 25—July 1, https://www.frontierweekly.com/articles/vol-49/49-51/49-51-Bhoomaiah.html. Accessed on 31 October 2021.

Ray, Arun. 2004. *National Human Rights Commission of India: Formation, Functioning and Future Proposals*, Vol. I. New Delhi: Khama Publications.

Reddy, K.V. Ramana. 1977. *Detenu Diary* (Telugu). Kavali: Jhanjha Publications.

Reddy, T. Nagi. 1978. *India Mortgaged.* Anantapuram: Tarimela Nagi Reddy Memorial Trust.

Satyanarayana, Cherukuri. 2016. *Suryodayam Kutrakaadu* (Sunrise Is No Conspiracy). Guntur: Tarimela Nagireddy Memorial Committee.

Saxena, Manohar Raj, ed. 2000. *Historic Telangana Peasants' Struggle and the Legal Battle*. Hyderabad: Telangana Martyrs' Memorial Trust.

'Second Report of Civil Rights Panel: Cold blooded Murder of 9 in Guntur'. 1977. *Indian Express*, 13 June, pp. 1, 9.

Sen, Ilina. 2018. 'The Life and Times of Saroj Dutta, Communist Poet and Thinker'. *Wire*, 3 October, https://thewire.in/film/the-life-and-times-of-saroj-dutta-communist-poet-and-thinker. Accessed on 28 November 2021.

Shirer, William L. 1960. *The Rise and Fall of the Third Reich: A History of Nazi Germany.* 2 Vols.: Simon & Schuster.

Shourie, Arun. 1980. *Institutions in the Janata Phase*. Bombay: Popular Prakashan.

'Shyamsunder to probe Bidar Riots'. 1988. *Indian Express* (Bangalore), 28 September.

Stone, Julius. 2000. *The Province and Function of Law: A Study in Jurisprudence*, Delhi: Universal Law Publishing Co. (first Indian reprint).

Suchitra, M. 2017. 'Charu and Son: Revisiting the Legacy of a Revolutionary Father 50 Years after Naxalbari'. Wire, 14 July, https://thewire.in/government/naxalbari-abhijit-mazumdar-charu-mazumdar. Accessed on 23 September 2021.

Sundarayya, P. 1972. *Telangana People's Struggle and Its Lessons*. Calcutta: Communist Party of India (Marxist).

Tendulkar, D.C. *Mahatma: Life of Mohandas Karamchand Gandhi*, Vol. 7. Delhi: Government of India.

Thakor, Harsh. 2018. 'Centenary of D.V. Rao and Nagi Reddy'. *Frontier*, Vol. 50, No. 31, February 4–10, https://www.frontierweekly.com/articles/vol-50/50-31/50-31-Centenary%20of%20D%20V%20Rao%20and%20Nagi%20Reddy.html. Accessed on 19 October 2021.

The Advocate (2007), documentary film on K.G. Kannabiran, direction: Deepa Dhanraj; cinematography: Navroze Contractor; editor: Jabeen Merchant. Part 2: https://www.youtube.com/watch?v=lrLStnOMP4s&t=10s. Accessed on 13 October 2021.

'Tobacco Growers' Stir Turns Violent: 3 Dead in Firing at Tangutur' *The Indian Express*, 15 March 1983.

Wilde, Oscar (1905) 2007. *De Profundis*. https://www.gutenberg.org/files/921/921-h/921-h.htm. Accessed on 26 October 2021.

Venugopal, N. 'Killing the dead all over again', *India Together*, 26 May 2014. https://indiatogether.org/court-verdict-on-tsundur-massacre-human-rights. Accessed on 17 October 2021.

'Watch Rajiv Gandhi make his infamous 'big tree falls' speech justifying the 1984 anti-Sikh riots'. Scroll.in, 20 November 2015. https://scroll.in/video/1558/watch-rajiv-gandhi-make-his-infamous-big-tree-falls-speech-justifying-the-1984-anti-sikh-riots. Accessed on 28 November 2021.

Index

Acknowledgements

The publication of this memoir—first in Telugu and now in English—is part of a larger project of archiving K.G. Kannabiran's stupendous work in defence of civil liberties in India, but especially in the composite state of Andhra Pradesh; an effort which was in important ways a lodestar for the movement for the protection of civil liberties in independent India.

There are three important pieces to this effort: in chronological order, his book *The Wages of Impunity: Power, Justice and Human Rights* (2004), which I helped him compile and prepare for publication; the documentary film *The Advocate* (2007) by Deepa Dhanraj and Navroze Contractor, which was made with his close and enthusiastic involvement; and *24 Gantalu: Atmakadhatmaka Samajika Chitram* (2009), his oral memoir recorded painstakingly by N. Venugopal over two years, and narrated at the insistence of Amar Devulapalli, who facilitated its publication in Telugu—first in weekly features over a year in *Prajatantra*, and then as a book in 2009. These three projects—spread out from 2000 to 2009—at one time were being carried out simultaneously with texts travelling between them. G.S. Vasu's support has been invaluable. None of the citations of news reports and legislative debates that enrich this volume could have happened without him. Volga's advice and feedback at various stages of this work has been vital. Vasanth Kannabiran, co-traveller in the stories told here, summoned the energy to run through and edit the draft chapters. I express my deep gratitude to them all.

In doing this work over five decades, K.G. Kannabiran had a large community of co-travellers—across vocation, political persuasion and generation—that worked with him on cases, fact-finding missions and tribunals, in courts and outside. Too many to name, I gratefully acknowledge their contribution to the collectively crafted defence of human rights, civil liberties and constitutionalism that Kannabiran speaks of in this book. Several friends have helped me in specific ways with cases, materials, information, advice, good humour and lending a sympathetic ear to my gripes during the various stages of this work. My sincere thanks to all.

This project has been carried out without any research funding or financial support/assistance from any source—but with inestimable emotional, moral and intellectual support from every quarter.

Vasanth, Chitra, Arvind, Raj Mohan, Ramya and Keertana are part of my life with K.G. Kannabiran—and my memories of him are inseparable from our shared, entangled, heterogeneous and ambivalent experiences as a family that lived that life.

I am grateful to Ajoy Devulapalli for permission to translate and adapt *24 Gantalu* (2009) for publication in English. My sincere thanks to the HarperCollins team—especially Siddhesh Inamdar, Suchismita Ukil, Shreya Chakravertty and S.K. Ray Chaudhuri—for their support in publishing this work.

Kalpana Kannabiran

May 2022

About the Authors

K.G. Kannabiran (1929–2010) was a leader of the civil liberties movement in India, known nationally and internationally for his tenacious defence of fundamental freedoms in courts of every jurisdiction, and his challenge of state impunity in independent India. Senior advocate at the Andhra Pradesh High Court, he was president of the Andhra Pradesh Civil Liberties Committee from 1978 to 1993, and national president of the People's Union for Civil Liberties from 1995 to 2009. He is the author of *The Wages of Impunity: Power, Justice and Human Rights* (2004) and *24 Gantalu: Atmakadhatmaka Samajika Chitram* (2009).

Kalpana Kannabiran is a sociologist and legal scholar based in Hyderabad, India, whose work focuses on the intersections of constitutional studies, human rights, law and literature, gender studies, and social movements. Among her books are: *Tools of Justice: Non-Discrimination and the Indian Constitution* (2012), *Gender Regimes and the Politics of Privacy: A Feminist Re-Reading of Puttaswamy v. Union of India* (2021), *Law, Justice and Human Rights in India: Short Reflections* (2021); and her edited volumes: *The Violence of Normal Times: Essays on Women's Lived Realities* (2005), *Women and Law: Critical Feminist Perspectives* (2014), *Violence Studies* (2016), *Routledge Readings on Law and Social Justice: Dispossessions, Marginalities, Rights* (2022) and *Routledge Readings on Law, Development and Legal Pluralism: Ecology, Families, Governance* (2022). She is the second of K.G. Kannabiran's three children.

30 Years *of*

HarperCollins *Publishers* India

At HarperCollins, we believe in telling the best stories and finding the widest possible readership for our books in every format possible. We started publishing 30 years ago; a great deal has changed since then, but what has remained constant is the passion with which our authors write their books, the love with which readers receive them, and the sheer joy and excitement that we as publishers feel in being a part of the publishing process.

Over the years, we've had the pleasure of publishing some of the finest writing from the subcontinent and around the world, and some of the biggest bestsellers in India's publishing history. Our books and authors have won a phenomenal range of awards, and we ourselves have been named Publisher of the Year the greatest number of times. But nothing has meant more to us than the fact that millions of people have read the books we published, and somewhere, a book of ours might have made a difference.

As we step into our fourth decade, we go back to that one word – a word which has been a driving force for us all these years.

Read.